PENSIONS HANDBOOK

7th edition

by

Anthony M Reardon, ACII

PEARSON EDUCATION LIMITED

London Office:
128 Long Acre, London WC2E 9AN
Tel: +44(0)20 7447 2000
Fax: +44(0)20 7240 5771
Website: www.pearsoned-ema.com

First published in Great Britain in 2000

ISBN 0 273 64174 3

British Library Cataloguing in Publication Data
A CIP catalogue record for this book can be obtained
from the British Library

Typeset by M Rules
Printed and bound in Great Britain by
Biddles Ltd, Guildford, Surrey

*The Publishers' policy is to use paper manufactured
from sustainable forests.*

CONTENTS

PREFACE

Since the publication of the 6th edition of this book in November 1996, there have been many changes in the field of pensions, both in terms of personnel and legislation, with many more changes planned for implementation during the next two years.

The election of a Labour Government in April 1997 consigned to the waste-basket the previous Conservative Government's proposals for pensions reform – 'Basic Pensions Plus' – which at the time caused much interest among pensions practitioners for its radicalism. The Labour Government has been very active in the pensions field since taking office. At the time of writing, three Government pensions ministers have come and gone, or moved on. All, however, have been keen to consult with the pensions industry on proposals to increase pensions coverage, especially among the low paid and those on middle incomes, through stakeholder pensions. This consultation phase, though lengthy, is now drawing to a close, with the Welfare Reform and Pensions Bill going through Parliament. However, the essential detail will not be known until regulations are laid, expected in April 2000, with draft regulations to be published towards the end of 1999. The introduction of stakeholder pensions will have a considerable impact on pensions generally as, inevitably, pension managers and employers will reassess all existing forms of pension provision.

Stakeholder pensions, due to start in April 2001, will be accompanied by major changes to state pensions, with replacement of the State Earnings Related Pension (SERPS) by the State Second Pension (SSP) in 2002. The SSP itself will change from being an earnings-related pension to a flat rate pension by 2007. The ability to contract out of SERPS and the SSP through stakeholder pensions is expected to give considerable encouragement to around 4½ million people who are not currently contrated out of SERPS to do so during the next few years.

While stakeholder pensions have not yet been introduced, many other pensions changes have taken effect, the most significant being the abolition of the reclaiming of tax credits on dividend payments on UK equities owned by pension funds. Many other, less significant changes have been introduced in terms of the financial impact on pension funds and on members' benefits, and these are covered in this edition.

I acknowledge with thanks the valuable assistance given to me by my colleagues, David Cheeseman BSc FIA, Stuart Reynolds LLB, Mike Rawle, Kate Griffin, Amanda Costain, Nigel Carter, Henry Tapper BA and Jonathan Poll.

A M Reardon
September 1999

ACKNOWLEDGEMENT

The following is Crown copyright and has been reproduced with permission of the Controller of HMSO.

Extra statutory concession A9, *Doctors' and dentists' superannuation contributions*

Inland Revenue note entitled *Medical or dental practitioners assessed under Schedule D: Retirement annuity relief for the year of assessment 1983/84*

Inland Revenue Memorandum 101 of October 1989 (Parts I and II)

Inland Revenue Practice Notes, IR 12 (1997, updated August 1999)

Inland Revenue Practice Notes 1997, containing subsequent amendments including some dated May 1999

ALLIED DUNBAR

Other titles in the Allied Dunbar Handbook series

TAX HANDBOOK 1999–2000

Whether you are a financial adviser, accountant, solicitor, company secretary, finance director or private individual who wants to find out about your own tax situation, this thorough guide has to be your first choice for shrewd advice and tax saving hints. Fully revised and updated, this edition incorporates all the latest changes following the Finance Act 1999. It offers sound advice on how to cope with self assessment, as well as offering detailed information on the complete range of taxes including CGT, VAT, stamp duty, inheritance tax, life assurance and national insurance.

BUSINESS TAX & LAW HANDBOOK

With detailed information and astute advice, the *Allied Dunbar Business Tax & Law Handbook* makes business planning easier. It details the important taxation and legal considerations that affect a business; and considers both the legal environment in which businesses operate and the taxation obligations which must be met.

ESTATE PLANNING & TAXATION OF CAPITAL HANDBOOK

An accessible guide to estate planning, which you can use to understand the legal obligations and minimise the tax strain. Discover the latest changes and new techniques for successful planning.

INVESTMENT AND SAVINGS HANDBOOK 1999–2000

The *Allied Dunbar Investment & Savings Handbook* delivers invaluable advice on developing and maintaining a sound savings plan and investment portfolio. It includes objective advice from the experts, changes to legislation following budgets of July 1997, November 1997, March 1998 and March 1999, plus a full introduction to ISAs.

EXPATRIATES TAX & INVESTMENT HANDBOOK (7th edition)

'Expat's bible' – *What Investment*

Written by experts, the *Allied Dunbar Expatriate Tax & Investment Handbook* gives you comprehensive coverage of every aspect of expatriate tax and investment from the effect of the single currency to advice on working abroad. It is the essential guide for expatriates wishing to manage their financial affairs to their greatest possible advantage.

RETIREMENT PLANNING HANDBOOK (7th edition)

The *Allied Dunbar Retirement Planning Handbook* is an essential addition to your bookshelf. It ensures that your are fully aware of long and short term investment opportunities and examines the options available for improving retirement prospects.

**For further information contact your local bookseller
or telephone Pearson Education Ltd on 01704 50 80 80.**

1

EMPLOYED V SELF-EMPLOYED

1.1 INTRODUCTION

Pensions for these two categories differ considerably: if you are employed, you may join a pension plan set up by your employer where the only limits on the benefits relate to your salary: if you are self-employed, you may contribute to a pension plan where the limits are related not to your salary, but to the contributions that you may pay. The potential for pension provision is far greater if you are employed.

Pension arrangements available to the employed, including directors, are usually known as executive pension plans, occupational pension schemes, company pension schemes, superannuation funds or variations on that theme. Such schemes can be introduced for the benefit of employees of not only companies, but also sole traders, partnerships, charities and other bodies.

If you are self-employed you are eligible for a personal pension scheme. The eligibility for personal pension schemes is extended to employed persons who are not members of a company scheme. The forerunner of the personal pension scheme was the retirement annuity contract, also commonly known as the self-employed retirement annuity: it is still possible to contribute to these contracts although new ones have not been allowed since 1988.

Company pension schemes and personal pension schemes enjoy considerable tax concessions which are broadly similar. The surrounding legislation, however, is separate and differs in many ways.

Provided a company pension plan or personal pension scheme is approved by the Inland Revenue, contributions paid by the employer and the employee are tax deductible. The fund is exempt from income tax on investments and deposits and capital gains tax on the disposal of investments. The benefits may be taken in the form of a tax-free lump sum and a pension which will be treated as earned income.

Benefits under new occupational pension schemes are restricted for high earners through the application of an earnings limit which stands at

1

£90,600 for the tax year 1999/2000. Under personal pension schemes higher contributions, as a percentage of earnings, can now be paid, compared with contributions to retirement annuities, although earnings are also restricted to £90,600. The basis for calculating maximum benefits under 'earmarked' pension schemes such as executive pension plans set up for a few members, usually directors and senior executives, was changed in September 1994 and June 1996. This reduced further the funding advantage previously enjoyed by employed people.

A comparison of the contributions that may be invested at intervals throughout the term to retirement, if salary increases at 6.9 per cent per annum compound, is set out below:

Table 1.1

Male aged 30, initial salary £20,000, retirement at 60.

Future age	Salary progression	Personal Pension Scheme		Executive Pension Plan	
		% Salary	Amount	% Initial salary	Amount
30	£ 20,000	17.5	£ 3,500	26	£ 5,200
40	£ 38,976	20.0	£ 7,795	26	£10,134
50	£ 75,960	25.0	£18,990	26	£19.750
55	£106,040	30.0	£31,812	26	£27,570

Table 1.2

Male aged 40, initial salary £30,000, retirement at 60.

Future age	Salary progression	Personal Pension Scheme		Executive Pension Plan	
		% Salary	Amount	% Initial salary	Amount
40	£30,000	20.0	£ 6,000	43	£12,900
50	£58,465	25.0	£14,616	43	£25,140
55	£81,618	30.0	£24,485	43	£35,096

Notes
(1) Under the Executive Pension Plan, allowance is made at outset for future salary increases, assumed to be 6.9 per cent per annum compound, and fund growth, assumed to be 8.5 per cent per annum. If the salary increases at a greater level and/or fund growth is lower, higher contributions may be paid in future. The cost of providing dependants' pensions and life assurance benefits has been excluded. The nominal rates of 6.9 and 8.5 per cent are

Table 1.2 *(cont.)*

---

high in today's environment of low interest rates. However, the real rate of growth of 1.6 per cent is a cautious assumption and is of more importance.

(2) Under the Personal Pension Scheme, the amount that can be paid is based on the actual salary and the percentage contribution which applies at that age.

The changes in 1994 and 1996 have reduced the gap between maximum contributions that may be paid under arrangements of the self-employed as compared to employees. However the differences in the underlying systems remain unchanged:

(1) For the self-employed there are no specific limits on benefits. The restrictions on contribution input, however, make it imperative that contributions are started as early as possible.
(2) For employees, whilst contributions are now restricted, the underlying limits on benefits remain. If, for example, there are substantial salary increases close to retirement, and the fund is insufficient to provide maximum benefits, then a further single contribution may be made just prior to retirement to bridge the shortfall.

The two different forms of pension arrangements, occupational pension schemes and personal pension plans, are considered in detail in the following chapters.

1.2 PENSIONS SIMPLIFICATION

One of the causes of the pensions complexity which has built up over the years is the difference in approach to pensions for employed and self-employed people, as described above.

There have been many calls for simplification of pensions, particularly in relation to occupational pension schemes. Legislative changes have generally affected occupational pensions rather than personal pensions and although these changes have usually benefited scheme members, schemes have become more complex and expensive to administer.

The mis-selling of personal pensions in the late 1980s and the early 1990s has cast a cloud over them but this relates to bad advice rather than to the structure of personal pensions which has been held up as the model for a simpler, unified pensions regime for both the employed and the self-employed. However, a unified regime is unlikely to happen in the short term. The arrival of stakeholder pension schemes from April 2001 will not simplify pensions, but it will increase complexity.

1.3 STAKEHOLDER PENSION SCHEMES

The Government wishes to see the formation of stakeholder pension schemes for the self-employed as well as for the employed. However, the major impetus of stakeholder schemes will come as a result of employed people contracting out of the State Earnings Related Pension Scheme (SERPS), and eventually the State Second Pension which will replace SERPS from 2002. As the self-employed are not currently eligible for SERPS, they will not be able to contract out of it. So, initially, stakeholder pension schemes will give more options to employed people. It is possible that self-employed affinity groups may set up and market stakeholder schemes for the self-employed.

The Government's Consultation Brief No 6 on the tax regime for stakeholder pensions proposes a major change which will bring together the two types of pension scheme for the employed and self-employed referred to in this chapter. Building on the legislation for personal pensions the Government proposes a new defined contribution tax regime which will apply to personal pensions, personal pensions designated as stakeholder schemes and employer schemes. Schemes for both employed and self-employed people will be on an equal footing, with contributions calculated in the same way (essentially the age and earnings limits which apply to personal pensions today). There will be no limitations on emerging benefits.

2

HISTORICAL NOTES

2.1 EARLY SCHEMES AND LEGISLATION

One early example of a scheme is seen in the famous case of *Hancock v General Reversionary and Investment Company Ltd* [1919] 1 KB 25, which established the important principle that a company which purchases an annuity for a retiring employee may set the cost against its profits for tax purposes as a business expense. It is still quite common for 'Hancock annuities' to be set up for retiring employees (see 16.10).

The 1918 Income Tax Act gave life assurance tax relief to employees contributing to a retirement benefit scheme using insurance policies. The Finance Acts of 1921 and 1930 provided, amongst other things, for the approval of superannuation funds set up under irrevocable trust and for the Commissioners of Inland Revenue to regulate such schemes.

New pensions legislation was introduced by the 1952 Income Tax Act and re-enacted in the consolidating Income and Corporation Taxes Act 1970. By 1970, however, the conditions for approval of pension schemes derived from a combination of legislation, case law and Inland Revenue practice. The Civil Service Superannuation Scheme was the model by which all private schemes were judged. The tax treatment of pension fund investments varied from total freedom to partial exemption from capital gains tax but no exemption from income tax, depending entirely on the type of benefit being provided, for example, cash, pension or death benefit. It was common for trustees of these old pension schemes to seek approval of three-quarters of the benefits under s 208 (giving complete tax-free treatment but requiring all benefits to be taken in pension form) and one-quarter of the benefits under s 222 of the Income and Corporation Taxes Act 1970 (allowing benefits to be taken in cash but giving limited relief) – giving rise to the expression '¾, ¼ Schemes'.

2.2 OLD AND NEW CODES

The case for simplification, if not outright reform, was recognised in the late 1960s resulting in a 'New Code' of approval introduced by FA 1970, Pt II, Chap II. The New Code introduced a concept of one single fund with total freedom from tax on both contributions and investment income.

By April 1980 all schemes, including existing Old Code schemes, had to be approved by the Inland Revenue under the New Code.

The differences between the Old and New Codes which had the most dramatic effect on the subsequent growth in pension schemes were probably as follows:

(1) The ability to fund for maximum pensions over ten rather than 20 years.
(2) Full tax relief on contributions paid by an employee and employer irrespective of the type of benefit being provided.
(3) The ability to set up a pension scheme which would provide a tax-free cash sum in isolation. Under the Old Code it was necessary to restrict the amount of the tax-free lump sum to one-quarter of the pension being provided, so that it was impossible to fund solely for a tax-free cash sum.
(4) Freedom from tax on all investments irrespective of the benefits being provided except for a period when development land tax was charged on real and deemed realisations of development value.
(5) The concept of approvable death in service benefits.

Section 15 of FA 1973 extended FA 1970 by allowing 'controlling directors' to be included in New Code pension schemes.

The Finance (No 2) Act 1987 brought in a number of significant changes to pension scheme practice. In some ways the changes meant a reversion to the Old Code regime in that:

(1) Maximum pensions for persons joining pension schemes on or after 17 March 1987 could be provided only if 20 years' service with the employer could be completed by retirement, rather than ten.
(2) Pension schemes set up to provide only tax-free cash sums on retirement are restricted. Generally, if the *maximum* tax-free cash sum is required the *maximum* pension benefit has to be provided under the scheme.
(3) Measures have been introduced to restrict the benefits which may be enjoyed by high earners, including 'controlling directors'.

Schedule 6 to FA 1989 introduced further limitations to all members of new occupational pension schemes set up from 14 March 1989 and, in respect of new members joining from 1 June 1989, schemes set up before that date. Details are given in later chapters but the principal change was the maximum level of earnings on which retirement benefits could be based. This was set at £60,000 in 1989/90 and is increased each year in line with increases in the Retail Prices Index, except in 1993/94 when no increase was applied. The maximum level stands at £90,600 in 1999/2000.

2.3 TOP HAT SCHEMES

The top hat scheme first gained prominence in the late 1940s as a simple but effective means of reducing the burden of income tax; in those days the top rate was 97.5 per cent. The proceeds of endowment schemes could be taken completely tax free at the end of a period of employment. The 1947 Finance Act was an attempt to make top hats less attractive by restricting the amount of pension which could be commuted for a tax-free lump sum to 25 per cent but in fact it only succeeded in boosting their popularity by giving them respectability.

The early top hat schemes were straightforward endowment assurance policies set up by a director giving up part of his income or an increment, a device known as 'salary sacrifice'. Top hat schemes were approved retirement benefit schemes offering the following advantages:

- The director paid no tax on his 'contribution' (because it had been sacrificed).
- On death the proceeds of the endowment assurance policy were free of estate duty.
- On retirement, up to one-quarter of the policy was available as a tax-free capital sum.

However, there were some disadvantages which gained greater significance as time passed:

- Insurance companies could not invest contributions from top hat schemes into their tax-exempt pension funds but only their life and annuity funds which did not offer such good returns.
- Direct personal contributions paid by the director were given only life assurance tax relief.
- Controlling directors, ie those owning more than 5 per cent of the equity in a company which the directors between them controlled, were ineligible and could only take advantage of retirement annuities where the scope for contributions was very limited.

Following the passing of the 1973 Finance Act, which allowed controlling directors to join New Code schemes, top hat schemes found a new lease of life. Because of the changes which were brought about by the New Code, the modern top hat policy became a much more sophisticated vehicle than its predecessor, offering maximum flexibility in terms of benefits and investment options. Indeed, executive pension plans, as they are now called, have become essential tools of tax planners with their ability to avoid income tax, capital gains tax, inheritance tax and corporation tax.

2.4 LIFETIME SERVICE AGREEMENTS

The FA 1973 allowing controlling directors to join New Code schemes was passed in July 1973. In April of the same year, many controlling directors had completed special whole of life death in service arrangements to beat the Old Code time limit. Because it had not been necessary to obtain approval to death benefits under the Old Code, it was realised that unlimited sums assured through insurance policies written under trust could be established for controlling directors by their companies and, provided the company did not claim corporation tax relief on the premiums, the proceeds would be payable to beneficiaries free of estate duty.

These old death in service arrangements were unapproved and were designed to be self-funding (by surrendering bonuses which had been allotted to the policy to pay future premiums) after April 1980, by which date all continuing schemes required re-approval under the New Code.

The director for whose benefit the policy was set up had to have a lifetime service agreement and could not, in respect of the same employment, enjoy the benefits of a self-employed retirement annuity policy. It is unlikely that many of these lifetime service agreements would have been completed had it been known that shortly afterwards, controlling directors could set up New Code pension schemes for the first time. The Revenue agreed to approve whole of life assurance policies issued by insurance companies as vehicles for retirement benefit schemes under the New Code, provided that there was genuine evidence of a lifetime service agreement and the amount of benefit fell within normal New Code limits – essentially that the lump sum payable on death would be within four times salary at the date of death.

It was even possible to adapt the pre-1973 death in service arrangements to make them approvable under the New Code. If this were done, the company could offset its premium payments against profits for corporation tax purposes and the insurance company could put the premiums into its tax-exempt fund instead of its tax-bearing life fund. In short, the premiums could be reduced.

Once again, many insurance companies marketed 'whole of life death in service' packages, and controlling directors with serious capital transfer tax (the forerunner of inheritance tax) problems took advantage of these schemes. The Inland Revenue effectively put a stop to the practice by issuing Memorandum No 41 which imposed a restriction on the discretionary distribution of death benefits on or after the age of 75. This Memorandum was followed by Memorandum No 59 which further tightened the rules. These rulings were not retrospective, however, so that some controlling directors still have advantageous arrangements which they are unable to change materially without causing the Memorandum No 59 restrictions to apply automatically.

Lifetime service agreements have little or no practical application nowadays.

2.5 GROWTH OF EXECUTIVE PENSION PLANS

The creation and growth of the executive pension plan for the controlling director coincided with the development of unit-linked life assurance policies, pioneered by such companies as Hambro Life Assurance (now Allied Dunbar Assurance plc). By the end of the 1970s these companies had been joined by many other new companies and also very old established life assurance companies, all offering unit-linked as well as with-profits policies.

The essential attraction of the unit-linked policy is the option given to the policyholder to decide his own investment strategy. He may choose to invest his contributions in a variety of sectors ranging from properties, equities, cash, gilts and overseas funds. Alternatively, the policyholder may leave the investment strategy to the insurance company under what is known as a 'managed fund'.

2.6 SMALL SELF-ADMINISTERED PENSION SCHEMES

The late 1970s saw the development of small self-administered pension schemes, sometimes known as 'captives', where the employer sets up a pension scheme himself, with the assistance of various experts, rather than using an insurance company. The trustees have wider powers of investment compared with those allowed under a straightforward insured arrangement, in particular the ability to lend part of the pension fund back to the employer to assist the expansion of the business, to purchase shares in the employer's business and to purchase property which is leased to the employer. However, the Social Security Act 1990 limited such 'self-investment' to 5 per cent of the value of the pension fund unless the scheme membership is limited to '20 per cent directors' of the company, and provided other conditions are met (see Chapter 9).

Insurance companies offer small self-administered schemes, usually providing all the necessary services and investment management if required but normally on the basis that a portion of the pension fund is invested in an insurance policy.

2.7 DEVELOPMENT OF STATE BENEFITS

The 1960s and 1970s were notorious for the frequency with which governments invented new state schemes. Some never reached the statute book while others were overturned by an incoming administration. All tended to bear the name of their creators – the Boyd-Carpenter Graduated Pension Scheme, the Crossman Plan, the Keith Joseph Funded Pension Scheme and the Barbara Castle State Earnings Related Scheme (SERPS).

Although there was all-party consensus on the Castle Scheme, Norman Fowler, as Secretary of State for Health and Social Security, introduced measures in the Social Security Act 1986 which reduced benefits under the earnings related part of the state scheme (see Chapter 11).

Recent commentaries on welfare provision have tended to question the continuation of the current universal nature of the state pension, suggesting that any future improvements should be targeted on the most needy.

As far as the director and senior executive of a company is concerned, however, it is only the earnings related part of the state scheme which has ever been of any influence in the provision of benefits.

The Conservative Government toyed with a radical restructure of state and private pensions in its proposals in 1997 for 'Basic Pension Plus'. However, this came too late in the lifetime of that government to generate much more than passing interest. The election a few months later of the Labour Government with its own ideas on reform of welfare and pensions, as set out in its Green Paper 'A new contract for welfare: partnership in pensions', will result in significant changes to state pensions. SERPS will be replaced by a new State Second Pension which initially will provide pensions on an earnings-related basis, but will eventually become flat-rate.

2.8 MORE RECENT CHANGES

The 1970s saw the start of legislative changes to improve the benefits of early leavers and provide for greater transferability between schemes. This continued into 1990 which saw further legislation to improve early leavers' benefits. The late 1980s saw significant changes to both occupational and personal pension schemes (see 2.11 below and later chapters), increased the awareness of 'unapproved pension schemes' (see Chapter 5) and saw the beginning of anti-sex discrimination law in the field of pensions. Under the Sex Discrimination Act 1986, it is unlawful for employers to require female employees to retire at an earlier age than male colleagues. In its judgment on the *Barber v Guardian Royal Exchange* case in May 1990 the European Court ruled that redundancy pay and membership of a contracted-out pension scheme are 'pay' for the purposes of equal treatment directives of the European Community Council and Art 119 of the Treaty of Rome and that Mr Barber had been discriminated against by his employer even though the reason for the different treatment between him and his female colleagues was the different state retirement ages for men and women.

In the *Coloroll Pension Trustees* case the court ruled that scheme trustees as well as employers are bound by Article 119. It also ruled that actuarial factors which vary according to sex do not fall within the scope of Article 119 where such factors are used by employers in establishing the funding levels of defined benefit schemes and in determining matters which are linked to those funding arrangements, eg commutation factors and the calculation of transfer values.

In the event of a transfer of pension rights from one occupational scheme to another, owing to a worker's change of job, the second scheme is obliged, on the member reaching retirement age, to increase the benefits it undertook to pay him when accepting the transfer. This increase in benefits is required in order to eliminate the effects which may have been suffered by the worker in consequence of the inadequacy of the cash equivalent transferred (this being due in turn to discriminatory treatment suffered by the worker by the first scheme in relation to benefits payable in respect of period of service, subsequent to the *Barber* judgment of 17 May 1990). Whether the second scheme can make a claim against the first scheme has yet to be established.

The court also ruled that in equalising pensions, scheme trustees are allowed to equalise down the benefits of men and women. However, scheme trustees have to improve benefits for men accruing between May 1990 and the date when the company took whatever action was required to implement equal pension rights.

In *Smith v Advel Systems*, five women, backed by the Equal Opportunities Commission, brought claims before the Industrial Tribunal in the United Kingdom arguing that they were financially worse off as a result of the employer raising their retirement age from 60 to 65 following the *Barber* ruling. The court ruled that it was legitimate for employers to worsen pension provision for women for the period of service after implementation of equal pension rights. For a period of service between 1990 and implementation of equal pension rights the benefits enjoyed by women as a result of lower retirement ages may not be reduced.

In *Vroege v NCIV* (a Dutch case) about the rights of access to pension schemes by part-time workers, the court ruled that the right to join an occupational pension scheme falls within the scope of Article 119 of the Treaty of Rome. The right is not time-limited by the *Barber* judgment and therefore stretches back to April 1976.

In *Fisscher v Voorhuis Hengelo* (another Dutch case), the court ruled that equal pay rules applied to access to a pension scheme which excluded married women. The court also ruled that a worker wishing to join a scheme retroactively must pay back contributions if the scheme is a contributory scheme.

In *Van Den Akker v Shell* the court ruled that, for a period between the *Barber* judgment in May 1990 and equalisation, conditions for male workers have to be improved to equal the benefits for female workers.

In *ABP v Beune*, the court ruled that the Dutch civil service occupational pension scheme is also covered by equal treatment rules and it is not permissible for such a scheme to discriminate against married men. This case also affects other national public service schemes.

The ruling that has caused most interest is that of *Vroege v NCIV*: backdated pension demands by part-timers could cost companies, and their pension funds, significant sums. In addition, there would be the administrative costs of tracing employees who may have left a company since 1976. The effect is likely to fall on those companies with high numbers of part-timers. However, the court's ruling affects companies that excluded part-timers from membership where the part-timers were generally of one sex (usually women). If the exclusion of part-timers could be shown to include men and women equally, the ruling would have no effect.

Doubt about the use of actuarial factors under money purchase schemes still exists: we still do not know whether it is sufficient for employers to pay *equal* contributions for men and women or whether equal pensions have to be paid. It appears likely that employers need pay only equal contributions which will generate equal funds at retirement, but that those funds will purchase unequal benefits because annuity rates differ for men and women. It is likely that another test case will have to be referred to the European Court before a definitive answer is obtained.

2.9 PENSIONS LAW REFORM: PENSIONS ACT 1995

This Act brought in many of the proposals of the Pension Law Review Committee to improve the security of occupational pensions. The main effects of the Act are as follows:

(1) The Occupational Pensions Regulatory Authority, known as 'OPRA', has wide-ranging powers. It may impose civil penalties of up to £5,000 in the case of individuals and £50,000 in the case of companies for breaches in their statutory duties by trustees, employers and their advisers. OPRA may prohibit a person from being a trustee of a scheme and appoint new trustees. It has the power to wind up a scheme and apply to the court for an injunction if it is likely that someone will misappropriate scheme assets.

(2) Member-nominated trustees – existing trustees were responsible for putting in place and obtaining the scheme members' approval to procedures for members to select one-third of the trustee board. Employers may decide that they wish to opt out of the requirement to have member-nominated trustees and introduce alternative arrangements for selecting trustees. Members must be given the opportunity to object to the employer's proposals.

(3) General aspects of trusteeship – a trustee and any person who is connected with the trustee cannot act as the auditor or actuary of the same scheme. A trustee will be disqualified from being a trustee of any scheme if he has been convicted of an offence (including deception or dishonesty), has been made bankrupt, has made an arrangement with his creditors, is subject to a disqualification order as a company director, and in the case of a corporate trustee, if any of the directors is disqualified from being a trustee. Trustees cannot be indemnified out of scheme assets for fines or penalties.

(4) Functions of trustees – the trustees must maintain a written statement of investment principles, including the kinds of investments to be held, risk, expected return and the balance between different kinds of investments. They must consider the advice of a suitable expert and consult the employer.

(5) Advisers – the trustees must appoint a scheme auditor and actuary, although most money purchase schemes are exempt from the requirement to appoint an actuary.

(6) Minimum funding requirement – every scheme, except money purchase schemes, is subject to a minimum funding requirement (MFR) that the value of its assets is not less than the amount of its liabilities. The trustees must maintain a schedule showing the contribution rates payable by the employer and members, and the due dates for payment. Contribution rates must be certified by the actuary. If the contributions schedule cannot be agreed between the trustees and the employer, the schedule must show the contribution rates decided by the trustees as adequate for MFR purposes. The trustees must notify OPRA and the scheme members of any unpaid contributions which will then be a debt on the employer.

(7) Equal treatment – all schemes will be treated as if they have a rule providing for equal treatment between men and women relating to

eligibility and scheme benefits (the latter relating to pensionable service from 17 May 1990). Sex-based factors, however, are permitted in calculating benefits in money purchase schemes and optional benefits in defined benefit scheme such as transfer values.

(8) Compensation scheme – a Pensions Compensation Board and scheme has been set up to cover schemes where the employer is insolvent and in the case of a defined benefits scheme, the value of the assets is less than 90 per cent of liabilities.

(9) Transfer values – the Act extended the right to receive a cash equivalent to those members whose pensionable service ended before 1 January 1986.

(10) Modification of schemes – any power to modify a pension scheme cannot be exercised if it would reduce or prejudice members' benefits and the members' consents have not been obtained.

(11) All occupational pension schemes, including money purchase, must provide pensions in payment which increase by 5 per cent per annum or RPI if lower, in respect of benefits arising from service after April 1997.

(12) A new scheme-based test (the 'reference test') replaced Guaranteed Minimum Pensions under contracted out final salary schemes: the scheme must provide an accrual rate of at least $\frac{1}{80}$ of final average salary based on 90 per cent of band earnings for each year of service after April 1997, and payable at a normal pension age of 65.

(13) The rebate payable under contracted-out money purchase schemes, and personal pension schemes, moved to an age-related basis from April 1997.

2.10 PERSONAL PENSIONS

The introduction of personal pensions in 1988 resulted in a considerable increase in pensions coverage, albeit at modest contribution levels. Around 6 million people have taken out personal pensions, of whom the vast majority are using these plans to contract out of SERPS.

These plans can also take contributions from individuals (employed and self-employed) and from employers, as well as from the Government where the plans are used for contracting out.

Personal pensions are truly portable, with no employer control, although many employers are prepared to contribute to employees' personal pensions.

2.11 PART-TIME WORKERS

The European Court decided in *Fisscher v Voorhuis Hengelo* and *Vroege v NCIV* (see 2.8) that the exclusion of part-time workers from occupational pension schemes could constitute indirect sex discrimination in contravention of Art 119 of the Treaty of Rome (see also 2.8 above). The court held that this could relate back to 8 April 1976. Subsequently, many claims from part-time workers who had been excluded from occupational schemes were lodged at industrial tribunals to clarify various issues, particularly in relation to the time limits for bringing actions against employers.

An industrial tribunal, in December 1996, presiding over various test cases, decided that the time limits of the Equal Pay Act 1970 do apply to claims for access to pension schemes and therefore applications from part-timers should have been made within six months of the end of the employment giving rise to the claims. The industrial tribunal also stated that access to schemes retrospectively can only be ordered by the tribunal for the two years before the application was made.

In July 1996 the Employment Appeal Tribunal stated that the six months' time limit applies to all part-timers' claims. As a result the vast majority of claims from part-timers will be ineffective under the six-month rule. Claims for those cases which are valid will be restricted by the overall two-year limit.

The European Advocate General has given his opinion in *Shirley Preston and Others v Wolverhampton Healthcare NHS Trust and Others, Dorothy Fletcher and Others v Midland Bank plc*. The opinion is not binding on the courts, although they are likely to follow it. It suggests that the six-month time limit for bringing actions after the date of employment ends is acceptable for EU law, but the two-year rule for limiting retroactive membership of the plans is not acceptable. So, if a claim is allowed it is possible the part-timer could claim membership backdated to the time of the *Barber* judgment.

2.12 MATERNITY LEAVE

The European Court of Justice in *Boyle v Equal Opportunities Commission* ruled that women are entitled to build up their full pension benefits during 14 weeks of maternity leave, and that employers are not allowed to restrict the period during which occupational pension rights accrue to the period of paid leave.

3

INLAND REVENUE APPROVAL

3.1 PENSION SCHEMES OFFICE

All pension schemes, to be tax effective, must be approved by the Inland Revenue. The United Kingdom is fortunate in the system of tax approval for pension schemes administered by the Inland Revenue Pension Schemes Office (PSO) in accordance with the broad discretionary powers conferred on it by the Income and Corporation Taxes Act 1988.

The PSO has built up a unique relationship with the pensions industry over many years and gives guidance and offers comment on proposals put to it by interested organisations.

Those aspects of pension schemes relating primarily to tax approval are regulated by a flexible code of practice, which can quickly accommodate changes in legislation and social custom, as well as react swiftly to counter tax avoidance. In recent years, however, the PSO has found it necessary to seek additional powers in the form of statutory regulation.

3.1.1 The purpose of approval

It is often forgotten by directors when drawing up their service agreements or contracts of employment that the mere promise of a pension constitutes a 'retirement benefit scheme' in the eyes of the Inland Revenue who will tax it as a benefit in kind in the hands of the director.

There are many directors who have service agreements which promise pension benefits but which have never been seen by the Inland Revenue and are potential tax traps: such agreements normally only come to light following a takeover or the merger of companies. These agreements will almost certainly be unapproved pension schemes requiring careful examination following FA 1989 (see Chapter 5).

One of the purposes of seeking approval from the PSO is to remove the liability for income tax from the employee. If the scheme is approved by the PSO as an exempt approved scheme, further advantages flow from this. If the promise to provide retirement benefits is funded by means of an exempt approved pension scheme the employer can claim tax relief on the payment as a business expense. Exempt approval also enables the trustees of funded schemes to invest fund monies without liability to income tax or capital gains tax.

Following a change of practice in October 1991, the Inland Revenue now maintains that an *ex gratia* payment can also constitute a retirement benefit scheme where the payment is made on retirement. Although many genuine redundancy payments are free from tax as 'golden handshakes' (if they are up to £30,000 in value), other *ex gratia* benefits need to be restricted to the normal limits and formal approval obtained.

3.1.2 Conditions for approval

The basic conditions which must be met before the PSO approves a scheme as an exempt approved scheme are:

(1) That the scheme is established under irrevocable trusts for the sole purpose of providing relevant benefits in respect of service as an employee: 'relevant benefits' is defined in ICTA 1988, s 612(1) (see Appendix 4) in very wide terms, and covers any type of financial benefit given in connection with the termination of an employee's service with a particular employer, including termination by reason of death, with the sole exception of benefits receivable only in the event of death by accident or disablement by accident during (though not necessarily arising out of) service.

(2) That the scheme is recognised by the employer and employees to whom it relates and that every employee who is or who has a right to be a member of the scheme has been given written particulars of all essential features of the scheme which concern him (sometimes known as an 'announcement letter').

(3) That there is a person resident in the United Kingdom who is responsible for the discharge of all duties imposed on the scheme's administrator.

(4) That the employer is a contributor to the scheme. (Generally, the level of contribution must be at least 10 per cent of the total contribution to the scheme.)

(5) That the scheme is established in connection with some trade or undertaking carried on in the United Kingdom by a person resident in the United Kingdom.

(6) That in no circumstances, whether during the subsistence of the scheme or later, can any amount be paid by way of repayment of an employee's contributions under the scheme (although this condition may be overridden by preservation provisions).

(7) That any benefit for an employee is a pension on retirement at a

specified age not earlier than 60 and not later than 75, which does not exceed one-sixtieth of the employee's final remuneration for each year of service up to a maximum of 40 years.

(8) That any benefit for any widow of an employee is a pension payable on his death after retirement such that the amount payable to the widow by way of pension does not exceed two-thirds of any pension or pensions payable to the employee.

(9) That no other benefits are payable under the scheme.

(10) That no pension is capable in whole or in part of surrender, commutation or assignment except so far as the scheme allows an employee on retirement to obtain by commutation of this pension, a lump sum or sums not exceeding in all three-eightieths of his final remuneration for each year of service up to a maximum of 40 years.

These are the primary conditions which, if met, entitle the scheme to all the tax advantages which approval can confer as of right and are contained in ICTA 1988, s 590 (see Appendix 4). Very few schemes, however, exist which do not infringe one or more of these primary conditions, and approval under s 590 is normally only sought in very limited circumstances such as where a scheme is to be set up for directors of investment companies (of which more is said in Chapter 18).

To cope with the vast majority of occupational pension schemes, the PSO relies on its discretionary powers which are extremely wide ranging and are set out in the PSO's Practice Notes on approval of Occupational Pension Schemes (IR 12 (1997)). These Practice Notes apply to schemes approved after 29 November 1997. Previous Practice Notes, IR 12 (1979) as amended, may continue to apply to schemes approved before 29 November 1991, although these may not necessarily be more advantageous. The Practice Notes have to be interpreted alongside separate Updates, and other notification of change of practice, published by the PSO.

In effect approval can be given to a scheme:

(1) which exceeds the limits imposed by the primary conditions as respects benefits for less than 40 years' service;

(2) which provides pensions for the widows or widowers of employees on death in service or for children or dependants of such employees;

(3) which provides, on death in service, a lump sum of up to four times the employee's final remuneration (exclusive of any refund of contributions);

(4) which allows benefits to be payable on retirement within ten years of the specified age, or on earlier incapacity;

(5) which provides for the return in certain contingencies of the employee's contributions;

(6) which relates to a trade or undertaking carried on only partly in the United Kingdom and by a person resident in the United Kingdom;

(7) which provides in certain contingencies for securing relevant benefits (but no other benefits) by means of an annuity contract approved by the Board and made with an insurance company of the employee's choice (ie a 'Section 32 annuity'); or

(8) to which the employer is not a contributor and which provides benefits additional to those provided by a scheme to which he is a contributor (ie a 'freestanding AVC').

The much wider benefits set out above are contained in ICTA 1988, s 591 (see Appendix 4).

The PSO has the power to withdraw approval at any time should it feel that the scheme is no longer meeting its requirements. The consequences of withdrawal of approval are penal since the contributions paid by the employers would be regarded as income in the hands of the members, tax relief on employees' contributions would be withdrawn, the fund itself would lose its tax exempt status and tax is charged at 40 per cent on an amount equal to the value of the assets immediately before the date of cessation of approval.

A scheme which meets all the other conditions of approval set out above but which is not established under irrevocable trust may be approved by the PSO, but not exempt approved. The effect of this is to avoid a charge to income tax on the employee or director, but none of the other tax advantages apply.

3.2 OTHER LEGISLATION

Although Chapter XIV of ICTA 1988 is the legislative base for approval of all pension schemes other legislation can have an influence on the scheme. The most important pieces of legislation are as follows.

3.2.1 The Pension Schemes Act 1993

This Act consolidates the pension provisions in social security legislation, commencing with the Social Security Act 1973, which contains the original preservation requirements. Other main provisions of this Act are:

(1) requirements and procedures to enable employees to be contracted out of the State Earnings Related Pension Scheme (Social Security Pensions Act 1975 and Social Security Act 1986);

(2) establishment of the register of occupational and personal pension schemes (Social Security Acts 1985 and 1990);

(3) those provisions of the Employment Protection (Consolidation) Act 1978 relating to information about pension rights to be included in contracts of employment, and also to the payment of employer contributions by the Secretary of State for Social Security if the employer is insolvent;

(4) improvements in the benefits of early leavers from pension schemes. With effect from 1 January 1986 employers were required to revalue the pension provided on leaving service at the lesser of the increase in the rate of the Retail Prices Index or 5 per cent compound for each year between the date of leaving and the date of retirement. Revaluation applies only in respect of service with the employer from 1 January 1985 which means that the Act is not retrospective and therefore does not increase an employer's liability in respect of members who left the schemes formerly nor does it apply in respect of service with an employer up to January 1985 (Social Security Act 1985);

(5) provision for pension scheme trustees to disclose information to prospective members, current members and early leavers. The information to be provided relates to the member's own benefits under the scheme and also information relating to the scheme as a whole including its investment policy and finances;

(6) provisions of the Act also compel scheme trustees to facilitate the payment of transfer values to another suitable scheme at the member's request (Social Security Act 1985);

(7) if there is a surplus under the pension scheme the first call on the surplus is to pay increases in pension to members for rights which they have built up before the 'appointed day'. When a scheme winds up, employers must ensure that any surplus is used to provide members with increases, in line with increases in the Retail Prices Index up to 5 per cent, to all pension rights. Increases for pension rights before the 'appointed day' depend on increases already guaranteed and any surplus on winding-up. These changes do not apply to money purchase schemes or to personal pension schemes. Regulations introduced on 1 July 1992 make any deficiency of pension funds that are wound up a debt due from the employer to the trustees of the scheme;

(8) establishment of the Pensions Ombudsman with powers to determine complaints by scheme members and their dependants.

3.2.2 Sex Discrimination Act 1986

This Act made it unlawful to require that a woman retires from work at an earlier age than a man in the same job. It also makes it illegal for an employer to refuse her training or to refuse to promote her because she is nearing retirement provided that these opportunities would have been offered to a man of the same age.

3.2.3 Finance (No 2) Act 1987

This Act contained the tax framework of personal pension schemes introduced in the Social Security Act 1986. It amends those provisions now contained in ICTA 1988 relating to pension schemes for the self-employed and those who are in non-pensionable employment as well as to occupational schemes. This Act also brought in restrictions on the benefits permitted under occupational pension schemes.

3.2.4 Finance Act 1989

This Act contained further limitations on benefits which may be provided by occupational pension schemes, by reference to an earnings ceiling, £90,600 in 1999/2000, and changes to contribution levels to personal pension schemes.

3.2.5 Pension Act 1995

This legislative landmark is the real legacy of Robert Maxwell; the need to allay public concern about the security of pension scheme assets created an opportunity to review many other aspects of pension provision in the UK. (See 2.9.)

3.3 TRUSTS

In order to obtain exempt approval, the scheme must be established under trust so that the pension scheme's assets are legally separated from those of the employer.

The employer establishes the trust, appoints the first trustees and lays down the conditions under which employees and their dependants will benefit.

3.3.1 Setting up the trust

For the purposes of approval a trust can be created in a number of ways, all of which are acceptable to the Inland Revenue.

Formal deed

This method is generally used for large group pension schemes and consists of a formal deed under which the employer creates a trust and appoints trustees giving them various powers of investment, and also adopts formal rules. Often the trust is established by an interim deed and is followed by a definitive deed at a later stage.

Declaration of trust

This is similar to, though much shorter than, a formal deed, and is normally used in connection with discretionary individual pension arrangements, for example executive pension plans, where benefits are to be provided by an insurance company.

Board resolution

Providing a company's memorandum and articles of association permit it, the Board of Directors may pass a board resolution which has the effect of creating a trust.

Employer trust

Sometimes a trust is created by an exchange of letters between the employer and the employee who is to benefit from the pension scheme. This is only used for individual pension arrangements where the scheme is being established for one employee or director.

The legislation requires the appointment of a UK resident person as scheme administrator who is liable for tax matters relating to the scheme. It is usual to appoint the scheme trustee(s) as administrator. The scheme's actual day-to-day administration is normally carried on by either an in-house office with the assistance of external advisors or, where the scheme is insured, by the insurance company.

3.4 HOW TO OBTAIN REVENUE APPROVAL

Applications for approval to schemes must be sent in writing to the PSO within at least six months from the scheme's establishment, possibly longer, depending on the date of establishment, as follows:

Date scheme established		*Date by which application must be received by PSO*	
In the 6 months ending	5 October	By the following	5 April
In the month ending	5 November	By the following	5 May
	5 December		5 June
	5 January		5 July
	5 February		5 August
	5 March		5 September
	5 April		5 October

Subject to provisions for spreading tax relief forward (see Chapter 7) employer's contributions are relieved for tax purposes in the accounting year in which they are paid.

The application for approval must be accompanied by the appropriate return. There are four types of return, in a form and colour prescribed and supplied by the PSO: one for the schemes open to more than one employee; one for individual arrangements; one for 'Hancock annuities'; and one for simplified defined contribution schemes.

Standard returns must be completed fully and accurately otherwise they will not be treated as valid applications for approval. The following information is included in the returns, but is not exhaustive.

(1) The employer's full name, address and registered office.
(2) The employer's status, for example, limited company, partnership, sole trader.
(3) The nature of the employer's business.
(4) The name of the scheme.
(5) The tax districts dealing with the employer's PAYE and corporation tax and the employer's reference numbers in those districts.
(6) A copy of the document establishing the scheme, for example, the trust deed, exchange of letters or declaration of trust if not already agreed as standard.
(7) A copy of the letter to employees describing the scheme's main features.
(8) The scheme's commencement date.
(9) Where appropriate (for example in the case of small self-administered schemes) actuarial reports concerning the scheme's funding.
(10) Details of any existing schemes and their interaction with the new scheme which has been set up.
(11) The name and address of the administrator and trustee.
(12) Details of the person or persons who will be responsible for paying pensions. This is normally the trustees but in insured schemes the insurance company often pays pensions as agent for the administrator.
(13) The employer's financial year end.
(14) The number of members.
(15) The amount of ordinary annual contributions and date of first payment.
(16) The amount of any special contributions.
(17) The method of funding, for example insured or self-administered, together with full details of the employer's ordinary annual contributions and any special contributions to any other schemes.
(18) The names of any directors joining the scheme who either on his/her own or with one or more associates beneficially owns or is able to control directly or indirectly or through other companies 20 per cent or more of the ordinary share capital of the company.

(19) Details of controlling directors including National Insurance number and current pensionable earnings.

(20) A list of all retained benefits – those earned from earlier membership of approved pension schemes or through self-employed retirement annuities, benefits under approved occupational pension schemes relating to earlier employments and under retirement annuity contracts and personal pension schemes relating to this or earlier employments. If the scheme is insured the insurance company automatically obtains the above information through its application forms and in turn passes them on to the PSO.

3.5 PSO APPROVAL

The PSO does not authorise provisional income tax relief on members' personal contributions until they have received the above items. Most insurance companies have agreed standard documents with the PSO so that final approval is normally a matter of waiting for the PSO to rubber stamp the documents.

Since 1 December 1987 the PSO has not notified the employer's Schedule D tax district that a scheme has been approved. Instead, the letter signifying approval lists the participating employers, and the date of approval, and it is the responsibility of the employer(s) or their agents to forward a copy to the appropriate tax district to support the initial claim for relief in respect of an employer's pension scheme contribution. This procedure ensures that tax inspectors have evidence of the entitlement to relief before them at a time a participating employer's accounts are examined for Schedule D or corporation tax liability.

If employees are contributing towards the cost of the pension scheme, they receive tax relief under PAYE: this means for example that if an employee's salary amounts to £800 per month and is proposing to pay £50 per month to the pension scheme the employer calculates tax by applying the employee's PAYE code to £750. This is known as the 'net pay arrangement' but an employer should not operate this until the local inspector has been notified that provisional tax relief has been allowed.

If approval is withdrawn, for example because definitive scheme documentation is not adopted within 24 months of the establishment of the scheme, any provisional tax reliefs will be withdrawn and the scheme will be taxed as a funded unapproved retirement benefits scheme (FURBS) from commencement (see Chapter 5).

3.6 SIMPLIFIED SCHEMES

A simplified procedure for tax approval is available to schemes providing a package of benefits which need to satisfy only the minimal basic Revenue requirements. The procedure is available to a simplified defined contribution scheme, which offers only money purchase benefits and to which no limits on benefits will apply, although there is an overall limit on contributions. It will not be possible for such schemes to be self-administered, unless they are contracted-out on a money purchase basis.

3.7 UNAPPROVED SCHEMES

Since the introduction of the limit on the benefits which can emerge from new occupational pension schemes there has been increasing interest in unapproved schemes. These are not subject to Inland Revenue limits; for example, an employer could provide a pension equal to an employer's retiring salary.

Under the current legislation however, the major drawback is the choice forced on the employee between an immediate Schedule E charge on employer contributions (treated as a taxable benefit in kind) and an unsecured benefit (if the arrangement is unfunded). (Full details are contained in Chapter 5.)

These arrangements may be either funded (in which case the employer contributions attract a Schedule E charge payable by the member) or unfunded (in which case the payment of the benefit will be tied closely to the financial position of the employer several years hence).

MAXIMUM PERMITTED BENEFITS

This chapter looks at the maximum levels of benefits which the PSO will approve for an employee including the considerable changes brought about by F(No 2)A 1987 and FA 1989. The restrictions which apply to company directors are contained in Chapter 6.

4.1 WHO CAN QUALIFY?

Any person who is an employee of an employer and therefore liable to pay tax under Schedule E may be provided with retirement and death benefits under an approved retirement benefit scheme. The term 'employee' includes:

(1) directors, whether controlling or not, whose income is assessable under Schedule E;
(2) part-time or temporary employees;
(3) genuinely employed spouses of professional persons such as accountants, solicitors, doctors and dentists;
(4) genuinely employed spouses of the self-employed;
(5) salaried, not equity, partners in a partnership;
(6) UK-resident employees of overseas employers;
(7) domestic servants.

4.2 WHO CANNOT QUALIFY?

It is not possible to provide benefits under an approved retirement benefit scheme for anyone whose income is assessable under Schedule D, for example:

(1) self-employed persons, whether sole proprietors or equity partners;
(2) consultants whose only source of income is assessable under Schedule D;
(3) directors of an investment company, although they are often entitled

to receive low levels of Schedule E income from the company (see Chapter 18).

The first two categories listed above may, however, pay contributions to personal pension schemes and/or to retirement annuity contracts (see Chapter 14).

4.3 RECENT CHANGES

Occupational pension schemes have been subject to many changes in recent years. While the Pensions Act 1995 will have a considerable impact primarily on the administration of pension schemes, the principal changes to permitted levels of benefit were brought about by F(No 2)A 1987 and FA 1989. The relevant provisions are now consolidated in Part XIV of ICTA 1988. In broad terms, there are three categories of benefit structure depending upon the date of membership of the scheme, as set out below.

While the legislation sets out basic conditions which entitle a scheme to mandatory approval, it also confers wide discretionary powers on the PSO to approve schemes which do not fully comply. Most schemes seek discretionary approval, to which end the PSO has issued its own guidance as to (among other requirements) calculation of maximum benefits. That guidance is set out in what are commonly referred to as the 'Practice Notes' of which there are two current versions. The 1979 Practice Notes apply, generally speaking, to all schemes approved before 29 November 1991 and the 1997 Practice Notes to schemes approved on or after that date.

Membership categories

In broad terms the maximum benefits that may be provided depend on the date of joining the scheme, which categorises membership as follows.

4.3.1 Pre-1987 members

Pre-1987 benefits may be provided under schemes which were established before 17 March 1987 for members who joined before that date.

4.3.2 1987–89 members

1987–89 benefits may be provided under schemes which were established before 14 March 1989 for members who joined on or after 17 March 1987 and before 1 June 1989.

4.3.3 Post-1989 members

Post-1989 benefits may be provided for members joining schemes from 1 June 1989, regardless of when the scheme was established and also for members who joined, before 1 June 1989, schemes established on or after 14 March 1989.

In general terms each category is subject to more restrictions on the benefits which may be provided than its predecessor: pre-1987 pension benefits are better than 1987–89 pension benefits which in turn are better than post-1989 pension benefits. However, it is possible to opt for post-1989 benefits where the result would be beneficial in certain circumstances, eg where enhanced early retirement benefits are required.

The benefits relating to the three categories are described later in this chapter.

4.3.4 Maximum funding

Revenue concern about overfunding of money purchase schemes resulted in the imposition of age-related contribution limits, at first on insured schemes from 1 September 1994, and then on small self-administered schemes from 1 June 1996. These contribution limits, based on assumptions which are more stringent than hitherto, have the effect of reducing funding rates, particularly at the lower end of the age scale. Accordingly, money purchase schemes are limited both in relation to contributions and emerging benefits.

Transitional arrangements apply for those who were members of money purchase schemes before the effective date of the new funding arrangements. For the five years ending 31 August 1999 the employer may continue to make contributions to an insured money purchase scheme at the level under the old basis. Any increase, however, during the five-year period will cause the new rules to bite.

Similar transitional arrangements apply to small self-administered schemes with the five-year period ending on 1 June 2001.

4.4 RETIREMENT AGES

To obtain PSO approval of scheme membership it is necessary to stipulate a normal retirement age, which should be the best estimate of an employee's retiring age.

Under schemes approved on or after 29 November 1991, the permitted age range for both men and women is normally 60 to 75, although an earlier or later normal retirement age is possible in individual cases at the PSO's discretion, eg in the case of a member who joins the scheme as a post-1989 member with the right to benefits on a pre-1987 basis.

Under schemes approved before 29 November 1991, post-1989 members of either sex are restricted to the age range 60 to 75. However, the permitted ranges for pre-1987 and 1987–89 members are 60 to 70 for men and 55 to 70 for women (subject to the special restrictions for controlling directors – see Chapter 6). Where it can be demonstrated that such a member is likely to continue working beyond age 70 it is possible to obtain approval of a later normal retirement age.

4.5 MAXIMUM BENEFITS

The maximum benefits available to an employee or director from a pension scheme normally depend on his years of service with the employer and his salary at or around retirement. Generally, the maximum pension which an employee can receive at his normal retirement date under Revenue rules is two-thirds of his final salary ('final salary' is explained below), of which he may be able to commute up to a maximum of 1.5 times final salary for a lump sum.

There is, however, a distinction between what the Revenue permits and what a particular pension scheme might provide: even if the pension fund has accumulated substantial amounts it is not possible to provide retirement benefits in excess of Revenue limits. Conversely a pension scheme may provide benefits well below the maximum permitted by the Revenue.

In the case of a post-1989 member who is a controlling director (see Chapter 6) and who retired on or after 31 August 1991, the Revenue also requires that the limits described below apply to the *aggregate* of the member's occupational scheme benefits and those derived from retirement annuity contract/personal pension schemes relating to earnings with the same employer.

4.6 MAXIMUM PENSION

4.6.1 60ths scale

The Revenue will always permit a pension benefit of up to one-sixtieth of final salary for each year of service (this is known as the '60ths scale' or 'straight 60ths') so that a maximum pension of two-thirds of final salary is obtained only after completing 40 years' service with the employer – an unlikely event for most people. If the period of service is less than 40 years the pension on retirement is calculated by multiplying the number of years of service with the employer by one-sixtieth of final salary.

Example 4.1

An employee retires after 27 years' service with his employer: his final salary is £20,000: the rules of the group pension scheme provide for a pension of $\frac{1}{60}$ of final salary for each year of service: his retirement pension from the scheme will therefore be £9,000:

$$\frac{27}{60} \times £20,000 = £9,000 \text{ pa}$$

Very few employees and directors will complete 40 years' service with the same employer. It is still possible, however, for them to receive the maximum pension of two-thirds of final salary under an enhanced accrual rate (if permitted by the rules of the scheme) depending on their category of membership.

4.6.2 Uplifted 60ths scale (pre-1987 members)

Under this scale the two-thirds maximum is permitted if at least ten years' service has been completed with the employer at normal retirement date. Provided at least five years' service can be completed with an employer, higher benefits can be provided than under the straight 60ths scale.

The following table shows how pension entitlement can be accelerated.

Table 4.1

Years of service normal retirement age	Maximum pension as a fraction of final salary
1–5	1/60th for each year
6	8/60
7	16/60
8	24/60
9	32/60
10 or more	40/60

Example 4.2

An employee retires after eight years' service with his company. His final salary is £28,000. The rules of the pension scheme provide for a pension calculated on the uplifted 60ths scale.

His retirement pension from the scheme will therefore be £11,200, calculated as follows:

$$^{24}\!/\!_{60} \times £28,000 = £11,200 \text{ pa}$$

If, as is usually the case, the period of service includes a part of a year, the uplifted 60ths scale is increased proportionately to reflect the service in the last year.

Example 4.3

The employee in the previous example retires after seven years and six months. His retirement pension from the scheme will be calculated as follows:

Number of 60ths after eight years	24
Number of 60ths after seven years	16
Increase obtained during twelve months	8
Increase obtained during six months	4
Number of 60ths after seven years and six months	16 + 4 = 20
Pension $^{20}\!/\!_{60} \times £28,000 = £9,333$ pa	

In arriving at the maximum pension obtainable on the 'uplifted 60ths scale', it is necessary to include a restriction to take account of additional pensions arising from any voluntary contributions and any 'retained benefits' (see below).

4.6.3 Accelerated scale (1987–89 members and post-1989 members)

In respect of members joining schemes on or after 17 March 1987 or where a new scheme was established on or after that date, the maximum pension is one-thirtieth of final salary for each year of service. The two-thirds maximum is therefore permitted only on completion of at least 20 years' service with the employer at normal retirement date (compared with ten under the uplifted 60ths scale).

Thus, the pension on the new accelerated scale is better than the maximum pension set out in Table 4.1 where the years of service to normal retirement age are seven or less. Where the years of service to normal retirement age are greater than seven the old uplifted 60ths scale is significantly better.

The following is a comparison of the two scales:

Table 4.2

Years of service	Pre-1987 members		1987–89 members and post-1989 members	
	Fraction of final salary	Percentage of final salary	Fraction of final salary	Percentage of final salary
1	1/60	1.66	2/60	3.33
2	2/60	3.33	4/60	6.66
3	3/60	5.00	6/60	10.00
4	4/60	6.66	8/60	13.33
5	5/60	8.33	10/60	16.66
6	8/60	13.33	12/60	20.00
7	16/60	26.66	14/60	23.33
8	24/60	40.00	16/60	26.66
9	32/60	53.33	18/60	30.00
10	40/60	66.66	20/60	33.30
11	40/60	66.66	22/60	36.60
12	40/60	66.66	24/60	40.00
13	40/60	66.66	26/60	43.33
14	40/60	66.66	28/60	46.66
15	40/60	66.66	30/60	50.00
16	40/60	66.66	32/60	53.33
17	40/60	66.66	34/60	56.66
18	40/60	66.66	36/60	60.00
19	40/60	66.66	38/60	63.30
20	40/60	66.66	40/60	66.66

4.7 DEFINITIONS OF 'FINAL SALARY'

The bases for calculating final salary permitted by the PSO are as follows:

(I) Remuneration (on which Schedule E income tax liability has been assessed as final and conclusive) for any one of the five years preceding the normal retirement date: remuneration includes basic salary for the year in question together with the average of fluctuating emoluments, such as bonus or commission, earned over a period of at least three consecutive years ending in the year in question.

(II) The annual average of total earnings (on which Schedule E income tax liability has been assessed as final and conclusive) over a period of at least three consecutive years ending not earlier than ten years before normal retirement date.

In the case of a controlling director, however, only definition (II) is acceptable.

'Fluctuating emoluments' means any earnings not paid on a fixed basis which are additional to basic wage or salary and, depending on the rules of the scheme, can include:

(1) Profit related pay (whether or not taxable).
(2) Overtime, commission, bonuses assessable to income tax under Schedule E.
(3) Benefits in kind which are assessable to income tax under Schedule E such as company car, company paid petrol, rent-free accommodation.

Where fluctuating emoluments have been paid for less than three years they should (when calculating final salary in accordance with definition (I) above) be averaged over the period starting with the date they commenced or, if later, the beginning of the three-year period and ending on the last day of the basic salary year in question. PSO permission must however be sought if it is intended to include a fluctuating emolument paid only once.

The F(No 2)A 1987 and FA 1989 brought about changes to the definition of 'final salary'. The changes apply to all members of occupational schemes, as follows:

(1) Income or gains from the acquisition or disposal of shares or interests in shares or options over shares acquired through share option, share incentive and profit sharing schemes, or from shares which give rise to a Schedule E tax liability, are excluded from the calculation of 'final salary'. However this exclusion does not apply:
  (a) where the shares or the option or other interest in shares which give rise, on or after 17 March 1987, to a Schedule E tax liability were acquired or granted before that date; or
  (b) where 'final salary' is determined for calculating maximum benefits on death in service (see below).
(2) Also excluded from 'final salary' is anything in respect of which tax is chargeable by virtue of ICTA 1988, s 148 (payments on termination of employment, eg golden handshakes) except where final salary is being used to calculate maximum benefits on death in service.
(3) In the case of a pre-1987 or 1987–89 member, if the 'final salary' calculated in accordance with definition (I) exceeds £100,000 (or such other figure as may be prescribed by the Treasury) in any year from 6 April 1987 onwards, actual 'final salary' must be restricted to the amount calculated in accordance with definition (II) or, if greater, £100,000.
(4) In the case of a post-1989 member, 'final salary' under either

definition is restricted to a maximum of £90,600 (for the 1999/2000 tax year). It is intended that this maximum will be adjusted annually in line with increases in the Retail Prices Index (measured from September to September) and rounded up to the next highest multiple of £600. A member who is subject to this upper limit may therefore be provided with a maximum pension of £60,200 per annum on normal retirement in the 1999/2000 tax year.

(5) Final remuneration may now also include:
   (a) remuneration received after termination of employment or retirement but on which the tax liability has been determined, provided that it was earned prior to termination and is treated as a fluctuating emolument;
   (b) remuneration assessable to tax under Schedule E but on which the tax liability has not yet been determined, provided that final remuneration is recalculated once the tax liability has been determined, but only for calculating immediate benefits.

4.8 DYNAMISED OR INDEXED FINAL REMUNERATION

Final salary may be re-calculated as a notional figure known as dynamised final remuneration or indexed final remuneration by increasing the actual salary earned in a particular year by the increase in the Retail Prices Index (RPI) between the end of the year in question and normal retirement date. The result is to produce a pension which is related to the salary which an employee would have received if his previous years' salaries had kept pace with the cost of living. Dynamisation however:

(1) may not be used to increase the tax-free lump sum (see below) payable to a pre-1987 member unless the pension is increased to the same proportionate extent – that is dynamisation must be justified by the increase to the overall entitlement to benefits;

(2) may not cause the final salary of a 1987–89 member used to calculate the tax-free lump sum to exceed £100,000 (or such other figure as may be prescribed by the Treasury);

(3) may not be used to increase the final salary of a post-1989 member beyond the value of the 'earnings cap' as at the date of retirement.

4.9 RETAINED PENSION BENEFITS

Depending on the context in which maximum permitted benefits under the current employer's scheme are being calculated, retained benefits can include:

(1) Deferred pensions and pensions in payment, in respect of previous employment, from:
   (a) any UK scheme which is approved or seeking approval, including any free standing additional voluntary scheme;
   (b) any statutory scheme (eg the Teacher's Superannuation Scheme);
   (c) any overseas scheme which the Revenue regards as approved for UK tax relief purposes.
(2) The annuity equivalent of lump sums received or receivable from previous pension schemes defined under (1) above.
(3) Pensions and/or the annuity equivalent of lump sums arising from personal pension schemes or retirement annuity contracts relating to service with the same or a former employer, or to previous self-employment.
(4) Benefits relating to transfer payments from overseas schemes made to any of the arrangements defined in (1), (2) or (3) above.
(5) Funds to which s 608 of ICTA 1988 (see Appendix 4) applies (ie 'Old Code' funds).
(6) Benefits arising from transfer payments received by the current employer's scheme.

Benefits which would otherwise have to be taken into account may however be disregarded as retained benefits in the following circumstances:

(1) If the member retires and
   (a) his earnings in the first year of membership of the scheme do not exceed one-quarter of the earnings cap in force at the date of entry (for the 1999/2000 tax year £90,600 ÷ 4 = £22,650), and
   (b) he is not, and has not been in the ten years prior to joining the scheme, a controlling director in respect of the employment being pensioned,
   although if the member is or was a member of more than one scheme of the employer it is the date of entry to the first of those schemes which determines if the exemption applies, so that there is no exemption if the member joined the first scheme before 31 August 1991.
(2) Where the benefits in question relate to a wholly concurrent employment/occupation.
(3) If the total retained benefits are equivalent to or less than a pension of £260 per annum.
(4) Where the benefits relate to a transfer value received from an occupational pension scheme of the same employer.

Effect of retained pension benefits on maximum benefits

If a member's benefits are calculated on the 'straight' 60ths scale it is not in any event necessary to take retained benefits into account, *unless* that member is a controlling director in which case

(1) If the controlling director is:
   (a) a pre-1987 member; or
   (b) a 1987–89 member; or
   (c) a post-1989 member who retired before 31 August 1991;
   the value of all personal pension scheme/retirement annuity contract benefits has to be deducted from the straight 60ths scale benefits in order to arrive at the occupational scheme maximum.
(2) If the controlling director is a post-1989 member who retires on or after 31 August 1991, the value of personal pension scheme/retirement annuity contract benefits are required to be taken into account by treating such benefits which relate to earnings from the same employer as if they were benefits which had been provided by the occupational scheme (other retained personal pension scheme/retirement annuity contract benefits relating to previous employment can be ignored).

Whenever pension benefits are to be provided on the pre-1987 member 'uplifted 60ths' scale or 1987–89/post-1989 member accelerated scale, the sum of the member's retained benefits and pension benefits from his current employment must not exceed two-thirds of his final salary. In this context the pension benefit of a post-1989 controlling director member from his current employment is the aggregate of that payable from the occupational scheme and from personal pension schemes/retirement annuity contracts relating to earnings from the same employer.

4.10 PENSION INCREASES (ESCALATION)

Pensions which have been paid to a retired employee or to his dependants may be increased to reflect increases in the RPI since retirement or up to the level of the maximum approvable pension payable on retirement and then subsequently increased in line with the RPI.

Example 4.4

An employee retires from the company on a final salary of £15,000 but receives only £4,000 from his pension scheme. It would be possible for his employer subsequently to increase his pension up to £10,000, ie two-thirds of his final salary (assuming that he had completed at least 20 years' service with the employer) with subsequent RPI increases on the pension of £10,000.

For members who retired before 31 August 1991, the maximum approvable pension at retirement includes any amount commuted for a lump sum. On retirement on or after 31 August 1991, however, the pension cannot be increased beyond the maximum residual pension as at the date of retirement, ie after deducting the annuity equivalent of any lump sum and any spouse's/dependant's pension provided by surrender of the member's pension from the maximum approvable before either or both of those events. The maximum residual may be subsequently increased in line with the RPI.

After 1 April 1997, the provisions of the Pensions Act 1995 require schemes to increase pensions by at least the lower of 5 per cent per annum or the increase in the RPI.

4.11 CASH LUMP SUMS

4.11.1 80ths scale

Most pension schemes allow an employee to give up part of his pension on retirement for a tax-free cash lump sum. Even if income is of paramount importance the tax-free lump sum should still be taken and then if necessary converted into an income which would be taxed more favourably (see Chapter 19).

The maximum tax-free lump sum that can be provided for an employee is 1.5 times his final salary after completing 40 years' service at normal retirement date: this represents three-eighteths of his final salary for each year of service.

Example 4.5

> If an employee retires after 27 years' service with his employer on a salary of £20,000, and his pension scheme provides that part of his pension may be given up for a tax-free cash sum of three-eighteths of his final salary for each year of service, his lump sum will therefore be £20,250.

4.11.2 Uplifted 80ths scale for pre-1987 members

Under Revenue limits pre-1987 members can obtain the maximum lump sum after 20 years' service with the same employer if the pension scheme provides lump sum benefits at an enhanced accrual rate known as the 'uplifted 80ths' scale. There is no advantage in using this scale unless the employee has achieved eight years' service before normal retirement age because the accrual rate is the same as the '80ths' scale, ie three-eighteths of final salary per year of service. Thereafter the lump sum accrual rate increases progressively until a lump sum of $^{120}\!/_{80}$ of final salary is obtained after 20 or more years' service.

Table 4.3

Years of service to normal retirement age	Maximum lump sum as a fraction of final salary
1–8	3/80ths for each year
9	30/80
10	36/80
11	42/80
12	48/80
13	54/80
14	63/80
15	72/80
16	81/80
17	90/80
18	99/80
19	108/80
20 or more	120/80

Example 4.6

An employee retires after 15 years' service with his employer. His final salary is £18,000. The rules of the pension scheme provide for a tax-free lump sum calculated on the uplifted 80ths scale.

His tax-free lump sum from the scheme will therefore be £16,200, calculated as follows: $^{72}\!/_{80} \times £18,000 = £16,200$.

If, as is usually the case, the period of service includes a part of a year, the uplifted 80ths scale is interpolated to reflect the service in the last year but the result must be a whole eightieth.

4.11.3 Accelerated scale (1987–89 members)

It is not possible for a 1987–89 member to be provided with a tax-free lump sum on the uplifted 80ths scale in isolation, although a lump sum on the 80ths scale is always permitted (ie three-eightieths of final salary for each year of service) regardless of the amount, if any, of pension benefit.

Even where the occupational scheme provides for both pension and tax-free lump sum it is only possible to provide the maximum lump sum cash on the uplifted 80ths scale if the scheme provides the maximum approvable pension benefits on the accelerated scale for pensions, ie one-thirtieth of final salary for each year of service. However, where the pension provided is between one-sixtieth and one-thirtieth of final salary for each year of service an enhanced cash lump sum may be payable. The formula and examples are shown below.

In calculating the maximum tax-free lump sum, final salary is still capped at a figure of £100,000 (although this may be increased by Treasury Order). For an individual who could complete 20 years' service by retirement and whose scheme provides him with a maximum approvable pension, his tax-free lump sum will be limited to £150,000 even though his final salary might be, say, £200,000.

The formula for calculating the amounts of tax-free cash on the new accelerated scale is as follows:

Formula

Step 1

$$\frac{\text{Actual pension} - \text{basic pension (on 60ths scale)}}{\text{maximum pension (30ths scale)} - \text{basic pension (60ths scale)}} = \%$$

Step 2   Maximum Tax-Free Cash – basic Tax-Free Cash × % in Step 1 above.

Step 3   Add result of Step 2 to basic Tax-Free Cash = Total Tax-Free Cash permitted

Example 4.7

	Service 20 years			
	Final Salary £30,000			
	Actual Pension Provided £19,000 pa			
Actual pension			=	£19,000
Basic pension (1/60 scale) =	$^{20}/_{60} \times$ FS		=	£10,000
Maximum pension	=	$^{40}/_{60} \times$ FS	=	£20,000
Basic cash (3/80 scale)	=	$^{60}/_{80} \times$ FS	=	£22,500
Maximum cash	=	$1^{1}/_{2} \times$ FS	=	£45,000
(a) $\dfrac{19,000 - 10,000}{20,000 - 10,000}$	=	$\dfrac{9,000}{10,000}$	=	90%
(b) 45,000 – 22,500	=	22,500 × 90%	=	£20,250
(c) 22,500 + 20,250	=	£42,750 = Tax-Free Cash permitted		

Example 4.8

Service 15 years
Final Salary £30,000
Actual Pension Provided £10,000 pa

Actual pension			$=$	£10,000
Basic pension (1/60)	$=$	$^{15}/_{60} \times$ FS	$=$	£ 7,500
Maximum pension	$=$	$^{30}/_{60} \times$ FS	$=$	£15,000
Basic cash (3/80)	$=$	$^{45}/_{80} \times$ FS	$=$	£16,875
Maximum cash	$=$	$90\% \times$ FS	$=$	£27,000

(a) $\dfrac{10,000 - 7,500}{15,000 - 7,500} \ \equiv \ \dfrac{2,500}{7,500} \ = \ 33\frac{1}{3}\%$

(b) $27,000 - 16,875 \ = \ 10,125 \times 33\frac{1}{3}\% \ = \ £3,375$

(c) $16,875 + 3,375 \ = \ £20,250 =$ Tax-Free Cash permitted

Example 4.9

Service 18 years
Final Salary £75,000
Actual Pension Provided £40,000 pa

Actual pension			$=$	£40,000
Basic pension	$=$	$^{18}/_{60} \times$ FS	$=$	£22,500
Maximum pension	$=$	$^{36}/_{60} \times$ FS	$=$	£45,000
Basic cash	$=$	$^{54}/_{80} \times$ FS	$=$	£50,625
Maximum cash	$=$	$123.75\% \times$ FS $=$		£92,812

(a) $\dfrac{40,000 - 22,500}{45,000 - 22,500} \ = \ \dfrac{17,500}{22,500} \ = \ 77.77\%$

(b) $92,812 - 50,625 \ = \ 42,187 \times 77.77\% \ = \ £32,808$

(c) $50,625 + 32,808 \ = \ £83,433 =$ Tax-Free Cash permitted

Example 4.10

Service 15 years
Final Salary £200,000
Actual Pension Provided £90,000 pa

Actual pension			$=$	£ 90,000
Basic pension	$=$	$^{15}/_{60} \times$ FS	$=$	£ 50,000
Maximum pension	$=$	$^{30}/_{60} \times$ FS	$=$	£100,000
Basic cash	$=$	$^{45}/_{80} \times £100,000$	$=$	£ 56,250
Maximum cash	$=$	$90\% \times £100,000$	$=$	£ 90,000

(a) $\dfrac{90,000 - 50,000}{100,000 - 50,000} \ = \ \dfrac{40,000}{50,000} \ = \ 80\%$

(b) $90,000 - 56,250 \ = \ 33,750 \times 80\% \ = \ £27,000$

(c) $56,250 + 27,000 \ = \ £83,250 =$ Tax-Free Cash permitted

4.11.4 Scale for post-1989 members

The maximum lump sum is the greater of three-eightieths of final salary (capped at £90,600 in 1999/2000) for each year of service and the pension multiplied by 2.25: 'Pension' is the amount before commutation or any reduction in favour of widows/dependants and is calculated on the basis on which it will actually be paid, eg in monthly instalments, increasing in payment at 5 per cent per annum compound.

In the case of a controlling director who retires on or after 31 August 1991 it is also required that the three-eightieths limit applies to the aggregate benefit payable from the occupational scheme and any personal pension scheme/retirement annuity contract relating to earnings from the same employer. Similarly such benefits are aggregated for the purposes of the '2.25 ×' calculation.

4.12 RETAINED LUMP SUM BENEFITS

The retained lump sum benefits which it might be necessary to take into account are those arising from the arrangements described under retained pension benefits above, as are the circumstances in which retained lump sums may be disregarded.

If a member's benefits are calculated on the three-eigh100ths scale it is not necessary to take retained benefits into account, unless that member is a controlling director in which case:

(1) If the controlling director is:
    (a) a pre-1987 member, or
    (b) a 1987–89 member, or
    (c) a post-1989 member who retired before 31 August 1991
    the three-eightieths scale benefits cannot exceed a maximum of 1.5 × final salary minus the value of all personal pension schemes/ retirement annuity contract retained benefits.
(2) If the controlling director is a post-1989 member who retires on or after 31 August 1991, the value of personal pension scheme/retirement annuity contract benefits is required to be taken into account by treating such benefits which relate to earnings from the same employer as if they were benefits provided by the occupational scheme (other retained personal pension scheme/retirement annuity contract benefits relating to previous employment can be ignored).

Where the date of retirement is before 31 August 1991 and lump sum benefit is to be provided for a pre-1987 or 1987–89 member on the 'uplifted 80ths' scale or is to be enhanced in the case of a post-1989 member, the sum of the member's retained benefits and lump sum benefits from his current employment must not exceed 1.5 × final salary. On retirement on or after 31 August 1991, however:

(1) Retained benefits of any 1987–89 non-controlling director can be disregarded in calculating benefit on the 'uplifted 80ths' scale.

(2) The 'uplifted 80ths' scale benefit for a 1987–89 controlling director is subject to a maximum of 1.5 × final salary minus retained benefits from personal pension schemes/retirement annuity contracts *only*.

(3) All retained benefits of any post-1989 member can be disregarded.

The lump sum benefit of a post-1989 controlling director, who retires on or after 31 August 1991, from his current employment is in any event the aggregate of that payable from the occupational scheme and from personal pension schemes/retirement annuity contracts relating to earnings from the same employer.

4.13 PENSION VALUES OF LUMP SUMS

If a lump sum is taken under a pension scheme, any pension benefit to which the employee would be otherwise entitled is reduced. For pre-1987 and 1987–89 members and post-1989 members retiring before 31 August 1991, the amount by which the member's pension is reduced depends on the member's age at retirement; the following table of factors was agreed between the PSO, the Association of British Insurers and the Association of Consulting Actuaries.

Table 4.4

	Age	Factor
Men	60	10.2
	65	9.0
	70	7.8
Women	55	12.2
	60	11.0
	65	9.8

Factors for intermediate ages are calculated by an increase or decrease of 0.02 per month of age difference.

The amount by which a pension reduces is obtained by dividing the factor into the cash available. For example, a male employee retiring at age 65 and accepting a tax-free lump sum of £18,000 will have his pension reduced by £2,000 per annum.

Where pensions increase at a greater rate than 5 per cent per annum compound, the PSO insist that different factors are used to reflect this. Thus, if a pension increases at, say, 8.5 per cent per annum compound automatically, the factor used for commutation purposes must incorporate an interest yield assumption of at least 11.5 per cent. In other words, the difference between the rate of increase in the pension and the yield assumed on investments must be 3 per cent at least.

Trustees of pension schemes are not bound by any of these factors and may use less generous ones reflecting economic conditions from time to time. Insurance companies may agree tables of commutation factors with the PSO.

However for post-1989 members retiring on or after 31 August 1991 the commutation factor which must be used in calculating Revenue limits is a unisex 12:1 regardless of escalation.

It is sometimes difficult for a retiring employee to decide whether he should take a tax-free lump sum or opt for a pension which will increase in payment. Chapter 19 deals with some of the considerations which should influence his decision.

4.14 DEATH BENEFITS

4.14.1 Benefits on death after retirement

A pension can be provided for the widow or dependants of a former employee who dies in retirement. The maximum amount is two-thirds of the maximum approvable pension which could have been provided for the employee himself ignoring his retained benefits from earlier occupations. As the maximum will normally be two-thirds of the employee's final salary, the widow or dependant's maximum pension is two-thirds of two-thirds of the employee's final salary (four-ninths).

If the member retired before 31 August 1991 then any widow's/dependant's pension payable from the arrangements described under retained pension benefits above must be deducted from the four-ninths maximum.

Whether or not retained benefits have to be taken into account, the widow's/dependant's maximum may be increased in line with the increase in the RPI since the date of the member's retirement.

The reduction in the maximum approvable member's pension for short-serving employees, which applies to 1987–89 members and post-1989 members, also has the effect of reducing dependants' pensions.

Where pensions are paid to a widow and one or more dependants (or if there is no widow, to more than one dependant) no individual pension can exceed the above maximum, nor can the aggregate of all the pensions exceed the maximum pension which could have been provided for the employee.

It is possible for these pensions to increase in line with the RPI calculated from the date at which the employee would have retired (rather than from the time the widow's or dependant's pension commences).

A widow's or dependant's pension can start at the date of the employee's death (unless the employee's pension was guaranteed to be paid for a period exceeding five years, when the pension cannot start until the end of the guarantee period). The widow's pension and dependant's pension can continue for life or can cease or reduce on remarriage. Any pension received by a child must cease when the child ceases to be a dependant. A dependant is someone who is financially dependent on the employee. A widow's or dependant's pension must cease on death: no guaranteed period may apply as in the case of an employee's own pension, unless the pension has been provided by surrender.

An employee may surrender part of his own pension to provide one for his widow or dependant on his death in retirement, either because the widow/dependant has no pension entitlement in his or her own right or because the employee wishes to enhance an own right pension. The maximum pension which is allocated in this way must not exceed the amount of the reduced pension (either before commutation, or including the annuity equivalent of any separate lump sum) which is payable to the employee and if more than one allocated pension is provided, the limit applies to their aggregate value. A widow's or dependant's pension provided by this method can start at the date of the employee's death, even if his residual pension continues to be paid under a guarantee not exceeding five years.

The employee's pension can be guaranteed for a period of up to ten years, even though he dies during that period. If the guaranteed period is five years or less the balance of the pension payable following the death of the retired employee in that period can be paid as a lump sum. For example, if the employee's pension amounted to £1,000 per annum, commencing at age 65 and the employee died at age 67, having received two instalments of pension, a lump sum could be paid to his dependants amounting to £3,000. The destination of these payments can be at the discretion of the scheme trustees to a wide range of beneficiaries and are normally exempt from income tax and inheritance tax.

Widowers' pensions can be provided on a similar basis to widows' pensions as set out above.

4.14.2 Benefits on death in service

If death occurs in service the following maximum benefits may be provided.

Lump sums

A lump sum may be provided not exceeding the greater of £5,000, and four times the final remuneration of the employee at the date of death (minus any retained benefits), together with a refund of any personal contributions paid by the employee with or without interest: the interest may represent the actual rate of growth on those contributions. For post-1989 members, final remuneration is subject to the earnings limit of £90,600 (in 1999/2000). Thus the maximum lump sum is £362,400 (plus a refund of personal contributions with growth, as before).

The retained benefits are those payable on death in service from the arrangements described under retained pension benefits above, but lump sum death benefits may be disregarded under the following conditions:

(1) where the member satisfied the one-quarter earnings cap exemption;
(2) if the benefits total £2,500 or less;
(3) where they represent a return of fund under a personal pension scheme or retirement annuity contract;
(4) when payable from a personal pension scheme providing contracted-out benefits only;
(5) when they are a refund of member contributions under an occupational scheme (other than a free standing AVC scheme);
(6) where the benefits in question relate to a wholly concurrent employment/occupation.

The destination of lump sum death-in-service payments can be at the discretion of the scheme's trustees in which case they are normally free of inheritance tax. The rules of the pension scheme will specify the classes of individual to whom such payments may be made. Normally the employee will have notified the trustees of his wishes regarding the person or persons to whom he would like the monies to be paid although the trustees are not bound by this nomination.

Spouses' and dependants' pensions

A pension for a spouse or dependant may be provided equal to two-thirds of the maximum pension that could have been approved for the employee assuming he or she had not died but had continued in employment to normal retirement age with the same final salary as he or she was earning at the time of death. The maximum pension, therefore, is four-ninths of the employee's salary at the date of death (subject to the earnings limit in the case of a post-1989 member).

Where the deceased member was a 1987–89 member the maximum pension for a spouse or dependant may again be lower, as a result of the reduction in the maximum approvable member's pension for short-serving employees.

In the same way as on death in retirement, pensions can also be provided for other dependants, including children, providing the total income payable to spouses and dependants does not exceed the maximum level of pension which could have been provided for the deceased, had he or she remained in service to normal retirement age. A widow's or widower's pension is normally payable for life but could cease or reduce on remarriage. Pensions for children must cease at the age of 18 or completion of full-time education or training, if later.

Escalation of death-in-service benefits

Spouse's and dependant's pensions may automatically increase in payment in a similar manner to that described above for members' pensions.

Dynamised final remuneration

In calculating maximum benefits on death in service, use may be made of dynamised final remuneration, as explained in 4.8.

Final remuneration need not be defined in the same terms as for the calculation of other benefits. It may be defined in the following ways:

(1) where basic salary only is involved, the annual rate of salary being received immediately before death;

(2) basic salary as above, plus the average of fluctuating emoluments during the three years (or the whole period of the employment if less) up to the date of death;

(3) the total earnings (fixed plus fluctuating) paid during a selected period of 12 months prior to death (the selected period may end either at the date of death, or on some convenient date, such as 5 April, or the end of the pension scheme year, falling not earlier than 36 months prior to the date of death).

Death in service after normal retirement date

Where an employee has deferred his retirement and dies during his extended service, benefits may be paid on either of the following bases:

(1) that he died before normal retirement date and therefore normal death-in-service benefits may be provided; or

(2) that he retired the day before he died and is, therefore, entitled to death-in-retirement benefits.

If an employee has taken any benefit at normal retirement date, for example the tax-free cash sum, and subsequently dies in service, any death benefits are limited to those payable on death after retirement.

The rules of the scheme will specify which method is to be used in the event of death during deferred retirement.

4.15 RETIREMENT

4.15.1 Retirement before normal retirement date

An employee can take an immediate pension and lump sum if his employment is terminated or if he retires early, from age 50. Female employees who joined schemes approved before November 1991 can take immediate benefits at age 45, provided they are within ten years of their normal retirement date.

4.15.2 Early retirement (not through ill-health)

Pre-1987 members and 1987–89 members

As an alternative to using the straight 60ths and 3/80ths scales, maximum benefits can be calculated in accordance with the formulae:

$$\frac{N}{NS} \times P \text{ or } \frac{N}{NS} \times LS$$

where 'N' is the number of years which have been completed in service to the point of early retirement (maximum 40).

'NS' is the number of years which could have been completed from the date of joining service to normal retirement date.

'P' and 'LS' are, respectively, the maximum pension and tax-free lump sum which could have been approved had the employee retired at his normal retirement date but based on his final remuneration at the date of his early retirement.

For example, a pre-1987 member who joined the scheme at the age of 25, expecting to retire at age 60 but who retires early at the age of 50 on a salary of £9,000 per annum, may be provided with a maximum early retirement pension of £4,285, calculated as follows:

£9,000 × $\frac{2}{3}$ × $\frac{25}{35}$ = £4,285 pa

He could exchange part of the above early retirement pension for a lump sum calculated on a similar basis as follows:

£9,000 × 1.5 × $\frac{25}{35}$ = £9,642

These are the overall limits and include the value of any retained benefits (see above) which must be deducted from the value of 'P' and 'LS' before applying N/NS. Any dependants' benefits are then directly related to the reduced pension.

Post-1989 members

The method of calculating the pension is much simpler. The alternative to the straight 60ths benefit is normally a maximum of one-thirtieth of final remuneration for each year of service completed up to the date of early retirement. Thus, if an employee has completed 20 years' service a maximum pension of two-thirds of final remuneration may be provided from age 50 onwards.

Money purchase schemes

Under money purchase schemes approved before 29 November 1991 whose rules have been suitably drafted and under all money purchase schemes approved on or after 29 November 1991, the 'normal' early retirement pension maxima described above do not apply. The permitted maximum (as an alternative to straight 60ths) is the same as that on early retirement through ill health (incapacity), ie based on potential service to normal retirement age and final salary at the date of early retirement.

4.15.3 Early retirement through incapacity

If the reason for early retirement is incapacity, the maximum benefits payable are those which could have been payable at normal retirement date but based on the level of final remuneration at the date of early retirement.

Thus, a person with potentially at least 20 years' service to normal retirement date may receive a maximum early retirement pension of two-thirds of his final salary in the event of early retirement through ill health. The same principle applies to his tax-free lump sum.

'Incapacity' means physical or mental deterioration which is bad enough to prevent the individual from following his or her normal employment, or which seriously impairs his or her earning capacity. It does not simply mean a decline in energy or ability.

Where an employee is in exceptional circumstances of ill health such that his life expectancy is undoubtedly very short (ie, less than one year) he may be able to exchange the whole of his early retirement pension for an immediate cash sum although this will not be totally free of tax. Commutation on those grounds should not take place unless the administrator is notified by adequate medical evidence that the expectation of life is measured in months rather than years and so short that a pension is not a reasonable provision. The value of the pension which, but for the seriousness of the ill health, would not have been commutable, will be subject to tax at 20 per cent.

4.15.4 Benefits on late retirement

An employee who remains in service after normal retirement date can be provided with such additional pension benefits up to the normal maximum as would be available assuming that his actual retirement date is his normal retirement date.

1987–89 members

If his total service exceeds 40 years, he will be entitled to an additional pension of one-sixtieth of his final salary in respect of each year in excess of 40 which occurs after reaching normal retirement date: there is an overall maximum of $^{45}\!/_{60}$ of final salary at the date of retirement.

As an alternative to accruing additional 60ths, the maximum benefits available at normal retirement date may be increased by the greater of the actuarial increase reflecting the period of deferment and the growth in the underlying fund, or the increase in the RPI during the period of deferment.

A similar basis is used for calculating the increased tax-free lump sum on late retirement. Where total service exceeds 40 years, each year over 40 occurring after normal retirement date can generate an additional lump sum of three-eightieths of final salary at the date of actual retirement, subject to a maximum lump sum of $^{135}\!/_{80}$ of final salary. Alternatively the lump sum available at normal retirement date can be increased on a reasonable basis – in line with the increase in the underlying pension funds investments.

Post-1989 membership

No additional benefits may be provided in respect of service completed beyond normal retirement date above the maximum approvable pension at normal retirement date.

14.15.5 **Options on retirement**

On reaching normal retirement date, it is normally possible (depending on the rules of the scheme) to:

(1) take all the benefits – cash and pension (it is likely in these circumstances that the employee will be retiring from the company);
(2) to defer all the benefits (consistent with continuing to work with the employer or joining a new employer);
(3) take the tax-free lump sum and defer the pension or vice versa (while continuing in service).

Special rules apply to 20 per cent directors, and are explained in Chapter 6.

In respect of post-1989 members, option (2) is of limited value because the maximum approvable pension is not increased beyond normal retirement date and option (3) is not permitted.

Greater flexibility may be achieved by transferring the fund into a personal pension plan (see Chapter 14).

4.16 TRIVIAL BENEFITS

Where the total annual value of all pensions to an employee from the same employer do not exceed £260 per annum it is possible for the whole of the pension to be commuted for a lump sum. This does not apply where the member who is entitled to a pension which exceeds £260 per annum, commutes part of it for a lump sum and has a residual pension of £260 per annum or less.

4.17 COMBINATIONS OF SCHEMES

The changes introduced by F(No 2)A 1987 and FA 1989 have given rise to questions about the levels of benefits which may be provided for members who move to new or reconstructed schemes or join schemes to provide additional benefits. It is the broad intention that members of a scheme who remain with the same employer or who effectively remain members of the same scheme should not be adversely affected by any subsequent changes.

4.18 FINANCE (NO 2) ACT 1987

Inland Revenue Memorandum No 87, issued in August 1987, describes those situations in which pre-1987 members will not normally be regarded as caught by the changes – which apply to 1987–89 members – introduced by the F(No 2)A 1987 as follows:

(1) Restructuring of a business (or re-organisation of pension arrangements) resulting in employees moving from one employer's scheme to another's, provided that both employers are within the same group and that such changes do not give accelerated rates of accrual under the pre-17 March rules where these were not previously available.

(2) A move (eg on promotion) from one scheme of an employer to another scheme of that same employer, or of another employer in the same group.

(3) The joining (eg on promotion) of a separate top-up scheme which provides additional benefits to those under the main scheme in respect of which the individual remains a member.

(4) A move to a new or existing scheme of a new employer who has taken over the old employer (or all or part of his business), provided that the individual was a member of the old employer's scheme.

(5) Changes in the benefits structure of an existing scheme, provided that such changes do not give accelerated rates of accrual under the pre-17 March rules where these were not previously available.

(6) The exercise of a power of augmentation under the rules of an existing scheme to improve the benefits available to a member who joined before 17 March 1987, provided that the rules contained such a power before that date.

(7) Schemes or arrangements established before 17 March 1987, even if by then all the relevant documentation had not been finalised or no application for tax approval had been made. This will usually depend on the facts of a particular case but, as a general rule, a scheme will be in this category if, before 17 March 1987, the employer had entered into a contractual obligation to provide benefits.

(8) Changes to an existing scheme to permit it to contract out of SERPS or the establishment of a new scheme to enable existing members to contract out.

(9) Employees who leave their employer's scheme as a result of a temporary posting or secondment to another employer (whether in the United Kingdom or abroad), provided that at the time of leaving the scheme there was a definite intention to return and that on return they rejoin a scheme of the original employer, or of another employer in the same group.

(10) Individuals not covered by (9) above who cease to be members of their employer's scheme (whether or not they leave the employer's

service), provided that they rejoin the scheme within one month. Where absence is due to maternity leave, temporary lay-off or redundancy a longer period may be appropriate.

(11) Employees serving a waiting period before becoming full members of the employer's scheme, provided that they were regarded as members before 17 March 1987, for preservation purposes.

The F(No 2)A 1987 restrictions applying to 1987–89 members, who, *after* 17 March 1987, joined schemes which were approved *before* the Act received Royal Assent on 23 July 1987, are set out in Sched 23 to ICTA 1988 (see Appendix 4). However that Schedule permits the Revenue to waive the 1987–89 restrictions in relation to an employee:

(1) in circumstances prescribed by the Occupational Pension Schemes (Transitional Provisions) Regulations 1988;

(2) by the exercise of Revenue discretion.

4.19 FINANCE ACT 1989

The Revenue published Memorandum 100 in October 1989 in which it reiterated its intention that, broadly speaking, scheme members whose benefit entitlement is on a pre-1987 or 1987–89 basis should not be adversely affected if, because of corporate changes, pension scheme reconstructions etc, they join new schemes to which the post-1989 restrictions apply. Regulations have now been made, the Retirement Benefits Schemes (Continuation of Rights of Members of Approved Schemes) Regulations 1990, which achieve this in relation to schemes approved before 27 July 1989.

In the 1991 Practice Notes the Revenue has repeated that it may grant continued rights to pre-1987 and 1987–89 members who would otherwise be joining schemes as post-1989 members in the following circumstances:

(1) Benefits on the old basis cease to accrue under a scheme for a member who:

    (a) changes schemes within an association of employers to which the new earnings restriction applies in aggregate; or

    (b) joins a scheme of an employer who has acquired, been acquired by, merged with or taken over the whole or part of the business of his employer; or

    (c) returns to the scheme (or joins an associated scheme as in (a) and (b) above) after a temporary secondment or posting, or within one month of returning to work after maternity leave, or

    (d) returns to the scheme (or joins an associated scheme as in (a) or (b) above) within one month of any unpaid absence, or

(e) in any other circumstance provided that the member rejoins the scheme within one month of ceasing to accrue benefits.

(2) Before 1 June 1989 the member joined a scheme established before 14 March 1989, and on or after 1 June 1989 joins a supplementary scheme.

(3) An employee who served a waiting period for a scheme established before 14 March 1989, provided he was regarded as a member before that date for preservation purposes.

(4) An employee who while not a member had a contractual right to benefits before 1 June 1989 in a scheme established before 14 March 1989.

The FA 1989 restrictions applying to post-1989 members who *after* 14 March 1989 join schemes approved *before* the Act received Royal Assent on 27 July 1987 are set out in Sched 6 to that Act. However, that Schedule permits the Revenue to waive the post-1989 restrictions:

(1) in the circumstances prescribed by The Retirement Benefit Schemes (Continuation of Rights of Members of Approved Schemes) Regulations 1990;

(2) by the exercise of Revenue discretion.

4.20 OPTING FOR POST-1989 BENEFITS

A pre-1987 member may opt to receive the benefits applicable to a post-1989 member if the scheme's trustees are prepared to allow his benefits to be augmented and if the scheme rules are amended. For example, a pre-1987 member may wish to retire at age 50 on a pension of two-thirds of his final remuneration: this would not be permissible under pre-1987 rules although under post-1989 rules this would be permissible subject to the earnings cap.

A 1987–89 member may opt to be classed as a post-1989 member should the result be beneficial. Once again the member has to accept the earnings cap but in these circumstances there is no requirement for the scheme's trustees to permit the election because the right to make that election is conferred by statute.

4.21 ASSOCIATED EMPLOYMENTS

It is not uncommon for an individual to draw earnings from two or more employments which are associated and for these employments to provide pension benefits for the individual.

The FA 1989 provides that employers are associated if one is controlled by the other (eg parent and wholly-owned subsidiary) or both are controlled by the same third party (eg wholly-owned subsidiaries of the same parent).

4.21.1 Connected schemes

For post-1989 members this means that:

(1) Two or more schemes of such associated employers are *connected schemes* if:
   (a) there is a period during which the member is an employee of the associated employers;
   (b) that period is one for which benefits are payable under the scheme of each associated employer;
   (c) under each scheme that period counts as service with the relevant associated employer.
(2) Under any occupational scheme the Revenue limits apply to the total benefits payable:
   (a) in respect of all associated employers participating in the scheme; and
   (b) from all connected schemes; and
   (c) if the member is a controlling director who retires on or after 31 August 1991, from personal pension schemes/retirement annuity contracts relating to earnings from associated employers participating in the scheme.
(3) The earnings cap applies to aggregate pensionable remuneration payable from associated employers providing benefits under the scheme and/or under any connected scheme.

For all members moves between such associated employers can (and for post-1989 members must) be regarded as constituting a single unbroken employment. Pre-1987 or 1987–89 members who make that move therefore have, usually, a continued right to benefits calculated on pre-1987 or 1987–89 limits, whether they remain in the same scheme or join another of the associated employers.

4.21.1 Permanent community of interests

The Revenue will also approve the inclusion in a scheme which although not an associated employer in terms of the statutory definition, is associated with the employer who established the scheme through a permanent community of interests, such as common management or shareholders, interchangeable or jointly employed staff or interdependent operations, eg one selling the bulk of the other's products.

Where employers are associated through a permanent community of interests

(1) Moves between them by pre-1987 and 1987–89 members who are not controlling directors can be regarded as constituting a single unbroken employment with continued benefit rights (ie they are treated the same as those who move between employers who are associated in terms of the statutory definition).

(2) The benefits of pre-1987 and 1987–89 and post-1989 controlling directors must be calculated separately for each employment and the limits applying to each will depend, generally speaking, on the date of joining the relevant employer.

If however the scheme was approved before 27 July 1989 any member will, where appropriate, have continued rights to pre-1989 limits if he joins an employer which participated in the scheme before 14 March 1989, irrespective of the nature of the association between the employers.

4.22 MULTIPLE EMPLOYMENTS

It is not uncommon for people to have two or more completely separate employments, one assessable under Schedule D and the other or others assessable under Schedule E. Examples might be a teacher working for a local authority who also does private tuition work, or an accountant in practice who is also a director in his family firm. In these cases retirement and death benefits may be provided through an approved retirement benefit scheme in respect of the service and income from the Schedule E employment while completely separate pension provision may be made through retirement annuity contracts and personal pension schemes in respect of the Schedule D income.

If the earnings from the multiple employments are classified under Schedule E then retirement benefit schemes may be set up in respect of each separate employment, although complications arise if the employments are neither associated (see above) nor wholly concurrent.

Where the concurrent employment extends to only part of the member's overall service with the employers, the benefits from one scheme relating to a period when the employments are not concurrent must be taken into account under the other as retained benefits, ie as if they were benefits of a previous employer, unless:

(1) In relation to a pre-1987 or 1987–89 member the employers are associated through control (see above) and:
    (a) each participates in the other's scheme; or

    (b) only one employer participates in both schemes, in which case the scheme with the single employer will have to take only the non-concurrent benefits relating to service with the associated employer under the other scheme into account as retained benefits.

(2) In relation to a post-1989 member, the schemes are connected schemes (see above).

5

UNAPPROVED PENSION SCHEMES

5.1 INTRODUCTION

The FA 1989 allowed employers to establish unapproved pension schemes providing benefits in excess of those permitted under approved schemes (see Chapter 4). This change in legislation was partly cosmetic in that it disguised the restrictions placed on new approved occupational schemes by FA 1989. The change also provides opportunities for employers to provide more flexible remuneration packages for high earners who would be restricted by the earnings cap under approved pension schemes and for those with less than 20 years' service to retirement who would be unable to obtain a maximum approvable pension. However, these opportunities are at the expense of the generous tax reliefs available to approved schemes, some or all of which will not be available to unapproved schemes. Guidance Notes on the tax treatment of top-up pension schemes were published in August 1991 by the Inland Revenue: these Notes have been used in parts of this chapter.

The FA 1994 introduced further changes to funded unapproved retirement benefit schemes which invest in assets which are not subject to UK income or capital gains tax, normally by means of an offshore trust.

The FA 1998, whilst having no direct impact on FURBS, brought about fundamental changes to capital gains tax which will have an adverse effect on the financial attraction of FURBS to higher earners. This, together with extension of employers' national insurance contributions on employer contributions to FURBS, means that the financial benefit in having a FURBS rather than cash in hand is finely balanced.

5.2 SUMMARY OF EFFECTS OF CHANGES

(1) The major change is that benefits from 'approved' and 'unapproved' schemes no longer need to be considered in aggregate. In the past,

membership of an unapproved scheme would render invalid membership of the approved scheme.

(2) The changes focus attention on the definition of 'retirement benefit schemes': this expression is generally assumed to include a conventional occupational scheme or arrangement set up under trust and approved by the Revenue for tax purposes. However, other arrangements may also fall within the meaning of this expression. For example, an insurance policy taken out by an employer on the life of a 'keyman' in the organisation might be regarded as an unapproved pension scheme if the employee can expect that it will be assigned to him on retirement – a form of 'golden handshake'. (A keyman policy is one which pays out benefits to the employer in the event of the keyman's death to provide a cushion until such time as the employer is able to employ another employee of similar calibre.)

(3) Employees are taxed on contributions to 'funded' schemes at the time the contributions are paid. A scheme is 'funded' for these purposes when the payment is made 'with a view to provision of' benefits for the employee. Employee contributions do not benefit from tax relief and may bring into play the special anti-avoidance rules applicable to trusts where the person establishing a trust can benefit. Most unapproved schemes do not permit employee contributions.

(4) The budget on 17 March 1998 introduced more changes to the rate of capital gains tax payable on trusts (considered by the Revenue to include a FURBS established under trust). The assets of a FURBS are now subject to capital gains tax starting at an initial rate of 34 per cent tapering to an effective rate of 20.4 per cent when the asset in the FURBS is held for more than ten years. The trustees normally benefit from half of the annual exemption from capital gains tax (currently £3,550).

(5) In the case of unfunded schemes employees are taxed on the benefits they receive, but funded schemes can provide a full tax-free lump sum as long as tax has been paid on the underlying fund. Pensions are always taxable, and, for this reason, funded schemes normally pay out their benefits as a lump sum allowing the employee to buy a purchased life annuity if he needs income. By doing this, at least part (the capital element) of the annuity escapes tax.

(6) The tax treatment of contributions by employers to funded unapproved pension schemes depends on the normal rules for the deductibility of business expenses. It is likely that in some cases these contributions are not deductible expenses particularly where very large contributions are paid by private limited companies to schemes set up for members who are directors of those companies. The changes to the maximum permissible funding rates that may be paid into typical directors' pension arrangements (see Chapter 7) make it more difficult for directors to make maximum use of the tax

advantages of approved pension schemes, leading to more interest in unapproved schemes.

(7) In November 1997 the DSS announced that employer's NIC would be payable in respect of contributions made by employers from 6 April 1998. However, NIC is also payable on any extra salary paid to the employee to compensate for the income tax due in respect of the employer's contributions.

(8) As long as the scheme satisfies certain conditions (broadly that the employer bears the running costs of the scheme and any death benefits are distributed at the discretion of the scheme's trustees) it is normally possible to avoid any inheritance tax on the contributions to and the benefits from an unapproved scheme.

5.3 RETIREMENT BENEFITS SCHEME

One feature of the development of unapproved pension schemes is that more attention has to be paid to the definition of 'retirement benefits scheme'. In the past employers generally knew when they were setting up a 'pension scheme' and approval was sought and obtained. However, the greater flexibility permitted by the amendment of FA 1989, s 590(7) permits the establishment of schemes which look less like a true pension scheme.

This focuses attention on what is a 'retirement benefits scheme' and what is not. This distinction is likely to be important as it may determine the tax treatment of both the contributions and the benefits.

A 'retirement benefits scheme' is 'a scheme for the provision of benefits consisting of or including relevant benefits' (see ICTA 1988, s 611(1) in Appendix 4). This definition makes it important to define the meaning of:

(1) 'Scheme'; and
(2) 'Relevant benefits'.

Scheme is defined by s 611(2) as including:

> 'Reference to a deed, agreement, series of agreements, or other arrangements providing for relevant benefits notwithstanding that it relates or they relate only to:
>
> (a) small number of employees, or to a single employee, or,
> (b) the payment of a pension starting immediately on the making of the arrangements.'

This definition is wide and is capable of encompassing many arrangements which would not perhaps be regarded as 'schemes' in the accepted sense. However, it is not as wide as it may at first appear because the word 'arrangement' must be read in the light of the preceding words 'deed' or 'agreement'. Both of these words denote a form of binding obligation (on the employer). It is possible that a letter from an employer promising a lump sum at retirement could constitute a scheme and that, theoretically at least, nothing in writing is needed at all. Following a Revenue change of practice in October 1991 the Revenue now considers that an *ex gratia* pension or a lump sum may be capable of constituting a retirement benefit scheme.

The difficulty in deciding whether a 'scheme' exists is quite simply how far can the employer go in informing the employee and making any form of commitment without creating a scheme? The answer is not likely to be far, especially where the employee is continuing in employment and is thus working for his potential entitlement.

5.3.1 Relevant benefits

The second part of the definition of retirement benefits scheme is the definition of 'relevant benefits'. These are defined by s 612(1) as:

> 'Any pension, lump sum, gratuity or other like benefit given or to be given on retirement or on death, or in anticipation of retirement, or, in connection with past service, after retirement or death, or to be given on or in anticipation of or in connection with any change in the nature of the service of the employee in question, except that it does not include any benefit which is to be afforded solely by reason of the disablement by accident of a person occurring during his service or of his death by accident so occurring and for no other reason.'

One commentary on the definition says that 'relevant benefits ... are defined so widely that they could possibly be stretched to cover practically every kind of benefit paid or provided by an employer except remuneration paid during service'.

The only clear feature of the definition is that accidental death and disability benefits are not relevant benefits. However, this only applies to accidental death and disability benefits (although the accident need not have occurred at work). It is clear that ordinary death benefits are relevant benefits although it is not clear whether disablement benefits generally are caught.

The answer probably depends on whether the individual can be said to have 'retired' and the better view is that there is a distinction between 'sick pay' (where the individual expects to return to work) which is not a relevant benefit, and a 'disability pension' or a lump sum disability benefit (where the individual does not expect to return to work) which are likely to be relevant benefits.

Finally it is not necessary for the creation of a scheme for there to be a direct contract between the employer and employee for the provision of the relevant benefits. Section 612(2) provides that references to the provision of relevant benefits include 'the provision of relevant benefits ... by means of a contract between the Administrator (of the scheme) or the employer or the employee and a third person'. The reference to the employee would appear to make it theoretically possible for an insurance policy effected by the employee himself to constitute a scheme providing relevant benefits. For this to be the case it is probably necessary for some employer involvement but this could be satisfied if the employer promised to pay the contributions for the employee. Of course, whether the Revenue would seek to extend the definition this far is doubtful.

5.4 TAXATION OF CONTRIBUTIONS – THE EMPLOYER'S POSITION

Contributions to an exempt approved scheme attract automatic tax relief for the employer by virtue of ICTA 1988, s 592(4) (see Appendix 4). Contributions paid by the employer to an unapproved scheme do not qualify for relief automatically but *may* be relievable under the ordinary rules of Schedule D.

In order to be deductible, expenditure has to be in broad terms:

(1) incurred wholly and exclusively for the purposes of the business;
(2) not incurred for any other non-business purpose;
(3) expenditure of an income nature and not a capital nature;
(4) the expenditure must actually have been incurred.

These rules impact on expenditure on a pension scheme in the following ways:

(1) It may be difficult to argue that pension schemes for directors are wholly and exclusively for the purposes of the business.
(2) It is easy to imply a non-business purpose (eg a personal benefit) where the employees also have a significant shareholding in the company (or are relatives of such persons).
(3) It is often common to put in a lump sum to start a pension scheme (in order to make provision for past service) which could be regarded as a capital payment.
(4) Merely saving money or investing it may not be expenditure for these purposes.

5.5 OBTAINING TAX RELIEF

As can be seen the test for obtaining tax relief is strict. The key features for schemes are:

(1) There is likely to be a need to put scheme's assets beyond the reach of the company perhaps directly in the hands of the employee or a trust for his benefit (the investment of scheme assets in the employer's business in the form of a loan, or in the purchase of shares, may make the obtaining of tax relief more difficult).

(2) The company should not be a 'long stop' beneficiary of the trust (eg the company should not be in the position where it can benefit from any undistributed funds).

(3) There is likely to be a 'reasonableness' test in the level of benefits (ie it might become more difficult to justify high levels of pension as being wholly and exclusively for the purposes of the trade).

(4) Deductibility is more likely in respect of arm's length employees (ie non-shareholder directors) than employees with a proprietary interest or relatives of such persons.

(5) If the company merely sets up an accounting reserve to meet a liability under an unfunded scheme payments into the reserve are not regarded as expenditure and, therefore, are non-deductible.

(6) Payments of lump sums and the purchase of annuities at retirement under unfunded schemes should be deductible if they satisfy the general rules for deductibility.

5.6 TAXATION OF CONTRIBUTIONS – THE EMPLOYEE'S POSITION

If an employee has an absolute right to benefit from a fund or policy the amounts paid in are taxable under ordinary principles and the specific rules relating to pension schemes do not apply. Those specific rules were introduced to catch a simple dodge. Rather than giving the employee an absolute right to benefit it was possible to make his benefits contingent on reaching retirement. This was actually quite common before FA 1947 imposed the charge to tax on schemes where the employee's benefit was contingent.

This legislation is contained in ICTA 1988, s 595 (see Appendix 4). Subsection (1) deals with 'where, pursuant to a retirement benefits scheme, the employer ... pays a sum with a view to the provision of any relevant benefits for any employee (whether or not the accrual of the benefits is dependent on any contingency)'. These are what the Revenue calls 'funded schemes', ie where the employer is actually making payments to provide the benefits.

However, s 595(1) is insufficient on its own to tax all situations where the employer has set up a scheme (ie made a commitment or promise of relevant benefits). If the employer did not fund in advance no tax would be payable.

Prior to FA 1989, s 595(2) and (3), ICTA 1988 provided for the notional cost of providing the relevant benefit, based on actuarial principles, to be taxed in the hands of the employee. Section 596(A) now replaces these sections the consequence of which is that no charge arises on 'unfunded' schemes but one would arise where the scheme is 'funded'.

The employee is chargeable to tax where, to reiterate the words of s 595(1), the employer: 'pays a sum with a view to the provision of relevant benefits'. In effect this is the Revenue's definition of 'funded schemes'. This could apply where, say, a trust fund is established for the benefit of an employee to provide him with a pension but the employer can wind up the trust, or if the employee were a director or substantial shareholder of the company.

Where employers make contributions to unapproved pension schemes employees see no immediate benefits, but rather a tax charge, which could lead to pressure to increase employees' salaries. This in itself is taxable and subject to employer's NIC (12.2 per cent) giving considerable extra costs.

If an employer wants to meet the employee's tax liability on the contributions they may agree a grossing arrangement. The grossed-up equivalent of the actual chargeable contribution, and the tax figure, should then be included on the employer's pay record (form P11) for the pay period in which the contributions are paid. Contributions paid by an employer without a grossing arrangement should be notified by the employer at the end of the year to the Tax Office on a form P9D or P11D.

5.7 TAXATION OF THE FUND

In the case of unapproved unfunded schemes, there is by definition no fund but in the case of unapproved funded schemes, the scheme assets do not enjoy tax benefits available to exempt approved pension funds. Prior to 17 March 1998, tax was payable at the basic rate on investment income and on chargeable capital gains. Since then the rate of capital gains tax on trusts has changed to 34 per cent, subject to tapering. Where the asset is held for ten years or more, the effective rate of tax for a FURBS trustee will be 20.4 per cent (as compared with 24 per cent had the asset been held by the individual outside a FURBS).

A FURBS trustee still has an annual capital gains tax exemption of £3,550 (in 1999/2000) but the capital gains tax indexation allowance (which was removed for increases in asset values in line with the price of inflation) is only available up to 5 April 1998. However, this annual exemption applies at the scheme level, not in respect of each individual member of the FURBS. Where a FURBS comprises a number of members, the claiming of the annual exemption and its equitable distribution across members may be costly and time-consuming.

Prior to 30 November 1993, it was attractive to establish a funded scheme using an offshore trust enabling the fund to accumulate free of UK income and capital gains tax (other than any withholding tax on dividends from UK companies). Care had to be taken to ensure that special anti-avoidance rules, designed to prevent the avoidance of tax by transfers of assets outside the United Kingdom, did not apply. For schemes set up from 30 November 1993 onwards, or existing schemes varied after that date (eg by adding a new member) the use of offshore trusts is no longer likely to be attractive (see 5.8 below).

If the fund is invested in a life assurance policy, even if the policy is a qualifying policy, or any annuity policy there is a potential tax charge under new rules introduced in FA 1989 (Sched 9). If the policy is held by a company or under a trust set up by a company any investment profit realised from the policy is liable to corporation tax under the chargeable event legislation contained in ICTA 1988. In any case, the life assurance company's fund is subject to tax as the policy does not form part of its pensions business exempt fund.

5.8 TAXATION OF LUMP SUM BENEFITS

Lump sum benefits from unfunded schemes are subject to income tax. In the case of funded schemes, where the employee can prove that he has already paid tax in respect of the employer contributions, lumps sums can be paid free of tax. From 30 November 1993, the exemption from tax on lump sums from unfunded schemes was removed where the fund was not itself subject to UK income tax.

This provision contained in ICTA 1988, s 596A was primarily directed at situations where the fund is subject to an offshore trust and the assets are likely to consist of investments which are not subject to UK income tax. In effect, these funds could grow tax free, similar to the funds of UK approved pension schemes. This was seen by the Government as an abuse and the legislation now provides that income tax is payable on lump sums payable out of funds which are not themselves subject to income tax.

5.9 TAXATION OF PENSIONS

At present it is unlikely that any funded unapproved scheme would pay out a pension. If a pension is required, the better route for the employee is to take a lump sum and purchase a purchased life annuity. All pensions payable by the scheme are taxed under the ordinary rules of Schedule E.

5.10 INHERITANCE TAX

Unapproved schemes can, like approved schemes, benefit from significant inheritance tax advantages.

Unapproved schemes can be set up as 'sponsored superannuation schemes' because even where the employee is charged to income tax under s 595(1), that tax does not cover the costs of setting up and running the scheme. For IHT, this means that unapproved schemes set up under trust may be sponsored schemes, if there are separately identifiable setting up and running costs, and such schemes fall within IHTA 1984, s 151. As a result, the normal IHT charges on settled property do not apply. So, for example, benefits paid out under such schemes are free of any IHT trust charges.

Tax may, however, be chargeable if the benefit is expressed to be payable only to the deceased's estate. But commonly, death benefits may be paid at the employer's or scheme administrator's discretion to one or more of a specified group of possible beneficiaries as under approved schemes. In these cases IHT is not generally payable if the employee's estate is excluded from this group. However, there remains the possibility of an inheritance tax gift with reservation (GWR) charge. Unlike tax approved schemes, where the GWR rules do not apply (see Inland Revenue press release of 9 July 1986) there remains the possibility of an IHT charge on benefits from an unapproved scheme if the employee is deemed by the Revenue to have retained a benefit from the scheme. However, so long as the scheme is operated in a similar way to an approved scheme and no employee contributions are made, the GWR rules should not apply.

5.11 NATIONAL INSURANCE CONTRIBUTIONS

National insurance contributions are payable on 'earnings'. These are broadly defined as 'any remuneration or profit derived from any trade, business, profession, office or vocation'.

Before November 1997, payments which were regarded as 'benefits in kind' were excluded for NIC purposes and, for example, if the scheme was set up under trust, payments to the trustees would be 'benefits in kind' and not 'earnings' (in the same way as payments to existing approved schemes).

However, the Contributions Agency believes some FURBS have been set up to avoid national insurance contributions rather than to provide retirement benefits. A scheme would be set up into which a payment would be made, equivalent to, say, a bonus to which the employee would otherwise be entitled. The trustees of the scheme would pay the benefits out of the scheme shortly afterwards. The payment into the scheme would be regarded as a 'benefit in kind' and not subject to national insurance. To prevent such avoidance, the Contributions Agency stated in November 1997 that employer contributions would no longer be regarded as benefits in kind and would be subject to national insurance.

5.12 USES OF UNAPPROVED SCHEMES

The Guidance Notes issued by the Revenue suggest that there are three situations where an unapproved scheme is likely to be attractive.

(1) Where an employer wants to offer some employees a pension greater than two-thirds of final salary.
(2) Where the employee has not completed the full 20 years' service to qualify for a full two-thirds pension.
(3) Where the employer wants to pension earnings over £90,600 (in 1999/2000).

The first situation is likely to be rare as few employers will want to offer a pension of more than two-thirds final salary as this is likely to be as much as the employer will want to pay or is able to afford. The second situation where employers wish to provide more for employees unable to obtain a full two-thirds final salary pension is marginally more likely. (The maximum pension can now be provided only after 20 years whereas previously it was possible after ten).

In some circumstances employers may wish to recruit staff who will be affected by the £90,600 (indexed) earnings cap under an approved retirement benefits scheme, initially or at a later date. Employees who are already in existing schemes and are pre-1987 members or 1987–1989 members are less likely to wish to move jobs if they are earning or anticipate earning more than the £90,600 limit.

It remains to be seen, however, the extent of which employers will be forced to provide 'top-ups' to recruit staff. This may be more likely in industries with skills shortages than elsewhere. Also, companies who have one or more key employees whom they wish to tie in (eg computer experts, top salesmen, key executives, etc) may wish to provide top-up schemes. Small private companies could find the prospect of providing pensions for the key directors appealing but the availability of tax relief is crucial. The charge to tax on the employer's contribution as a 'benefit in kind' is a disadvantage for funded schemes (except perhaps in the case of death in service schemes where the premiums are smaller in relation to the emerging benefits). The alternative of an unfunded arrangement – where a lump sum is paid to the employee on retirement – while much more financially attractive offers little security for the employee.

5.13 DEATH IN SERVICE BENEFITS

The unattractiveness of unapproved as compared with approved pension schemes in relation to tax benefits is not so evident where the employer wishes to provide additional death in service benefits for an employee where there is a possibility of a substantial benefit compared with the tax liability.

Take an employee, aged 45, earning £120,000 who is a post-1989 member of an approved pension scheme and is subject to the earnings cap of £90,600. The scheme provides maximum approved death in service benefits on death before retirement, assumed to be at age 60, as follows:

(1) A lump sum of four times capped earnings, ie £362,400.
(2) A pension for his widow payable on his death before retirement of £40,266 (two-thirds of his maximum approvable pension which is assumed to be £60,400). The widow's pension is assumed to be capitalised at a lump sum of £644,250 so that the total value of the death in service benefit amounts to £1,006,650.

The employer wishes to provide the above scale of death in service benefits in relation to total earnings of £120,000 which would have a capitalised value of £1,333,333. The difference which could be provided by an ordinary term life assurance policy with a sum assured of £326,683 would be payable by the employer by means of an unapproved funded scheme written under a discretionary trust. The annual premium would amount to around £1,000, increasing each year in line with the Average Earnings Index, assumed to be at 4 per cent a year (assuming that the employee is male and is a non-smoker). The premium would be regarded as income in the hands of the employee and subject to income tax. The contribution, however, could no longer be regarded as a 'benefit in kind' and would be subject to national insurance. The employer would obtain tax relief on the premiums.

On death the benefits would be paid to the trustees and distributed according to the trust provisions. Inheritance tax would not be payable as long as the unapproved scheme is seen to have been 'sponsored' by the employer. However, 'sponsorship' requires more than payment of the premium by the employer: it is likely that this will be satisfied by separate and identifiable payments to meet expenses in setting up and administering the scheme.

Finance Act 1989 charges to tax gains made by companies in respect of company-owned life policies and annuity contracts and those held in trusts set up by companies. The gain is the difference between the premiums paid and the proceeds of the policy and in the case of a life assurance policy the gain on death is calculated by deducting total premiums paid. If a group policy is used, say, for a group of members, death benefits paid in respect of previous deaths may come into the computation for calculating the surrender value on a subsequent death. To avoid this, individual assurance policies should be used for each member.

5.14 ACCOUNTING FOR COSTS

Provisions for unfunded schemes made in company accounts are not allowable as business expenses but it may be possible to obtain allowance for deferred tax relief.

5.15 FUTURE TRENDS

Although unapproved pension schemes are still in their infancy (apart from ones set up inadvertently before FA 1989) a common approach by employers is beginning to emerge. The earnings cap becomes significant each year as wages inflation, which excludes price inflation (by which the earnings cap is increased), catches more employees. Large employers are becoming more interested in setting up unapproved pension schemes as they are keen to be able to offer an attractive financial package to high-flyers whom they may wish to recruit. Equally, smaller employers, attracted by the flexibility of unapproved schemes, are becoming more interested in the tax planning opportunities presented by them (including the opportunity of a 'self-invested' option). In the last few years, changes to national insurance contributions and the taxation of FURBS investments have reduced the financial benefits in receiving part remuneration by means of a FURBS investment. However, some employers will prefer to use FURBS for high earners in order to complement approved schemes and to ensure a discipline of retirement saving which would disappear if remuneration were to be paid wholly as salary. However, as seen from this chapter, the taxation of unapproved pension schemes can give rise to considerable complexity. Other options worth considering are as follows:

(1) By maximising the benefits under approved pension schemes in relation to earnings up to the cap, eg providing a maximum pension of two-thirds of final remuneration after completion of 20 years' service, together with cost of living increases in pensions in payment: these benefit scales may be more generous than those for employees who are not subject to the cap.

(2) High earners could pay Additional Voluntary Contributions of up to 15 per cent of their remuneration (subject to a cash limit of £13,590 in 1999/2000) in order to maximise benefits up to the cap.

(3) Rather than using a combination of approved occupational schemes and unapproved pension schemes (whether funded or unfunded), it may be worthwhile considering a personal pension scheme for the employee. Where earnings are high and the employee is young it is possible that personal pension plans might provide higher benefits than under an approved pension scheme in any case, without having to resort to an unapproved scheme.

(4) Other 'benefits in kind' such as share option schemes or increased remuneration which gives the employee the means to maximise contributions to personal investment arrangements like an individual savings account (ISA).

According to a survey in January 1998 of total remuneration of directors and key executives of the top UK companies by Executive Remuneration Review Ltd, the responses of companies with 'earnings capped' executives were as follows:

Benefit	Companies
Approved benefits augmented	16%
Cash supplements paid to compensate	8%
Unfunded unapproved promises made	34%
Funded unapproved benefits provided	42%

Table 5.1 Summary of tax position

	Funded	Unfunded
Employer's contributions	allowable as business expenses subject to NI taxed in hands of employee	allowable as business expenses
Employee's contributions	paid out of taxed income, so no tax relief	not applicable
Growth of fund	subject to income tax and capital gains tax in excess of annual exemption after taking into account indexation allowance to April 1998 less tapering relief. No further tax to pay on investment income accompanied by tax credit	not applicable
Benefit payments	if lump sum, tax free, provided that the fund has suffered tax as above. If the fund is established offshore, and tax has not been paid on the investment growth, tax will be paid on the emerging lump sum. If pension, subject to income tax (therefore an ineffective alternative)	lump sum or pension paid subject to income tax
Death benefits	free of inheritance tax under a 'sponsored' superannuation scheme	as for funded

6

COMPANY DIRECTORS

6.1 INTRODUCTION

The Inland Revenue has long regarded company directors – especially those with a controlling interest – as a special category for whom membership of an approved pension scheme is permitted only subject to certain restrictions. In recent years, the PSO has increased its monitoring of pension schemes with controlling director members.

The earnings cap (£90,600 in 1999/2000) has hit this particular group more than others. In addition, from 1 September 1994, the Revenue announced further limitations on levels of contributions to 'earmarked' money purchase schemes. Although there has been no restriction on the benefits which can be provided for directors, the funding of those benefits has to take place uniformly, without the scope for accelerated funding as had been possible previously. A similar limit on contribution levels has been applied to small self-administered schemes from 1 June 1996.

Directors of companies which are regarded for tax purposes as investment companies are ineligible to become members of a pension scheme approved by the PSO under its discretionary powers if they are controlling directors (see below) or are members of a family who together control more than 50 per cent of the company (see Chapter 18). The PSO does not, however, object to such schemes for these directors if the investment company is the holding company for a group of trading companies for which it acts as coordinator.

The benefits which may be provided for a director who is described by the Revenue as a *controlling director* are restricted as follows.

6.1.1 All members

The definition of 'final remuneration' and 'dynamised final remuneration' must not be based on one year only but must be averaged over a period of at least three consecutive years.

6.1.2 **Pre-1987 and 1987–89 members only**

(1) The earliest normal retirement age is 60. This means that female controlling directors of schemes approved before 29 November 1991 are restricted to a normal retirement range of 60–70 and cannot retire on maximum benefits at age 55 (see 4.4).

(2) If the director defers drawing benefits beyond his normal retirement date the limits on pension and tax-free cash up to age 70 are the same limits as would have applied had he chosen the actual date of his retirement as his normal retirement date and there is no entitlement to the additional benefits described in 4.15.4.

(3) For deferment beyond age 70, benefits based on final remuneration and service determined at age 70 may be increased by the greater of an actuarial increase and the increase in the RPI. Alternatively, full service to and final remuneration at the actual date of retirement can be taken into account, with an extra one-sixtieth of final remuneration given for each year of service after age 70 in excess of 40 years, up to a maximum of forty-five-sixtieths.

(4) If the cash lump sum is taken at the normal retirement date or later (but before age 70) during deferred retirement, the maximum deferred residual pension may only be increased by reference to the RPI up to age 70. Thereafter, it may be increased by the greater of an actuarial increase and the increase in the RPI.

(5) Normally lump sum death in service payments from a pension scheme are made at the discretion of the trustee of the scheme to a wide range of beneficiaries, free of inheritance tax. However, in the case of a controlling director with continued rights, remaining in service on or after age 75, the rules of the pension scheme may provide only that any death in service payment should be made either to the surviving spouse or to the director's estate.

(Death benefits for scheme members (including controlling directors) *without continued rights* must be provided on a death-after-retirement basis, and a lump sum benefit will take the form therefore of a guarantee payment, which may be made subject to the trust's discretionary disposal provisions.)

6.2 **CONTROLLING DIRECTOR – DEFINITION**

There are currently two operative definitions of controlling director. The definition applicable to an individual director depends on the date on which he joins the pension scheme. Therefore:

(1) A director joining a pension scheme *on or after* 1 December 1987 is treated as a controlling director to whom the relevant above-

mentioned restrictions apply if he has at any time after 16 March 1987 and within ten years of retirement or leaving (pensionable) service been a director and either on his own or with one or more associates beneficially owned or been able to control directly or indirectly or through other companies 20 per cent or more of the ordinary share capital of the company. 'Associate' means:

(a) any relative or partner,

(b) the trustees of any settlement in relation to which the director is a settlor,

(c) the trustees of any settlement in relation to which any relative of the director (living or dead) is or was a settlor,

(d) if the director has an interest in any shares or obligations of the company which are subject to any trust (or are part of the estate of a deceased person) the trustees of that trust (or the personal representatives of the deceased as the case may be).

'Either on his own or with one or more associates' means a director is treated as owning or controlling what any associate owns or controls, even if the director in question does not own or control any share capital himself. Benefits for a director who joined a pension scheme *before* 1 December 1987 to whom the above definition applies are restricted to the definition of final remuneration which is based on an average of three or more consecutive years. None of the other restrictions, however, are effective unless (2) below applies.

(2) A director who joined a pension scheme *before* 1 December 1987 is only treated as a controlling director to whom all the relevant restrictions apply if he could at that date be described as a director who, either alone or together with his/her spouse and minor children, is or becomes the beneficial owner of shares which when added to any shares held by the trustees of any settlement to which the director or his/her spouse had transferred assets carry more than 20 per cent of the voting rights in the company providing the pension or in a company which controls that company.

Regulations relating to transfers to personal pension schemes, and early retirement of members on ill-health grounds, apply the definition in (1) above to all members.

6.3 RETAINED BENEFITS

6.3.1 Controlling directors

Retained benefits cannot always be disregarded for a controlling director, or a person who has been a controlling director in the ten years prior to first joining a scheme of the employer, even if earnings in the first year of scheme membership do not exceed one-quarter of the earnings cap at the date of entry.

Pre-1987 and 1987–89 controlling directors

Unless benefits from the company scheme are to be provided on an uplifted/accelerated accrual basis, the maximum can be calculated ignoring retained benefits from:

(1) occupational schemes of previous employment,
(2) retirement annuity contracts and personal pension schemes of previous self-employment,
(3) retirement annuity contracts and personal pension schemes of the same employment.

Post-1989 controlling directors

Benefits from retirement annuity contracts and personal pension schemes relating to earnings from the same employment must always be taken into account, and treated as if they were further benefits provided by the company scheme. Retained benefits from occupational schemes, retirement annuity contracts and personal pension schemes relating to previous employments or self-employment can be ignored unless benefits from the company scheme are to be provided on an uplifted/accelerated accrual basis.

6.4 PENSIONABLE SERVICE

It may be possible by prior application to the Inland Revenue to pension the service of a director even though no remuneration is paid by the company. The reasoning appears to be that directors are included in the definition of 'employee' under ICTA 1988, s 612(1) (see Appendix 4) and any employee can become a member of a retirement benefit scheme. Obviously the director has to receive at least one year's remuneration on which to base the calculation of final remuneration.

6.5 SERIOUS ILL-HEALTH AND INCAPACITY

Full commutation of a member's benefits for a cash lump sum may be permissible where the member is in serious ill-health such that the expectation of life is so short that it is measured in months rather than years. In the case of controlling directors, the prior agreement of the

PSO must be obtained before a member's benefits are commuted on these grounds.

Similarly, if retirement is caused by incapacity, a scheme member may take benefits immediately, but calculated on the assumption that service with the employer has continued to the normal retirement date. Again, the prior agreement of the PSO must be obtained.

6.6 CONTINUOUS SERVICE/CONTINUED RIGHTS

Where a controlling director is a member of a scheme set up by an employer which is later reconstructed (eg on a company takeover) there may be implications for the way in which 'pensionable service' is calculated. Neither continuous service nor continued rights are granted on a move to employers associated only by a 'community of interest'. Continuous service may not be granted following a takeover unless continuity of trade, involving the assumption of at least 75 per cent of the vendor's liabilities, can be demonstrated.

Also, in a centralised scheme for employers associated only by a community of interests, cross-subsidy is not permitted in relation to controlling directors: each employer must contribute only in respect of the controlling director's salary and service with that employer, and the benefits payable must also be calculated separately in respect of each employer, the applicable limits usually depending on the date of joining the relevant employer.

Claims for continuous service where the individual is a controlling director of either or both the employers concerned must be submitted to the PSO for approval on a special form, PS 155.

7

FUNDING METHODS

The techniques used for funding group pension schemes and individual pension arrangements differ considerably. Although this book is aimed primarily at the personal position of a company director or self-employed person whose benefits will normally be provided by means of an individual arrangement it is important to be aware of the differences in the techniques used as it is not uncommon for a director to receive benefits from a group pension scheme and also an individual pension arrangement.

7.1 FUNDING OF GROUP SCHEMES

Most group schemes promise benefits related to final salary so that as salaries increase, so do prospective pensions: it is obvious therefore that it is difficult to quantify in advance the exact pension benefit and therefore the cost of providing it. Under group pension schemes, it is usual for employers to pay contributions which are expressed as a percentage of the total pensionable salaries of employees. This percentage, known as the 'funding rate', will be calculated by the actuary after making various assumptions of which the most important are that:

(1) salaries will increase uniformly at, say, 5 per cent per annum compound;
(2) the yield on the fund will be, say, 6 per cent compound after expenses;
(3) mortality will be experienced in line with an appropriate mortality table;
(4) the salary/age profile of the group will remain more or less constant;
(5) the ratio of males and females in the scheme will remain constant;
(6) persons retiring will be replaced by new entrants within a certain age range, usually at the younger ages.

In recent years funding rates have been affected by external factors not allowed for in actuarial calculations: legislation changes, which have usually benefited scheme members or have increased the compliance burdens on trustees but have resulted in increases in funding rates.

At least every three years, the actuary checks the actual performance of the fund against the assumptions made originally. If the assumptions have not been borne out in practice, an adjustment may have to be made to the funding rate.

If salaries have increased substantially without corresponding increases in the yield on the fund, there will be a deficit which may have to be made good by the injection of a lump sum.

However in recent years two factors have generated surpluses in some pension schemes, particularly those of large, public companies:

(1) The rate of pension fund growth has outstripped the growth in earnings.
(2) Pension schemes have made a profit out of early leavers. Large companies have shed large numbers of employees in recent years, many of whom will have been in the company pension scheme. As redundancy often works on the basis of 'last in, first out,' pension schemes have gained by having to provide minimal benefits for persons leaving service after a short period (see Chapter 20 for material on 'Surpluses'). However, legislation has improved the benefits of the 'early leaver' by providing for inflation-proofing of preserved benefits in line with price, but not earnings, inflation.

7.1.1 Minimum funding requirement

The Pensions Act 1995 has introduced a new requirement aimed at ensuring that group schemes providing benefits related to final salary have sufficient funds to meet the pension rights of their members. The objective is that at all times the scheme should be 100 per cent funded. If it proves not to be the case then the employer must make payments to the scheme to restore it to 100 per cent funding within timescales.

Being 100 per cent funded means that the scheme's assets are sufficient to buy annuities for all retiring members and to pay cash equivalents (ie transfer values) for active and deferred pension members as if the scheme is being wound up.

Actuarial valuations will continue to be required at least every three years. However, at annual dates between valuations an actuarial certificate will be needed to confirm that the scheme is on track to meet the minimum funding requirement.

If a scheme proves to be less than 100 per cent funded action is required. If it is at least 90 per cent funded then a revised funding basis must be put in place to reach the 100 per cent level within five years. If, however, it is less than 90 per cent funded immediate steps must be taken. Normally this will require an immediate payment from the employer such that the 90 per ent level is reached within 12 months, and 100 per cent within five years.

Since 6 April 1997, schemes subject to the minimum funding requirements must prepare and keep up to date a schedule of contributions (employees' and employers'). This schedule enables the trustees to ensure that contributions are paid promptly and at the right rate. Any non-payment can easily be spotted and rectified. Contributions deducted from the employee's salary must be paid within 19 days of the end of the calendar month in which they were deducted.

If the scheme fails to meet the MFR, the trustees must inform the members, with reasons for the failure. If the employer does not make good any shortfall to 90 per cent within one year, the trustees must inform OPRA and the scheme members within 14 days.

7.2 FUNDING INDIVIDUAL ARRANGEMENTS

The funding of individual pension arrangements or executive pension plans also involves making assumptions about salary growth and investment return, but these are related directly to the individual member concerned. The benefits to which he will be entitled will normally represent the proceeds of the fund at the end of the day and will therefore be a function of the contributions paid and the growth thereon: this differs from the final salary type scheme where the employer promises that benefits will be directly related to salary.

7.2.1 Funding for capital

The principle behind executive pension plans is to accumulate capital in the hands of the trustees which can be used to purchase an annuity on retirement. The trustees purchase annuities at the most competitive rates available at the time of retirement from any life office – not necessarily the one which has been used to accumulate the capital before retirement. Thus the executive pension plan can be split into two parts: the first part relates to the period when contributions are paid and invested in order to accumulate the maximum amount of capital, within Revenue limits, and the second part consists of buying an annuity with the accumulated capital.

The various ways in which capital can be accumulated are explored in Chapter 8.

The amount of capital needed at retirement depends on the annuity rates available at that time.

7.2.2 **Annuity rates**

The actual rate of annuity – or periodical payment by an insurance company in return for a capital investment – depends not only on the age of the person retiring, but on the following factors:

(1) whether the annuity is payable monthly, quarterly, or yearly;
(2) whether the annuity is level or increases (or 'escalates') in payment;
(3) whether it will be guaranteed for a minimum period of five or ten years or not guaranteed; and
(4) whether or not the annuity continues to be paid to the surviving spouse on the prior death of the annuitant.

With regard to (1) above, under the Pensions Act 1995, pensions accruing after 5 April 1997 in occupational pension schemes must increase payment in line with the Limited Prices Index (RPI with a ceiling of 5 per cent per year).

Annuity rates are also volatile as they relate directly to interest rates and also on the desire of an insurance company to come in or out of the annuity market. The following table is an example of annuity rates per annum for males and females based on a purchase price of £1,000 available in September 1999, although it does not represent the most competitive available at that time. It is assumed that the annuity is payable by quarterly instalments in advance and is payable for a minimum of five years and is based on an underlying interest rate of 5.25 per cent. The table shows annuities which are level throughout and annuities which escalate each year at 5 per cent compound.

Table 7.1

Age next birthday	Male level	Male 5% esc.	Female level	Female 5% esc.
55	56.06	30.76	50.69	25.43
56	57.03	31.77	51.35	26.16
57	58.06	32.83	52.05	26.92
58	59.15	33.95	52.80	27.73
59	60.30	35.13	53.59	28.59
60	61.53	36.38	54.44	29.49
61	62.82	37.71	55.34	30.45
62	64.19	39.11	56.30	31.46
63	65.63	40.58	57.33	32.54
64	67.15	42.14	58.42	33.68
65	68.75	43.78	59.59	34.90
66	70.43	45.51	60.84	36.18
67	72.19	47.33	62.17	37.56
68	74.06	49.26	63.58	39.01
69	76.03	51.30	65.10	40.57
70	78.12	53.46	66.71	42.22
71	80.31	55.75	68.43	43.98
72	82.63	58.16	70.27	45.87
73	85.07	60.71	72.23	47.87
74	87.64	63.40	74.32	50.01
75	90.34	66.24	76.55	52.29

Annuities purchased by trustees of pension schemes are known as 'compulsory purchase annuities' and are treated as earned income. These contrast with 'purchased life annuities' which are available to individuals to purchase with their own money and which receive different tax treatment in that they are regarded as partly a return of capital which is tax free with the balance being taxed as unearned income.

7.2.3 Salary increases

In order to calculate how much capital would be required at retirement, it is necessary to project current salary forward to retirement.

In March 1994 the Inland Revenue announced through the Association of British Insurers a revised method of calculating maximum contributions, to take effect from 1 September 1994 and updated from 1 June 1996. The latest (1996) method applies to 'earmarked insurance policies'. For schemes commencing from that date salaries should be assumed to increase at no more than 6.9 per cent per annum compound. The earnings cap, £90,600 in 1999/2000, should be assumed to increase at 5.3 per cent.

Example 7.1

A director, aged 30, proposing to retire at age 60, currently earning £70,000, may have the cost of his benefits calculated on a projected final salary of £426,000 (actual final salary would be £518,000 assuming increases at 6.9% pa but limited to the earnings cap increased at 5.3% pa).

7.3 YIELD ASSUMPTION

Having established the amount of capital required at age 60, it is then necessary to make an assumption about the return which will be earned on the investment to achieve that capital sum.

For schemes set up from 1 September 1994 the yield assumption is 1.5 per cent in excess of that assumed for salary inflation and 3 per cent in excess of that assumed for the increase in the earnings cap. In consequence, based on an 8.5 per cent per annum yield, the salary inflation rate is 6.9 per cent per annum (1.085 ÷ 1.015) and the earnings cap increase rate is 5.3 per cent per annum (1.085 ÷ 1.03). For schemes set up before then a yield assumption of 0.5 per cent per annum above salary inflation was acceptable, but that method ended in September 1999.

7.3.1 Maximum permissible contributions – Inland Revenue changes

As stated above, in 1994 the Inland Revenue introduced more realistic assumptions to be made about future salary increases and pension fund growth. It is now permissible to fund for pensions increasing in payment at only 5.3 per cent per annum: prior to the introduction of the changes it was possible to fund for pensions increasing in payment at 8.5 per cent per annum. The increase in the real rate of fund growth over salary inflation to 1.5 per cent per annum and the reduction in the assumed increase in pensions in payment had the effect of reducing the input needed to fund maximum benefits at retirement. There is another change which has a considerable impact: before 1994 maximum contributions were calculated on a 'level' basis. Under the current basis, contributions are assumed to increase in line with earnings, again reducing the initial contribution.

The following table shows a comparison of the previous and current contribution levels in respect of males and females retiring at age 60, with 20 years' service completed at retirement, with no provision for widow(er)s' pensions and where earnings are not affected by the earnings cap. The previous basis ended in September 1999 and any scheme which benefited from it should have recalculated contributions on the current basis by now.

Table 7.2

Males Aged	Previous basis %	Current basis %
30	88	26
35	94	33
40	102	43
45	117	61
50	151	99
55	261	231
Females Aged		
30	103	31
35	109	39
40	119	51
45	137	72
50	176	116
55	306	272

7.3.2 New schemes

The following examples show the contribution levels for a director or key executive.

Example 7.2

Male aged 40 with a salary of £50,000 and a retirement age of 60. The maximum regular annual contribution payable on the current basis (43%) starts at £21,500 and, if earnings grow in line with the assumed rate of salary inflation of 6.9% per annum, rises to £81,650 just before retirement.

Example 7.3

Female aged 35 with a salary of £45,000 and a selected retirement age of 60. The maximum regular annual contribution payable on the current basis (39%) starts at £17,550 and, if earnings grow in line with the assumed 6.9% per annum, rises to £93,050 just before retirement.

Whilst the two bases are quite different the objective remains the same, to build up a fund sufficient to provide a two-thirds pension at retirement. However, the scope for accelerated funding under the previous basis is no longer available.

7.3.3 *De minimis* rule

There is a *de minimis* contribution limit below which the initial benefit testing does not have to be carried out.

The *de minimis* limit applies where the aggregate contributions to all schemes, excluding contributions for death in service benefits, for the same employment do not exceed 17½ per cent of earnings provided contributions to all schemes of the employer have always been below this limit.

Before 31 March 1998 the limit was higher than this. Pension schemes set up on the higher basis will have to be reviewed by 31 March 2001.

7.4 ANNUAL AND SPECIAL/SINGLE CONTRIBUTIONS – TAX RELIEF

7.4.1 The employer – regular contributions

Regular contributions to approved executive pension plans (being an exempt approved scheme) are deductible for tax purposes in the year of payment provided that they can be classified as 'ordinary annual contributions'. As a rule of thumb this means that the rate of contribution (eg a fixed amount or a fixed percentage of payroll) should continue for no less than three consecutive years.

There are, however, circumstances in which regular contributions may be treated as single contributions (see 'The employer – single contributions' below) in which case tax relief could be spread for up to four years. Where a regular contribution plan is set up and the contribution is either reduced or stopped in a later year, the Revenue has discretion to go back and treat the previous contribution as single instead of regular.

7.4.2 The employer – special single contributions

The tax relief on single or 'special' contributions (usually paid in respect of past service) to an occupational pension scheme is determined as follows:

- The maximum term over which tax relief on single contributions will be spread is four years.
- The period of the spread is determined solely by the size of the aggregate special contributions to that scheme.

Special contributions which amount to £500,000 or over and exceed the total of other contributions made by the employer to that scheme in the same chargeable period will normally be spread on the basis set out below. Aggregate special contributions amounting to less than £500,000 will not be spread for tax relief purposes:

£500,000 or over but less than £1m	2 years
£1m or over but less than £2m	3 years
£2m or over	4 years

The allowance of the contribution(s) will be spread evenly over the period (eg an aggregate *special contribution* of £800,000 will be allowed on the basis of £400,000 in year 1 (the chargeable period in which it was paid) and £400,000 in year 2 (the next chargeable period)). Where a chargeable period is not a period of 12 months, allowance will be given on a *pro rata* basis.

Where there is evidence of manipulation to reduce the period of spread, the Revenue's Pension Schemes Office reserves the right to determine the spread on some other basis.

Once the period of spread has been determined, it will not be changed subsequently, even if the underlying ordinary annual contributions were to be reduced.

In arriving at this spread of relief, all single contributions paid to the scheme are aggregated.

The period of spread may be changed if the employer ceases to trade or its trade is taken over by another employer. In these circumstances the unrelieved balance of the single contribution will normally be allowed against the profits of the employer whose trade has ceased in the final chargeable period before cessation. Alternatively the single contribution may be re-apportioned over the period between the date of payment and cessation.

7.5 DEPENDANT'S DEATH IN RETIREMENT BENEFITS

The amount of additional capital required to provide a widow(er)'s death in retirement pension varies according to the difference in ages between husband and wife and retirement age. For example, if the wife is three years younger than her husband, between 21 per cent and 25 per cent additional capital would be required to provide the maximum widow's pension on the husband's death after retirement ages of 60 and 65 respectively. If a female director wishes to provide a widower's death in retirement pension for her husband, who is three years older, around 5–6 per cent additional capital would be required to provide the maximum widower's pension on the wife's death after retirement ages of 60 and 65 respectively.

7.6 PERSONAL CONTRIBUTIONS

The maximum levels of contribution given above include any contributions paid personally by the employee or director from his own remuneration as follows:

(1) Any personal contributions which the employer requires the member to pay towards the cost of his benefits.
(2) Any Additional Voluntary Contributions (AVCs) which the member chooses to pay to top up his benefits within the employer's scheme.

Contributions in (1) above are fully tax deductible through the PAYE system but contributions under (2) above are paid net of basic rate tax with any higher relief given through the individual's tax assessment.

There is an overall limit on personal contributions of 15 per cent of remuneration (subject to the earnings cap in the case of post-1989 members) in any one tax year.

7.7 OVER-FUNDING

As the maximum levels of contribution at the outset incorporate a projection of future salary, it is necessary to monitor the performance of the fund in relation to actual increases in salary, especially as retirement draws near, when a change in annuity rates upwards or downwards can seriously affect the provision of maximum benefits. If there is too much capital in the fund to provide the benefits promised, or the maximum levels of benefit, any excess must be returned to the employer and will be taxed as a trading receipt at a special rate of 40 per cent. Alternatively, if there are other members in the fund it may usually be re-applied to purchase pensions for those other members. The changes in the basis of calculating the maximum contribution levels will reduce the likelihood of a build up of too much capital in the fund.

7.8 DEATH IN SERVICE BENEFITS

Under executive pension plans, lump sums and dependants' pensions are provided by means of a straightforward term assurance which normally ceases at retirement age.

The cost of death in service benefits are in addition to the maximum contribution for retirement benefits shown in Table 7.2.

The following table shows the approximate multiple of salary that can be provided at outset as a lump sum for a widow(er)'s death in service pension in addition to the four times salary life assurance benefit.

Table 7.3

Age of wife	Multiple of salary	Age of husband	Multiple of salary
up to 29	12	up to 23	12
30 to 38	11	24 to 32	11
39 to 45	10	33 to 39	10
46 to 51	9	40 to 45	9
52 to 57	8	46 to 51	8
58 to 62	7	52 to 56	7
63 to 67	6	57 to 61	6
68 to 70	5	62 to 67	5
		68 to 70	4

On death in service, any life assurance in excess of four times final salary is used to purchase a widow(er)'s death in service pension.

These multiples assume the member can complete at least 20 years' service to retirement age and are subject to the following funding limits.

7.9 ANNUAL AND SINGLE PREMIUMS

Some insurance companies quote death in service benefits on the basis of single premiums. Thus, a premium paid at the beginning of a year will be sufficient to cover the cost of the risk for 12 months only. The following year, the same amount of cover will be slightly more expensive because the member will be one year older. Single premiums, therefore, involve an increase in cost for the same amount of cover.

Annual premiums, however, are level amounts paid throughout the term of the policy irrespective of any change in health and will be higher than single contributions in the early years, but less in later years.

7.10 DECREASING TERM ASSURANCE

Because the capital fund which is building up for retirement is normally returned in the event of death this itself will provide part of the required level of death in service benefit: some companies, therefore, are prepared to insure death in service benefits on the basis of a decreasing term assurance which provides the difference between the total desired level of death in service benefit and the amount building up under the fund.

This is a useful way of keeping the cost of life assurance requirements to a minimum, especially in the case of older employees and directors.

8

INSURED PENSION ARRANGEMENTS

Insured pension arrangements can be divided into four broad categories, as follows:

(1) with-profits policies;
(2) unit-linked policies;
(3) deposit administration policies;
(4) unitised with-profits policies.

8.1 WITH-PROFITS POLICIES

Many old insurance plans on the market fall into this category. Typically they are operated by traditional life offices, many of which have been in existence for over a century, although these companies, particularly mutuals, have undergone considerable structural change in recent years as a result of takeovers and mergers. The pension policies are similar to with-profits endowment life assurance policies although life cover is generally optional. The policy is either a pure endowment where a guaranteed capital sum is payable on retirement, or a deferred annuity with a guaranteed annuity payable on retirement.

The pure endowment policy is converted into an annuity at an annuity rate that may be guaranteed in the policy, whereas the deferred annuity policy may provide a guaranteed cash option. Most with-profits policies, however, offer an 'open market option' whereby the trustees may purchase an annuity on the open market from another insurance company.

An individual who is considering investing in a conventional with-profits policy is normally offered a 'projected capital fund per £1,000 of annual contribution' made up of three elements:

(1) a minimum guaranteed amount payable at retiring age, plus
(2) an additional sum, which is not guaranteed, and which depends on the actual results achieved over the full investment period; this additional 'bonus' (known as a reversionary bonus) is normally expressed as a percentage of the minimum guaranteed amount in (1) above and usually benefits from a compounding effect, plus
(3) a final additional amount which depends on economic and financial

conditions prevailing at the time of retirement – known as a 'terminal bonus'.

Once a reversionary bonus has been declared by the insurance company, it cannot be subsequently removed even if future investment results fail to match expectations.

In recent years there has been a stabilising of reversionary bonuses and more emphasis on variations in terminal bonuses.

There is no such guarantee with terminal bonuses, however, as these are discretionary payments depending upon investment conditions when the policy matures.

In the event of the member's death before retirement the policy may provide one of the following:

(1) No return of premiums paid.
(2) A return of the premiums paid without interest.
(3) A return of the premiums paid together with compound interest at around 3–6 per cent per annum.
(4) A return of the fund up to the date of death.

Obviously to the extent that the return on death is improved then the eventual benefits which may be received on retirement will be smaller. The fourth option set out above does not, of course, necessarily represent the face value of the policy including attaching bonuses but represents the 'value' of the policy as determined by the actuary.

The management charges made by the insurance company for issuing a with-profits policy and running the pension plan are not disclosed in the policy document, although sometimes a separate policy fee is specified in addition to the contributions.

It is only possible to monitor the performance of this type of contract when the policy is determined, for example, by analysing the amount paid in the event of death or the policy's surrender value should it be discontinued on, say, early retirement or should the policy actually mature at retiring age.

The guarantees inherent in these old policies may be very valuable in the current environment where annuity rates are very low. It may be advantageous to convert the accumulated fund at retirement into an annuity at the rate guaranteed in the policy rather than transferring the fund to another provider under an open-market option where current annuity rates would be used. However, the guaranteed route may not offer so many options as to the *type* of annuity that may be taken, for example level, joint level, with or without escalation.

8.2 UNIT-LINKED POLICIES

The 1970s saw an upsurge of insurance companies offering policies on unit-linked principles. The FA 1973 allowing controlling directors to have executive pension plans gave a timely boost to this business and today, life offices offer unit-linked policies as well as conventional with-profits policies.

Under a unit-linked policy, the investor is able to choose the investment sector in which he would like his contributions to be invested and he may switch between sectors from time to time. The contributions paid are used to buy units in one or more of the chosen investment sectors and the value of the units at any time is dependent on the value of the underlying assets.

On retirement, the units are encashed and the proceeds are used to purchase an annuity on the open market. No bonuses are declared and no guarantee attaches to the value of the units.

8.3 CHARGING STRUCTURES

The methods by which insurance companies take their charges for administering a unit-linked policy vary from one to another but will normally be based on one or more of a combination of the following principles.

8.3.1 Allocation to units

In most plans up to 100 per cent of each contribution is allocated to units but sometimes there is a smaller allocation in respect of investment terms of ten years or less. The following table is fairly typical.

Table 8.1

Years to pension age from commencement of the contract	Allocation to units
10 or more	100%
9	99%
8	98%
7	97%
6	96%
5 and less	95%

Some insurance companies offer allocations in excess of 100 per cent but often with the requirement that contributions have to be paid throughout the term, some give an increased rate of allocation, provided a proportion of the contributions payable within, say, the first ten years have actually been paid, and some companies give a higher allocation to units in respect of contributions paid towards the end of the term of the contract.

Many contracts have a reduced allocation to units in the first two years, although in recent years there has been a trend away from these front-end-loaded structures towards ones with level allocation to units throughout the term of the contract.

8.3.2 Type of units

It is still common to find the first one or two years' contributions allocated to 'capital' or 'initial' units, under which the insurance company takes an additional charge of between 3.5 and 6 per cent per annum of the units' value. Subsequent contributions purchase 'accumulation' or 'ordinary' units under which all the income and growth from the underlying investment accrues to the planholders (except for the 'annual management' charge – see below).

Another method of charging is where insurance companies allocate a reduced percentage of the first one or two years' contributions to 'accumulation' or 'ordinary' units. As an example, the insurance company may allocate between 25 and 85 per cent of the first year's contribution depending upon the contract's term. Both of these methods are examples of front-end-loaded structures.

Yet another method is for no explicit charge to be made in the first one or two years' contributions. Instead all contributions are allocated to accumulation or ordinary units, but if contributions stop or reduce (a frequent occurrence under pensions plans) a reduction is made to the fund at that time.

8.3.3 Management charges

In addition to the charges mentioned above, most insurance companies make a management charge which is expressed as a percentage of the total value of the units and might lie anywhere between 0.75 and 1.0 per cent per annum, although insurance companies market unit-linked policies which have unlimited annual management charges or have the ability to increase management charges from, say, 0.75 to 1.5 per cent per annum at some stage in the future. Also, it is not uncommon particularly in the case of property investments for the cost of buying, selling and managing properties, fees to independent valuers and other dealing costs to be borne by the fund.

8.3.4 Bid/offer prices

As with unit trusts, units are allocated on the basis of offer prices and are subsequently sold at lower bid prices when the policyholder takes his benefits. The difference between bid and offer prices is usually around 5 per cent.

8.3.5 Policy charges

In addition some companies take an initial instalment charge and a fixed policy amount in real terms every year (the initial amount is thus increased every year in line with an index such as the National Average Earnings Index or Retail Prices Index) which actually reflects the cost of servicing the policy.

8.3.6 Disclosure of charges

The Personal Investment Authority (PIA) introduced changes to the basis on which insurers disclose charges taken under pension contracts. The basis, which came into effect from January 1995, includes the following:

(1) Disclosure of the actual deductions taken from the policy by the insurer in certain years throughout its term.
(2) The policy's surrender value (or transfer) during each of the first five years, every five years thereafter and during each of the last five years. A comparison of these surrender values gives an indication of the charges under different contracts.

Under PIA rules on illustrations pension benefits must be illustrated assuming rates of return of 5 per cent per annum, 7 per cent per annum and 9 per cent per annum based on the insurer's own charging structure. This enables investors to compare the contracts of competing pension providers.

The PIA rules require insurers to show the reduction in investment yield brought about by the charges under unit-linked contracts. (Under with-profits and unitised with-profits contracts only the effect of expenses need to be shown; expenses do not include the profits which accrue to the insurer.)

8.4 TYPES OF INVESTMENT FUNDS

Most companies offer separate property, equity, gilt-edged and cash funds, but the majority of investors choose the 'managed' approach where the insurance company itself invests each contribution in whatever proportions and between whichever different investment sectors it feels appropriate for the longer term. This normally means a mixture of property, equities and gilt-edged investments. Cash deposit funds or building society related funds are usually intended to be used as a means of consolidating gains (or losses) at or near retirement age. Policyholders need not direct all their contributions into one fund but normally have the choice of investing in all funds or in any combination. Investment choice extends to overseas areas such as North America and Canada, Japan, Hong Kong, Australia and Europe and, in recent years, South America. Sometimes an international managed fund is available incorporating all these areas.

8.5 DEPOSIT ADMINISTRATION

Deposit administration contracts sought to combine the best features of conventional with-profits and unit-linked policies although these are now rarely used. The principle behind deposit administration is that, after deducting charges for administration, the policyholder has a deposit account with the insurance company – similar to a bank account – to which interest is added from time to time. The amount of interest that is actually guaranteed (if any) in the contract varies widely with some offices linking the rates to the building society lending rate and others crediting interest on a basis reflecting interest rates generally.

There are considerable variations in the method of charging expenses. For example, the credited interest rate may take account of expenses or a fixed policy amount may be deducted from the contribution before interest is credited, an annual charge may be made, or a lower interest may be applied to the initial contributions. The pension obtained from the accumulated fund at the time of retirement depends on annuity rates prevailing at the time and therefore it is not normally guaranteed.

8.6 UNITISED WITH-PROFITS POLICIES

The unitised with-profits policy is a variation on the conventional with-profits policy, although it has the hallmarks of a unit-linked policy. However, there are a number of important differences: under unitised with-profits, there is no annual management charge and the unit prices are generally guaranteed to increase at a minimum rate of growth, eg 4 per cent per annum although this price guarantee normally only applies at maturity or on early death. At any other time the unit price is not guaranteed and may be reduced by the actuary.

Investment performance is not reflected immediately but is smoothed over a period of years. The excess over the minimum guaranteed rate is added as a bonus which, once added, cannot be taken away.

The benefits are expressed in the form of units with bid and offer prices, allocation rates and initial charges, similar to unit-linked contracts.

Policyholders are permitted to switch into and out of the unitised with-profits fund although companies normally reserve the right to reduce the unit price on a switch-out by applying a Market Value Adjuster (MVA) and some do not allow switches-in within five years of the retirement date.

In recent years unitised with-profits annuities have become popular, giving annuitants the combination of a guaranteed amount of income together with exposure to equity investments through annual bonuses (see also Chapter 19).

8.7 GUARANTEED EQUITY FUNDS

A recent innovation has been the guaranteed equity fund, designed to provide planholders with the benefits of equity investments, but without the associated risk of loss of capital. Typically these funds, using financial instruments such as derivatives, guarantee a minimum return of capital together with a proportion of the growth in the Financial Times Stock Exchange 100 Index over a specified period. (The FTSE 100 Index reflects the total collective value of the top 100 companies in the UK stock market, not including the dividends paid by these companies to shareholders.) Because a minimum return of capital is guaranteed, the potential for equity growth is limited.

Growth in these funds is usually based on two elements:

(1) the level of guarantee and
(2) the gearing mechanism.

The level of guarantee limits the loss in the value of the pension units to which the planholder is exposed in any specified period; for example, the guarantee is typically 97–100 per cent of capital.

The gearing mechanisms represent the growth in the FT-SE index over a period, for example, three months, one year, three years (known as set dates). At the end of the period the unit price is adjusted by a percentage (known as the gearing). Gearings are higher where the planholder is prepared to accept some loss of capital, for example under a 97 per cent guarantee. Where the planholder requires a 100 per cent capital guarantee the gearings are lower.

Investment growth as measured by the gearings is calculated on the set dates and is 'locked in' to the planholder's fund. Planholders are not generally permitted to switch out of these funds during the set dates without incurring a surrender penalty.

8.8 COMPARISONS OF UNIT-LINKED FUNDS

The most important factor determining the value for money which a unit-linked planholder receives is the performance of the investment fund to which his plan is linked. How is the investor to assess the likely future performance of different life companies' investment funds?

Performance league tables are not by themselves the answer. The fact that one fund has performed particularly well over a period in the past – especially a short period – is no assurance that it will perform well in the period which matters to the new planholder, which is the future. Past performance over that period may have been the result of special circumstances which will not be relevant in the future.

The best solution is to look for the features which are likely to result in consistent long-term performance. No one can guarantee future performance, but certain features can point to the likelihood of consistent long-term performance, or act as a warning that future performance is likely to be volatile. The following checklist may be helpful.

- Does the fund have the benefit of a regular cash inflow?
- Has the fund a consistent long-term performance record?
- How long has the fund been in existence?
- What is the size of the fund?
- How has the fund coped with market upheavals?
- Is the fund broadly based or is it a specialised fund?
- How have the company's other funds performed?
- Does the fund have continuity of investment management?
- Does the name of the fund reflect its composition?

The significance of these factors is analysed in detail below.

8.8.1 Assured regular cash inflow

Investment managers often state that nothing assists them more than the knowledge that there is a regular cash inflow, and nothing can harm investment performance more than a sudden drying-up of funds or, worse still, a sudden need to liquidate investments to meet cash requirements of investors wishing to take out their money. A regular cash inflow makes it easy for an investment manager to change the weighting of investments in the fund without bearing the heavy costs of selling some shares in order to buy others. A sudden outflow can involve not merely the expense and the difficulty of selling shares on a falling market, but can force a fund to change its unit valuation from an 'offer price' to a 'bid price', which may in the most exceptional circumstances reduce the unit price by 6 or 7 per cent overnight. So a fund which shows up well in a short-term league table might still be highly vulnerable if it does not have a source of regular cash inflow.

8.8.2 Assessing a fund's future prospects

When assessing the future prospect of a fund which has shown up well in a past performance league table, the following other factors should be taken into account:

(1) If the table is for a relatively short term, check up on the fund's performance over other periods, particularly long-term periods. It is not uncommon for funds which are in the 'Top Ten' of this year's one-year performance tables to figure in the 'Bottom Ten' of next year's tables. What matters to a planholder is consistent, long-term performance.
(2) How long has the fund been in existence? Many new funds have shown very good performance in their first year or two, only to lapse into disappointing performance in later years. Although many new funds have performed well in their early years, other new funds have performed badly.
(3) Is the fund still a small fund? As there are a large number of small funds in existence, often with specialised investment policies, there are frequently a number of small funds near the top of the yearly league tables. The following year there may still be a number of small funds among the leaders, but they are likely to be different small funds. Any successful fund with a regular cash flow will soon become a large fund – and the real test is the ability to show consistent long-term performance.
(4) How did the fund cope with market upheavals, for example in 1974 when share prices suffered the largest fall this century? A fund should be judged in bad conditions as well as good. Similarly,

how did the fund cope with the 'Black Monday' crash in October 1987 or the currency crisis in October 1992?

(5) Does the fund have a broadly based investment policy or is it a specialist fund? Specialist funds (invested in one type of share or one country) often lead the short-term league tables because that type of share is in fashion during that year or that country's stock market has a good run for a year. These funds frequently fall sharply the following year; for example, over the last ten years there have been a number of specialist funds such as commodities, Far Eastern and American funds in the top ten performance tables in one year but many of those same funds also appear in the bottom ten tables in other years.

(6) Where one fund of a life company or unit trust group shows up well in a performance table, how did the other funds managed by the same company or group perform over that period? Some life companies and unit trust groups have anything up to 40 different funds, so that a few of their funds are generally in the upper levels of the league table in any one period, even if most of their funds do not perform well – but of course no one knows in advance which of their funds will perform well.

(7) Does the fund manager describe each fund in terms of relative risk (eg cautious, balanced or adventurous)?

(8) Pension scheme trustees are coming under pressure to specify their policy over ethical investments. The Government has made regulations requiring trustees to disclose their policy by 3 July 2000. The regulations also require trustees to disclose by that date their policy on the exercise of voting rights relating to the shares they hold. These requirements may affect fund performance.

8.8.3 Assessing property funds' performance

In assessing the performance of property funds these additional factors should be considered:

(1) Is the fund large enough to include a broad spread of properties? Some small funds have in the past achieved very good performance for a year or two when invested in only two or three properties, including one 'special situation' property which gives the fund a non-repeatable boost to performance – and leaves it vulnerable to a fall if there is a change in the marketability of that particular property (eg a change in business conditions in that area, perhaps because one large firm closes down).

(2) Is the fund invested directly in property or in shares of property companies? Shares of property companies tend to be volatile, as exemplified by the October 1987 crash, whereas direct investment in property has a more stable history.

8.8.4 Continuity of investment management

Good past performance is not necessarily even a pointer to the future if the investment management has changed hands. Some smaller funds have changed hands on a number of occasions, and may well be sold on again in the future.

8.8.5 The fund's name and composition

A property fund investor would probably expect the fund to consist of shops, offices, industrial units and cash. However, small 'property' funds could consist of a large amount of cash and only a few properties. A 'managed' fund might comprise a mixed portfolio of equities, properties, gilt edged securities and deposits or it might be largely concentrated in one sector in which case 'managed' might really mean 'managed equity'.

9

SMALL SELF-ADMINISTERED SCHEMES AND INSURANCE COMPANY HYBRID SCHEMES

9.1 INTRODUCTION

Small self-administered schemes are similar to insured schemes in that the emerging benefits which may be enjoyed by the members are exactly the same, being governed by the same legislation and to a large extent the same Inland Revenue practice. In a self-administered scheme, however, the trustees, either directly or indirectly, are responsible for managing the scheme's investments and administration. This contrasts with an insured scheme where the trustees pay contributions to an insurance company which manages the scheme and is responsible for investing the contributions.

Under a small self-administered scheme the directors of a company are the scheme's sole or principal members and also normally act as a scheme's trustees. They are then able to exert a considerable degree of control over the fund's investments and the level of benefits provided. A small self-administered scheme is defined as a self-administered scheme with less than 12 members.

A scheme is regarded as self-administered if some or all of the income and other assets are invested otherwise than in insurance policies. Scheme assets, of small amounts, held in a current account (whether interest-bearing or not) with a bank or building society for these purposes are not treated as an investment 'otherwise than in insurance policies'.

A small self-administered scheme may not earmark particular investments for particular members, although the calculation of the amount of a member's benefits may be notionally linked to the value of specific investments. The trust provisions will ensure that the member's entitlement to benefits is against the funds of the trust as a whole.

9.1.1 Self-investment

The main attraction of self-administered schemes to directors is the scope to exercise wide investment powers available to the company through *self-investment* rather than *self-administration.*

Self-investment in areas which would assist the employer in its operations can be achieved through:

(1) loans to the company and/or its subsidiaries,
(2) the purchase of property from the company (but not from its directors or connected persons),
(3) investment in the company's own shares.

The above areas are considered in more depth later in this chapter.

9.2 GUIDELINES FOR SCHEME INVESTMENTS

The Inland Revenue was concerned about some aspects of potential abuse and issued guidance on the approval of small self-administered schemes in February 1979 in the form of Memorandum 58. The Revenue's major concern related to the problems which could arise if the potential beneficiaries under the trust decided to wind up the trust and distribute the assets amongst themselves. Under a normal pension scheme this would be a practical impossibility because there would be so many members and potential beneficiaries; under a small insured scheme the insurance company could be expected to prevent this, but under a small self-administered scheme providing benefits for possibly only one person the enforced termination of the trust by all potential beneficiaries is a real possibility.

The Retirement Benefit Schemes (Restriction on Discretion to Approve) Small Self-Administered Schemes Regulations 1991, which were made on 15 July 1991 and came into force on 5 August 1991, limit the Revenue's discretion relating to the approval of small self-administered schemes and specify certain requirements for the approval of a small self-administered scheme. Chapter 20 of the latest Inland Revenue Practice Notes (reproduced in Appendix 3) amplifies the effects of the regulations.

The Social Security Act 1990 also introduced restrictions on self-investment by self-administered pension schemes to not more than 5 per cent of the value of pension fund assets through the Occupational Pension Schemes (Investment of Scheme Resources) Regulations 1992. However, these restrictions are relaxed under small self-administered schemes provided that the following conditions are met:

(1) That all scheme members are trustees of the scheme (this is not as unwieldy as it seems because these schemes are generally only set up for a small group of people, normally the company directors), and the scheme requires the written consent of all members to any self-investment.

(2) That the trust deed requires trustees' decisions on investment policy to be unanimous.

(3) That all members are party to investment decisions.

Most small self-administered schemes are exempt from the DSS Regulations as they are in a position to ensure compliance.

9.2.1 Company loans

The scope for a small self-administered scheme to make available loans to assist the company represents a valuable and flexible facility. The lenders, however, (normally the directors as trustees of the scheme) should ensure that the employer has the ability to repay the loan. The following conditions apply:

(1) The loan should not exceed 50 per cent of the scheme's total assets (in the first two years 25 per cent of the total assets excluding transfers received from other schemes).

(2) There should not be a regular pattern of lending back to the company part of successive employers' contributions.

(3) The loan should be on commercial terms at a realistic rate of interest: the Inland Revenue specifies a rate of 3 per cent per annum above Clearing Bank Base Rate (unless the borrower can show in writing that he could have obtained a loan at less than this rate from another lender on otherwise similar terms). Interest must be charged and paid. The loan agreement should state the terms of the loan including the circumstances when the borrower would be in breach of the conditions of the agreement.

(4) The loan must be used for a genuine commercial purpose, for example to purchase capital equipment or another specific capital requirement. Loans made solely to keep an ailing business afloat or to employers who are technically insolvent may lead to the withdrawal of approval of the scheme.

(5) Loans, being generally required on an unsecured basis, are normally made short term. If the loan to the employer is to be on a long-term basis, the trustees may wish to take security, for example a charge on company assets, such as property owned by the employer. In any event the loan should be subject to a written agreement under which repayment can be legally enforced.

(6) The loan must be for a fixed term as agreed between the parties to

the loan agreement. A series of 364 day loans (to enable interest to be paid to the trustees gross without deduction of tax) is not permitted. Also, it is not acceptable for the term to be longer than necessary. It may be possible to roll over these loans into a fresh loan agreement for a further period (but not more than twice) provided the interest is paid to date.

(7) Loans to scheme members or any other members with a contingent interest (eg relatives) are prohibited as is the sale, purchase or lease of any assets from or to scheme members or anyone connected with a scheme member.

9.2.2 Commercial and residential property

If the trustees are considering buying commercial property from the sponsoring employer, the Revenue will normally want to be satisfied that:

(1) The trustees of the self-administered scheme buy the property at current market value, supported by an independent surveyor's valuation.

(2) The rental income should give a reasonable yield – currently 8–10 per cent per annum, again supported by the advice of an independent surveyor.

(3) With regard to residential property, investments in residential property for use by, or leasing to, a director or shareholder or to the employer will not be approved unless the property is occupied by an arm's length employee (such as a caretaker).

(4) Investment in residential property may also be acceptable if it is occupied by someone unrelated to the members of the scheme (or to a person connected with a scheme member) in connection with his or her occupation of business premises (eg a shop with a flat above it) where those premises are held by trustees of the scheme as an asset.

Investment by trustees in holiday property is not regarded as consistent with approval.

Other factors which the trustees will have to consider are:

(1) The concentration of scheme investments in property may result in liquidity problems should funds be needed to provide benefits on death or on transfer to another scheme. However, the need to sell a property to provide a member with retirement benefits is now not so essential as it was in the past as the trustees may pay an income out of the fund, deferring the purchase of an annuity until the member's 75th birthday.

(2) There should be adequate funds elsewhere so that the property would not have to be sold at an inopportune time to provide death benefits.

(3) The trustees of the self-administered scheme will normally have the powers in the trust deed to effect a short-term commercial mortgage

to finance the initial purchase of a property which may well prove attractive because:

(a) the company contributions to the scheme to enable the trustees to purchase the property and pay off the loan will attract tax relief,

(b) rental income paid by the employer to the trustees can be offset as an expense for the purposes of corporation tax,

(c) rental income from the property accumulates tax free in the self-administered scheme, and

(d) when the property is sold by the self-administered scheme trustees they do not have to pay capital gains tax on the sale.

9.2.3 **Company shares**

Although the trustees of a small self-administered scheme may invest in shares of the sponsoring employer, this is not common. The practice has been that most private companies operated by shareholding directors do not declare dividends or pay minimal dividends on ordinary share-holdings. This can cause problems when the trustees of a small self-administered scheme wish to acquire such shares because the Inland Revenue will want to be satisfied that the holding will represent a rea-sonable investment in terms of expected annual dividends whereas normally the directors will not wish to declare substantial dividends.

In considering the purchase of company shares, the trustees will have had to have ensured that:

(1) advance clearance has been obtained from the Inspector of Taxes of whether the transaction gives rise to an assessment for income tax under ICTA 1988, s 703;

(2) there is a genuine commercial reason for the share transaction and it is not an exercise in tax avoidance;

(3) the shareholding in the company is taken into account when looking at the overall degree of self-investment, including loans;

(4) the shares have been professionally valued;

(5) the value of the shareholdings in the company is reasonable in rela-tion to the overall value of the pension fund. In practice, this means that the Revenue may object if it is proposed that more than, say, 25 per cent of the pension fund is invested in company shares, although the Revenue may be prepared to agree a higher proportion if a sound case is put up;

(6) investments in the company shares should not exceed 30 per cent of the company's issued share capital; and

(7) shares in the company will have to be realised when the members retire and this may be difficult simply because shares in private companies tend not to be marketable.

9.2.4 Unlisted company shares

If scheme trustees acquire shares in an unlisted trading company (a company not listed on a recognised stock exchange within the meaning of ICTA 1988, s 841) they may be able to control or convert what would otherwise be taxable trading profits into a dividend which, being investment income, is exempt from tax in their hands. To limit tax avoidance in this area the trustees of a small self-administered scheme are prohibited from investing in shares in any unlisted company which:

- carry more than 30 per cent of the voting rights in the company; or
- entitle the holder of the shares to more than 30 per cent of any dividends disclosed by the company.

Shares in unlisted public limited companies, and in companies listed on the Alternative Investment Market (AIM), are subject to the above restrictions.

9.2.5 Notification of transactions

The Regulations require automatic notification of any transactions between the scheme and a 'connected person'. This is normally taken to include the principal employer, another employer which participates in the scheme, a company associated with the principal employer or participating employer because it is a subsidiary or it shares a common trade, shareholdings or directorships and scheme members, the member's spouse, relative or the relative's spouse. This information has to be furnished to the Inland Revenue within 90 days from the date of the transaction; failure to do so could result in a penalty.

9.2.6 Conventional investments

These include:

(1) quoted shares or stocks listed on a recognised stock exchange;
(2) gilt-edged stocks (eg UK Government loan stocks);
(3) bank and building society deposits;
(4) insurance policies (subject to possible restrictions on second-hand policies (usually endowment policies)); and
(5) unit trusts and open-ended investment companies.

9.2.7 Investments in works of art, valuable chattels, etc

Investments in such 'pride in possession' assets such as antiques, works of art, rare books, gold bullion, jewellery, etc are not permitted.

9.2.8 Borrowings

It is not uncommon for a scheme to borrow money to help finance the purchase of investment. Borrowings are limited to three times the amount of the employer's ordinary annual contributions to the scheme and three times the annual contributions paid by scheme members in the year of assessment ending immediately before the time of borrowing (excluding any additional voluntary contributions) plus 45 per cent of the market value of the existing scheme investments.

'Ordinary annual contributions' means the smaller of:

(1) the annual average of the contributions paid by the employer in the three scheme accounting periods preceding the date on which the ordinary annual contribution is to be determined (or, where the scheme has been established for less than three years, the total amount paid to the scheme by the employer divided by the number of years since the scheme was established (a part year counting as one), and

(2) the amount of the annual contribution which has been advised by an actuary in writing within three years of the date on which the ordinary annual contribution is determined, and is necessary to secure the benefits payable under the scheme.

9.2.9 Provision of information

In addition to the general requirement under small self-administered schemes that trustees provide actuarial valuations every three years at least, schemes now have to volunteer other items of information relating to investments in the areas outlined above (using the statutory forms) together with an undertaking that the transaction does not infringe current Inland Revenue requirements.

9.3 OTHER REVENUE REQUIREMENTS

9.3.1 Pensioneer trustee

The Regulations require that all small self-administered schemes appoint a 'pensioneer trustee'. If this is not done the scheme will not be approved or existing approval will be withdrawn.

If the scheme ceases to have a pensioneer trustee the Revenue must be notified in writing within 30 days and a replacement pensioneer trustee must be appointed within 60 days. Also, the Revenue has to be given written notification of the name of the new pensioneer trustee within 30 days of appointment.

The main functions of the pensioneer trustee are to prevent the premature winding-up of the scheme other than in accordance with the approved terms for winding-up in the scheme rules and to undertake to notify the Revenue of any transaction undertaken by the scheme which, in his opinion, is likely to infringe requirements for approval.

A pensioneer trustee is an individual or body widely involved with occupational pension schemes and known to the Revenue who approve the appointment. It is generally accepted that the pensioneer trustee is jointly and severally liable for the trust's administration with the other trustees, although some pensioneer trustees have sought to limit their responsibilities to the primary function above.

9.3.2 Investment strategy

Full details of the funding assumptions and the investment strategy must be submitted when Revenue approval of the scheme is sought.

In addition to the initial actuarial report the Revenue requires subsequent actuarial reports every three years containing details of investments.

9.3.3 Revenue scrutiny

As the Inland Revenue scrutinises the investment strategy adopted by the trustees of a small self-administered scheme to ensure that it is suitable, the trustees must satisfy themselves that the main purpose of the scheme is the provision of retirement benefits, rather than the avoidance of tax, and that any substantial investment in a particular area is appropriate to the benefits being provided for the members: in particular if all members are close to retirement, then purchasing a property may be regarded as inappropriate because of the possible problems in selling the investment to provide pensions.

9.3.4 Death-in-service benefits

If the death benefit formula provided under the scheme exceeds the value of the member's share in the scheme's assets, then the balance of any death-in-service benefits promised must be insured with a life office.

9.3.5 **Purchase of pensions and income drawdown**

The PSO announced in May 1994 (Memorandum No 119) that small self-administered scheme rules may permit the purchase of an annuity to be deferred for retiring members until they reach age 75. During this period (potentially 25 years) the member's pension may be paid directly from the scheme assets.

The scheme actuary must provide the PSO with a certificate, initially and thereafter at triennial reviews, comparing the pension being paid direct from the scheme's resources with an annuity on the same terms that could be secured on the open market. The actuary must explain any divergence of more than 10 per cent.

At the end of the period – if the scheme assets have not been exhausted – the trustees must purchase an annuity. This will be an important decision for the trustees as investment conditions may vary considerably during this period. However, unless inflation proofing is at the fixed rate of 3 per cent per annum the trustees may retain the right to pay any increases in pension in line with movements in the Retail Prices Index directly to the pensioner out of the plan assets. The decision on when to purchase an annuity rests with the trustees.

As an alternative to the above method of deferring the outright purchase of an annuity, scheme trustees may now adopt the procedures available under personal pension schemes (explained in Chapter 19). This method also enables the trustees to defer annuity purchase until the member's 75th birthday, paying an income which lies between 35 and 100 per cent of the annuity which could have been purchased for the member based on annuity tables published by the Government Actuary. As with personal pensions, the income must be reviewed every three years and adjusted if necessary in accordance with annuity rates at that time. Under this method the decision on when to purchase an annuity rests with the member.

However, the treatment of death benefits is different: whereas under personal pensions the fund can be paid as a lump sum subject to a 35 per cent tax charge, under a small self-administered scheme the member is treated as if he or she had retired on the day before death. The death benefit becomes the guaranteed period under the notional annuity (usually five years) minus the income payments already paid out. This method of 'drawdown' or 'income withdrawal' is not so attractive as under personal pensions.

9.3.6 **Provision of information to Inland Revenue**

The Inland Revenue must be notified by scheme administrators of specified transactions on relevant Revenue forms (see Appendix 3) covering the following:

- Loans to employer or an associated employer
- Acquisition or disposal of land including buildings
- Acquisition or disposal of shares in the employer, associated employers or unlisted companies
- Borrowing of money
- Purchase or sale from or to an employer
- Commutation for serious ill health.

These transactions must be reported to the Revenue within a period of 90 days from the date of acquisition or at the date when the scheme is submitted to the Revenue if this is later.

In the case of the last item above, a scheme may permit a member who is in exceptional circumstances of ill health to commute the whole of his or her pension. Members of small self-administered schemes, in the majority of cases, will be controlling directors in which case the *prior* approval of the PSO to the commutation is required. The scheme administrator must give the PSO 14 days' notice and supply copies of medical reports. The PSO is then obliged to say before the end of the 14 days whether the proposal is acceptable.

9.3.7 Self-assessment for tax

Trustees of small self-administered schemes have been within the scope of self-assessment from 6 April 1996.

9.4 COST OF SETTING UP AND RUNNING A SMALL SELF-ADMINISTERED SCHEME

The costs involved in a small self-administered scheme vary considerably depending on the services given. The services required in order to establish and run a small self-administered scheme include:

(1) **Documentation and Revenue negotiations.** These include drafting the definitive deed and rules, and preparing announcements to members setting out benefits under the scheme. The documents then have to be submitted to the Revenue for approval and from time to time the employer will require advice in connection with the interpretation of the scheme rules and Revenue practice.

(2) **Actuarial services.** These involve an initial actuarial report and triennial actuarial reports. From time to time, interim actuarial reports may be required, for example on company takeovers or if a claim is made on the scheme trustees, for example, on a member's death or early retirement.

(3) **Pensioneer trusteeship.** See 9.3.1 above.
(4) **Accounting and financial management.** This includes keeping records of assets and payments in and out of the scheme and how they are allocated between members; it includes, for example:
  (a) reconciling bank statements;
  (b) preparing audited annual accounts;
  (c) completing annual tax returns;
  (d) settling tax liabilities;
  (e) reclaiming any tax;
  (f) collecting dividends, interest and rental income.
(5) **Payment of benefits.** This includes the payment of death benefits to beneficiaries, the purchase of annuities for scheme members and their dependants and the payment and acceptance of transfers from other approved pension schemes.

The cost of obtaining all these services varies enormously from specialist to specialist and depends on the method of charging fees which can be either on a time cost basis or as a percentage of the assets under management, or even a combination of the two. The amount of work involved in setting up a small self-administered scheme tends to be the same whether £10,000 or £100,000 is being invested.

These costs usually relate solely to the day-to-day administration. They do not take into account the cost of managing the assets, such as the legal costs involved in purchasing property, the stockbroking costs incurred in managing an investment portfolio and the costs of seeking and obtaining Revenue approval to the types of investment covered in this chapter such as loans and investment in shares in the employer.

9.5 KEY ADVANTAGES AND DISADVANTAGES OF SMALL SELF-ADMINISTERED SCHEMES

The potential advantages include:

(1) The scope to assist company finances through self-investment in own company assets, particularly commercial premises used by the business.
(2) Loans to the company of up to 50 per cent of the fund (or 25 per cent during the first two years of the scheme's establishment). This requirement is also normally satisfied by policy loans available under executive pension plans offered by insurance companies – see below.
(3) The opportunity to achieve a high investment return where the directors have an interest or expertise in a particular investment sector.
(4) If the fund is large, the cost may be cheaper than under insured arrangements.

(5) The personal satisfaction of direct personal control over investment selection and administration of the scheme.

(6) The ability to defer purchase of a pension (see 9.3.5 above).

(7) The ability to allocate scheme assets across a number of members, so avoiding or mitigating the effects of a surplus.

Disadvantages of self-administered schemes include:

(1) The cost of appointing outside specialists to provide actuarial reports, legal advice and pensioneer trustee services.

(2) The cost in terms of executive time required to manage investments and carry out trustee responsibilities.

(3) Most directors of small family companies are not likely to be expert in long-term investment; they do not have the time, ability and resources to research markets in depth in order to maximise gains and minimise losses.

(4) The possible loss of control if company assets, such as properties, are switched to form part of a small self-administered plan. In particular a property which has been purchased by the small self-administered scheme from the company cannot then be put up as security for loans to the company as it no longer forms part of a company's asset base.

(5) A small self-administered scheme is a common trust fund which means that the assets are held for the benefit of all the members (in practice, a small number of directors) as a whole. This contrasts with executive pension plans where assets are earmarked for each individual member.

Under a common trust fund, in the event of a claim being made by a beneficiary, for example on the death of a member, the beneficiary is entitled to a proportion of the assets of the common trust fund, say one-third. The trustees then have to realise one-third of the fund in order to meet their liabilities to the beneficiary. This could cause problems for the trustees if the deceased member, when alive, had invested what he regarded as 'his share' of the fund in an area of investment which had shown poor returns, as the remaining two members of the scheme could have to subsidise the deceased member from other investments of the fund which had performed better.

The inability to earmark assets under common trust funds is a problem which has come to the fore over the past few years as more insurance companies have been prepared to set up and administer small self-administered schemes where a portion of the assets are invested in insurance policies. These policies are, by their very nature, taken out by the trustees in respect of individual scheme members but they represent merely an investment vehicle on the trustees' part. The proceeds of the policy are not earmarked for individual members.

This contrasts with a straightforward executive pension plan, which is not a common trust fund, and where the proceeds of each separate policy are indisputably earmarked for the member concerned.

9.6 PROPERTY PURCHASE

Many small self-administered schemes are set up with a view to purchasing property (although the scheme may not purchase a property from the director(s)). The property may already be owned by the company, or it may be one which the director or the company is considering purchasing, and from which the company will operate. The following tables set out the pros and cons of the methods of property purchase.

Table 9.1 Property purchase by the director

Pros	Cons
(1) The property is separate from the company and can be sold independently.	(1) Additional life assurance is required by the lender as collateral.
(2) The property does not have to be sold at retirement and could generate rental income which supplements any pension received.	(2) The director may have given personal guarantees to his company creditors so that the property is not necessarily free from creditors.
(3) When the property is sold by the director there is a potential CGT liability but this should be substantially mitigated by the indexation allowance.	(3) When obtaining a loan to buy the property it is unlikely that the director will be able to obtain a 100% mortgage so that he may have to put up additional security such as his own private residence: this may be emotionally unacceptable, or may conflict with personal guarantees given to other lenders.
(4) The increasing value of the property could be used as collateral security for further ventures of a personal or corporate nature.	(4) If a full market rent is received from his company he is not entitled to business retirement relief. A proportion of the business retirement relief is given if the rent received is less than the full market rent.
(5) If the director does not charge the company rent for the use of his property he is entitled to business retirement relief usually from age 50 onwards.	(5) The director may be unable to obtain a personal long-term interest-only loan.

Table 9.1 Property purchase by the director *(cont.)*

(6) If the director uses the tax-free cash emerging from his pension plan to repay the capital he effectively obtains tax relief on the capital repayment.	(6) Other directors may be unhappy about the property being owned by one director.
(7) IHT relief for business property may be available.	

Table 9.2 Property purchase by the company

Pros	*Cons*
(1) It is the most natural place for the property to be held and the property can be used for future expansion.	(1) The company will probably be unable to obtain a loan on a long-term interest-only basis. It is likely to be of a fairly short term with capital repayments every year.
(2) The company rather than an individual director is much more likely to be able to obtain a loan if a substantial amount is involved.	(2) When the property is sold there is a potential corporation tax liability on the gain and when the director sells his shares he has a potential CGT liability. It may be possible to avoid this double tax charge if the company is sold as a whole, rather than individual elements of it.
(3) The company although paying interest and capital on the loan does not have to pay rent.	(3) Although life assurance is not necessary as collateral security, it is advisable.
(4) Collateral life assurance is not necessarily needed. The death of one of the directors would not necessarily affect the loan (unless the deceased was a keyman in the company).	
(5) IHT relief for business property may be available.	
(6) The method is simple.	

Table 9.3 Property purchase by the SSAS

Pros	Cons
(1) When the property is sold by the fund to provide the director with his retirement benefits there is no CGT to pay.	(1) The scheme is a common trust fund and the individual members lose their personal investment choice; see above.
(2) The capital growth of the property does not increase the value of the director's shares for CGT and IHT purposes.	(2) Death, ill health, leaving service and early retirement could involve the scheme's trustees in having to sell the property, or obtain a loan at an inopportune time.
(3) If there are younger directors in the scheme the property could effectively remain in the fund when older directors retire. There is no need to sell the property if the share of the fund which belongs to the retiring director can be met from other scheme assets.	(3) The proposed property investment may not be a suitable investment for a scheme as it would not satisfy Revenue rules.
(4) The rent paid by the company to the trustees of the fund reduces corporation tax liability.	(4) The property could not be used as collateral for future loans to the company.
(5) The property is free from creditors (provided there has been no attempt to defraud creditors)	(5) The company would have to pay a commercial rent to the scheme.
	(6) As an actuarial valuation of the fund is required every three years this requires a valuation of the property, an added cost.
	(7) If the scheme borrows to purchase the property, it is faced with high capital repayments so as to keep the term of the loan to a minimum: interest payable on the loan by the trustees does not rank for tax relief—the scheme does not pay tax.

9.6.1 Property purchase – summary

Some companies make the mistake of setting up a small self-administered scheme to purchase a property, while the real aim should be to purchase the property on the most commercial and cost-effective terms to the company, with the pension fund as a secondary objective.

Example 9.1

The company is considering purchasing a property which will cost £200,000. Whilst it is feasible that a small self-administered scheme could be used to purchase the property, in practice this may be an unacceptable option as the cost of financing the project would be too expensive for the following reasons:

(1) The annual contribution to the scheme would be around £50,000.

(2) The maximum loan which the scheme's trustees could obtain would be £150,000 (three times the regular annual contribution, averaged over the previous three years in line with Revenue practice).

(3) The trustees now have £200,000 to purchase the property, assuming the lender is prepared to lend 75% of the valuation of the property. However in the case of an existing scheme, the facility to borrow an additional amount equal to 45% of scheme assets will assist the purchase.

(4) The company directors may have to increase their salaries and/or bonuses from the company to justify regular contributions to a scheme of £50,000, affecting the directors' personal tax liability and the company's NIC liability.

(5) The company will have to pay a commercial rent to the scheme for the use of the property, say, £15,000 per annum.

(6) Even with corporation tax relief on the annual contribution of £50,000 and rent of £15,000, and on the cost of the directors' remuneration, the total cost commitment may well be beyond the company's resources.

An alternative method would be to regard the purchase of the property and the setting up of a pension scheme as two completely separate free-standing objectives. The property purchase would be financed by the directors or by the company on a long-term basis which would reduce the strain on cash flow and a pension plan could be set up at modest levels. If, for various reasons, the company were unable to pay contributions to the pension plan this would not prejudice mortgage payments in respect of the property purchase and if the property had to be sold at an inopportune time it would not undermine the pension benefits of the directors and their beneficiaries.

9.7 INSURANCE-BASED HYBRID SCHEMES

Insured executive pension plans are often adapted to provide some or all of the features of a small self-administered scheme. This is done quite simply by:

(1) Including the executive pension plan policy within a fully fledged small self-administered scheme on the basis set out above. The fund's balance is invested by the trustees in other areas. The insurance company then carries out either limited administration of the scheme or provides a full service including preparation of documents, negotiations with the Revenue, accounting services, actuarial services and acting as pensioneer trustee. The Revenue and DSS regulations summarised above also apply to these schemes.

(2) Offering a loan facility alongside its executive pension plan on the basis that this normally satisfies the requirements of most directors of small family companies. However, this type of arrangement does *not* constitute a small self-administered scheme. Under this method the insurance company lends to the employer an amount currently not exceeding one-half of the pension fund, taking as security the pension policy itself. A loan made within two years of setting up the pension plan may not, however, exceed 25 per cent of the fund value, excluding the value of transfer payments included in the fund. The loan to the employing company must be for a genuine commercial purpose and interest is payable at a commercial rate (3 per cent above the current base rate of a particular clearing bank).

The loan must be repaid 12 months before the member's retiring age (or if the member leaves the company, or dies, or the company becomes insolvent). Failure by the borrowing company to repay the loan may result in the reduction of the member's benefits – and in particular of the tax-free cash sum available at retirement.

The member must give his consent to the policy being used by the trustees as security, but in practice the member is a controlling director of the company directly involved in using the money borrowed from the insurance company for a commercial purpose.

On 26 August 1999 the PSO announced new restrictions on insured loanback arrangements, set out in new practice notes (see Appendix 2). A brief summary of the main impact of the changes, which take effect from 1 December 1999, follows:

- normally the duration of the loan is expected to be no more than five years and for some purposes, for example where the loan is for stock-in-trade, a duration of one year would be more appropriate;
- the duration of the loan may not exceed two years unless level capital repayments are made at least every six months;
- before the trustees grant the pensions policies as security for the loan they must undertake a credit check on the borrower (the employer) ideally containing a rating on the borrower;
- the securing of an 'injudicious' loan on the insured policies may lead to loss of approval of the scheme;
- a certificate PS 8 (also reprinted in Appendix 2) signed by the employer and the trustees of the scheme must be sent to the PSO within 90 days of making the loan;
- if the insurer forecloses on the loan and therefore reduces the policies by the amount of the outstanding loan the scheme trustees have right of action against the employer. This could result in the scheme being regarded as a small self-administered scheme rather than a simple insured scheme.

10

TOPPING-UP GROUP SCHEMES

Most directors or senior executives have some form of retirement provision but very few enjoy benefits in line with the absolute maximum levels permitted by the Inland Revenue. This chapter identifies the ways in which existing benefits can be topped up either by the director himself or with the help of his company or a combination of the two.

The methods of increasing benefits depends to a large extent on the type of scheme from which the director's main benefits will emerge from and the date on which he joined it as this determines whether he is classed as a pre-1987 member, a 1987–89 member or a post-1989 member.

10.1 GROUP SCHEMES

The vast majority of group schemes provide benefits related to final salary. For directors and senior executives this is likely to be at least one-sixtieth of final salary for each year of service as a scheme member: in the event of death a widow's or widower's death-in-retirement pension is payable and, in the event of death in service, there will probably be a lump sum payable of between twice and four times salary together with a spouse's death-in-service pension of one-half of the prospective personal pension. When in payment, the pension is likely to remain level or increase at a rate of around 5 per cent per annum compound. Retirement age is usually at age 65, although in recent years age 60 has become common. The following comparison table shows the benefits which a director who enters a scheme aged 35, earning £50,000 per annum, is likely to receive under a typical group pension scheme compared with the maximum levels permitted.

Table 10.1

Benefit	Typical group scheme	Maximum benefits
Member's pension	$^{30}/_{60} \times$ £50,000 = £25,000 pa	$^2/_3$ of £50,000 = £33,333 pa
Pension increases at	3% to 5%	In line with Retail Prices Index
Widow's pension	50% of member's pension = £12,500	$^2/_3$ of member's pension = £22,222 pa
Lump sum death benefit	2 × £50,000 = £100,000	4 × £50,000 = £200,000

The difference between actual benefits received under a typical group scheme and the maximum benefits approvable are even greater than those set out above. Maximum benefits can be paid from age 60 rather than 65, total remuneration may be pensioned including such items as bonuses, commissions, director's fees, and the taxable element of fringe benefits: a typical group scheme limits pensionable salary to basic salary only and excludes fluctuating items. Thus there is usually plenty of scope for topping-up the benefits of a director or executive even if he is a post-1989 member and might be affected by the earnings ceiling of £90,600 (in 1999/2000).

10.2 ADDITIONAL VOLUNTARY CONTRIBUTIONS (AVCs)

The Inland Revenue allows contributions by members of up to 15 per cent of their total remuneration. If the member is already paying normal contributions to the scheme of, say, 5 per cent, he may increase this by a further 10 per cent. Since 26 October 1987, scheme members have a choice between investing AVCs through either:

(1) their employer's scheme (scheme AVCs or 'in house' AVCs); or
(2) free-standing AVCs.

The choice of investment vehicle for voluntary contributions is wide, including insurance contracts, building society and bank accounts and unit trusts. AVCs started after 8 April 1987 are not permitted to generate directly a lump sum but only pension.

(1) **Scheme AVCs** – The whole of the member's additional contributions are deductible from his/her pay before tax, thus giving relief from income tax at the highest rate (known as the net pay system).
(2) **Free-standing AVCs** – This is a contract which is completely separate from any employer sponsored scheme, to which a scheme member can pay AVCs. Tax relief is not given through the net pay system. Instead the individual obtains basic rate tax relief at source

and claims any higher rate relief through his tax assessment. (For further details see 10.9.)

(3) **Added years** – Public sector schemes often allow 'added years of service' to be purchased but very few private schemes adopt this approach since it requires a commitment on the part of the employer to underwrite salary inflation. For example, a voluntary contribution of 5 per cent of salary might secure three or four years' additional pensionable service for a young member. If, however, his salary increases substantially later in life, the pension fund would have to meet the additional liabilities which have not been matched by the voluntary contributions paid by the member. From the member's point of view, this would be very attractive but is unsatisfactory to the employer.

10.3 AUGMENTATION UNDER THE GROUP SCHEME

Most group schemes contain rules allowing the trustees to augment the benefits of selected individuals or groups and in recent years some large schemes have reduced surpluses in this way. Although this involves a financial commitment on the employer's part, it may be attractive to the individual director, since the cost of the additional benefit can be lost in the scheme's group funding arrangements. However, moves to improve corporate governance may make this more difficult to achieve (as a result of recommendations of the Greenbury Committee). The employer normally writes to the director or key executive concerned advising him of the extent to which his benefits under the scheme are being topped-up. This method of augmentation does involve a loss of confidentiality, and in the case of directors of profitable family companies tends to be inflexible in dealing with tax problems. It is much more likely that the following method, which involves setting up a separate arrangement, will be more suitable.

10.4 TOPPING-UP THROUGH EXECUTIVE PENSION PLANS

The Revenue permits categories of employees to have (effectively) two normal retirement dates: a director or executive could, for example, be a member of a group pension scheme with a normal retirement age of 65 when the majority of employees will retire, and also be a member of an executive pension plan arranged specially for him with a retirement age of 60 if this age is the best estimate of his date of retirement. For the purpose of deciding the maximum approvable benefits under the executive pension plan there must be taken into account the benefits payable under the main scheme on retirement at the supplementary scheme age, ie the benefits on early retirement.

When setting up a pension plan to top up group scheme benefits, it is important to consider the member's status, ie pre-1987, 1987–89 or post-1989 (see 4.3).

By combining an executive pension plan with a group pension scheme sufficient funds can be accumulated to provide:

(1) A full two-thirds pension at 60 rather than at 65.
(2) Increases in dependants' benefits.
(3) Increases in pensions in line with increases in the cost of living.
(4) Increases in the tax-free lump sum up to the maximum permitted.

Further features of adopting the executive pension plan route are:

(1) Improved rights in the event of leaving service; if the director or executive leaves service, his benefits (often in the form of an individual policy) can be transferred to his new employer (and even if it is not transferred, they continue to benefit from future growth).
(2) Improved death-in-service protection.
(3) The use of dynamised final remuneration (as explained in 4.8).
(4) Improved benefits on early retirement.
(5) The director has greater control over the investment medium in which his contributions are invested and greater privacy over his retirement provisions.
(6) Items which are not normally pensionable (eg bonus, commission) are more easily handled under an executive pension plan.
(7) The employer may use it for discretionary payments in respect of certain directors from time to time, and as a benefit when recruiting executives who do not wish to join a group salary-related scheme.

The following example shows the extent to which a director could top up his benefits.

Example 10.1

A is a member of a group pension scheme which provides him with two-thirds of his final salary as a pension from the age of 65, having joined the scheme when he was 25, and is now aged 38. Current salary is £50,000. The scope for investment in an executive pension plan may be calculated as follows:

Prospective pension at age 65 based on
current basic salary $= \frac{2}{3} \times £50,000$
$= £33,333$ pa

Early retirement at age 60 $= \frac{35}{60} \times £50,000 \times 0.7*$
$= £20,416$ pa

Salary required to support this pension
if he were entitled to maximum benefits
at age 60 $= £20,416 \div \frac{2}{3}$
$= £30,624$

Non-pensioned basic salary	= £50,000 – £30,624
	= £19,376
Add other items averaged over three years, eg bonus, taxable element of fringe benefits, say,	£2,000
Total non-pensioned remuneration	£21,376

*Early retirement actuarial factor to bring forward group scheme pension from age 65 to 60.

The approximate initial contribution which could be paid to an executive pension plan in this example to provide a maximum member's pension is around £7,268 (increasing in future in line with salary increases).

No allowance has been made for increasing any widow's pension or making provision for post-retirement increases in the group scheme pension.

10.5 SALARY SACRIFICE

If a director's benefits are to be topped-up by means of a separate executive pension plan, which requires approval by the Revenue in the usual way, the employer must contribute towards the costs. If the employer is unwilling to bear any additional expenditure, the employer's contribution can be made by the director giving up part of his salary voluntarily – a practice known as 'salary sacrifice'. Because the employer is paying a lower salary to the director, it has the funds to contribute to an executive pension plan. Amounts sacrificed in this way must be documented usually in the form of an exchange of letters, for example:

Dear Mr X,

This is to inform you that with effect from 1 October your salary will be reduced from £50,000 pa to £46,000 pa.

Yours sincerely,

For the Company . . . .   Date . . . .

I agree to this reduction in salary.

Signed . . . .   Date . . . .

Director

It is essential that the letter makes no reference to the application of the forgone amount to pension contributions and that it is exchanged before the reduction in salary commences. Failure to observe these rules almost certainly results in the treatment of the sacrifice as ineffective by the local Inspector of Taxes.

Details of the amount of salary sacrifice should be sent by the employer direct to the Schedule E tax district where the amount is £5,000 or over. The Schedule E tax district decides whether the sacrifice is an effective reduction of the employee's remuneration assessable to income tax.

If the director is considering paying personal contributions in addition to salary sacrifice the Revenue requires that the employer's contribution is not a derisory proportion of the total, and normally wishes to see 10 per cent of the total contribution paid by the employer.

The effect of salary sacrifice is that the director never receives the sacrificed salary so that he therefore cannot pay tax or National Insurance contributions on it. The company obtains tax relief whether it pays a level of salary to the director or a lower level of salary plus a pension contribution. The director's salary must, however, be reduced for all purposes including his pensionable salary on which his pension benefits are calculated.

The following example shows how contributions may be paid:

Example 10.2

		Total contribution £
Salary	£50,000	
Salary sacrifice	£ 4,000	4,000 from employer
Revised salary	£46,000	
Personal contribution of, say, 15%	£ 6,900	6,900 from employee
		10,900

The employer will contribute £10,900 and deduct the member's share of £6,900 from his salary under a net PAY arrangement.

If, however, the company intends recouping the member's share in monthly instalments over a period of 12 months, then it is effectively giving him an interest-free loan on a reducing basis which might be in breach of the Companies Act 1985, s 330 if the member is a director of a public company or of a company in a group which includes a public company. If there is any likelihood of such a breach then the employer should recoup the member's share in one lump.

10.6 DIVIDEND WAIVER

The principle of dividend waiver is that the shareholder (who will be a working director or employee of the company) renounces in advance his entitlement to any dividend that may be declared in respect of his holdings so that he never becomes entitled to the dividend. The waiver should take the form of a unilateral deed under seal executed by the shareholder only. The waiver should be executed before payment in the case of an interim dividend and before declaration in the case of a final dividend. The waiver must relate only to dividends payable within 12 months of execution and there must be no connection between the dividend waiver and the provision of pension benefits.

10.7 BONUS SACRIFICE

Some employees are entitled to a bonus or commission which is calculated when the employer's accounts have been certified. For income tax purposes the bonus or commission is treated as accruing during the period to which it relates, for example by reference to annual, quarterly or monthly accounts. A bonus or commission sacrifice which is made after the end of the relative period is regarded by the Revenue as retrospective and therefore as ineffective. The Revenue takes the view that the employee's entitlement is fixed at the end of the relative accounting period. When that point is reached the employee cannot sacrifice any part of his bonus or commission even though the exact amount may not be quantified until a later date.

However, the Revenue is prepared to accept a reduction which is agreed sufficiently long before the year end so that the reduced annual sum is not less than the remuneration which has already accrued at the former rate. Ultimately, however, the question of whether a sacrifice is effective is a matter for the local Inspector of Taxes.

10.8 EFFECT OF INCOME SACRIFICE ON NATIONAL INSURANCE CONTRIBUTIONS

To the extent that an individual sacrifices income (whether salary, bonus, commission, etc) there is a saving in the employer's national insurance contributions.

Since 6 October 1985 national insurance contributions have been payable by employers on all earnings (prior to that time they were limited to the upper earnings level, which still applies to employees' national insurance contributions).

Example 10.3

- An executive sacrifices a bonus of £10,000.
- The employer saves £1,220 in NIC.
- Employer's contributions to pension plan can be between £10,000 and £11,220.
- Net income sacrified by executive £6,000 (assuming a 40% taxpayer).

Example 10.4

- The employer is prepared to spend £10,000 including National Insurance contributions.
- If the executive opts to receive a bonus he obtains £8,913 gross, £5,348 net (assuming a 40% taxpayer).
- If the executive sacrifices his bonus the company invests £10,000 in a pension plan.

10.9 FREE-STANDING AVCS

From 6 April 1988 the Social Security Act 1986 required employers to offer members of their occupational schemes the facility to pay additional voluntary contributions to top-up their benefits, although many schemes had provided such facilities for years and had encouraged scheme members to take advantage of the tax efficiency of AVC arrangements.

From 26 October 1987 a different type of AVC arrangement became available, known as a 'free-standing AVC' (FSAVC). This type of pension contract was introduced by F(No 2)A 1987 and has the following characteristics:

(1) It must be used to provide income in retirement only, not tax-free lump sums. This restriction also applies to scheme AVCs which started after 7 April 1987.
(2) Contributions are subject to the normal limits applying under occupational schemes approved under ICTA 1988, ss 590–612 (see Appendix 4). There are two main restrictions:
  (a) The maximum contributions that may be paid by an individual amount to 15 per cent of his remuneration (including any personal contributions which his employer may require him to pay under an occupational scheme or under a separate executive pension plan).
  (b) Benefits will also be subject to the normal limits applying under occupational schemes approved under ICTA 1988 (see Chapter 4), but broadly there is a maximum pension on retirement from all sources of two-thirds of final remuneration.

(3) The FSAVC scheme is completely separate from the employer's occupational scheme although there is liaison between the trustees of the employer's occupational scheme and the pension provider of the AVC, when benefits become payable, eg on retirement. The trustees of the employer's scheme inform the pension provider of the maximum benefits permitted under Revenue rules, and the amount being provided under the employer's scheme. The balance may be provided by the FSAVC scheme. If there is a surplus when benefits become payable it has to be returned to the members minus a tax charge (see below).

(4) Prior to 6 April 1987 the Revenue required AVCs to be paid for at least five years, or to retirement if earlier, in order to attract tax relief. From 6 April 1987 members have been permitted to vary the amount and timing of AVCs, making these arrangements even more flexible.

(5) They may be arranged through an extended number of pension providers which includes insurance companies, banks, building societies and unit trusts.

(6) Because contributions are paid directly by the individual to the pension provider, tax relief is not obtained in the same manner as tax relief on contributions to an occupational pension scheme or executive pension plan where the 'net pay arrangement' normally operates. Instead, the individual pays contributions net of basic rate tax: for example an individual wishing to pay £100 per month to an FSAVC contract therefore has to pay only £77 per month net to the pension provider who reclaims the tax deducted, ie £23 per month from the Revenue, and credits the additional £23 per month to the contract (this example assumes basic rate tax relief of 23 per cent). Any higher rate tax relief is obtained by application to the Revenue, ie through the individual's tax return.

Leading scheme procedures

The Inland Revenue has issued revised FSAVC Guidance Notes which confirm leading scheme administration requirements. These have now been enacted in the form of regulations.

A member of an occupational scheme may contribute to an in-house AVC, an FSAVC, or both at the same time (within the overall contribution limit). Furthermore he may have contributed to more than one FSAVC during his employment (but contributions may not be made to more than one such FSAVC in any one financial year).

The leading scheme is defined as:

- the last FSAVC, where the member has not made any contributions to an in-house AVC;

- the employer's scheme, if any in-house AVC contributions have been made.

The Administrator of the leading scheme is required to instruct the various FSAVC schemes involved (if applicable) as to what benefits should be paid, including any surplus amounts payable as cash arising from over-provision.

In order to determine whether or not maximum benefits have been exceeded the employer's scheme must certify the maximum member's pension payable from all approved occupational/statutory schemes in respect of the member's service with the employer. For this purpose the employer's scheme may use the best definition of final remuneration allowed by the Revenue, or the definition upon which the employer's scheme benefits are calculated (which may be more restrictive than Revenue rules, eg the definition of final remuneration may be basic salary only).

If the total pension benefits from the main scheme and FSAVCs taken together exceed maximum benefits certified by the employer's scheme, then the member may choose either to:

- take the whole of the surplus fund as cash sum subject to tax; or
- to maximise pension benefits in accordance with Revenue rules, hence only taking a cash refund if a surplus still exists.

10.9.1 Over-provision

If the combination of benefits under the main occupational scheme and the FSAVC provides excessive benefits the main scheme benefits are not reduced but the surplus arises under the FSAVC. The scheme administrator of the FSAVC must deduct tax at 33 per cent of the surplus fund if the individual is a basic rate taxpayer. Assuming a surplus of £1,000, tax is deducted of £330 with £670 payable to the member. This amount, £670, is treated as income which has suffered basic rate tax (taken to be 23 per cent). The net amount received by the individual of £670 has a grossed up equivalent of £870 but there is no further liability to tax in the case of a basic rate taxpayer. Even if the individual is not liable to tax the amount paid by the scheme administrator cannot be recovered. If the individual is a higher rate taxpayer, further tax at 17 per cent is payable on the grossed up amount, in this case £139 further liability. In the case of a higher rate taxpayer, therefore, there is total tax to pay of £479, representing an effective tax rate of approximately 48 per cent on the surplus of £1,000. Any surplus arising on death is taxed at 33 per cent.

10.9.2 Estimating benefits

An individual wishing to pay AVCs will wish to ascertain how much could be contributed to the FSAVC to top up the overall benefits to the Revenue maximum. An indication of the scope for AVCs can be provided by the main scheme trustees or by the pension provider which runs the FSAVC. An individual wishing to pay contributions of £2,400 per annum or more must provide the FSAVC provider information relating to his main scheme and previous retained benefits. The pension provider then tests the possibility of over-provision, known as a 'headroom test'. If this is likely the pension provider informs the intending contributor of the reduced level of contributions which should be paid to ensure that overall benefits do not exceed Revenue limits. If contributions, however, are less than £2,400 per annum the FSAVC provider does not have to carry out an initial check (but will do so should the contributions exceed £2,400 per annum in the future).

Although a disadvantage of the FSAVC scheme is the inability to take any of the emerging benefits in the form of a tax-free lump sum, in practice this problem may be overcome by looking at the combined benefits emerging from the FSAVC scheme and the individual's other pension arrangements. To the extent that an individual takes a tax-free lump sum from any pension scheme, his pension is bound to be lower: in practice, many pensioners reinvest any lump sum in other areas to provide additional income in order to maintain a reasonable standard of living. If, however, an individual is deterred from paying contributions to an FSAVC scheme because it does not provide a tax-free lump sum, he should investigate the rules of his main occupational scheme. Although it might provide a cash lump sum of, say, only three-eighths of his final salary for each year of service, the rules often contain powers of augmentation allowing the trustees to increase the tax-free lump sum (and other benefits) up to the maximum permitted by the Revenue (not available under statutory schemes). The individual, therefore, could take increased cash from his occupational scheme leaving a lower income from that scheme which would be topped up by the pension emerging from his FSAVC scheme.

Example 10.5

> Company pension scheme provides:
>
> - a pension of £6,666 pa ($^{20}\!/_{60}$ of pensionable salary of £20,000); or
> - a cash lump sum of £15,000 ($^{3}\!/_{80}$ of pensionable salary for each year of pensionable service, ie $^{60}\!/_{80}$ plus a reduced pension of around £5,416 pa).
>
> The Inland Revenue allows tax-free cash to be calculated using the greater of $^{3}\!/_{80}$ of pensionable salary for each year of pensionable service or 2.25 × the pension before commutation. Both methods would produce the same result. If the member contributes to an FSAVC scheme which produces an additional pension of £1,000 pa, this can be taken into account in the calculation. The member could then take £17,250 under the main company scheme as a cash lump sum (2.25 × £7,666, plus a reduced pension of £5,229 pa together with the FSAVC pension of £1,000 pa).

10.9.3 Transitional arrangements

The F(No 2)A 1987 introduced changes affecting AVCs. Only new AVC arrangements entered into after 7 April 1987, including contributions to FSAVC schemes, are affected by the 'no commutation rule'. The following (which is an extract from Memorandum 87 published by the Inland Revenue on the subject) will not be affected:

(1) An arrangement whereby a contractual obligation was entered into before 8 April 1987, even if the first contribution had not been paid until after that date.
(2) Continuation of an arrangement following the re-organisation of an employer's pension arrangements, or the restructuring or sale of part or all of the employer's business.
(3) A change in the amount or timing of AVCs; examples are an increase in the percentage of salary being paid or a change from a monthly to annual payment basis.
(4) A break in contributions, provided that on recommencement the AVCs are paid to the original arrangement or to another arrangement which is part of the employer's scheme.
(5) A change in investment medium for the AVCs (eg a switch from an insurance contract to a building society deposit) provided that the new investments are held under an AVC arrangement first entered into before 8 April 1987.

10.9.4 Recent improvements in AVCs

In July 1999, the Revenue announced greater flexibility for in-house and free-standing AVCs. Benefits under these arrangements no longer have to be taken at the same time as the main scheme benefits. This facility will be readily available under FSAVCs. However, because in-house AVCs form part of the main scheme, the separation of the AVC fund from the rest of the benefits will depend on the scheme's administration systems and the willingness of the scheme trustees to offer the facility.

The recent improvements also extend to allowing 'income drawdown' (also known as 'income withdrawal') under AVCs and FSAVCs rather than the straightforward purchase of an annuity. This concept is described in Chapter 19 in relation to personal pensions.

Where benefits under AVCs and FSAVCs are taken before the main scheme benefits, income drawdown must be used. This is of dubious benefit because income drawdown is a complex procedure under personal pensions, often applying only when the accumulated fund is at least £100,000. Under income drawdown arrangements, the fund is not converted into an annuity. Instead, an income is withdrawn from the fund, subject to Revenue rules, with annuity purchase deferred until age 75. In the meantime, the fund has to be invested in a manner which gives a sufficient return to ensure that income can be maintained or even increased in later years while not exposing the pensioner to unnecessary risk. Under personal pensions, the risk is borne by the individual member: under an AVC, the scheme trustees will bear some responsibility for the ongoing investment management of the drawdown fund but will seek to limit their liabilities insofar as their overall trustee duties and responsibilities allow.

10.10 TIERED SCHEMES AND MATCHING ARRANGEMENTS

Some schemes allow choice over levels of accrual rate (under defined benefits schemes) or over levels of contribution (under defined contribution schemes).

For example, a defined benefit scheme provides a pension of $1/60$ of final salary for each year of service, with members paying contractual contributions of 5 per cent per year. The tiered arrangements allow, say, members to opt for a higher rate of pension accrual of $1/50$ of final salary for each year of service but with members' contributions at 6 per cent per year. The member who opts for the increased pension will also obtain an employer subsidy because the additional benefit ($1/50 – 1/60$) of final salary will not be met purely by the increased member's contribution of 1 per cent. The balance of the cost will be met by the employer.

Under a defined contribution scheme the employer may pay, for example, 6 per cent of pay with members paying 4 per cent of pay, giving a total of 10 per cent. Under a matching arrangement the employer may offer to match every 1 per cent of additional contribution paid by the member, on a one-for-one basis (or more): if, say, the member increases contributions to 6 per cent the employer will increase contributions to 8 per cent, giving a total contribution of 14 per cent.

Under tiered or matching arrangements the member increases the rate of *contractual* contributions, up to retirement: the member does not pay additional *voluntary* contributions. Taking advantage of tiered or matching arrangements is almost certainly likely to be better than paying AVCs or FSAVCs.

11

STATE BENEFITS

11.1 THE CURRENT SYSTEM

On 6 April 1978, the present state scheme started, following the Social Security Pensions Act 1975 and replacing the State Graduated Scheme. The scheme consists of two pensions – a basic old age pension and an earnings related additional pension (known as 'SERPS'). At that time employers with a good occupational pension scheme (providing pensions on a defined basis) could 'contract out' of SERPS. Those employees who were contracted out on this basis will receive the old age pension from the state and an additional earnings related pension from their occupational scheme.

In 1988 contracting out on a money purchase basis through either an occupational pension scheme set up by the employer or a personal pension plan became available. Those employees who are contracted-out on a money purchase basis will receive the old age pension from the state and a 'protected rights' pension (see Chapter 12). Self-employed persons, however, are entitled only to the old age pension, not the earnings related pension (their national insurance contributions are substantially lower than those paid by and on behalf of an employed person). The scheme has been the subject of amendments since its introduction, and this chapter considers the scheme as it is (in amended form) and also the changes which took effect from 6 April 1988.

The Government announced in the November 1993 Budget that the state pension age for men and women is to be equalised at age 65. The revised pension age for women will not apply immediately but will be phased in over a ten-year period commencing April 2010.

The phasing in will operate as follows:

- the state pension age for women born during or before March 1950 will remain at 60.
- the state pension age for women born during or after April 1955 will be 65.
- the state pension age for women born in the period April 1950 to March 1955 will be on a transitional basis.

For example:

Date of birth	Pension age
6 April to 5 May 1950	60 years 1 month
6 October to 5 November 1950	60 years 7 months
6 April to 5 May 1951	61 years 1 month
6 October to 5 November 1951	61 years 7 months
6 April to 5 May 1952	62 years 1 month
6 October to 5 November 1952	62 years 7 months
6 April to 5 May 1953	63 years 1 month
6 October to 5 November 1953	63 years 7 months
6 April to 5 May 1954	64 years 1 month
6 October to 5 November 1954	64 years 7 months

For dates of birth between those shown the retirement age will be on a corresponding basis. Thus, a woman born on 9 July 1953 would have a retirement date of 9 November 2016 (ie 63 years 4 months).

11.1.1 Objective of the earnings related state pension

The single person's old age pension was around 25 per cent of the national average earnings but now stands at around only 19 per cent. (This is a result of increasing the old age pension in line with increases in the retail prices index rather than the national average earnings index, as applied previously.) The original objective of the earnings related part of the state scheme (which is not a funded scheme) was to increase the general level of state pension for single persons by a further 25 per cent of national average earnings over a period of 20 years starting from April 1978. Thus, employed persons retiring in 1998 could expect to receive a full earnings related pension when they finally retired. Employed males who were over the age of 45 in 1978 and most working females over the age of 40 in 1978 will receive a proportion of the full pension depending upon the number of years that they participate before retirement and their own level of earnings.

The Social Security Act 1986, however, brought about major changes to the earnings related part of the state scheme (SERPS). These changes will result in the reduction in SERPS mainly for people retiring in the next century. The Social Security Act 1986 has also had a major impact on occupational schemes as it is simpler for employers to set up pension schemes to contract out of SERPS and it is also possible for individuals to decide whether or not to contract out of SERPS through the use of personal pension schemes (see Chapter 12).

Table 11.1

Tax year	Employer			Employee		
	Contracted out					
	COSR (%)	COMP (%)	Contracted in (%)	Initial (%)	Contracted out (%)	Contracted in (%)
6.4.98–5.4.99						
Earnings per week						
£64–£109.99	0.0	1.5	3.0	2.0	8.4	10.0
£110–£154.99	2.0	3.5	5.0	2.0	8.4	10.0
£155–£209.99	4.0	5.5	7.0	2.0	8.4	10.0
£210–£485	7.0	8.5	10.0	2.0	8.4	10.0
6.4.99–5.4.00						
Earnings per week						
£66–£82.99	nil	nil	nil	N/A	8.4	10.0
£83–£500	9.2	11.6	12.2	N/A	8.4	10.0
above £500	12.2	12.2	12.2	N/A	nil	nil

(1) 'COSR' means contracted out salary related and 'COMP' means contracted out money purchase.

(2) These tables show how the contribution rates have become complicated over the past few years. There have been four changes to the structure of the rebates over the past 15 years.

(3) From 6 October 1985, lower band rates were introduced for both employers and employees. This meant that the rate payable depended on the level of the employee's earnings. Contributions were payable at the relevant rate on all earnings between the UEL (lower earnings limit) and the UEL (upper earnings limit) and at the corresponding contracted-in rate on earnings below the LEL. No contributions were required from the employees on earnings above the UEL but employer's contributions on earnings above the UEL were paid at the full contracted-in rate. Lower and upper earnings limits are set out in Table 11.2 below.

(4) From 5 October 1989, changes were made to the structure of NICs. If employee earnings exceeded the LEL, contributions were payable by the employee at the 'initial' rate on earnings below the LEL and at the 'main rate' on all earnings between the LEL and UEL.

(5) From 6 April 1997, further changes were made. These meant that contracted-out money purchase schemes received a small flat rate rebate with the balance of monies due paid as an age-related rebate by the DSS. The extent of these age-related rebates were designed when aggregated with the flat rate rebate to be broadly equivalent to the value of the SERPS benefit given up.

(6) From 6 April 1999, a major simplification of contributions was introduced. Employees only paid contributions on earnings between the LEL and UEL. Employers paid contributions on income above £83 per week (in line with the income tax threshold) but rather than contributions being paid against earnings bands, they were paid at single rate on all earnings above £83 per week.

11.2 STATE SCHEME CONTRIBUTIONS

Pensions are paid by levying national insurance contributions on the working population on a 'pay as you go basis'. The employer's contributions may be set against profits for corporation tax purposes but employee contributions are not tax deductible. (National insurance contributions are collected through the PAYE system.)

National insurance contribution rates incorporate other National insurance benefits such as short-term sickness, National Health and redundancy payments. They do not therefore represent the actual cost of state pensions alone.

Table 11.1 sets out contracted-in and contracted-out national insurance contributions payable by employers and employees in 1998/1999 and 1999/2000.

11.3 UPPER AND LOWER EARNINGS LIMITS

There is a ceiling on earnings for national insurance purposes known as the upper earnings limit. The lower earnings limit corresponds roughly with the flat rate pension for a single person while the upper earnings limit is around seven times the lower earnings limit: both limits are adjusted in April each year. Table 11.2 sets out upper and lower earnings limits for 1981 to 1999 inclusive.

Table 11.2

Earnings limits		
	Lower earnings limit	Upper earnings limit
Tax year	£ pa(a)	£ pa(a)
1981/82	1,404	10,400
1982/83	1,534	11,440
1983/84	1,690	12,220
1984/85	1,768	13,000
1985/86	1,846	13,780
1986/87	1,976	14,820
1987/88	2,028	15,340
1988/89	2,132	15,860
1989/90	2,236	16,900
1990/91	2,392	18,200
1991/92	2,704	20,280
1992/93	2,808	21,060
1993/94	2,912	21,840
1994/95	2,964	22,360
1995/96	3,260	22,880

Table 11.2 *(cont.)*

1996/97	3,430	23,660
1997/98	3,224	24,180
1998/99	3,328	25,220
1999/2000	3,432	26,000

Note
(a)   52 times the weekly amount

11.4 QUALIFYING CONDITIONS

SERPS is paid as part of the old age pension, and the qualifying conditions are therefore the same, namely that the individual:

● has reached pensionable age (currently 65 males, 60 females); and
● has retired from regular employment (see below); and
● satisfies the contribution condition (in SERPS terms, this is the requirement that the Class 1 national insurance contributions paid in at least one tax year from 1978/79 onwards generate a 'surplus' – see 11.6 below).

Currently a person who ceases employment in order to care for children, or sick or disabled persons can claim home responsibilities protection (HRP) which has the effect of reducing the number of years over which Class 1 national insurance contributions must be paid to secure a full basic state pension. HRP does not currently apply to SERPS.

At present, the provisions cover the basic pension only. However, arrangements are being made to extend HRP coverage to SERPS for those retiring (or widowed) on or after 6 April 1999.

11.5 EMPLOYMENT BEYOND PENSIONABLE AGE

An individual who continues to work after reaching pensionable age is usually still regarded as having retired from regular employment if the employment falls within no more than one of the following:

(1) the work does not normally involve more than 12 hours per week; or
(2) the work is 'occasional' (ie no normal weekly commitment).

Individuals are automatically treated as having retired on attaining the age of (currently) 70 (males) or 65 (females) if they have not already done so. The individual still needs to submit a claim for SERPS even on attaining the age of 70/65.

Widow(er)s

A widow(er) may also be able to claim SERPS benefits based on the contribution record of the deceased spouse (see widow(er)s benefits at 11.13).

11.6 AMOUNT OF PENSION

The total earnings figure on which SERPS depends is calculated as follows:

(1) Earnings on which Class 1 national insurance contributions have been paid in each tax year commencing 1978/79 are calculated.
(2) Each earnings figure is then 'revalued' by increasing it by a percentage reflecting the increase in national earnings since the tax year concerned (no revaluation takes place for the tax year in which age 64 (males) or age 59 (females) is attained).
(3) Each annual figure is then reduced by the qualifying level for basic pension applicable to the tax year in which age 64 (males) or 59 (females) is attained. The 1995 Pensions Act introduced a change to this calculation. In respect of earnings after 5 April 1999, each annual figure is reduced by the qualifying level for basic pension for that financial year.
(4) The resulting reduced amounts represent the 'surplus' for each of the tax years in question.
(5) The relevant ages for females will be amended in due course to take account of the change in the state retirement age for women.

11.7 ANNUAL RATE OF SERPS

11.7.1 Pre-April 1988 calculation

The annual rate of SERPS is then determined according to the tax year in which the individual retires as follows:

(1) **Retirement in 1998/99 or earlier.** The total of one-eightieth of each of the surpluses as calculated above.
(2) **Retirement in 1999/2000 or later.** SERPS will be based on a maximum of 20 years of earnings on which national insurance contributions have been paid. Employees who make national insurance contributions for more than 20 years will receive an earnings related pension based on the best of one-eightieth of each of the surpluses for each of the best 20 years, giving a maximum pension of 25 per cent of surpluses.

11.7.2 Post-April 1988 calculation

(1) **Retirement in 1998/99 or earlier**: the total of one-eightieth of each of the surpluses as calculated above.

(2) **Retirement in 1999/2000 – 2008/09**:

$\dfrac{25\%}{N}$ of the surpluses for the tax years 1978/79 to 1987/88 inclusive,

plus

$\dfrac{20 + X\%}{N}$ of the surpluses for the tax years 1988/89 onwards.

(3) **Retirement in 2009/10 onwards**

$\dfrac{25\%}{N}$ of the surpluses for the tax years 1978/79 to 1987/88 inclusive,

plus

$\dfrac{20\%}{N}$ of the surpluses for the tax years 1988/89 onwards.

Where:

N = the number of tax years in the pensioner's working life after 5 April 1978

X = 0.5 for each tax year by which retirement precedes the tax year 2009/10

and may be reduced in respect of tax years after 5 April 1978 in which:

(a) contributions or earnings were credited to enable a person to satisfy contribution conditions, or

(b) the pensioner was precluded from regular employment by responsibilities at home;

but not to the extent that N would fall below 20.

11.7.3 Major differences

The two major differences between the original and modified bases are:

(1) The reduction in the level of SERPS from a maximum of 25 per cent to 20 per cent in respect of surpluses for the tax years 1988/89 onwards (with a sliding scale for ten years); and

(2) The removal of the 'best 20 years' rule which will have the effect of reducing the level of earnings/surpluses on which SERPS is calculated.

Example 11.1

Person retiring in 2006/07 with a working life (since 1978/79) of 28 years.

Original basis: 1.25% of surpluses for the best 20 of the 28 years (ie the worst eight years are ignored), giving a total of 25% of surpluses.

Revised basis: $\dfrac{25\%}{28}$ of the surpluses for tax years 1978/79 to 1987/88 inclusive plus

$\dfrac{(20+1.5)\%}{28}$ of surpluses for the tax years 1988/89 onwards, giving a total of 22.75% of surpluses.

11.8 INCREASES DURING PAYMENT

The amount of SERPS benefit is increased each year by the state (along with the basic old age pension) in line with increases in the Retail Prices Index.

11.9 DEFERRED PENSION

If an individual, on reaching pensionable age, is still in regular employment (see above) or defers claiming the state pension, additional pension benefits will accrue at a rate of 7.5 per cent for each full year deferred. The rate of increase for those who reach state pension age in 2010 or later will be 10.4 per cent for each full year deferred.

The maximum period of deferment is currently five years to age 70 (males), 65 (females), and no further National Insurance contributions are payable by the individual during this period (although employers' Class 1 contributions continue for as long as the employment continues with no upper age limit). The maximum additional pension which may be earned over a full five years' deferment is approximately 37 per cent. However, from 2010 there will be no limit on the period of deferment.

If any social security benefits (except attendance allowance, mobility or benefit for a child) are received, or an unemployability supplement is paid with a disablement pension in any week, no additional pension will accrue for that week.

Any additional pension earned by deferment may also be inherited by a widow(er) on the individual's death.

11.10 WIDOWS' BENEFITS (CURRENT RULES)

The availability of any SERPS benefits in the event of a husband's death is dependent on:

- the husband's age at date of death, and
- the widow's age at date of husband's death, and
- whether any children under the age of 19 are resident with the widow.

The following paragraphs show the various benefits which may be claimed and should be read in conjunction with the following notes:

Notes

(1) Widow's payment, a lump sum of £1,000, cannot be claimed if:
    (a) the widow was over age 60 when her husband died and he was then over age 65 and then entitled to a retirement pension (this does not include a retirement pension which has been deferred), or
    (b) the 'contribution conditions' are not fulfilled.

(2) Widowed mother's allowance is payable immediately on bereavement until the youngest child ceases to be dependent.

(3) Where SERPS is claimed on the contribution record of the late husband in order to supplement the contribution record of the widow, the maximum benefit is that which a single person could have earned by paying maximum contributions.

(4) Widow's pension continues to be paid after age 60 unless the widow retires and she is automatically treated as having retired at age 65. When she retires, widow's pension is replaced with retirement pension.

(5) Both widowed mother's allowance and widow's pension cease permanently if the widow remarries, and are suspended if she lives with another man as his wife.

(6) Where SERPS is 'inherited' from a deceased husband, the current amount is 100 per cent of the SERPS earned up to the date of the husband's death, but will be reduced to 50 per cent of this amount if the husband dies after 5 April 2000.

11.11 HUSBAND DIES LEAVING CHILDREN

The benefits payable to the widow are:

(1) Widow's payment (but see Note 1 above);

(2) Widowed mother's allowance and SERPS based on husband's contribution record; followed by

(3) A widow's pension based on her age at the time the widowed mother's allowance ends as follows:

Table 11.3

Widow's age	Widow's pension
Over 60	Basic and SERPS on own and/or husband's contribution records (see Note 3).
55–60	(a) Basic and SERPS on husband's contribution record payable to age 60; then (b) Basic and SERPS on own and/or husband's contribution records (see Note 3) but with a minimum of the pension payable immediately before age 60.
45–54	(a) Basic and SERPS on husband's contribution record, reduced by 7% for each year (or part) by which widow's age falls short of 50, payable to age 60; then (b) Basic and SERPS on own and/or husband's contribution records (see Note 3) but with a minimum of the pension payable immediately before age 60.
Under 45	(a) No further benefit to age 60; then (b) Basic and SERPS on own contribution record.

11.12 HUSBAND DIES LEAVING NO CHILDREN

The benefits payable to the widow are:

(1) Widow's allowance (but see Notes (1) and (2) above); followed by

(2) A widow's pension based on her age *at the time of her husband's death* as follows:

Table 11.4

Widow's age	Widow's pension
Over 60	Basic and SERPS on own and/or husband's contribution records (see Note 3).
55–60	(a) Basic and SERPS on husband's contribution record payable to age 60; then (b) Basic and SERPS on own and/or husband's contribution records (see Note 3) but with a minimum of the pension payable immediately before age 60.
45–54	(a) Basic and SERPS on husband's contribution record, reduced by 7% for each year (or part) by which widow's age falls short of 50, payable to age 60; then (b) Basic and SERPS on own and/or husband's contribution records (see Note 3) but with a minimum of the pension payable immediately before age 60.
Under 45	(a) No further benefit to age 60; then (b) Basic and SERPS on own contribution record.

11.13   WIDOWERS' BENEFITS (CURRENT RULES)

11.13.1   Original basis

A widower may only claim any SERPS based on his late wife's contribution record if:

(1) both he and his wife had reached pensionable age before she died; and

(2) he had retired from regular employment.

The maximum SERPS a widower may inherit is such that, when added to his own SERPS entitlement, it does not exceed the maximum SERPS an individual would be entitled to based on maximum contributions.

11.13.2   Modified basis

The amount of SERPS which a widower may inherit from his late wife will be 50 per cent of that calculated on the original basis if she dies after 5 April 2010.

11.14 SUMMARY OF STATE PENSIONS

Table 11.5

Basic Old Age Pensions

From	Single person £ per annum	Married couple £ per annum
23 November 1981	1,539.20	2,462.20
22 November 1982	1,708.20	2,732.60
21 November 1983	1,770.60	2,834.00
26 November 1984	1,861.60	2,979.60
25 November 1985	1,991.60	3,187.60
28 July 1986	2,012.40	3,221.40
6 April 1987	2,054.00	3,289.00
6 April 1988	2,139.80	3,426.80
6 April 1989	2,267.20	3,629.60
6 April 1990	2,438.80	3,905.20
6 April 1991	2,704.00	4,329.00
6 April 1992	2,815.80	4,508.40
6 April 1993	2,917.20	4,669.60
6 April 1994	2,995.20	4,789.20
6 April 1995	3,060.20	4,893.20
6 April 1996	3,179.80	5,083.00
6 April 1997	3,247.40	5,189.60
6 April 1998	3,364.40	5,376.80
6 April 1999	3,471.00	5,548.40

Table 11.6 sets out the projected pension (SERPS and basic old age) for a single person retiring after 2010, who did not contribute to SERPS before 1988, as a percentage of salary. These are based on retirement at age 65. Women born before April 1955 will have their state pension phased in between ages 60 and 65.

Table 11.6

				Salary			
£8,000	£9,000	£10,000	£15,000	£20,000	£25,000	£26,000	£40,000
54.8	50.9	47.8	38.6	33.9	31.1	30.7	20.0

Table 11.7 shows the Married Couples' Additional Amount as a percentage of salary.

Table 11.7

| | | | | *Salary* | | | |
£8,000	£9,000	£10,000	£15,000	£20,000	£25,000	£26,000	£40,000
26.0	23.1	20.8	13.8	10.4	8.3	8.0	5.2

Notes to Tables 11.6 and 11.7

(1) The age shown is the age attained on the birthday falling within the 1999/2000 tax year.

(2) It is assumed that salary, lower earnings limit, upper earnings limit and old age pension all increase at the same rate.

(3) Amounts assumed: lower earnings limit £3,432
upper earnings limit £26,000
old age pension £3,471
married couples'
additional amount £2,077.40

(4) The self-employed will only receive the old age pension and where applicable the married couples' additional amount.

(5) The figures assume that individuals have been in contracted-in employment since 1978 or age 16 if later.

(6) The married couples' additional amount assumes the wife is unable to claim state scheme benefits in her own right.

(7) Individuals who contributed to SERPS before 1988 will have that part of their SERPS pension calculated by reference to the original 25 per cent formula.

(8) It is very difficult for individuals to calculate their own SERPS pension with any accuracy (especially if they have been contracted out for part of their working lives); the best course of action is to contact the DSS for a pensions forecast (see 11.17).

11.15 WIDOW(ER)'S BENEFITS – FUTURE BASIS

The Government has announced proposals to equalise the benefits and conditions for the payment of widows' and widowers' benefits. From 2010 the benefits for widowers will be improved to correspond with the more favourable widows' basis.

11.16 ADEQUACY OF STATE PENSIONS

The combination of the basic flat rate pension and the earnings related pension will provide reasonable benefits for employees earning up to national average earnings (approximately £18,000 per annum). For employees whose earnings are above the national average there are serious inadequacies including:

(1) The inability to obtain a pension on earnings which exceed the upper earnings limit.

(2) The maximum additional state pension obtainable of around 20 to 25 per cent of revalued earnings is substantially less than the maximum pension which could be provided from an occupational scheme or an executive pension plan.

(3) The state does not allow any part of the pension to be commuted for a tax-free lump sum.

(4) The state does not provide any lump sum benefits in the event of death in service or after retirement.

(5) The state makes no provision for benefits to be payable on early retirement.

The major advantage of the state scheme, however, is the degree of inflation-proofing provided.

In view of the above limitations it is advisable to top up state benefits through additional voluntary contributions, individual savings accounts (ISAs), executive pension plans (particularly in the case of directors who are able to fund for maximum benefits) and through personal pension schemes which have the added advantage of being able to contract out of SERPS which may be particularly beneficial for younger employees (see Chapter 12).

11.17 DSS LEAFLETS

In general the calculation of state benefits is a complicated exercise especially as so many conditions attach to the benefits. In practice the benefits themselves will probably be inadequate so that the need to top up state benefits through private provision, eg by membership of an occupational scheme or through a personal pension scheme, is of paramount importance, particularly in relation to widow(er)s' benefits.

The DSS publishes a number of leaflets describing state benefits and these are essential reading for anyone who wishes to comprehend fully all the conditions which apply. The principal leaflets are *A Guide to Retirement Pensions*, ref NP46 and *New Pensions Choices*, refs NP 40, NP 41, NP 42.

In addition, the DSS has produced some easy to understand explanatory pages on their website at <www.dss.gov.uk>. The pages are marked

PMI-8. The DSS also publishes a series of manuals which explain how to set up and change the status of contracted-out occupational schemes.

To obtain an estimate of state benefits, an individual should send a completed form BR19, 'Retirement Pension Forecast' to the DSS (the form is available from DSS offices). The DSS also runs a Pensions Info-Line on 0345 313233, and has an information address at DSS Pensions, Freepost, BS 5555/1, Bristol BS99 1BL.

The Revenue also provides details about the operation of the Contracted-Out Employments Group (COEG) at its website at <www.inlandrevenue.gov.uk>.

11.18 CONTRACTING OUT

This chapter has concentrated mainly on benefits provided under the State Earnings Related Pension Scheme. The next chapter looks at how it is possible to contract out of SERPS.

CONTRACTING OUT OF THE STATE EARNINGS RELATED SCHEME

12.1 CONDITIONS FOR CONTRACTING OUT

Contracting out of SERPS may be achieved either through membership of an occupational scheme set up by the employer or by taking out a personal pension scheme. However contracting out through a personal pension scheme was not possible before 1 July 1988.

Since 6 April 1978 it has been possible for occupational schemes to contract out. However this can be achieved on either a defined benefit or money purchase basis; the latter was not available before 6 April 1988. Around one-half of the working population are members of contracted out occupational pension schemes. Many of these schemes which had been in existence prior to 1978 provided worthwhile benefits so that in 1978 they required only fine-tuning to enable them to meet the original conditions for contracting out.

These conditions were two-fold: the scheme had to provide a reasonable level of benefits generally, known as 'requisite benefits', and, at the very least, the scheme had to match SERPS by providing 'Guaranteed Minimum Pension', ie the pension which an individual would have received from SERPS if he had never been contracted out.

The basic minimum conditions which had to be satisfied were as follows:

(1) The occupational pension scheme has to provide pensions based on an accrual rate of one-eightieth of final salary (or average salary revalued in line with National Average Earnings) for each year of contracted-out service subject to a maximum of 40 years (a 'requisite benefit').

(2) There had to be a widow's pension payable on death either before or after retirement of at least one-sixtieth of the employee's final salary for each year of contracted-out service (a 'requisite benefit').

(3) The occupational scheme had to meet certain minimum requirements laid down by the Occupational Pensions Board.

(4) The pension in respect of a member and the widow's pension in

respect of a deceased member must never have fallen below the Guaranteed Minimum Pension.

(5) Employees leaving service before retirement age would enjoy revaluation of their Guaranteed Minimum Pensions between leaving and retirement age.

12.1.1 Abolition of requisite benefit test

From November 1986, occupational schemes no longer had to satisfy the requisite benefit test referred to in the previous paragraph. It became sufficient for schemes to provide Guaranteed Minimum Pensions for contracting-out purposes. This was particularly beneficial for occupational schemes which had a younger age distribution because the Guaranteed Minimum Pension was considerably lower than requisite benefits. Under the requisite benefit test an individual aged 25 would have been provided with a pension of forty-eightieths, ie 50 per cent, of his total salary on retirement at 65. The Guaranteed Minimum Pension, which matched SERPS, amounted to a maximum of 25 per cent of earnings between the lower and upper earnings levels. Whilst the removal of the requisite benefit made it easier for employers to contract out of SERPS, in practice the pensions payable to individual members in many cases did no more than match SERPS. However, most occupational schemes, particularly those set up prior to November 1986, provide a level of benefits greater than SERPS.

12.1.2 Introduction of protected rights and COSR

Where an occupational scheme is used to contract out of SERPS the employer and employee pay national insurance contributions at contracted-out rates. As from 5 April 1997, schemes contracted-out on a money purchase scheme were no longer obliged to provide a guaranteed minimum pension, being only required to pay national insurance rebates into a money purchase account to provide 'protected rights'. Consequently, the benefit conditions attaching to the contracted-out contributions were equivalent to those afforded to personal pensions. At this point, the last link with the guarantees offered by SERPS was broken.

From 6 April, occupational schemes that promised a benefit based on the member's final salary were given the choice of whether to contract a member out using protected rights (COMP – see 12.14.2) or to promise a broad equivalence with SERPS (using a reference test known as COSR – see 12.14.1).

Members of defined benefit schemes that contract out on a protected rights basis (COMP) are required to offer a pension which is at least as good as that which could have been bought from the protected rights. This is often referred to as a 'protected rights underpin'. Final salary schemes that have chosen to contract out in this way did so either because they could not pass the quality test for COSR schemes (see below) or because the age and salaries of their membership made it financially beneficial to receive COMP rather than COSR rebates.

Members of COSR schemes do not earn any entitlement to a GMP. Instead, the scheme itself must meet a quality test to ensure that at least 90 per cent of its members would, as judged by guidelines laid down by the Institute and Faculty of Actuaries, receive at least as good a benefit from the scheme as they would have done from SERPS.

Occupational schemes can also choose to contract out some members on a COMP basis and others on a COSR basis. Such schemes are known as contracted-out mixed benefit schemes (COMBS – see 12.14.14).

Schemes that provide only money purchase benefits can, from April 1997, only contract out as a COMP scheme using protected rights.

Where an occupational scheme is not contracted out of SERPS, the employer and employee have to pay the full contracted-in national insurance contribution. This represents an increase in contribution for the employee of 1.6 per cent of band earnings, and between 3 and 0.6 per cent of band earnings for the employer (depending on whether the scheme uses the COSR or COMP method).

12.2 GUARANTEED MINIMUM PENSION (GMP)

12.2.1 Original basis

Although GMPs only affect contracted-out contributions paid to schemes between November 1986 and April 1997, schemes are obliged to treat these contributions separately and to preserve the rights attaching to them on the following basis.

The GMP and widow's GMP mirror SERPS and are calculated as follows:

Retirement in 1997/98 or earlier: 1.25 per cent of the total of earnings factors (see Chapter 11 for a description of earnings factor).

Retirement in 1998/99 or later: 25 per cent/N of the total of the earnings factors.

12.2.2 Revised basis

Retirement in 1997/98 or earlier:

1.25 per cent of the earnings factors for the tax years 1978/79 to 1987/88 inclusive, plus 1 per cent of the earnings factors for the tax years 1988/89 onwards.

Retirement in 1998/99 onwards:

$\dfrac{25\%}{N}$ of the earnings factors for the tax years 1978/79 to 1987/88 inclusive,

plus

$\dfrac{20\%}{N}$ of the earnings factors for the tax years 1988/89 onwards

Where 'N' is the number of contracted-out tax years in the pensioner's working life after 5 April 1978 and 'retirement' is age 65 (men), age 60 (women).

12.2.3 Major difference

The major difference between the current and revised bases is the reduction in the accrual of GMP from a maximum of 25 per cent to 20 per cent in respect of earnings for the tax years 1988/89 onwards.

Example 12.1

Person retiring in 2006/07 with a contracted-out working life (since 1978/79) of 28 years.		
Original basis:	$\dfrac{25\%}{28}$	of earnings factors for the 28 years (ie 25% of the total earnings factors).
Revised basis:	$\dfrac{25\%}{28}$	of earnings factors for the tax years 1978/79 to 1987/88 inclusive,
plus	$\dfrac{20\%}{28}$	of earnings factors for the tax year 1988/89 onwards.

12.3 DEFERRED GMP

If an individual continues in employment beyond state pensionable age, the scheme may provide for the GMP to be postponed for any period of continued employment.

The member's consent, however, is required for any postponement beyond five years after state pensionable age or where the continuing employment is not that to which the scheme relates.

Where GMP is deferred, the amount is increased by 0.14 per cent for each full week of deferral. Unlike SERPS, the minimum period of deferral before an increase is payable is just one week, and GMP may be deferred for longer than five years.

12.4 WIDOW'S GMP

Since the abolition of the requisite benefit test on 1 November 1986, it has only been necessary for a contracted-out scheme to provide members with a widow's GMP of half the member's GMP, whether the member dies before or after the pensionable age.

The widow's GMP must be payable for any period for which a widow's pension, widowed mother's allowance or retirement pension based on the deceased member's contribution record is payable.

A widow's GMP can only be paid to the widow and not to any other dependant.

The amount of total pension benefits a widow may inherit is calculated in the same way as for the member's own pension, ie SERPS is calculated as if the member had never been contracted out and then reduced by the amount of any GMP payable.

12.5 INCREASES DURING PAYMENT

The amount of GMP payable is increased each year (along with the basic old age pension) in line with prices. In respect of the GMP attributable to earnings factors for tax years prior to 1988/89, this increase is provided by the state. However, in respect of GMP attributable to earnings factors for the tax years 1988/89 or later, it is necessary for the occupational scheme to increase the GMP each year by the lessor of:

(1) the increase in the general level of prices; and
(2) 3 per cent.

As the GMP is not provided by the state, the total amount of increase to be paid by the state is calculated as follows:

(1) An amount of SERPS is calculated as if the employee had never been contracted out. This provides a base figure on which all future increases will be based.

(2) The amount of 'revalued' SERPS is then reduced by the amount of any GMP payable (including any increases to GMP provided by the scheme).

(3) The net amount is then paid each week along with the basic old age pension.

This method also allows SERPS to be calculated where the individual is entitled to both an element of SERPS and GMP as a result of not having been contracted out for his entire working life.

12.6 CONTRACTING OUT AFTER 1988

The Social Security Act 1986 resulted in an increase in the number of contracted-out people because:

(1) Since 1 July 1988 individuals have been allowed to effect a personal pension scheme and contract out. Any person acting before 6 April 1989 was allowed to contract out retrospectively from 6 April 1987. The DSS pays into the personal pension scheme a rebate in national insurance contributions. The rebate was originally a flat-rate rebate, ie it was not age- or sex-related, and as a result favoured the young. However, in order to reduce the numbers of people ceasing to contract out and opting back into SERPS, the Government introduced age-related rebates from 1997/98. The payment of an additional incentive of 1 per cent to personal pensions for persons aged 30 and over from 1993/94 to 1996/97 was a step in that direction.

(2) Since 6 April 1988 employers have been allowed to contract out through occupational schemes which provide benefits on a money-purchase basis. Prior to that time employers could contract out only if the scheme provided benefits on a defined benefit basis, as described above.

After 1997, the whole of any deferred salary-related pension must increase up to retirement by 5 per cent, or the increase in RPI if lower. After retirement the State is no longer responsible for indexing any part of contracted-out occupational pension entitlements earned after 1997. Instead, the whole of the occupational pension, including the contracted-out component, must be increased by 5 per cent per annum or the increase in RPI if lower.

12.7 CONTRACTING OUT THROUGH PERSONAL PENSIONS

About one-half of the working population are not members of an occupational scheme which means that their only benefits on retirement will come from SERPS, and old age pension.

Employees not in pensionable employment were eligible for retirement annuity contracts between 1956 and 30 June 1988. Nevertheless the number of employees taking out retirement annuity contracts was insignificant. Personal pension schemes, which became available on 1 July 1988 and are very similar to retirement annuity contracts (both of which are covered fully in Chapter 14) have the added advantage of allowing individuals to contract out. This has resulted in a substantial increase in the number of individuals taking out personal pension schemes. The increase has come from younger people as the rebate in national insurance contributions is currently flat-rate, rather than age- or sex-related, and is particularly beneficial for young people.

12.8 MECHANICS OF CONTRACTING OUT THROUGH PERSONAL PENSION SCHEMES

The individual, having examined the options open to him (see 12.11 below for 'Who should contract out'), decides he wishes to contract out. The process which follows this decision is as follows:

(1) The individual and the pension provider complete a joint notice which is sent to the DSS. The employer continues to deduct national insurance contributions at the contracted-in rate. The employer need not necessarily be aware of the employee's decision. Individuals wishing to contract out through personal pension schemes are either in non-pensionable employment or are members of a contracted-in occupational pension scheme.

(2) At the end of the tax year the DSS, having been informed by the Inland Revenue of the National Insurance contributions paid during the tax year, pays directly into the personal pension scheme a sum calculated as follows:
   (a) the contracted-out rebate, plus
   (b) an incentive payment (see below), if appropriate.

(3) The rebates for appropriate personal pensions are outlined in 12.14.3 and Table 12.2.

(4) A change in legislation in 1989, to allow members to take protected rights benefits from age 60 under a COMP scheme to prevent sex-discrimination in favour of females, was followed by a similar change to personal pensions with effect from April 1996.

The contributions paid by the DSS constitute 'protected rights', and are separated from any other contributions paid by the employee and/or employer, and are subject to the following conditions:

(1) Protected rights may be used to provide a pension only in retirement,

from State pensionable age (currently 65 men, 60 women), there being no provision for early retirement.

(2) It will not be possible to take protected rights in the form of a cash lump sum.

(3) As a move towards a reduction in sex discrimination, protected rights must buy annuities on a unisex and unistatus basis. This means that there must be no discrimination between males and females and single and married people (in practice, this means a downward movement in annuity rates for men). Unisex/unistatus rates, however, do not have to be used in respect of annuities purchased in the event of the death of the member whilst in service before state pensionable age.

(4) For benefits arising from rebates before 5 April 1997 the annuity must be increased by the lower of the increase in the Retail Prices Index (RPI) and 3 per cent per annum. This also applies to any widow(er)'s annuity. The basis has changed for benefits arising from rebates in respect of 1997/98 and beyond; the annuity must be increased by the lower of the increase in RPI and 5 per cent a year.

(5) Protected rights do not have to provide a guaranteed minimum pension. If at state pensionable age protected rights purchase benefits lower than what SERPS would have provided if the individual had not been contracted out, the State will not make up the shortfall. However, any excess benefits the individual.

(6) An open-market option must be available.

An individual may have a series of personal pension schemes but only one of these schemes may accept the rebate from the DSS.

When personal pensions started on 1 July 1988 it was possible to use them to contract out retrospectively from 6 April 1987 provided that the individual had not already been contracted out by reference to an occupational scheme during that period.

However, an election to contract out for a particular tax year must now be made by 5 April of that year.

12.9 INCENTIVES FOR PERSONAL PENSIONS

Initially the Government offered a 2 per cent incentive to encourage contracting out of SERPS. Originally it was to be payable for five years from 6 April 1988. It was then extended to six years for those taking out personal pension schemes contracted out retrospectively to 6 April 1987.

The incentive was then reduced to 1 per cent of band earnings, a rate which applied to anyone aged 30 and over on 6 April. It was payable during 1993/94, 1994/95, 1995/96 and 1996/97. Since 6 April 1997 a full age-related basis has applied.

12.10 WHO SHOULD CONTRACT OUT?

Currently, the emphasis is in favour of contracting out at the younger ages. The decision to contract out will have to be reviewed regularly, especially when changes in rebate are announced – every five years.

The break-even point in 1999/2000 is around age 54 for men, and age 42 for women. In recent years the guarantees given by SERPS have become more valuable as mortality improvements have reduced the annuities available under private schemes (occupational and private) without any corresponding improvement in the rebates. However, the break-even ages may increase again in later years if the rebates for contracting out improve in the future.

Employers are permitted to pay contributions to their employees' personal pension schemes thereby meeting a requirement or wish to provide retirement benefits but without having to undertake the responsibilities and administration of an employer's in-house occupational scheme. The bulk of the administration is carried out by the DSS as it pays directly into the personal pension scheme the flat rate in respect of those individual employees who have chosen to contract out. There is no need for the employer to rearrange his payroll systems to deduct National Insurance contributions at the contracted-out rate.

12.11 CONTRACTING OUT THROUGH MONEY PURCHASE SCHEMES

Contracting out on a money purchase basis is beneficial to small businesses which would like to offer employees a remuneration package which includes a good pension on retirement, and which wish to use the scheme for contracting-out purposes but not take on the open-ended liability inherent in a scheme which guarantees benefits on retirement.

It has been possible for employers to contract out on a money purchase basis since 6 April 1988. As with occupational schemes operating on a defined benefit basis, the employer and employees pay national insurance contributions at the contracted-out rate (see Table 11.1). This means a reduction in national insurance contributions for the employee of 1.6 per cent and for the employer of 0.6 per cent. Before the introduction of age-related rebates, the scheme could simply receive the balance between the reduced rate contribution and the full rate national insurance contribution as what was known as a 'minimum payment'. Since the introduction of age-related rebates, the minimum payment has been topped up by age-related rebates which are received by the scheme from the DSS in the same way as operates for contracted-out personal pensions. The total that an individual receives by way of minimum payments and age-related rebates may be more or less than under the old system, depending on age. Some employers choose to pay only the minimum payment into their occupational scheme.

Although this contribution is merely a re-direction of what would have been paid to the DSS, employers may consider that this route is worthwhile in fostering good employer/employee relations. Whatever other benefits are provided under the scheme in respect of additional contributions paid by the employee and employer, the benefits generated by the reduction in national insurance contributions secure 'protected rights' and are subject to the conditions described above.

The fact that a contracted-out money purchase scheme does not have to provide an ultimate guarantee on retirement means that many more employers have been prepared to contract out. The only 'guarantee' which applies is the requirement that the saving in national insurance contributions is directed into this scheme to secure 'protected rights'.

In the case of a controlling director of a company it may be advisable not to contract out of SERPS but to use an executive pension plan to provide the maximum approvable pension of two-thirds of final salary. In this way the overall benefits on retirement will exceed two-thirds of remuneration because SERPS will be paid in addition as it does not count towards the two-thirds limit. However, if a controlling director, or employee, contracts out through an occupational scheme (of any description) the overall maximum potential benefits will be lower because the equivalent of SERPS is provided within the scheme and therefore within the normal two-thirds limit.

Alternatively, the director or executive could take out a personal pension scheme to contract out personally: the sole permitted contribution will be from the DSS – no contributions may be paid by the individual or his employer. Because this scheme is being used as SERPS replacement the protected rights within it may be in addition to the maximum benefits available under the executive pension plan.

12.12 CONTRACTING BACK INTO SERPS

Persons approaching the pivotal ages when contracting out ceases to be attractive (see 12.10 above) should consider informing the DSS that they no longer wish to be contracted out. This is done by sending a completed form APP 2 'Cancellation Notice' to the DSS. A member of a COMP scheme has to approach his pension scheme trustees to find out his options, which might include switching into a 'not contracted-out' category of membership whilst remaining in the scheme.

12.13 THE EFFECT OF CONTRACTING OUT ON EMPLOYERS' SCHEMES

The facility to contract out through a personal pension scheme applies not only to individuals who are in non-pensionable employment and those who are in contracted-in occupational schemes but also to members who leave their existing occupational schemes. From 6 April 1988, the Social Security Act 1986 has prevented employers insisting that employees join their occupational pension schemes (except schemes providing death in service benefits only) and also allows members of schemes to opt out, in favour of personal pensions, or even back into SERPS. Prior to 6 April 1988 most employers required employees to join their schemes as a condition of service, and usually prevented members leaving their schemes unless they left service.

Although the member may obtain greater flexibility under the personal pension scheme the cost of sacrificing the employer's contribution is too great. Before making a decision to opt out of an occupational scheme, especially one which relates benefits to final salary, the member must consider very carefully the benefits which he will be giving up. These include not just the pension itself but widow's pensions, death in service benefits, escalation of pensions payment, early retirement benefits and incapacity benefits. Opting-out is rarely a sensible option.

Regrettably, significant numbers of potential new entrants to schemes have decided not to join occupational schemes; some are relying purely on SERPS and have not even taken out a personal pension scheme. Higher take-home pay (because they do not have to pay the member's contribution under the occupational scheme) is seen as the immediate 'benefit' to the employee. Inevitably employers will recruit individuals who are in favour of personal pension schemes and as the years go by there will be an increasing number of individuals who have been contributing to personal pension schemes in the past. Failure to attract new members to a final salary scheme will result in the average age of the scheme increasing so that the cost as a percentage of payroll is likely to increase (although the cost will of course be related to a smaller number of members and a smaller payroll). Some employers will also allow individuals to opt back into the occupational scheme at a later date, perhaps imposing an age limit of, say, 40. If employers allow individuals to opt back into the occupational scheme, then only future service in the scheme is likely to be pensioned.

The initial resistance to personal pensions by employers running occupational schemes is beginning to diminish and more employers will offer a money purchase alternative to a final salary scheme by running a separate money purchase scheme often for younger employees. Smaller organisations rather than large ones are more likely to contribute to personal pension schemes taken out by individual employees.

The Government has recently announced that it intends to reintroduce legislation enabling employers to make entry into their pension scheme a condition of employment.

The 1998 Annual Survey of Occupational Pension Schemes by the National Association of Pension Funds shows that where there was automatic entry to final salary schemes, around 91 per cent of those eligible actually joined: where new entrants had to apply for membership, the take-up rate was reduced to 81 per cent.

Around two-thirds of employers allow employees who have opted-out of schemes to be re-admitted later. Around 38 per cent of schemes provided death in service for employees who opted-out.

Only 5 per cent of employers are willing to contribute to personal pension schemes.

12.14 CONTRACTING OUT AFTER 1997

The Pensions Act 1995 introduced major changes to the contracting out conditions for both occupational schemes and personal pension plans.

12.14.1 Occupational schemes – abolition of GMPs

Contracted out salary related schemes will no longer have to provide GMPs for service after 5 April 1997. However, they must still provide GMPs for benefits accruing up to that time.

To replace the GMP requirement from 6 April 1997 a new form of requisite benefit test will be introduced.

In order to continue to contract out of SERPS, schemes must obtain an actuarial certificate confirming that at least 90 per cent of scheme members will receive benefits no lower than those provided under a 'reference scheme'.

The benefit structure must be at least as generous as the following:

- An accrual rate of one-eightieth of pensionable salary averaged over the final three years prior to the pension age of 65 (males and females), with a maximum for 40 years' service to count.
- Pensionable salary to be at least 90 per cent of earnings between the lower earnings level and upper earnings level.
- A spouse's pension before or after retirement of 50 per cent of the member's pension.
- The resulting pensions must increase in payment by the lesser of 5 per cent per annum or RPI.

Existing schemes must therefore provide pension benefits which incorporate a combination of the two contracting out tests for service before or after April 1997. The reduction in National Insurance contributions for salary-related contracted-out schemes from 6 April 1997 will be 4.6 per cent split 1.6 per cent to employees and 3 per cent employers.

12.14.2 Contracted-out money purchase schemes

Contracted-out money purchase schemes (COMPS) enable employers to contract out employees on a money purchase basis similar to that available under personal pension plans.

From 6 April 1997 an age-related basis was introduced similar to that under personal pension plans.

Payments into the scheme to provide protected rights came from two sources: the employer pays an amount equal to savings in national insurance contributions direct into the scheme each month, and after the end of each tax year the Government makes age-related payments based upon the members' ages.

For 1997/98 the national insurance contribution saving for COMPS members totalled 3.1 per cent being a reduction of 1.6 per cent to the member and 1.5 per cent to the employer. Thus 3.1 per cent was by the employer into the COMPS.

From April 1999, the national insurance reduction for an employer paying into a COMPS reduced from 1.5 per cent to 0.6 per cent. The age-related rebate scales also changed. The additional DSS payment has been based on the following table which shows, for example, quinquennial ages. The amount paid by the DSS will be as in the table less 3.1 per cent for the years 1997/98 and 1998/99 and 2.2 per cent for subsequent years.

Table 12.1 COMPS age-related rebates (percentage of band earnings)

Age last birthday on 5 April 1997	1997/98	1998/99	1999/2000	2000/01	2001/02
15	3.1	3.2	2.3	2.3	2.4
20	3.4	3.4	2.5	2.6	2.6
25	3.6	3.7	2.8	2.9	2.9
30	3.9	4.0	3.1	3.2	3.3
35	4.3	4.4	3.5	3.6	3.7
40	5.2	5.3	4.4	4.5	4.6
45	8.0	8.1	7.1	7.2	7.4
50+	9.0	9.0	9.0	9.0	9.0

The capping of the rebate at 9 per cent will mean that members should continue to contract back into SERPS after they reach the break-even point which is around age 54 for males and age 42 for females in 1999/2000.

12.14.3 Personal pension plans

From 1997/98 DSS payments into personal pension plans for those contracted out of SERPS have been on an age-related basis.

The mechanics of contracting out will remain as in 12.8 but the amount paid will be as shown in the following table which, for example, shows quinquennial ages.

Table 12.2 Personal pension plan age-related rebates (% of band earnings)

Age last birthday on 5 April 1997	1997/98	1998/99	1999/2000	2000/01	2001/02
20	3.6	3.7	4.1	4.2	4.2
25	3.9	3.9	4.4	4.4	4.5
30	4.2	4.2	4.6	4.7	4.7
35	4.5	4.6	5.0	5.0	5.1
40	5.4	5.5	5.9	5.9	6.0
45	8.2	8.3	8.7	8.8	8.9
50+	9.0	9.0	9.0	9.0	9.0

The table does not include tax relief on the employee's share of the rebate.

The capping of the payment at 9 per cent will mean that employees should continue to contract back into SERPS after they reach the break-even point which is around 53 for males and 44 for females in 1999/2000.

12.14.4 Contracted-out mixed benefit schemes

From April 1997 it has been possible for employers to set up contracted-out mixed benefit schemes (COMBS) in order to allow contracted-out salary-related benefits and protected rights in the same scheme.

The introduction of COMBS enables an employer with an existing contracted-out final salary scheme providing GMP benefits to move to a money purchase protected rights basis for benefits accruing after April 1997 instead of using the new 'reference scheme' salary-related benefits test.

A COMBS is able to mix both types of contracting out, with the split being between pre- and post-April 1997 service or between different sections of members.

13

EXECUTIVE PENSIONS AND INHERITANCE TAX PLANNING

13.1 INTRODUCTION

Lump sums on death payable under retirement benefit schemes approved under ICTA 1988, ss 590–612 (see Appendix 4), retirement annuity contracts approved under ICTA 1988, ss 619–627 (ICTA 1970, s 226: see Appendix 4) and personal pension schemes approved under ICTA 1988, ss 630–655 (see Appendix 4), are largely free of inheritance tax. The methods of inheritance tax planning through retirement annuity contracts and personal pension schemes are set out in Chapter 14. This chapter deals with the use of executive pension plans in assisting a director in passing on his company to future generations without saddling his family with inheritance tax liabilities.

The FA 1989 has lessened the effectiveness of executive pension plans for inheritance tax planning in the case of directors who are categorised as 'post-1989 members' because of the cap on earnings.

In general terms a director should try to make provision for his spouse through the inter-spouse exemptions: all life-time gifts and property left by one spouse to the other on death are exempt from inheritance tax (although there is a restriction if the donor spouse is domiciled in the United Kingdom but the donee spouse is not).

In order to make provision for future generations, however, it is advisable to use death benefits arising from an executive pension plan. The rules of a pension scheme which has been designed specifically for controlling directors and key executives will contain a list of persons to whom the lump sum benefit may be paid such as the director's spouse, children, dependants and other individuals whom he has nominated. The rule will give the trustees power to pay to such one or more of the persons specified as they may in their discretion choose. Ideally the rules should also allow the trustees to pay monies to a separate trust (outside the trust governing the executive pension plan) for the benefit of the deceased's children: the trust could also provide for sums to be lent to the widow(er) for immediate needs.

Since the trustees exercise their discretion on who will receive the benefit after the director's death, it cannot form part of his freely disposable estate for inheritance tax purposes, and the pension plan is exempt from the normal charging provisions relating to discretionary trusts because it comes within IHTA 1984, s 58(1)(d).

The director will normally indicate his preference to the trustees in advance of his death by completing a nomination form or expression of wish letter, although this will not bind the trustees who may decide to disregard his wishes.

As the trustees are often fellow directors (eg his wife) or the limited company itself the director may be reasonably happy that his wishes will be complied with and by this simple device he can pass to his children and grandchildren considerable sums which will escape inheritance tax altogether.

13.2 DEFERRING RETIREMENT

A director who defers his retirement may have benefits paid in the event of his subsequent death on either of the following bases:

(1) The usual death in service benefit of a lump sum equal to four times final remuneration (subject to the earnings cap of £90,600 in 1999/2000 for post-1989 members) together with a refund of his own personal contributions plus growth; or

(2) The benefits based on the assumption that he had retired on the day before his death, ie a lump sum payment equal to five years' pension payments, which is the usual guarantee period attached to pensions.

Although in both situations the payment will be free of inheritance tax, where the guarantee under the pension itself is more than five years, the guarantee payments as they fall due must be paid to the deceased's estate – it is not possible to commute them.

In addition, a widow(er)'s pension can also be paid in either circumstance which would of course be free of inheritance tax.

Phased retirement

A director may transfer his benefits which have accumulated under the executive pension plan to a personal pension scheme (subject to the trustees of the executive pension plan providing a certificate to the effect that it is not 'overfunded' (ie that the fund would provide benefits which do not exceed Inland Revenue limits)).

The subsequent payment of benefits, on retirement, or on death, would then be subject to personal pension scheme rules; more flexibility might be provided on retirement because under the personal pension scheme benefits may be taken in stages up to age 75 at which point the remaining fund must be used to provide a pension. On death, however, the benefits under the personal pension scheme may not be so advantageous as they would have been under the executive pension plan; on death only one quarter of the fund under the personal pension scheme may be paid in the form of a lump sum (unless there is no widow(er)) whereas under the executive pension scheme, as stated above, it is generally possible to pay a larger lump sum. Thus, although the personal pension scheme, through the use of 'phased retirement' options, can provide flexibility in retirement benefits, its facility to provide lump sums free of inheritance tax are less advantageous.

Also, it is by no means certain that such a transfer into a personal pension scheme, even if written in trust, would necessarily provide inheritance tax-free benefits on death. In the event of death within two years of the transfer, it is highly unlikely that death benefits would escape inheritance tax.

Under a personal pension scheme it is no longer necessary to purchase an annuity to obtain income benefits. Instead, an income may be withdrawn from the fund, within certain limits, with the purchase of an annuity being deferred until age 75 at the latest. On death during the period when income is being withdrawn the fund may be paid to the deceased's dependants subject to a 35 per cent tax charge. This will be free of inheritance tax provided that the scheme is subject to a suitable trust. (Income withdrawal schemes are covered in detail in Chapter 19.)

13.3 PERSONAL CONTRIBUTIONS

As the object of the exercise is to pass as much capital to the next generation free of inheritance tax, basis (1) under 13.2 above is normally the most favourable. In fact, a director who is setting up an executive pension plan should, where there is a need, ensure that part of the contributions are paid in the form of personal contributions from his own salary to maximise death in service benefits. If he already has an executive pension plan in existence where the contributions are paid wholly by the employer, then, if necessary, he should take a larger salary from the company enabling him to pay personal contributions and reduce the employer's contributions appropriately. The following example and table show the effect of paying personal contributions.

Example 13.1

Current position

(1) Director's remuneration = £50,000
Company's contribution to executive pension plan = £10,000 pa
Company's total expenditure in remuneration and pensions = £60,000 pa
Maximum lump sum death in service benefit which can be provided under the plan = £200,000 (4 × £50,000).

Alternative position

(2) Director's revised remuneration = £58,823
Director's personal contribution under PAYE = £8,823 (15% of £58,823)
Company's contribution to executive pension plan = £1,177 pa
Company's total expenditure in remuneration and pensions = £60,000 pa
Maximum lump sum death in service benefit which can be provided under the plan = £235,292 (4 × £58,823) *and* £8,823, plus growth, for each year of payment.

Notes

(1) The director's remuneration has been increased by 17.65%, a factor that can be applied to any level of remuneration.
(2) Any increase in remuneration increases national insurance contributions. In this example the extra contributions would be 12.20% of £8,823, ie £1,076 which is not included in the company's total expenditure above.
(3) Where the director is a post-1989 member the lump sum will be restricted to four times capped remuneration, so the above method of increasing the lump sum through the use of personal contributions is of even greater value (although the personal contribution will also be restricted to 15% of capped remuneration).

Table 13.1

A member of an executive pension plan has an initial salary of £10,000 pa, which increases by 6% pa. He pays personal contributions of 15% of salary. The lump sum that could be paid free of inheritance tax on death in service is shown below, assuming pension fund growth of 8% pa after charges. The member is not subject to the cap on earnings applicable to post-1989 members.

At the end of:	4 × salary death in service benefit £	Increasing additional cover £	Total permissible cover £
5 years	53,530	10,120	63,650
10 years	71,630	28,420	100,650
15 years	95,860	59,890	155,750
20 years	128,280	112,260	240,540
25 years	171,670	197,420	369,090

13.4 RESTRICTIONS ON 20 PER CENT DIRECTORS

In March 1979, the Inland Revenue, through Memorandum No 59, limited the ability of a 20 per cent director to ensure that monies could be paid to succeeding generations free of capital transfer tax, the forerunner of inheritance tax. If he is still in service at the age of 75, then in the event of his subsequent death the lump sum payable must be made either to the legal personal representatives, or to the surviving spouse, or in the absence of any surviving spouse, to the legal personal representatives.

If however, the member had retired and died during the first five years following his retirement, and there was a five-year guarantee attaching to his pension, then the value of the outstanding pension instalments may be paid to the trustees who can then pay them at their discretion to the usual range of beneficiaries.

13.5 OPTIONS AT RETIREMENT

On reaching normal retirement date, it is possible to:

(1) take all the benefits, ie cash and pension,
(2) defer all the benefits and continue working, or
(3) take the tax-free lump sum, but defer the pension benefits (provided that the director is not classed as a post-1989 member).

From an inheritance tax point of view, however, taking cash and deferring pension is not to be recommended as this effectively triggers the director's retirement for the purposes of determining future benefits. In the event of his subsequent death while still working with the company, he will be regarded as having retired on the day before he died.

Example 13.2

Salary at date of death £24,000.

Maximum pension is £16,000 per annum or a reduced pension of around £12,000 per annum plus a tax-free cash sum of £36,000.

(1) If tax-free cash of £36,000 has been taken the maximum death benefit will be $5 \times$ the reduced pension of £12,000 per annum, ie £60,000.

(2) If all benefits have been deferred the maximum death benefit will be calculated on the normal death in service basis, ie $4 \times$ salary, ie £96,000.

The difference between the two bases is magnified where the length of time between the taking of tax-free cash and death is increased.

13.6 CONTINUATION FACILITIES

Term assurance is the usual means of providing death in service benefits under executive pension plans. However if the director takes his benefits on retirement, or if he leaves service, death in service benefits will usually cease. Most executive pension plans offer an option to the director to convert the term assurance into an ordinary life assurance policy, for example, a whole of life policy in his own name, without the need to produce medical evidence. The whole of life policy will be a personal contract where contributions are paid by the director himself at the rate applicable to his age when he effects the contract. Thus, a director can convert term assurance to permanent insurance. These policies can be written in trust and can provide a way of mitigating inheritance tax liability for the rest of his life. If he takes his pension from his pension plan the cost of the whole of life policy may be met from the pension payments.

13.7 SUMMARY

Executive pension plans, although appearing to emphasise the word 'pension', should not be looked at in this narrow sense. They offer flexibility for the director who wishes to build up his business rapidly over the short term and sell out, as benefits can be provided on early retirement from age 50 onwards, or more commonly, they can be used for the director who has virtually no intention of ever retiring from the business.

In the latter situation the director is almost certain to build up an inheritance tax problem. Thus an executive pension plan is unlikely to ever produce a pension simply because he will continue to take an income from the company and defer taking his pension benefits, although for directors categorised as post-1989 members this facility is not available beyond age 75, by which time benefits under the executive pension plan must be taken. What he requires, however, is an effective means of transferring capital to succeeding generations to enable them to pay inheritance tax and to continue the business if they wish. A pension plan is an extremely tax-efficient way of building up this capital.

An occupational pension scheme will very rarely provide this degree of flexibility – in fact, it should not really be used as a tax planning vehicle. Traditionally an occupational pension scheme should be regarded as a means of providing an adequate standard of living in retirement, whereas the executive pension plan provides not only deferred pay, but also a tax planning medium.

14

PERSONAL PENSION SCHEMES AND RETIREMENT ANNUITIES

14.1 BACKGROUND

Traditionally, retirement annuities were the means by which the self-employed provided for retirement. The term 'self-employed retirement annuity' (the common generic title for these contracts) is misleading as it suggests that eligibility was confined to one group; in fact people in non-pensionable employment may have taken out these contracts although the vast majority were self-employed.

On 1 July 1988 there was a considerable development in the legislation surrounding retirement annuities and their successors, personal pension schemes. From that date personal pension schemes, introduced by F(No 2)A 1987 and now incorporated in ICTA 1988, Chapter IV, came into force and no new retirement annuities (governed by ICTA 1970, ss 226–228, now incorporated in ICTA 1988, Chapter III) were available from that date.

Personal pension schemes are similar to retirement annuities but there are important differences, notably the facility to use the former to contract out of the earnings-related part of the state pension scheme (see Chapter 12).

Retirement annuities taken out before 1 July 1988 may continue beyond that date, and may be concurrent with personal pension schemes. In order to distinguish between the two contracts a 'retirement annuity' denotes an ICTA 1988, ss 618–629 contract (see Appendix 4) and a 'personal pension scheme' denotes an ICTA 1988, ss 630–655 contract (see Appendix 4).

Because many people contribute to both types of contract, and the inter-action of the two can be significant, both types are described in this chapter.

14.1.1 **How personal pension schemes and retirement annuities work**

Under the terms of a personal pension scheme which is effected between the individual and the pension provider (which can be an insurance company, friendly society, bank, building society or unit trust company), the individual pays contributions in order to secure benefits in the form of pension and a tax-free lump sum. The contributions may be payable:

(1) annually on a level basis, or with provision for increases each year,
(2) monthly, but with provision for increases to be made, or
(3) as single contributions.

Personal pension schemes often have the facility to convert from a monthly to an annual basis, and vice versa, and also to take additional single contributions from time to time.

If the personal pension scheme is used for contracting out of SERPS contributions are also paid by the DSS. Personal pension schemes may also take contributions from an employer: the employer's contributions are treated as a deductible business expense like an employer's contributions to an approved retirement benefits scheme.

The contributions, excluding any paid by the DSS, are subject to maximum limits arising from the legislation (set out below).

Retirement annuities, the forerunners of personal pension schemes, work in a similar way except that they cannot be used to contract out of SERPS. They do not receive contributions from the DSS, and nor can they accept contributions from an employer.

14.1.2 **Comparison of personal pension schemes and retirement annuities**

Although full information on the differences between retirement annuity contracts and personal pension schemes is given throughout this chapter, a brief comparison of the major differences is set out in the following table.

Table 14.1

	Retirement annuity	*Personal pension scheme*
Benefit ages	Between 60 and 75	Between 50 and 75
Basis of calculating tax-free cash	3 × the annuity remaining after cash has been taken	25% of fund used to provide the member's pension*
Facility to carry back/carry forward contributions	Yes	Yes
Ancillary benefits eg life assurance, waiver of contribution	Yes	Yes
Ability to contract-out	No	Yes
Cash limit	£150,000 (unless effected before 17 March 1987)	None
Tax relief on contributions at source	No	Yes, for employed only
Ability to accept employer's contributions	No	Yes
Facility to accept transfers from other schemes	No**	Yes
Facility to pay transfer to other schemes	Yes	Yes
Ability to write in trust	Yes	Yes
Open market option available	Yes	Yes
Income withdrawal***	No	Yes

Notes

* Any part of the fund which consists of 'Protected Rights' will have to be excluded for this purpose when the scheme was taken out after 27 July 1989. In the case of a scheme taken out before 27 July 1989 although Protected Rights do not have to be excluded, any part of the fund which is used to buy a widow(er)'s annuity may have to be excluded. This means that, in practice, around 20 per cent of the total fund may be taken in cash.

** Except other retirement annuities.

*** For details of income withdrawal see Chapter 19.

14.1.3 **Benefits**

Income in retirement

The sole purpose of the personal pension scheme is to provide an annuity in retirement commencing at any time between the ages of 50 and 75 but an annuity can be drawn regardless of whether the individual is working. Indeed it is possible to stagger the benefits over that period either by having a series of separate schemes or one scheme within which there are a number of arrangements which provide for the benefits to be paid at intervals.

The facility to take benefits under a personal pension scheme from age 50 compared with age 60 under a retirement annuity was a welcome improvement, although in practice it is unlikely to be seen as a sufficient reason for stopping contributions to a retirement annuity in favour of a personal pension scheme. Most planholders will not have had the opportunity of building up sufficient funds to provide a worthwhile income at age 50.

Lump sums

Generally, up to one-quarter of the fund accumulated in a personal pension scheme may be taken as a tax-free lump sum. The retirement annuity legislation restricts the maximum tax-free lump sum to three times the remaining pension after the cash has been taken. Although more complicated than the personal pension scheme legislation this method can provide more tax-free cash, depending on the level of annuity rates.

These options are very valuable as they give the member the flexibility of having more tax-free money in his hands, but if he is more interested in income he can use the tax-free cash to buy a purchased life annuity (ICTA 1988, s 656) which is taxed only on the interest content.

Assuming a retirement fund of £100,000 the amounts which could be taken in the form of a tax-free cash sum are as follows:

Table 14.2 Comparison of PPP and RAC tax-free cash (Fund value £100,000)

	Age	Personal pension scheme	Retirement annuity	
			Yield 5.25%	Yield 8%
Men	60	£25,000	£19,735	£23,740
	65	£25,000	£21,849	£25,659
	70	£25,000	£24,560	£28,142
	75	£25,000	£28,094	£31,414

Table 14.2 *(cont.)*

	Age	Personal pension scheme	Retirement annuity	
			Yield 5.25%	Yield 8%
Women	60	£25,000	£17,630	£21,820
	65	£25,000	£19,159	£23,155
	70	£25,000	£21,246	£25,029
	75	£25,000	£24,102	£27,650

Notes

(1) Under the retirement annuity the tax-free cash increases as age increases, and differs according to sex.

(2) It will be seen that a retirement annuity (which will have been effected before 1 July 1988) may give a higher proportion of tax-free cash sum than a personal pension scheme. Of course there is nothing to prevent an individual paying contributions to both contracts concurrently (within the overall maximum contribution limits).

(3) Under a retirement annuity, the Inland Revenue allows the tax-free lump sum to be calculated as though the most favourable annuity basis (ie annually in arrears without guarantee) had been selected. After the lump sum has been taken, the balance of the fund can be used to provide an annuity on a different basis, normally payable quarterly or monthly in advance, guaranteed for five years.

(4) If an open market option is exercised under a retirement annuity and transferred to a personal pension scheme, tax-free cash will be limited to 25 per cent of the fund.

Example 14.1

A fund of £100,000 built up under a personal pension scheme might provide an income payable in monthly instalments throughout the life of a man aged 65, guaranteed for five years, of £8,700 per annum, but subject to tax at, say, 23 per cent, leaving a net income of £6,714 per annum.

Alternatively the fund could be taken in the form of a tax-free lump sum of, say, £25,000 plus a reduced income of £6,509 gross, netting down to £5,011: the cash of £25,000 could be used to buy a purchased life annuity. Part of the annuity is regarded as a return of the purchase price – known as the capital content – and is not subject to tax: the balance is interest and is subject to tax.

The cash lump sum of £25,000 could be used to buy a purchased life annuity of, say, £2,223. Of this, £816 is interest and would be taxed (leaving a net income of £2,035 for a basic rate taxpayer).

The combination of the two net annuities is £7,046, an increase of £332 over the income obtained if the whole fund is used to buy an annuity. This demonstrates the benefit of taking advantage of the tax-free lump sum even if income is a priority.

14.1.4 Open market option

Retirement annuities usually permit an 'open market option' where the accumulated fund can be transferred, when the benefits are being cashed, to another insurance company. The policyholder takes advantage of the open market option if another insurance company offers annuity rates better than those of the original insurance company. The policyholder is normally given an indication of the insurance companies who are at the top of the market and the money passes from insurer to insurer (not through the policyholder). Sometimes the policyholder incurs a penalty if the money is transferred to another insurance company.

Under retirement annuities, when the open market option is exercised, the new insurance company issues a 'substituted contract' to provide the pension *and* the tax-free lump sum. Thus the whole fund is transferred from the first insurance company to the second with both cash and pension paid by the second. There is no objection, however, to a transfer of only part of the value of the planholder's benefit under the contract. In that event, both the original and the substituted contracts must limit the tax-free lump sum by reference to the pensions payable under the respective contracts.

Since 1 July 1988 no new retirement annuities can be effected including substituted contracts. This means that if an open market option is exercised money must be transferred from the retirement annuity either to another retirement annuity (which must have been effected before 1 July 1988) or to a personal pension scheme and subject to its rules which include a limitation on the tax-free cash to 25 per cent of the fund used to provide the member's pension. In recent years, however, this has not caused hardship because low annuity rates have often meant that the tax-free cash under the retirement annuity would be less than 25 per cent of the fund (see Table 14.2 above).

Personal pension schemes arranged through banks, building societies and unit trusts are not allowed to provide pension benefits on retirement directly; the underlying funds after tax-free cash has been paid have to be transferred to an insurance company which then provides the annuity.

Personal pension schemes arranged through insurance companies have to offer the right to a transfer as a condition of approval.

14.1.5 Types of pension available

On taking the benefits from the personal pension scheme or retirement annuity, the member normally has various options including the facility to take a reduced pension on his own life, which will continue, in the event of his death, to the spouse. For example, £100,000 would, at the time of writing, purchase the following types of annuity on the open market for a man aged 65. These annuities are not necessarily at the top of the market as annuity rates change frequently. (Further comments on this topic are given in Chapter 19.)

Table 14.3

Type of Annuity	Amount per annum
Single life annuity payable annually in arrears	£9,324
Single life annuity payable monthly in advance	£8,865
Single life annuity payable monthly in advance but for a minimum of five years	£8,720
Single life annuity payable monthly in advance but for a minimum of ten years	£8,328
Single life annuity payable quarterly in advance for a minimum of five years, increasing each year by 3% pa compound	£6,744
Joint life annuity, during the lives of the man and his wife, aged 62, payable quarterly in advance	£6,616

14.1.6 Death before taking benefits

The amounts payable vary widely between different contracts but the choices include:

- No return of contributions (rare).
- Return of contributions without interest (old contracts).
- Return of contributions with interest at around 4 per cent (old contracts).
- Return of the accumulated fund.

Example 14.2

Return on death after various periods of years, where the annual contribution is £1,000

| | After | | |
	10 years £	20 years £	30 years £
No return of contributions	–	–	–
Return of contributions without interest	10,000	20,000	30,000
Return of contributions with interest at 4% pa compound	12,486	30,969	58,328
Return of accumulated fund, assuming unit growth of 7% pa after charges	12,600	36,000	79,400

14.1.7 **Life cover**

Personal pension schemes allow life assurance to be provided through an authorised insurance company, under ICTA 1988, s 637 (see Appendix 4). The advantage of paying contributions to a policy approved under this section as opposed to an ordinary life assurance policy of a similar class is that the contributions for the former are fully deductible from earnings for income tax purposes. Under ordinary life assurance policies, however, no tax relief is given to policies effected following the 1984 Budget (although policies effected before that time benefit from tax relief at 12.5 per cent.

The relief under a s 637 policy in 1999/2000 is at 23 per cent (22 per cent from 6 April 2000) of the contribution for an employee who pays tax at the basic rate of 23 per cent so that the net outlay would be only 77 per cent of the contribution payable. For the self-employed and higher rate taxpayers higher rate relief will be given as appropriate, but relief will be at only 10 per cent on the part of their taxable earnings subject to the 10 per cent band.

Example 14.3

The annual cost of providing £100,000 worth of life cover up to age 60 for a male non-smoker aged 29 would amount to around £16 per month gross, £12.32 net for a 23% taxpayer under a s 637 policy. For a 40% taxpayer, the net annual cost of the s 637 policy would drop to £9.60 per month.

It is possible to assign s 637 policies with the result that they are often used to provide collateral security where the individual is borrowing money; they are also used for partnership assurance.

Life assurance may also be provided under the retirement annuity legislation (ICTA 1988, s 621(1)(b) (see Appendix 4)) provided that the policy was effected before 1 July 1988. These policies may also be assigned.

14.2 PERSONAL PENSION SCHEMES IN MORE DETAIL

The relevant legislation is ICTA 1988, Chapter IV, ss 630–655 (see Appendix 4). Under a personal pension scheme various types of benefit may be provided within the scheme rather than by means of separately approved contracts as applies to retirement annuity contracts under ICTA 1988, ss 620–621 (see Appendix 4). In this way a personal pension scheme is rather similar to an approved retirement benefit scheme. The benefits that may be provided within the scheme are as follows:

(1) An annuity must be payable by an authorised insurance company chosen by the member. The annuity may commence between the ages of 50 and 75. However, earlier commencement than age 50 is possible in the event of permanent incapacity or where earlier retirement ages are agreed for special occupations. Alternatively the member may use an income withdrawal facility and defer the purchase of the annuity until no later than age 75. Until the purchase of the annuity the member may draw varying amounts of income from the fund. (For details of income withdrawal see Chapter 19.)

(2) A lump sum may be provided for the member provided it is payable when the annuity is first payable (it is not possible to provide for a lump sum alone). It must not exceed one-quarter of the value of the retirement benefits provided for the member.

(3) A dependant's annuity may be provided for the surviving spouse or dependants if pension provision is being made for the member.

(4) Life assurance may be provided by an authorised insurance company on the death of the individual before he attains the age of 75. (This is the same as the benefit allowed under ICTA 1988, s 621(1)(b) for retirement annuities set up before 1 July 1988.)

14.2.1 Existing retirement annuities

The relevant legislation is found in ICTA 1988, ss 618–629: an extract from the legislation is contained in Appendix 4.

It has not been possible to take out a retirement annuity approved under the above legislation since 30 June 1988, but contracts already in existence at that time may continue in force and will be able to accept subsequent increases in contributions (provided that the contract is sufficiently flexible). Contracts taken out from 1 July 1988 will be personal pension schemes approved under ICTA 1988, ss 630–655 (see Appendix 4).

Three types of benefit can be provided within the retirement annuity legislation:

(1) A retirement annuity approved under s 620, having for its main object the provision of an annuity in old age, but with provision for commutation of part of the annuity for a lump sum. Contracts effected on or after 17 March 1987 must limit the lump sum to £150,000. (This £150,000 limit may be raised by Treasury Order.) The annuity may commence between the ages of 60 and 75. However, earlier commencement is possible in the event of permanent incapacity or where earlier retirement ages are agreed for special occupations.

(2) A dependant's annuity approved under s 621(1)(a). This is a contract which provides an annuity for the individual's spouse or any one or more dependants of the individual.

(3) Life assurance approved under s 621(1)(b). This is a contract the *sole object* of which is the provision of a lump sum on death of the individual before he attains the age of 75. The lump sum can be paid in instalments to provide income for dependants.

14.2.2 Earnings and eligibility

For the purpose of a personal pension scheme 'relevant earnings' is defined in s 623(2) and means:

(1) Emoluments chargeable under Schedule E from an office or employment held by the individual. This includes benefits in kind and emoluments from an employment which are paid in accordance with a profit-related pay scheme, but excludes anything arising from the acquisition or disposal of shares or an interest in shares or from a right to acquire shares (share option schemes) and anything in respect of which tax is chargeable by virtue of s 148 ('golden handshakes').

(2) Income from property which is attached to or forms part of the emoluments of any such office or employment held by the individual.

(3) Income which is chargeable under Schedule A, Schedule B or Schedule D and is immediately derived by the individual from the carrying on or exercise by him of his trade, profession or vocation either as an individual, or, in the case of a partnership, as a partner personally acting therein. In practice income under Schedules A and B is investment income and does not constitute relevant earnings.

(4) Income treated as earned income by virtue of ICTA 1988, s 529 (patent rights).

(5) Earnings from certain commercial lettings of furnished holiday accommodation, although assessed to tax under Schedule D Case IV, are treated as a trade for the purposes of s 623(2) and regarded as relevant earnings.

'Relevant earnings' do not include:

(1) Any remuneration as director of a company whose income consists solely or mainly of investment income if the individual, either alone or together with any other persons who are or have been at any time directors of the company, controls the company.

(2) Any remuneration from a company in which the individual
    (a) was a controlling director in the year of assessment or has been a controlling director of the company at any time in the ten years immediately preceding that year of assessment, and
    (b) is in receipt of benefits under a superannuation scheme of the

company or where benefits have been transferred from that superannuation scheme into a personal pension scheme.

These exclusions prevent a controlling director of a company pensioning his service through an occupational pension scheme, retiring and taking his benefits and then continuing to receive an income from that company which is pensioned by means of a personal pension scheme.

However for the purposes of an existing retirement annuity, relevant earnings can include share options and 'golden handshake' payments from non-pensionable employment and the pensioning of earnings of a director who is already in receipt of a pension from that company.

In summary, membership of a personal pension scheme can be extended to:

(1) Persons holding an office or employment which is not pensionable (but *not* controlling directors of investment companies).
(2) Persons engaged in business on their own account.
(3) Partners engaged in a trade, profession or vocation.

An occupation or office or employment is pensionable if an individual is a member of a relevant superannuation scheme from which he expects to receive retirement benefits. 'Relevant superannuation scheme' is defined in s 645(1), and is one which provides relevant benefits as defined in s 612 and is established by someone other than the individual; however, note the following points.

Membership of a scheme which provides lump sum life assurance benefits only on death before age 75 or some lower age and/or an annuity to the surviving spouse or a dependant does not make the occupation count as pensionable. An occupational pension scheme which provides a cash lump sum on retirement would be regarded as 'pensionable' preventing membership of a personal pension scheme or a retirement annuity contract. If, however, the scheme provides in addition to life asssurance benefits a widow's or dependant's pension this would render the occupation pensionable for *retirement annuity purposes* (unless extra statutory concession A38 applies).

The following points are also relevant for the purposes of both personal pension schemes and retirement annuities:

(1) A scheme does not have to be insured, or even funded at all. A formal promise to an employee of a pension to be paid when he reaches pension age, with no previous provision made for it, is a sponsored superannuation scheme (although it may be regarded as an unapproved pension scheme – see Chapter 5).
(2) An employee may not supplement his employer's scheme, however inadequate, by a personal pension scheme, or retirement annuity.
(3) Membership of an overseas scheme which is not approved in the

United Kingdom is regarded as pensionable employment for the purposes of the retirement annuity legislation, but does not preclude membership of a personal pension scheme.

(4) Where an employee is covered by a permanent health insurance (PHI) arrangement providing only for the continuation of what in effect is long-term sick pay up to state pension age, or if earlier, the normal retirement date of the employee (the employee remaining in the service of the employer until the date when the PHI contract ceases to provide benefits), such an arrangement will not be regarded as pensionable employment.

(5) Membership of the state pension scheme is not regarded as pensionable employment.

The relevant earnings for an employee or director taxed under Schedule E would be his actual earnings during the fiscal year beginning on 6 April and ending on 5 April, but for a self-employed individual relevant earnings for the year of assessment will be based on the earnings in his accounting year which ends in the fiscal year.

14.2.3 Net relevant earnings

Although it is necessary to have relevant earnings to be eligible to pay contributions to a personal pension scheme or retirement annuity, the tax efficiency of the arrangement depends on having *net* relevant earnings. The contributions which an individual may pay are calculated with reference to net relevant earnings (see ICTA 1988, s 646(b) and s 623 in Appendix 4).

Net relevant earnings means the amount of relevant earnings less business expenses including any deductions in respect of losses or capital allowances.

Personal charges such as alimony, charitable covenants and non-business interest do not reduce net relevant earnings.

14.2.4 Allowable maximum

In arriving at an individual's net relevant earnings for the purposes of a personal pension scheme, any amount in excess of the allowable maximum is ignored.

Table 14.4

The allowable maximum amounts are:

Tax year	Amount
1988/89	none
1989/90	£60,000
1990/91	£64,800
1991/92	£71,400
1992/93	£75,000
1993/94	£75,000
1994/95	£76,800
1995/96	£78,600
1996/97	£82,200
1997/98	£84,000
1998/99	£87,600
1999/00	£90,600

There is no allowable maximum for the purposes of a retirement annuity contract.

14.2.5 Associated employments

For the purposes of a personal pension scheme, if an individual has earnings from two or more employments which are associated and both are non-pensionable the earnings are aggregated for the purposes of assessing net relevant earnings and the earnings cap (see (1) and (2) in Example 14.4 below).

If one of the employments is pensioned through an Occupational Pension Scheme or Executive Pension Plan the earnings from the second employment on which contributions may be based is restricted to the excess of the earnings cap over the pensionable earnings (see (3) in Example 14.4 below).

However if an individual has two sources of earnings, one from employment which is pensioned and the other from self-employment, then the pensionable earnings may be disregarded (see (4) in Example 14.4 below).

Example 14.4

(1)	Two jobs – neither pensioned	
	Earnings from Job A	£70,000
	Earnings from Job B	£30,000
	Total non-pensionable earnings	£100,000
	Capped NRE from Job A plus Job B	£90,600

(2)	Two jobs – Job A fully pensioned through a personal pension scheme and Job B unpensioned	
	Earnings from Job A	£70,000
	Earnings from Job B	£30,000
	Total non-pensionable earnings	£100,000
	Capped NRE from Job B (ie, £90,600, less £70,000 already pensioned)	£20,600
(3)	Two jobs – Job A pensioned through an occupational pension scheme and Job B non-pensionable	
	Earnings from Job A	£70,000
	Earnings from Job B	£30,000
	Total non-pensionable earnings	£30,000
	Capped NRE from Job B (ie, £30,000 restricted to £90,600 less pensionable earnings)	£20,600
(4)	Two jobs – Job A pensioned through an occupational scheme, Job B self-employed	
	Earnings from Job A	£70,000
	Self-employed earnings	£30,000
	NRE from self-employment (£30,000 is not restricted by pensionable earnings)	£30,000

Personal pension scheme and retirement annuity contributions themselves, although requiring to be deducted in order to arrive at total income for tax purposes, are not deductible for the purposes of arriving at net relevant earnings.

The net relevant earnings in the year of assessment in which the annuity commences, or in which a personal pension scheme providing a lump sum on death terminates, are the earnings for the whole of the year.

14.2.6 Summary of calculation

Those in non-pensionable employment (taxed under Schedule E) normally have no deductions to make from their relevant earnings. Their gross earnings from their employment are their net relevant earnings and all deductions (such as tax, National Insurance contributions, alimony, covenants and interest) whether or not allowable for tax are ignored.

In the case of an approved personal pension scheme any employer's contributions are not regarded as emoluments of the employment chargeable to Schedule E income tax.

The self-employed (taxed under Schedule D) have to make the following deductions from their gross profits in order to arrive at their net relevant earnings:

(1) all expenses incurred in earning the profits, such as rent, rates, business interest, employee's salaries, etc;
(2) losses, whether
    (a) incurred in the current tax year, or
    (b) incurred in a previous tax year and carried forward to set against profits in the current tax year under ICTA 1988, s 385(1), or
    (c) incurred in a previous tax year, relieved against other income under s 380, and not yet deducted from net relevant earnings;
(3) capital allowances.

Personal mortgage interest and covenants to charity can be ignored. All self-employed individuals are now taxed on the 'current year' basis.

14.2.7 Capital allowances, Business Expansion Schemes and Venture Capital Trusts

Only capital allowances relating to the trade reduce net relevant earnings. Investments in Business Expansion Schemes (prior to 31 December 1993 when the scheme ended) and Enterprise Zones are personal investments and do not reduce NRE. Similarly, subscriptions to Venture Capital Trusts are not treated as reducing NRE.

14.2.8 Interest

Interest payable on money borrowed to buy into a partnership or buy shares in a close company is statutorily deductible, but it does not reduce NRE because it is money laid out for a personal purpose. The principle appears to be that interest on money borrowed for the purpose of running the business, which is deductible on normal accounting principles as an expense and not prohibited under ICTA 1988, s 74, reduces NRE while interest paid on money borrowed for personal purposes which is specifically allowable under ICTA 1988, Part IX does not reduce NRE.

This gives some scope for tax planning because a partnership, for instance, could provide extra finance for work in progress either by the partners applying to increase their business overdraft or by an individual partner borrowing money in a personal capacity to buy into (or increase his share in) the partnership. The money would be available for the partnership's business purposes either way but interest on the first loan would reduce the NRE of the partners concerned, while that on the second would not.

14.2.9 Maximum contributions (as a percentage of net relevant earnings)

The contributions which may be made from the tax year 1991/92 onwards to a personal pension scheme are:

(1)

Age on 6 April	Maximum contribution	1991/92 £	1992/93 & 1993/94 £	1994/95 £	1995/96 £
Up to 35	17.5%	12,495	13,125	13,440	13,755
36 to 45	20.0%	14,280	15,000	15,360	15,720
46 to 50	25.0%	17,850	18,750	19,200	19,650
51 to 55	30.0%	21,420	22,500	23,040	23,580
56 to 60	35.0%	24,990	26,250	26,880	27,510
61 to 74	40.0%	28,560	30,000	30,720	31,440
Maximum contributions for life assurance		3,570	3,750	3,840	3,930

Monetary limit (header spanning 1991/92 through 1995/96 columns)

Age on 6 April	Maximum contribution	1996/97 £	1997/98 £	1998/99 £	1999/ 2000 £
Up to 35	17.5%	14,385	14,700	15,330	15,855
36 to 45	20.0%	16,440	16,800	17,520	18,120
46 to 50	25.0%	20,550	21,000	21,900	22,650
51 to 55	30.0%	24,660	25,200	26,280	27,180
56 to 60	35.0%	28,770	29,400	30,600	31,710
61 to 74	40.0%	32,880	33,600	35,040	36,240
Maximum contributions for life assurance		4,110	4,200	4,380	4,530

Monetary limit

(2) up to 5 per cent of net relevant earnings for life assurance/dependants' pension contracts are included in the maximum contributions above, as is the cost of waiver of contribution benefit,

(3) where a personal pension scheme is used for contracting-out purposes, the minimum contributions made by the Secretary of State (in effect, the DSS) are payable in addition to the maximum contributions above,

(4) for the tax year 1988/89 there was no monetary limit and the maximum contributions were the same as for retirement annuity contracts, as below:

Age on 6 April	Maximum contributions
Up to 50	17.5%
51 to 55	20.0%
56 to 60	22.5%
61 to 74	27.5%

Note: All the above figures are inclusive of any contributions for life assurance and waiver of contribution benefit.

14.2.10 Interaction of contributions to personal pension schemes and retirement annuities

Many people who contribute to existing retirement annuities also wish to take advantage of the higher contribution limits available under personal pension schemes. However, special conditions apply in these circumstances.

The maximum amount that may be paid to a personal pension scheme includes any contributions being paid to a retirement annuity contract; if the latter is to continue this may mean that no contributions can be paid to the personal pension scheme.

Example 14.5

An individual aged 53 has net relevant earnings of £80,000. He currently contributes 20% to a retirement annuity contract, ie £16,000.

He wishes to top up through a personal pension scheme in 1999/2000 where the maximum contribution is £27,180 (30% of £90,600).

As £16,000 is already paid to the retirement annuity he has scope to pay £11,180 to the personal pension scheme.

Example 14.6

An individual aged 43 has net relevant earnings of £120,000. He currently contributes 17.5% to a retirement annuity contract, ie £21,000.

He is unable to top up with a personal pension scheme as the maximum contribution to a personal pension scheme is £18,120 (20% of £90,600), which is less than his contribution to the retirement annuity contract.

Further examples showing the scope for contributions to a personal pension, if the maximum contributions are being paid to a retirement annuity, are contained in Table 14.5 opposite.

Table 14.5 Tax year 1999/2000 Scope for contributions to Personal Pensions (if maximum paid to retirement annuity contract)

NRE	Ages											
	35 or less		36–45		46–50		51–55		56–60		61–74	
	RAC	PP	RAC	PP	RAC	PP	RAC	PP	RAC	PP	RAC	PP
Up to £90,600	17.5%	Nil	17.5%	2.5%	17.5%	7.5%	20%	10%	22.5%	12.5%	27.5%	12.5%
£100,000	£17,500	Nil	£17,500	£620	£17,500	£5,150	£20,000	£7,180	£22,500	£9,210	£27,500	£8,740
£110,000	£19,250	Nil	£19,250	Nil	£19,250	£3,400	£22,000	£5,180	£24,750	£6,960	£30,250	£5,990
£120,000	£21,000	Nil	£21,000	Nil	£21,000	£1,650	£24,000	£3,180	£27,000	£4,710	£33,000	£3,240
Earnings above which PP contributions is Nil	£0		£103,542		£129,428		£135,900		£140,933		£131,781	

Notes
(1) If NRE is £140,993 or higher then it can be seen that if maximum RA contributions have been paid, there is *no* scope for a PP contribution *regardless of age.*
(2) If an RA contribution is paid at a level lower than the maximum, then a PP can be used to top-up (but only to PP maximum).

14.2.11 Overfunding

The personal pension scheme must make provision, under ICTA 1988, s 640 (see Appendix 4), to ensure that the member's and any employer's contributions to the arrangement, in aggregate, do not exceed the permitted maximum. Any excess must be repaid to the contributor, as appropriate.

Excess contributions to retirement annuity contracts are not expressly prohibited under ICTA 1988 but insurers will not knowingly accept excess contributions from policyholders.

14.2.12 Tax relief

Contributions under approved personal pension schemes and retirement annuity contracts are treated as deductions from relevant earnings before their assessment to income tax. For the self-employed, the deductions are effective in the year of assessment in which they are paid (subject to the carry back provisions described later) rather than in the business year. Income tax relief is obtained at the highest tax rates paid by the individual on any part of his income. If the amount of the contribution exceeds the part of the income attracting tax relief at the highest rate, the remainder of the contribution attracts tax relief at the next highest rate and so on. For the self-employed and higher rate taxpayers relief will be given at only 10 per cent on the part of their earnings subject to the 10 per cent band.

Example 14.7

If an individual's taxable earned income in 1999/2000 amounted to £30,000, a contribution to a personal pension scheme or retirement annuity contract of £8,000 would attract tax relief of:

£2,000 at 40%	=	£ 800
£6,000 at 23%	=	£1,380
		£2,180

The tax relief obtained can be affected by the amount of investment income of an individual. For example, if net relevant earnings (ie earned income) in 1999/2000 amounted to £10,000 and investment income amounted to £20,000, a contribution of £1,750 (17.5 per cent of net relevant earnings of £10,000) would reduce taxable earnings and effectively obtain tax relief at 40 per cent.

The fact that deductions such as personal pension scheme contributions are applied to income before allowances has some favourable and unfavourable implications.

Income for the purposes of calculating age allowance is income after deduction of the contribution, so that the net income (after tax relief) is looked at when arriving at the abatement of the age allowance (on the £1 for every £2 basis) when it exceeds the statutory level (£16,800 for 1999/2000).

On the other hand, personal allowances are given on an actual basis, with no provision for carrying forward unused allowances from one year to the next. This means that tax relief on a personal pension scheme or retirement annuity contribution may be wasted or reduced if the income would have been covered by personal allowances, or investments in Venture Capital Trusts so that no tax or only reduced tax would have been payable in any case. In the case of a person who is assessed to tax under Schedule E, however, contributions to a personal pension scheme may only be paid net of basic rate tax in which case the benefit of the personal allowance is not lost.

14.2.13 Pension relief at source

Under retirement annuities, contributions are paid gross and tax relief is given later. In the case of an employee this is normally done by an adjustment to his tax coding.

Contributions to personal pension schemes by employed persons (but not the self-employed) are paid net of basic rate tax. The scheme administrator has to accept the net payment in the same way as if no deduction had been made and recovers the amount withheld from the Inland Revenue. If the individual is a higher rate taxpayer the difference between the actual rate of tax and the basic rate of tax may be reclaimed later when the individual completes his tax return and normally results in an adjustment to the individual's tax coding. This system is known as 'PRAS' or 'pension relief at source'.

This system gives a considerable cash-flow advantage over the system used under retirement annuity contracts. Even when the employed individual's earnings would not be chargeable to tax because they are low, or have been reduced for tax purposes by personal allowances, contributions are still paid net of basic rate tax. The basic rate of tax is 23 per cent (in 1999/2000) even though the first £1,500 of income is taxed at 10 per cent.

14.2.14 Carry forward/carry back facilities

It is possible for eligible persons to take advantage of two valuable facilities to maximise pension contributions and obtain the best possible taxation advantages on those contributions. The facilities are generally referred to as 'carry forward of unused relief' and 'carry back provisions'.

Carry forward of unused relief

(1) This facility enables a planholder to pay a higher contribution than normally available for the current year in order to catch up for missed contributions from the previous six years.

(2) Tax relief is, however, available against the current year, *having no effect on tax paid in past years*, and is therefore calculated according to current tax rates. It is important to note that tax relief is only available up to the level of tax payable on earned income for the current year. Thus there is no tax relief available upon payments in excess of the level of taxable earnings, except where contributions are paid to personal pension schemes by employees taxed under Schedule E: these contributions are payable net of basic rate tax, and the sum of the contributions for the current year and previous years may not exceed the net relevant earnings in the current year even though taxable earned income will be lower than NRE as a result of personal allowances and mortgage interest relief (before 6 April 2000). However, tax relief is at the highest rates, reflecting any investment income and income from pensionable employment.

(3) If the individual pays more than the year's normal maximum contribution in order to take advantage of this facility, then his local tax inspector automatically refers back over the previous six years in order to discover any unused relief which can be carried forward to absorb the excess contribution. Under a personal pension scheme a special form has to be completed, form PP42, and submitted to the tax inspector. Unused relief is only carried forward from previous years after the maximum contribution has been paid for the current year.

Carry back provisions

(1) A contribution (or part of a contribution) may be carried back to the tax year preceding the year of payment, regardless of the date of assessment and regardless of whether or not there are relevant earnings in the year in which the contribution is paid. A contribution cannot be carried back more than one year, except that if there were no net relevant earnings in the preceding tax year then the contributions may be carried back one further year. However, contributions may never be carried back more than two years.

(2) Carrying back a contribution in this way means that it will be treated for tax purposes exactly as if it had been paid in the year to which it is carried back and the maximum contribution is based on the limits

for that year, ie the normal maximum for that year plus any unused relief from the six previous years.

Thus a contribution paid in 1999/2000 and carried back to 1998/1999 would, for tax relief purposes, be allowed against the 1998/1999 tax bill (subject to the limits applicable to 1998/99) and could include an amount relating to missed contributions carried forward from 1992/93.

Mechanics of carry back

In order to carry back a contribution to the previous tax year, the following procedures must be followed:

(1) The contribution must be received by the pension provider before 6 April in the *current* tax year.
(2) An election must normally be made in writing to the Inspector of Taxes before 31 January following the tax year in which the contributions were made.
(3) The contract must have been issued by 6 April in the *current* tax year.
(4) An election for carry back may be made in the middle of a tax year. Normally, the Inland Revenue treats all methods of payment (annual, monthly or single) alike for tax relief purposes. Under a personal pension scheme an election to carry back has to be accompanied by a completed Inland Revenue form PP43.

It is important to be aware that the Inland Revenue adheres very strictly to these rules.

Carry back – effect of status

The fact that self-employed people pay contributions to a personal pension scheme on a gross basis but employed persons pay on a PRAS basis (ie 'Pension Relief At Source' – which is net of basic rate tax) raises questions on how contributions should be paid if contributions are to be carried back to a previous year when the status of the individual was different, eg self-employed today, employed last year. Table 14.6 sets out the procedure.

14.2.15 Administrative requirements

In March 1988 the Inland Revenue published guidance notes on personal pension schemes (updated in September 1999). These include the administrative requirements which have to be carried out by the individual and by the pension provider. The individual when applying to the pension provider has to provide details of his name and address, national insurance number, the Inspector of Taxes office dealing with his affairs and its reference number for him, whether he is employed or self-employed and details of any other retirement annuity contracts or personal pension schemes to which contributions are being paid by the individual or by his employer.

The individual also has to provide evidence to the pension provider of his earnings. The administrator of the personal pension scheme also has to obtain fresh evidence if the individual wishes to increase his contributions.

If the individual is employed and wishes to carry back his contributions to a previous year or carry forward unused relief, the pension provider, before accepting contributions, has to obtain from the member a statement giving details of the earnings in each of the years involved and the total contributions paid to personal pension schemes and retirement annuity contracts in those years.

14.2.16 Late assessments

In the fairly unusual case where an assessment to tax becomes final and conclusive more than six years after the end of the tax year to which it relates, relief may be obtained on a contribution paid within six months of the assessment becoming final and conclusive, provided an election is also made to the Inspector of Taxes within the same six months in respect of any relief arising out of the assessment, even though the usual six-year time limit will have gone.

Relief is given in the year in which the contribution is paid and not in the earlier years. This special provision entitles the taxpayer to absorb unused relief in respect of a year more than six years earlier, only insofar as it related to *extra* net relevant earnings which have only become apparent *because of the assessment*. The current year's entitlement is still set against the contribution first.

14.2.17 Investigation settlements

Where incorrect returns and accounts are found to have been submitted, offers in settlement of liability to tax, interest and penalties are often accepted by the Inland Revenue without a formal assessment. In the absence of the assessment, it would not be strictly possible to make use of the provisions for later assessments described in the previous paragraph where the year to which the investigation settlement related ended more than six years prior to the settlement.

The Revenue operates a special practice which applies to all investigation settlements where the letter of offer is made after 6 April 1981. This

Table 14.6

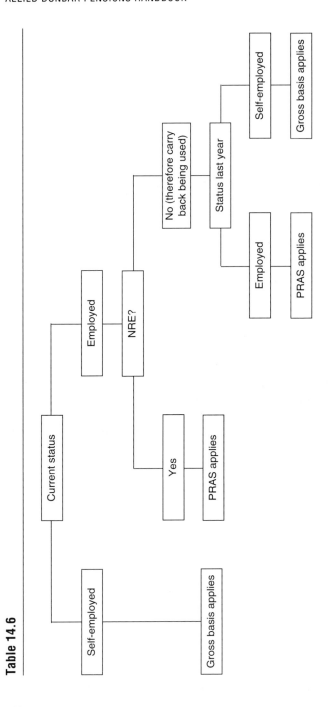

practice enables an individual to pay a contribution and make an election as described in the previous section within a period of six months from the date of the letter from the Revenue accepting the offer. Relief is granted against tax in the year in which it is paid. The individual is not obliged to pay during that period the maximum contribution applicable for the year in which the excess contribution is paid. He has in the usual way until the end of the following tax year in which to pay that maximum contribution.

14.3 SPECIFIC BENEFITS UNDER PERSONAL PENSION SCHEMES AND RETIREMENT ANNUITY CONTRACTS

14.3.1 Death benefits

Personal pension schemes and existing retirement annuity contracts

Death benefits are largely assimilated with ordinary life assurance policies, in that they can be written in trust using similar procedures and with similar inheritance tax consequences, except that they are treated more favourably.

Where the contract also provides for a pension, this remains under the control of the policyholder and he will continue to decide when and how to take his pension (within the limits imposed by the legislation) and in unit-linked contracts, for example, whether to switch or change the combination of investment funds at his disposal. The pension in payment and the tax-free cash sum are still required by law to be personal to the policyholder and cannot be assigned.

14.3.2 Flexible trusts

It is possible to write death benefits emerging from personal pension schemes and retirement annuity contracts in a form of flexible trust which provides for:

(1) **an immediate beneficiary** to whom it is intended benefits should go on death immediately after setting up the trust, and
(2) **a class of potential beneficiaries** with a power of appointment under which the death benefit may be appointed to any potential beneficiary, in addition to or to the exclusion of the current immediate beneficiary.

The power of appointment (revocable or irrevocable) is exercised by the policyholder during his life or by the trustees within 79 years from the commencement of the trust, although the appointment has to be made within two years of death to avoid inheritance tax liability.

The policyholder's lifetime power of appointment is subject to the exception that appointments back to the planholder himself must be made by at least two trustees (of whom the planholder may be one).

It is desirable to have a second trustee in addition to the policyholder himself so that the death benefit can be paid to the surviving trustee without waiting for probate.

14.3.3 Inheritance tax implications

Regular contributions

Under personal pension schemes and retirement annuity contracts, regular contributions on which tax relief is obtained are ignored for inheritance tax purposes. The principle is that they are paid primarily to provide the planholder with a personal benefit (his pension) and that the death benefit, which has been gifted to the trust beneficiaries, is incidental. Additional contributions paid from time to time, for example to pick up unused relief, or putting an existing contract in trust, are treated differently.

Under ICTA 1988, s 621 (see Appendix 4) regular contributions for life assurance contracts and the life assurance benefit within a personal pension scheme are not ignored because by definition they are not paid to provide a personal benefit, but to provide the in-trust death benefit, but in virtually every case they are exempt as normal expenditure out of income.

Proceeds on death

Payment is made on death to the trustees who use the money in accordance with the trust provisions. Normally they pass the money to the immediate beneficiary under the trust chosen by the planholder. Since the money is paid to the trustees and not to the deceased's estate, there is no inheritance tax liability.

Discretionary trusts

Provided the trust has been drawn up correctly and, in effect, is the same as the type of trust used for retirement benefit schemes approved under ICTA 1988, ss 590–612 (see Appendix 4), the normal rules for discretionary trusts do not apply, ie there are no exit charges or ten-year periodic charges, as it falls within IHTA 1984, s 58(1)(d). Also, there is no 'interest in possession' so there is no charge to inheritance tax should there be any change in the destination of the death benefits away from the person nominated by the member during his lifetime, provided this occurs within two years of death.

Interest in possession trusts

Under this type of trust the chosen beneficiary or beneficiaries have an immediate entitlement to any income produced by the trust. This means that for inheritance tax purposes the beneficiary is treated as owning the capital and it is included in his estate. In an interest in possession trust every appointment of a potential beneficiary to immediate entitlement involves the reduction (or disappearance) of the entitlement of the current immediate beneficiary. For example, if A alone is entitled to the benefits and B and C are appointed in addition, then A, B and C are each entitled to a one-third interest and the interest of A, who was previously entitled to the whole benefit, has been reduced by two-thirds. If B and C had been appointed to the whole interest to the exclusion of A, his interest would have disappeared altogether.

On each such occasion, the value of the policy is treated as passing for inheritance tax purposes as a potentially exempt transfer to the extent that the current immediate beneficiary's entitlement is reduced. The tax is calculated on the personal 'meter' of the beneficiary from whom the benefit was switched but it is payable by the trustees. There will be no inheritance tax to pay if the beneficiary losing his interest survives for seven years.

On lifetime appointments, the value switched is the market value of the death benefit and this is usually too small to attract inheritance tax. The value is only significant in the exceptional case where the planholder is in such poor health that a benefit payable on his death is imminent enough to make it attractive to a notional buyer of the policy.

If appointments are made in the two years after the planholder's death, the value switched is the actual death benefit paid, and in that case there may well be inheritance tax payable, unless the appointment is to the planholder's spouse, which would be exempt.

Protected rights

Some personal pension schemes have discretionary trust provisions contained in the rules of the scheme. Other personal pension schemes will allow individual trusts to be declared in respect of the death benefit, as with retirement annuities described above. If the personal pension scheme is used to contract out, the protected rights, which cannot be assigned, can still be subject to discretionary disposal provisions in accordance with the rules, with nominated beneficiaries.

14.3.4 Putting existing policies in trust

Declaring a trust of an existing retirement annuity policy or personal pension is also in principle a gift for inheritance tax purposes. The value transferred is the market value of the death benefit unless the immediate beneficiary is the planholder's spouse, in which case the transfer is exempt because it is between spouses.

Non-regular contributions to a personal pension scheme, or to a retirement annuity contract, eg an additional contribution in respect of unused relief carried forward from previous years, are treated in the same way.

In practice, however, such transfers are likely to be treated as negligible unless the planholder dies from natural causes within two years of making the declaration of trust. In these cases, the Capital Taxes Office (CTO) of the Inland Revenue may treat the market value at the time of the transfer as a transfer made at the time of the declaration with inheritance tax being payable at death rates. On the other hand, if the declaration had not been made, the entire fund value (not its market value at the date of the declaration) would have fallen into the estate on death and been chargeable at the death rates. So while it is sometimes difficult to say whether a declaration is liable to precipitate a charge to inheritance tax and at what level, as a general rule planholders have something to gain by declaring trusts of their policies and little or nothing to lose.

Retirement annuity contracts, including life assurance contracts under s 621 and personal pension schemes, should be written in trust. If they are not written in trust then the planholder is missing out on an obvious way of passing monies to beneficiaries free of inheritance tax, and the pension provider cannot pay out the proceeds until probate has been granted. It is essential, therefore, when considering retirement planning, to ensure that the pension provider can offer a suitable trust and should any existing policies not be written in trust to put them into trust.

Deferring benefits

From age 50 (or age 60 in the case of a retirement annuity) a policyholder may elect to take retirement benefits. Where the policyholder does not take benefits at the specified age and has still not done so when he or she dies, the CTO may consider that the failure to take retirement benefits before death gives rise to a charge to inheritance tax. This may arise where there is prima facie evidence that the policyholder's intention was to increase the estate of someone else – ie the beneficiaries of the death benefit. The CTO will look closely at arrangements where the policyholder became aware that he was suffering from a terminal illness or was uninsurable and at that time or after that time the policyholder took out a new policy and:

(1) assigned the death benefit on trust;
(2) assigned on trust the death benefit of an existing policy;
(3) paid further contributions to a single premium policy or increased contributions to a regular premium policy where the death benefit had been previously assigned on trust; or
(4) deferred the date for taking retirement benefits.

A claim by the CTO is unlikely to be pursued where the policyholder survived for two or more years after making these arrangements, or where the death benefit was paid to the policyholder's spouse and/or dependants.

14.3.5 Disability benefits

The past few years have seen an increase in the number of life offices offering different types of disability cover. Most offer a waiver of premium benefit while a few offer disability incomes and incapacity pensions.

Waiver of premium benefit

This benefit protects the planholder's commitment to pay pension contributions during disability at modest cost. Under personal pension schemes it is possible to obtain a waiver of premium benefit in respect of both the investment content and the life assurance element.

Each life office offering waiver of premium benefit naturally has its own embellishments but some characteristics are common to most of them:

(1) the waiver of premium element tends to cost around 2 to 6 per cent of the premium, depending on age at entry and sex;
(2) the waiver of premium element is a risk premium, and is not invested in order to provide retirement benefits, so that it is not normally returnable in the event of death;
(3) the waiver of premium element is considered as part of the premium under retirement annuities and personal pension schemes and the whole contribution including the waiver of premium element is eligible for tax relief;
(4) during periods of incapacity, the planholder is unlikely to have net relevant earnings, which is sometimes raised as an objection to the whole concept of waiver of premium benefit. The difficulty, however, falls away because premiums are not paid for the period in which the waiver of premium comes into operation so that the question of the life office accepting premiums or the planholder getting tax relief on them does not arise. The life office does not *pay* the contributions, it *waives* the contributions.

The benefit is usually only available to those not over age 55 at entry and normally ceases at age 60 or 65. There is usually a deferment period of three to six months, during which disability has to exist before the waiver of premium benefit comes into operation.

Example 14.8

A man aged 33 takes out a personal pension plan paying £1,000 per annum with a pension age of 65 without waiver of premium benefit.

At the end of the third year he falls ill, and, having no net relevant earnings, is unable to pay his fourth annual contribution. He recovers and restarts contributions in the fifth year.

His fund will be approximately £85,500. If he had opted for waiver of premium benefits costing around 2.5 per cent of the investment contribution of £975 (ie £25), giving the same outlay of £1,000, his fund at age 65 would be approximately £90,100, a difference of £4,600. Obviously, the greater the number of contributions missed which are not covered by waiver of premium benefit, the greater the difference in retirement benefit.

The above figures are based on a typical unit-linked contract and assume an annual growth rate of 7% before charges.

Disability incomes and incapacity pensions

Sections 620(4)(b) and 643(3)(c) of ICTA 1988 (see Appendix 4) allow for annuity payments to commence on incapacity: this means permanent incapacity – long-term incapacity is insufficient. This type of benefit should not be confused with permanent health insurance.

Insurance companies normally issue contracts containing a provision for the annuity to come into payment early in the event of incapacity; the annuity may be based on the premiums paid or, alternatively, there may be an insured element, in which case the life office will have charged an extra premium for what is an extra benefit in that should the planholder become disabled, the income which he receives will be more than that which could have been generated by the premiums actually paid.

14.3.6 Tax treatment of pensions

Pensions payable under retirement annuity contracts and personal pension schemes to:

- the planholder
- the planholder's dependant under the continuation of a joint life pension
- the planholder's dependant under a nomination

are taxed as earned income. (The only situation in which the above pensions are taxed as investment income is where the contributions under a retirement annuity contract from which the pension arises were not all completely relieved for tax.)

Retirement annuities are taxed under Schedule D of the Taxes Acts, for both employees and the self-employed. In practice this means that the annuities are paid net of basic rate tax with any additional tax being payable by the annuitant to the Inland Revenue. Any excess tax deducted from the annuity will be refunded by the Revenue.

Personal pensions are taxed under Schedule E for both employees and the self-employed. Usually the first one or two annuity payments are taxed at an emergency rate, with subsequent payments taxed at the correct rate, as confirmed by the Revenue to the pension provider.

Where a planholder dies during the period for which his pension is guaranteed (normally five years), the remaining guaranteed instalments (the right to which will have passed under the planholder's will) are taxed as investment income.

14.3.7 Overseas aspects

The overseas aspects of retirement annuities and personal pension schemes can be split into two parts: the first relates to foreign earnings and whether they constitute relevant earnings and so support contributions; the second is the effect on the payment of a pension to a planholder living abroad at the time.

Overseas earnings

These may be treated in one of four ways.

(1) UK residents are in principle liable to tax on earnings from all sources, including foreign earnings, and any such earnings which are liable to tax are correspondingly potentially relevant earnings.

(2) If virtually the whole year is spent abroad, Schedule E taxpayers may be eligible for a 100 per cent deduction (which does not apply to Schedule D taxpayers) although the 100 per cent deduction ceased to be available from 17 March 1998 except to seafarers. Nevertheless, the principle may still be relevant for the purposes of carry forward.

The principle of the 100 per cent deduction was that the whole of overseas earnings derived from non-pensionable employment constituted relevant earnings. A contribution to a retirement annuity or personal pension scheme may be effected in respect of the whole of it, despite the fact that effectively no tax would be payable in these circumstances on the overseas earnings. The 100 per cent allowance was not itself a deduction in arriving at net relevant earnings and therefore a retirement annuity or personal pension scheme contribution may have been paid. However, because no tax was payable this would have the effect of giving the individual relief to which he was not entitled. As a result, the Revenue would raise an assessment to claim back any relief given on the contribution (an employee contributing to a personal pension scheme will have paid the contribution net of basic rate tax). It may be possible to carry forward unused relief from a year to which the 100 per cent deduction applied to a later year when tax was charged.

(3) Where a UK resident takes a job abroad with a foreign employer which involves him in actually living abroad, as opposed to a job with a UK employer which usually involves spending long periods abroad, then he usually becomes non-resident for tax purposes. In that case, his foreign earnings are outside the UK tax net altogether, there is no question of their being liable to UK tax and, as a result, he is not eligible for a contribution in respect of those earnings to a retirement annuity or to a personal pension scheme.

Payment of pensions

Pensions payable from a UK source, including the pension emerging from a retirement annuity and from a personal pension scheme, are in principle liable to UK tax regardless of the residence of the pensioner.

In practice the position is governed by the double tax agreement, if any, in operation between the United Kingdom and the pensioner's country of residence. Most modern double tax agreements provide that private pensions (as opposed to ones paid by the Government to former civil servants) are liable to tax in the country of residence and therefore not in the country of origin.

Where this situation applies, the life office can obtain permission from the Inland Revenue to pay the pension gross. A lump sum which may be tax free when paid to a UK resident may not enjoy the same favourable treatment in the country of residence.

If permission has not been obtained to pay a gross pension, the pension provider will adopt its normal procedure which applies to UK residents and deduct tax at basic rate from the instalments of pension.

14.4 SPECIALISED OCCUPATIONS

The Revenue permits a pension age lower than age 50 under personal pension schemes and 60 under retirement annuity contracts in the case of occupations where early retirement is customary. The following is the list of early retirement ages which have been agreed by the Revenue.

Table 14.7

Profession or occupation	Maximum retirement age
Air Pilots	55*
Athletes (appearance and prize money only)	35
Badminton Players	35
Boxers	35
Brass Instrumentalists	55*
Circus animal trainers	50
Cricketers	40
Croupiers	50
Cyclists (Professional)	35
Dancers	35
Distant Water Trawlermen	55*
Divers (Saturation, Deep Sea and Free Swimming)	40
Downhill Skiers	30
Firemen (Part-Time)	55*
Footballers	35
Golfers (tournament earnings)	40
Ice Hockey Players	35
Inshore Fishermen	55*
Inter Dealer Brokers	50
Jockeys	
– Flat Racing	45
– National Hunt	35
Martial Arts Instructors	50
Members of the Reserve Forces	45
Models	35
Moneybroker Dealers (excluding Directors and Managers responsible for dealers)	50
Moneybroker Dealers (Directors and Managers responsible for dealers)	55*
Motorcross Motorcycle Riders	40
Motor-cycle Road Racing Riders	40
Motor Racing Drivers	40
Newscasters (ITV)	50
Nurses, Physiotherapists, Midwives or Health Visitors who are females	55*
Off-shore Riggers	50
Psychiatrists (who are also maximum part-time specialists employed within the National Health Service solely in the treatment of the mentally disordered)	55*
Real Tennis Players	35

Table 14.7 *(cont.)*

Royal Marine Reservists (non-commissioned)	45
Royal Naval Reservists	50
Rugby League Players	35
Rugby League Referees	50
Rugby Union Players	35
Singers	55*
Speedway Riders	40
Squash Players	35
Table Tennis Players	35
Tennis Players	35
Territorial Army Members	50
Trapeze Artists	40
Wrestlers	35

Note: Under personal pension schemes there is provision to take benefits between ages 50 and 75 so that individuals falling within those professions or occupations, and marked with an asterisk, may prefer a personal pension scheme if they wish to have access to benefits earlier than age 55.

From time to time new occupations and professions are added to the list, usually as a result of representations made by a trade body or professional association.

An individual falling into one of the above categories has the option of paying contributions into a personal pension scheme which will provide for benefits to commence at the earlier pension age shown above: he is entitled to defer the benefits in the usual way.

The earlier pension ages are intended to benefit individuals who fall into one of the specialised occupations. If the individual's job changes to one which would not fall into one of the above categories, he should stop paying contributions to the original contract and divert future contributions to a separate personal pension scheme which will specify the normal range of pension ages, 50 to 75.

An individual who falls into one of the above occupations but was not aware of the earlier pension ages, or where they have been reduced since he effected his original contract, may nevertheless take benefits at the earlier pension age provided that he can show that his occupation fell into one of the above categories at the time he took out the contract.

Although the earlier pension ages may appear to be attractive to an individual whose occupation is such that his earning capacity will drop considerably after an early age, this does not necessarily mean that his retirement income will be adequate because the period of time during which he is contributing will be short, whereas the period during which he will be receiving an income will be long.

Example 14.9

A deep-sea diver, with high earnings, pays £5,000 per annum for 15 years to a personal pension scheme starting when he is 25: at age 40 he has built up a fund of £119,000 (assuming growth of 7% per annum before charges) which provides him with immediate benefits of a £29,800 tax-free lump sum plus a level income of £5,650 per annum.

It will be seen from the above example that even though the earning capacity may have been high, the contributions are restricted to 17.5 per cent up to age 35 and 20 per cent between ages 35 and 40 with the result that the emerging benefits are unlikely to be adequate so that additional provision will have to be made elsewhere to supplement the income. By age 55, the income will be worth around £3,600 if inflation over the 15-year period is 3 per cent per annum.

14.4.1 Lloyd's underwriters

The ability to pay a contribution and to elect to have it treated as having been paid in the previous year generally did not assist Lloyd's under-writers who are generally unable to establish net relevant earnings until several years have elapsed. From 1993/94 onwards both earnings from being a Lloyd's underwriter and investment income from being a Lloyd's Name are treated as net relevant earnings and are pensionable.

The extended system of carry back which allowed Lloyd's underwriters to have a pension contribution treated as paid in the last year but two (ie three-year carry back) came to an end in 1997/98.

14.4.2 Doctors and dentists

It may seem surprising that a large section of this chapter is devoted to doctors and dentists, but the reason for this is that considerable planning opportunities are available to this section of the community through personal pension schemes and retirement annuities. A doctor or dentist is likely to be a member of the NHS Superannuation Scheme. The opportunities available, however, depend upon whether he is assessed to tax under Schedule E or under Schedule D.

Doctors and dentists assessable under Schedule E

A doctor or dentist who is in salaried employment in the NHS is assessable to tax under Schedule E and pays a contribution of 6 per cent of his remuneration to the NHS Superannuation Scheme (NHSSS). He is eligible for tax relief on these contributions under ICTA 1988, s 594. As his job is pensionable, the remuneration is not relevant earnings for the purpose of personal pension schemes and existing retirement annuity contracts.

It is possible that such an individual may have private earnings, assessable under Schedule D. For instance, it is common for a hospital doctor to carry out private consultancy work which is normally non-pensionable and regarded as relevant earnings. Retirement annuity contracts and personal pension schemes may be effected within the usual limits in respect of these non-pensionable earnings (see the earlier part of this chapter dealing with provisions relating to people with more than one job).

Doctors and dentists assessable under Schedule D

A doctor or dentist who is engaged in the NHS and who is assessable under Schedule D is a self-employed person. He is in the unusual position of being a member of a sponsored superannuation scheme, the NHSSS. Thus although he is not an employee, he is nevertheless a member of a pension scheme. The contribution which he pays to the NHSSS does not rank for tax relief. There is, however, an extra-statutory concession (A9), reproduced below, under which the Revenue is normally prepared to allow such contributions as deductions from the earnings assessed to tax.

A9 Doctors' and dentists' superannuation contributions

Under ICTA 1988, section 594, contributions required to be made in pursuance of a public general Act of Parliament by the holder of an office or employment towards the provision of superannuation benefits may be deducted in assessing his emoluments. This section is in practice treated as extending to assessments under Schedule D on the profits of a medical or dental practitioner who is required to make superannuation contributions in pursuance of National Health Service Acts. Where, however, the practitioner also pays premium or contributions towards a retirement annuity within ICTA 1988, sections 619 *et seq*, a restriction is imposed either on the amount of the deduction for his statutory contribution or on the amount of retirement annuity relief allowable.

For 1980/81 onwards, concessionary relief is allowable on either of the following bases. Either practitioners may have relief on the amount of their NHS contributions together with a relief on the amount of any retirement annuity premium in relation to their non-NHS earnings. For this purpose:

(a) Non-NHS earnings are taken as the amount of net relevant earnings (as defined in ICTA 1988, section 623) less the sum produced by multiplying the amount of the NHS contributions by $16\frac{2}{3}$.

(b) Retirement annuity relief will be allowable within the normal limit of 17.5 per cent (or the higher percentages for older contributors) of the non-NHS earnings plus any unused relief for earlier years. For this

purpose unused relief should be calculated on the appropriate concessional basis for years in which relief has been allowed on NHS
contributions.

Or, practitioners may have relief on the amount of their NHS contributions
together with relief on any retirement annuity premiums paid up to the
amount of the largest premium on which tax relief was allowed for any of the
three years 1969/70 to 1971/72 but with a restriction, if necessary, to keep the
total relief (on NHS contributions and retirement annuity premiums) within
the pre-1971/72 limits for retirement annuity relief of 10 per cent of net relevant earnings or £750 – or the higher limits permitted to older people. Any
surplus of premiums paid over the amount allowable on this basis will not be
available for carry-forward.

Finally, practitioners may, instead, have relief on a statutory basis. In this
case, they would take retirement annuity relief, up to the limits appropriate for
a particular year, on their full net relevant earnings (ie including NHS earnings). But in that event no concessionary relief would be available in respect
of NHS contributions.

A practitioner assessed under Schedule D has three options in relation to
the tax treatment of personal pension scheme contributions and any
retirement annuity contributions and NHSSS contributions which he
pays: the following is a reproduction with permission of a note produced
by the Inland Revenue Pension Schemes Office on the subject. The note
also applies unchanged in respect of personal pension schemes taken out
from 1 July 1988.

Medical or dental practitioners assessed under Schedule D
Retirement annuity relief for the year of assessment 1983/84
1   For the year 1983/84 a practitioner will have three options in relation to
     the tax treatment of any retirement annuity premiums and National
     Health Service Superannuation Scheme contributions which he pays –
     (A) to claim retirement annuity relief up to the statutory maxima by ref-
          erence to his net relevant earnings, both from National Health
          Service and private practice; this option will preclude any conces-
          sional relief on his NHS Superannuation Scheme contributions;
     (B) to claim concessional relief on NHS Superannuation Scheme con-
          tributions against his NHS earnings, and to claim in addition
          retirement annuity relief up to the statutory maxima by reference to
          non-NHS earnings only;
     (C) to claim concessional relief on NHS Superannuation Scheme con-
          tributions, and to claim in addition retirement annuity relief up to the
          amount of the largest premium on which tax relief was allowed for
          any of the 3 years 1969/70, 1970/71 and 1971/72, but with a restric-
          tion if necessary to keep the total relief (on NHS Superannuation
          Scheme contributions and retirement annuity premiums taken
          together) within the pre-1971 statutory limits.
2   In the preceding paragraph –
     (a) 'statutory maxima' means the present limits of 17.5 per cent (or the
          higher figures for older persons) plus any unused relief for earlier years.

201

(b) 'pre-1971 statutory limits' means 10 per cent and £750 and the other figures corresponding thereto in sections 227 and 228 Income and Corporation Taxes Act 1970.

(c) 'NHS earnings' will be computed by multiplying the amount of NHS Superannuation Scheme contributions paid in the year of assessment by 100/6.

(d) 'non-NHS earnings' means the remainder of the profits as assessed under Schedule D.

3   If NHS Superannuation Scheme contributions are inflated because of an addition for 'added years', only the normal annual NHS contributions should be used when computing NHS earnings for the purposes of Option 1(B) above.

4   The total relief to be kept within pre-1971 statutory limits under option 1(C) must be based on total NHS Superannuation Scheme contributions, including those relating to 'added years' and retirement annuity premiums taken together.

Special Note

A doctor or dentist holding a full or part time hospital appointment is an employee and the remuneration therefrom is assessed under Schedule E. Generally speaking, such an office would be pensionable (see Part 2 of the booklet relating to NHS Superannuation). If the individual is also in receipt of fees from a private practice assessed under Schedule D then he is able to pay retirement annuity premiums and claim relief to the extent of the statutory maxima as in 2(a) above.

Although the total benefits from the NHSSS and retirement annuities under basis (A) might exceed the maximum benefits approvable by the Revenue (see Chapter 4) the individual's benefits under the NHSSS would not be restricted by the Revenue.

Example 14.10

(1) Option (A)

A GP has net relevant earnings of £38,000. His NHS contributions (excluding any for added years) amount to £1,600.

NHS Pensionable Earnings (included in the NRE of £38,000) are £26,666 ($1,600 \times 100$%).

A GP can claim retirement annuity relief or personal pension scheme relief in relation to NRE of £38,000, provided that he does not claim tax relief on his NHS contributions of £1,600 and on any contributions for added years.

(2) Option (B)

In the above example the non-NHS earnings amount to £11,334 (£38,000 – £26,666) on which he may claim retirement annuity relief or personal pension scheme relief without giving up relief on his NHS contributions.

> **Notes**
>
> (1) In some circumstances NHS pensionable earnings are more than NRE because the former is a multiple of NHS contributions paid in the actual tax year whereas NRE represents adjusted profits in the accounting period which ended in the previous tax year.
>
> (2) NHS pensionable earnings may be lower than NRE even though there are no genuine private earnings because NHS Pensionable Earnings are an average.

Added years – personal pension schemes

A practitioner who is considering increasing his pension benefits will normally have the option of:

(1) Paying additional voluntary contributions to purchase added years under the NHSSS.
(2) Paying contributions to a personal pension scheme, either in respect of his total net relevant earnings under option (A) or in respect of any non-NHS earnings under option (B).
(3) A combination of the two.
(4) Paying contributions to a retirement annuity contract taken out before 1 July 1988.
(5) Paying additional voluntary contributions to a freestanding scheme (only available if he is claiming tax relief on his NHSSS contributions).

Under option (B), it would be possible for the practitioner to buy added years under the NHSSS and also pay maximum retirement annuity or personal pension scheme contributions in respect of any non-NHS earnings. If, however, the practitioner opts for option (A) he will be precluded from claiming concessional relief on his NHS contributions, *including* those to buy added years so that the cost might become prohibitive.

Other factors which have to be considered are as follows:

(1) the NHSSS currently inflation-proofs pensions;
(2) contributions for added years are limited to 9 per cent of NHS pensionable earnings because the maximum personal contribution that can be paid to an approved scheme amounts to 15 per cent;
(3) the personal pension scheme, or existing retirement annuity contract, affords greater flexibility in taking the benefits: benefits from separate contracts may be phased over a period of years between 50 and 75 (60 and 75 under the retirement annuity contract) regardless of whether or not the practitioner is working or has completely or partially retired; the personal pension scheme gives even greater flexibility in allowing benefits to be taken between 50 and 75;
(4) life assurance under ICTA 1988, s 637 can be provided with full tax relief on the contributions.

Retired practitioners

A doctor or dentist who has retired from the NHS but is continuing to practise privately, full time or part time, is eligible to contribute to a retirement annuity and/or personal pension scheme.

Carry back provisions

A doctor or dentist is entitled in the usual way to pay a contribution and elect under ICTA 1988, s 619(4)(a) or 641(1)(a) to have it treated as having been paid in the previous tax year. If he wishes to carry back in this way and use option (B), whereby he does not claim tax relief on his NHSSS contributions, a complication arises because he will probably have claimed tax relief on those NHSSS contributions already, as an expense against his profits. Nevertheless he may effectively 'unclaim' that relief and pay a personal pension scheme contribution and/or retirement annuity contribution in respect of net relevant earnings under option (B). If he is using option (A) there will be no problem, as he will not have claimed tax relief on his NHSSS contributions in the first place.

14.5 BENEFIT LEVELS

This chapter, so far, has dealt with technical matters such as eligibility, the meaning of 'net relevant earnings' and how to obtain tax relief in the current year and previous years, but it is important not to lose sight of the principal purpose of retirement annuities and personal pension schemes, namely to provide a worthwhile income in retirement.

In practice, the only way of doing this within the legislation is to contribute the maximum tax-relievable contributions allowed. Many people, however, do not contribute anything like the maximum contributions because they are not aware of the effect that inflation will have on their current pension planning.

Table 14.8 below shows the benefits emerging from a typical personal pension scheme at age 60 based on:

- contributions commencing at 10 per cent of income, but not increasing in line with increases in income, and
- contributions starting at 10 per cent of income and continuing at that level in line with salary increases.

The table is based on an initial income level of £10,000 per annum, and assumes that income increases by 4 per cent per annum to age 60, and that fund growth amounts to 7 per cent per annum after charges.

Table 14.8

Man aged	Projected income at age 60	Projected level pension produced by £1,000 pa investment contribution			
		level		Indexed at 4% pa	
24	£41,039	£10,100	(24.6%)	£17,400	(42.3%)
29	£33,731	£6,970	(20.6%)	£11,300	(33.5%)
34	£27,724	£4,780	(17.2%)	£7,310	(26.3%)
39	£22,787	£3,190	(13.9%)	£4,540	(19.9%)
44	£18,729	£2,030	(10.8%)	£2,670	(14.2%)
49	£15,394	£1,170	(7.6%)	£1,410	(9.1%)
54	£12,653	£542	(4.2%)	£598	(4.7%)

The table clearly demonstrates the importance of keeping pension provision under regular review and of planning for retirement many years before the event – in fact, it may be rather daunting to some people. The above figures, however, could be increased by 75 per cent if maximum contributions were made (or even doubled for a man over age 45); in addition contributions could be paid representing unused relief carried forward from previous years.

The most important figures in the above table are not the projected incomes on retirement and the projected pensions emerging from the pension plan, but the relationship between the two, for example, the individual aged 39 retiring at age 60 will receive an income from his personal pension of either 13.9 or 19.9 per cent of his final income depending upon whether or not he has increased contributions throughout the previous 20 years.

Table 14.9 below shows the pension emerging from a personal pension scheme as a *percentage* of final income in retirement. Income at retirement and the benefits under a personal pension scheme may appear extremely high in relation to today's earnings but in relation to final earnings, they may well be a very small percentage. The pension is based on contributions of 10 per cent of income throughout (ie an increasing contribution) on the same assumptions as the previous table.

Table 14.9

Age	Males		Females	
	Pension age 60	Pension age 65	Pension age 60	Pension age 65
24	42.3%	58.6%	38.7%	52.6%
29	33.5%	47.5%	30.8%	42.6%
34	26.3%	37.6%	24.1%	33.7%
39	19.9%	29.5%	18.2%	26.4%
44	14.2%	22.3%	13.0%	20.0%
49	9.1%	15.9%	8.3%	14.3%
54	4.7%	10.3%	4.3%	9.2%

The purpose of this table is to show what a future pension will be *worth* rather than showing the pension as a sterling amount.

The pensions are level: pensions increasing at 5 per cent per annum compound would be approximately 60 per cent of the pensions illustrated.

Example 14.11

A man aged 39 paying contributions of 10% of his income throughout could expect to receive an income of 19.9% of his income at age 60.

If he requires 50% of his income to live on, the contribution level required, as a percentage of his income, is as follows:

$$\frac{50.0}{19.9} \times 10 = 25\%$$

This exceeds the permitted amount for an individual aged 39 (20%) and demonstrates the need to start pension planning at an earlier age.

14.6 OTHER SCHEMES FOR PARTNERS

14.6.1 Retired partners' annuities

A partner who has made no provision for income through the retirement annuity or personal pension scheme legislation may nevertheless receive a pension from his firm on retirement.

Such a pension, because of old age or ill health, is normally treated as a charge for basic and higher rates of tax on the earned income of the paying partners under ICTA 1988, s 683(1) although it cannot be deducted from the investment income except to the extent that the pension exceeds the allowable limits under ICTA 1988, s 628.

In order for the pension to be regarded as earned income at the hands of the recipient, under the provision of s 628, it must be within the allowable limits, ie not more than 50 per cent of the average profits of the retiring partner for the best three out of the last seven years prior to his retirement during which he had devoted substantially the whole of his time to acting as a partner.

The payment must be in accordance with the partnership agreement or a supplementary agreement. The firm may make increases in the pension paid to a former partner in order that it may keep pace with inflation, as measured by the retail prices index for the December preceding the year of assessment for which the revised pension is to be paid compared with the December in the year of assessment in which he ceased to be a member of the partnership. It is permissible for the pension to continue for a widow or dependant.

Payments made by continuing partners to a retired partner do not reduce the net relevant earnings of the former.

There are several disadvantages in relying on a pension from the firm:

(1) The pension is usually limited to a period of, say, ten years simply because the continuing partners are unlikely to commit themselves to continue paying a pension for the life of a retired partner or even the life of his dependant.
(2) If several of the retiring partners leave the firm either on death or on retirement, the pension liability could be too great a burden on the continuing partners which might result in the dissolution of the partnership or a reduction in the pension paid to the retired partners. In fact it may be difficult for the firm to enter into mergers with other firms which might otherwise be desirable or it may prevent new partners from joining the firm.
(3) The continuation of the pension paid to the retired partner will depend on the continued success of the firm over which the retired partner has no control.

14.7 SELF-INVESTED PERSONAL PENSIONS

Prior to the introduction of personal pension schemes on 1 July 1988, a few insurance companies had introduced a variation on the retirement annuity contract whereby contributions were paid by a number of partners to the insurance company which would issue a policy to the partners as policyholders in an approved retirement annuity contract. The insurance company was the beneficial owner of the investments. The partners had an influence on the investment of the policies in a similar way to a self-managed or personalised life assurance mini-bond to the extent that the insurance company was prepared to take account of the preferences for investment as expressed by the policyholders. The partners could invest only in approved investments for the retirement annuity fund, but these could include, for example, approved quoted investments or, more commonly, the premises occupied by the partnership.

The main attraction of these schemes was the possibility of transferring property owned by the partnership into the retirement annuity or using the funds built up to purchase a property from which the partnership would operate.

Under the personal pension scheme legislation this is no longer possible. Inland Revenue practice on 'self-investment' is now much more restricted and is contained in their 'Memorandum 101', dated October 1989, an extract of which follows:

Part I   Investment of members contributions

1. In his Budget statement the Chancellor proposed that personal pension scheme (PPS) members should have the opportunity to become more involved in decisions about how their contributions are invested. This Memorandum contains the further guidance promised in paragraph 59 of Memorandum No 99.

2. This guidance applies to all personal pension schemes, regardless of the type of provider (bank, building society, friendly society etc), which wish to give members a degree of investment choice.

3. Decisions on the extent of choice which scheme members can have are matters for each scheme to decide. There will be no Revenue requirements on this point. Some schemes may choose to limit individual involvement to selecting the parameters of the investment portfolio, leaving the selection of particular investments to a fund manager. On the other hand, others may give the members a direct say as to the specific investments to be held and when they should be bought or sold.

Range of acceptable investments

4. The SFO will, therefore, now consider for approval schemes whose rules allow members to choose, if they wish, how their contributions should be invested. Investments available can be any of the following.

   Stocks and shares (eg equities, gilts, debentures etc.) quoted on the UK Stock Exchange including securities traded on the Unlisted Securities Market.

   Stocks and shares traded on a recognised overseas stock exchange.

   Unit trusts and investment trusts.

   Insurance company managed funds and unit-linked funds.

   Deposit accounts.

   Commercial property.

Part II Use of scheme funds

5. There will need to be some controls on investment activities and the way in which the scheme is administered. This is because the sole purpose of an approved PPS must be the provision of annuities or lump sums as required by Section 633 of the Taxes Act. So, from the date of this Memorandum it will be a condition of approval for all personal pension schemes, irrespective of the type of provider, that the documents must contain provisions expressly prohibiting investments of the types described in paragraphs 6 to 8 below.

Loans

6. Scheme funds must not be used to provide loans to members or any persons connected with a member. Further, no loan from any source made to an individual who is a member of the scheme should in any way affect the return on the investments representing that member's interest in the scheme.

Other investments

7. Schemes must not, except in the circumstances described in paragraph 8, enter into any investment transactions with a member or any person connected with a member. The acquisitions by the scheme of a member's commercial property or portfolio of stocks and shares are such transactions, as is the subsequent acquisition by the member of any of the scheme's assets. All transactions in quoted UK or overseas securities should take place through a recognised stock exchange.

8. Schemes must not hold directly as an investment residential property or land connected with such a property, or personal chattels capable in any way of private use. This does not apply to commercial land and property (subject to paragraph 7 above). Where commercial property is leased to a business or partnership connected with the member, the scheme rules should ensure that the lease, including the rent payable, is on commercial terms determined by a professional valuation.

Connected transactions

9. For the purposes of paragraphs 6 to 8 above a person is connected with a member if that person falls within the definition of connected persons in Section 839 of the Taxes Act. The duty of ensuring that a transaction is not one with a connected person must be placed on the scheme administrator.

Transactions completed before the issue of this Memorandum

10. Investment transactions which conflict with the requirements in paragraphs 6 to 8 above, but which were completed by an approved (or provisionally approved) scheme before the issue of this Memorandum will not normally be treated as giving rise to unapprovable benefits.

Existing schemes

11. Schemes which have already received full approval will be required to amend their rules accordingly, and should submit appropriate amendments to this Office. In the meantime no transactions as described in paragraphs 6 and 8 above should be entered into.

12. Schemes which have received provisional approval will be required to include the new restrictions in the rules before substantive approval is given. In the meantime the administrator's undertaking that the scheme does not make provision for any benefit other than those mentioned in the Taxes Act should be regarded as preventing any of the transactions described in paragraphs 6 to 8 above.

13. Schemes which have already submitted rules, and which are capable of, but have not yet received provisional approval in all respects except for paragraphs 6 to 8 above will be granted provisional approval on the understanding that the administrator will interpret his undertaking as in paragraph 12 above.

New schemes

14. The rules should contain the restrictions in paragraphs 6 to 8 above before provisional approval can be given. The form of application for approval (SFPP1) will be amended in due course to require an indication of where in the scheme documents the new restrictions are to be found. In the meantime applications should include in part 3 of the SFPP1 a note showing which rules contain these provisions. If rules have already been executed without these provisions this Office may be prepared to grant provisional approval upon receipt of an assurance from the administrator that he will interpret his undertaking as in paragraph 12 above.

Model rules

15. The model rules coded IMR/APP/88 and IR/PP/88 will be amended in due course to incorporate provisions permitting members' investment choice and the restrictions described above.

When personal pension schemes first started in July 1988 new providers such as banks, building societies and unit trusts were permitted to offer them, not just insurance companies. The above guidelines show the extended choice available to individuals by allowing all providers to offer members the facility to decide exactly how their fund can be invested. In effect the member can take advantage of a 'portfolio management' type service if this is offered by the pension provider.

The scheme may borrow to purchase a commercial property and there is no restriction on the amount (as applies to small self-administered schemes for directors – see Chapter 9 – where borrowings are limited to three times the ordinary annual contribution to the scheme plus an amount equal to 45 per cent of scheme assets).

It will be seen that loans and other transactions with scheme members and their associates are banned. Loans to the employer/company and unsecured loans generally are not permitted (in contrast to small self-administered schemes for directors where the scheme trustees may make an unsecured loan – generally for a short period – and to the company). Although investment in commercial property is allowed and the property may be used in connection with the member's (or his associate's) business, because of the prohibition on transactions with the member it will not be possible for the member to transfer to his personal pension scheme an *existing property* owned by his business. If a property is bought on the open market by the personal pension scheme and then leased back to the member's business the terms of the lease and the level of rent must be on commercial terms.

As with small self-administered schemes run by small limited companies, investments in residential property or 'pride in possession' assets is not permitted.

The above guidelines also prohibit any associated loans from a third party, eg a bank, where the return on the member's personal pension scheme fund would be affected. Under similar arrangements operated within the retirement annuity legislation it was not uncommon for a loan to be granted to a member on condition that a switch was made from his investment fund into another fund where the future return was linked in some way to the rate of interest charged on the loan. This is prohibited under personal pension schemes offering these facilities.

The documentation required for self-managed schemes is similar to that required for personal pension schemes offered by other providers, although the paperwork will increase significantly if investments are made outside insurance company pension funds. Actuarial valuations are not required at inception or for continued approval (as applies under small self-administered schemes for directors) but regular fund valuations will be needed from time to time.

The income withdrawal facility (see Chapter 19) allowing members of personal pension schemes to defer the purchase of an annuity until no later than age 75, drawing income from the fund, in the meantime, is also available under self invested personal pensions.

14.7.1 Friendly societies

Having their own friendly society enables a group of partners to make retirement provision with all the advantages normally enjoyed under an insured arrangement. By avoiding an insurance company the partners will hope that their expenses will be lower. They will, however, incur expenses in setting up their friendly society. The main steps to be undertaken are:

(1) At least seven partners of the same firm will be required to establish the arrangement, and the group will have to be approved by the Chief Registrar of Friendly Societies.
(2) A set of rules will have to be submitted to the Registrar who will need to be satisfied that suitable accounting systems will operate.

(3) A policy document will need to be approved by the Inland Revenue.

(4) Audited annual returns will have to be made to the Registrar.

Further changes to the legislation affecting friendly societies will come into force when the Friendly Societies Act 1992 takes effect.

Self-managed investments of this nature will require professional advice, especially as the effort involved in the above process is likely to be time consuming. They will also have to comply with the provisions of the Trustee Investment Act 1961 which requires at least 50 per cent of the fund to be invested in 'narrow-range' investments – mainly government securities.

14.8 DEFERRED ANNUiTY PURCHASE

Legislation now allows those with personal pension schemes to take 25 per cent as a lump sum at any time from age 50 and defer the purchase of an annuity to a later date, up to age 75. Until the actual purchase of the annuity, the planholder can draw down varying amounts of income subject to certain limits. This option has become increasingly popular as annuity rates have fallen in recent years, although the improved flexibility has resulted in greater complexity. This is covered in Chapter 19.

14.9 BANKRUPTCY

On a member becoming bankrupt under the 1986 Insolvency Act, control of the assets passes to the Trustee in Bankruptcy, who will be either the Official Receiver or a licensed insolvency practitioner. What this effectively means is that the Trustee in Bankruptcy can make any financial decisions that the bankrupt could have made prior to being made bankrupt (eg the sale of a house).

To put this into the context of a personal pension, the Trustee in Bankruptcy has the same powers in relation to the PPP as the bankrupt did. Therefore, when the bankrupt reaches age 50 (or an earlier retirement age if in a special occupation), the Trustee in Bankruptcy can access any benefits from a PPP (excluding the protected rights). It is not true that placing a PPP in trust can avoid this situation, as a trust only relates to death benefits.

Before reaching age 50 (or an earlier retirement age if in a special occupation), the Trustee in Bankruptcy cannot access any of the benefits whatsoever.

In the event of death before retirement, any lump sum death benefits which are subject to a trust must be distributed by the trustees under the trust rules. The Trustee in Bankruptcy cannot claim these benefits. In certain circumstances the Trustee in Bankruptcy can apply to the court for an order to set aside the trust, eg if it was set up within two years of the person being declared bankrupt. In this case the plan would pass to the Trustee in Bankruptcy as if there had been no trust.

Any personal pension which has passed to the Trustee in Bankruptcy is not automatically returned following discharge. Unless the personal pension is specifically reassigned by the Trustee in Bankruptcy, the position remains as described above.

If an individual who is or has been bankrupt continues or restarts contributions under the pension plan he or she had when he or she went bankrupt, it is possible the Trustee in Bankruptcy's rights to the bankrupt's pension may extend to any pension 'purchased' by the new contributions. Therefore, any bankrupt who wants to restart pension contributions should do so under a new plan, having obtained permission from the Trustee in Bankruptcy to do this.

The vesting powers in the Trustee in Bankruptcy under a personal pension is based on the judgment in a court case, *re Landau*. Whilst this case was about a retirement annuity contract, the principle that the Trustee in Bankruptcy can claim the retirement benefits without an Income Payments Order from the court also extends to personal pensions. However, the legal position will not be certain until it is clarified by the courts.

The powers of a Trustee in Bankruptcy apply equally to retirement annuity contracts, but the minimum age for taking retirement benefits from these contracts is age 60 (unless in a special occuption, or where benefits are transferred to a personal pension plan). Any decision to invoke these powers is for the Trustee in Bankruptcy and may vary from case to case.

Any lump sum benefit payable on death is paid to the Trustee in Bankruptcy, unless it is held in trust. However, the Trustee in Bankruptcy could still apply to the court for an order to set aside the trust, although the court's decision would depend upon a number of factors including the length of time the plan has been in trust.

It has recently been possible to include a forfeiture clause in the personal pension plan rules. This would have the effect that on bankruptcy, the member would forfeit rights to benefits and hence the Trustee in Bankruptcy would have no right to claim on the policy. However, it is not yet clear if such a forfeiture clause is a real solution, as once forfeited it may not be possible for the policyholder to regain rights to the benefits if discharged from bankruptcy. Also if a typical forfeiture clause is being used the scheme trustees may only be able to pay out scheme benefits if the member and/or his dependants are in financial hardship. Further, it is not clear that such clauses will be effective. However, the Welfare Reform and Pensions Act 1999, which includes the setting-up of stakeholder pension schemes from April 2001, also allows for stakeholder schemes and personal pensions to have protection against Trustees in Bankruptcy.

14.10 TAX REGIME FOR STAKEHOLDER PENSIONS

The Government's Consultative Brief on the tax regime for stakeholder pensions proposes a number of changes which will simplify pensions, including personal pensions (retirement annuities will not be affected). If the proposals are adopted they will have a significant impact on a number of areas covered in this chapter, as follows:

(1) Contribution limits: contributions into a stakeholder scheme will be limited to an annual maximum of the higher of:

- £3,600, and
- the amount which the member could pay into a personal pension under the current tax regime (see 14.2.9 above).

(2) Eligibility conditions: individuals will be able to contribute up to £3,600 a year to a stakeholder pension whether or not they have earnings from employment (eg carers or married spouses without earnings).

(3) A member whose annual contribution limit was higher than £3,600 when he was working will be able to contribute up to this limit for up to five years after ceasing work. The upper limit will be based on the highest relief available (by reference to age and earnings) in the year the member ceased working or in the two immediately preceding years. After five years the upper limit of £3,600 will apply. The current method of carry back and carry forward will end on 5 April 2001.

(4) There will be a new residence test: an individual must be resident and ordinarily resident in the United Kingdom for tax purposes, or have taxable earnings in the United Kingdom, or be a Crown servant treated as performing duties in the United Kingdom.

(5) Individuals will pay contributions net of basic rate tax and the provider will reclaim basic rate tax from the Inland Revenue (this also applies to the self-employed). Higher rate taxpayers will be able to claim higher rate tax relief through their tax returns.

(6) 'Rider' benefits: the ending of waiver of premium and pension life assurance benefits. It is not clear whether existing plans with these rider benefits will be able to retain them or whether they will have to cease.

15

TAX PLANNING HINTS THROUGH PENSIONS

This chapter contains brief notes on ways of using pension schemes in order to achieve not only retirement income for the member and his family, but also a means of overall tax planning.

The first part of this chapter deals with executive pension plans and the second half with personal pension schemes and existing retirement annuity contracts. It is suggested, however, that the whole of the chapter is read by both the company director and the self-employed person, because they may well change status throughout their careers. Indeed, it is not uncommon for persons to have income from limited companies and also from sole proprietorships or partnerships, in which case executive pension plans, personal pension schemes and retirement annuity contracts may be used concurrently.

15.1 EXECUTIVE PENSION PLANS: PLANNING HINTS

(1) Ensure that employers' contributions are paid by the end of the accounting period otherwise tax relief will be lost – there is no provision for carrying back pension contributions.

(2) Pension contributions can create, or augment, a trading loss which can be carried back one year or carried forward indefinitely.

(3) A trading loss (possibly caused by payment of a pension contribution) can be set against chargeable gains in the same year or in the previous year.

(4) Special, one-off contributions can be paid to purchase past service benefits. Tax relief will be given on the special contribution in the year in which it is paid unless it amounts to more than £500,000 in which case it may be spread (see Chapter 7).

(5) Any personal contributions paid by the director (not exceeding 15 per cent of remuneration) are relieved in the fiscal year in which they are paid (not the company's accounting year). Thus any personal contributions should be paid by 5 April in any year. Since 6

April 1987 it has been possible to vary the amount and timing of any additional voluntary contributions.

(6) Apart from specialised occupations the earliest normal retirement date that you may specify under an executive pension plan is age 60. This, therefore, is normally the best possible date to choose even if you are considering working beyond this date. Having chosen age 60, you may still defer the benefits if you continue working. A normal retirement date of age 60 is the earliest date at which you are entitled to take maximum benefits from your pension plan, ie a pension of two-thirds of your final salary, part of which you may exchange for a maximum tax-free lump sum of 1.5 times your final salary.

If you are classed as a pre-1987 member and choose a normal retirement date of 65, but subsequently decided to retire at, for example, age 63, you will not be entitled to maximum benefits even though you may well have completed 20 years' service by age 63. You will be treated as going on early retirement with resulting limitations on your maximum benefits.

The only exception to this recommendation is that if you can only complete 20 years' service with the company by, say, age 63 and are proposing to fund for maximum benefits, then you should choose a normal retirement date of 63.

(7) Although you cannot choose a normal retirement date before age 60, it is still possible to take substantial benefits from age 50 onwards on early retirement from the company.

If you are classed as a 'post-1989 member' of an executive pension plan you will be entitled to a pension of two-thirds of your final (capped) remuneration from age 50 onwards if you have completed 20 years' service by that date, so that if funds are available, an executive pension plan could provide maximum benefits from an early age. However, advance funding by the employer is not permitted in these circumstances; contributions may only be paid into the executive pension plan to provide the maximum benefits at age 60 but in the event of immediate early retirement at age 50 the short-fall may be provided by means of a one-off contribution into the plan at that time or in the case of a large group occupational scheme the required amount to provide the maximum pension could be drawn from the fund.

(8) As maximum benefits are related to 'final remuneration' which is usually based on the average of the best three consecutive years' remuneration in the last 12 years before retirement (whether normal retirement or early retirement), ensure that you pay yourself remuneration at higher levels for at least three consecutive years in the period. These three consecutive years do not necessarily have to be the *last* three: for example, they may be the levels of remuneration in the 12, 11 and 10 years prior to retirement increased in line with the Retail Prices Index, up to retirement.

(9) If you are classed as a pre-1987 member for an executive pension plan, it is possible to fund purely for the tax-free lump sum of 1.5 times final remuneration if you can complete 20 years' service: on reaching normal retirement date (ideally age 60 for the reasons set out above) the whole of the pension fund can be taken in the form of a tax-free lump sum but you can continue working for the company. There is no necessity to retire, but you cannot receive any further lump sum retirement benefits, and any death benefits will have to be calculated as if you had retired before your death. Pre-1987 membership is particularly valuable because it is possible to fund for a two-thirds pension over ten years rather than 20 years under post-1987 membership.

(10) If the remuneration which you draw from the company is less than the upper earnings limit (£26,000 in 1999/2000), the 'tax' saving by taking a lower salary is not just the basic rate of income tax but also the saving in national insurance contributions.

Example 15.1

Current situation

Director draws remuneration of £23,000

Alternative

Director draws reduced remuneration of £20,000

Company pays £3,000 to an executive pension plan.

Personal tax saving	=	£690 (23% of £3,000)
Personal NIC saving	=	£300 (10% of £3,000)
Company's NIC saving	=	£366 (12.2% of £3,000)
		£1,356

Thus £3,000 is invested at a net cost of £1,644 (£3,000 − £1,356 saving).

(11) Because of the effect of compound interest, it is the early years' pension contributions which generate most of the pension fund as the following examples show, so that provided profits permit, it is preferable to pay contributions in the early years rather than waiting until retirement approaches:

(a) A director pays contributions of £3,000 per annum for ten years between ages 40 and 50 and builds up a fund of £87,000 at age 60, assuming 7 per cent growth before charges.

(b) Another director pays contributions of £1,500 per annum between the ages of 40 and 60 and builds up a fund of £65,000 assuming 7 per cent growth before charges.

(12) The pension fund represents an additional source of borrowing: up

to one-half of the pension fund (normally in respect of controlling directors) may be loaned back to the company for a genuine commercial purpose. This type of loan can be a useful addition to short-term bank loans, although it will normally be limited to a maximum term of five years.

(13) Personal loans to the director can be arranged alongside pension plans. Banks and building societies are prepared to lend on an interest only basis, long term, usually on the security of property with capital being repaid at retirement. The tax-free lump sum which emerges from the pension fund has been built up in a tax-free fund and tax relief has been given on the pension contributions so this represents an extremely tax efficient way of repaying a mortgage (see Chapter 17).

(14) Where pension fund contributions are paid out of company profits, which lie between £300,000 and £1,500,000, tax relief is obtained at marginal rates. The rates of corporation tax for 1999/2000 have been set at the following levels:

Over £1,500,000	30%
Up to £300,000	20%
Marginal rate	32.5%

(15) If you own a property, for example, a commercial property which is used by your company, resist the temptation to transfer it to a self-administered pension fund which you may set up. Apart from incurring a possible CGT charge on the disposal of the asset, and conveyancing costs and stamp duty, you will be converting a capital asset over which you have personal control into earned income. When the trustees of the self-administered scheme sell the property it will be paid to you largely in the form of earned income with only a proportion of the total pension fund assets being paid to you in the form of tax-free cash. In practice, it is now only possible to transfer a personally owned property to a self-administered pension fund via a third party which must hold it for three years.

(16) You may consider taking dividends from your company, rather than salary, avoiding national insurance contributions. The disadvantages in taking this course of action are:

(a) by not taking salary, you will not be able to pay pension contributions;

(b) any periods of service with the company which were not salaried cannot generally be pensioned at a later date;

(c) State Earnings Related Pension may be lost;

(d) the payment of a dividend by the company may form a base for valuing the company and this may have an adverse effect on future inheritance tax;

(e) if the company is paying corporation tax at other than the 'small companies rate' (ie it has taxable profits over £300,000) the saving in national insurance contributions may be balanced by higher corporation tax (because dividends, unlike salary, are not tax deductible). Thus, there would be no financial advantage in taking dividends.

The following table shows a comparison of effective tax rates using £10,000 of profits to provide benefits for a director. In the case of the last column the figures show, for simplicity, that one-half of the £10,000 available profits are paid into an executive pension plan.

Table 15.1

	Salary	Dividend (Corp Tax at 20%)	Dividend (Corp Tax at 32.5%)	Salary plus Executive Pension Plan
Company outlay	£10,000	£10,000	£10,000	£10,000
Salary	(£8,913)	–	–	(£4,456)
NIC	(£1,087)	–	–	(£544)
Executive pension plan	–	–	–	(£5,000)
Taxable profits	Nil	£10,000	£10,000	Nil
Corporation tax	Nil	(£2,000)	(£3,250)	Nil
Dividend	Nil	(£8,000)	(£6,750)	–
Gross dividend including tax credit (100/90 of dividend)	–	£8,889)	(£7,500)	–
Director's income (gross)	£8,913	£8,889	£7,500	£4,456
Income tax at, say, 40%*	(£3,565)	(£2,889)	(£2,438)	(£1,782)
Balance of income tax	–	(£2,000)	(£1,688)	(£1,782)
Company's NIC	(£1,087)	Nil	Nil	(£544)
Tax and NIC	£4,652	£4,000	£4,938	£2,326
Effective 'tax' rate	46.52%	40.0%	49.38%	23.26%

*Higher rate income tax on dividends is at 32.5%

(17) If you are classed as a pre-1987 member or a 1987–89 member you may, on retirement, opt to be treated as a post-1989 member. Although you would be subject to the post-1989 rules relating to the earnings cap, years of service required to achieve maximum benefits and lump sum restrictions, you may still be better off, especially if you are proposing to retire early from age 50 onwards.

15.2 PERSONAL PENSION SCHEMES AND RETIREMENT ANNUITY CONTRACTS: PLANNING HINTS

Contributions do not have to be paid by the end of your accounting period in order to attract tax relief; contributions are relieved in the tax year in which they are paid, or the previous tax year.

Even though you may not have paid contributions in previous years, you can carry forward the unused reliefs for up to six years, and by using the carry back facility you can effectively carry forward unused relief for seven years.

Although you may have retired having sold your business, there may still be scope for paying personal pension scheme contributions and carrying them back one year or, in some circumstances, two years, to a period when you were in business in order to obtain a tax refund.

If on reaching retirement you have sources of capital and/or income, you should exhaust these before drawing on your pension benefits simply because the pension fund does not pay tax and will usually grow faster than your other investments. Arrange to pay contributions into a series of separate personal pension schemes or into one scheme which consists of a number of 'arrangements' or 'contracts' so that you can phase your retirement benefits in stages between the ages of 50 and 75.

To the extent that you defer your benefits, you are deferring an increasing capital sum which, in the event of your death, can be returned to a wide range of beneficiaries free of inheritance tax (provided the policy is written under a suitable trust).

If you are considering increasing contributions an existing retirement annuity may give a higher proportion of the fund in the form of a tax-free lump sum (see Chapter 14). However, the retirement annuity has to be sufficiently flexible to take increases in contributions.

Consider making use of personal loans alongside existing retirement annuities and personal pension schemes (see Chapter 17).

The life assurance benefits under the retirement annuity and personal pension scheme legislation can provide substantial amounts free of inheritance tax, provided the policy is written under a suitable trust. The contributions attract tax relief up to the highest rate on earned income, whereas ordinary life assurance policies taken out since March 1984 do not attract tax relief. This type of policy can be used to provide life cover for your family and also business associates, for example, co-partners.

By taking advantage of the ability to carry forward unused relief from previous years you can reduce current tax liability substantially. For example, you may carry forward unused relief from previous years when you were paying tax at lower rates to the current year when you may be paying tax at higher rates.

If you are already paying maximum contributions for yourself and you employ your spouse, you should set up an executive pension plan for your spouse: the contributions that you may pay to an approved pension scheme of that nature are generally much higher than the contributions that you could pay to your own personal pension scheme or retirement annuity contract (see Chapter 14). Typically these plans are set up for working wives. If your wife works in your business, you can pay her a salary which will be a deductible expense provided, of course, that her employment can be justified. Traditionally, the level of remuneration paid to the wife of a partner will be set at a figure which is below the lower earnings limit (and therefore not be subject to national insurance contributions) and also lower than the personal allowance (and not taxable in her hands, provided she does not have other income).

Example 15.2

Current situation	
Taxable earnings (top slice)	£10,000
23% tax	2,300
Net	7,700
Revised situation	
Taxable earnings	£10,000
Wife's salary £3,431	
Pension plan contribution £1,025	4,456
Taxable earnings	5,544
23% tax	1,275
Husband's net income	4,269
Add back wife's salary	3,431
Total net income	7,700

The pension plan has been set up for the individual's wife at no reduction in net spendable income.

The above example has an added advantage for the sole proprietor or partner in that as profits have been reduced by £4,156, this may also have the effect of reducing the employer's Class 4 national insurance contributions (6 per cent of profits between £7,530 and £26,000). When the benefits are taken from the executive pension plan at retirement, they will be taxable as earned income but effectively tax free as the wife's earned income relief continues in retirement and can be set against the wife's pension.

16

LEAVING SERVICE BENEFITS

16.1 PRESERVATION OF BENEFITS

Much of the publicity relating to pension schemes over the past few years has related to the treatment of members who change their jobs. Until 1975, many pension schemes provided nothing for the job mover whether he was dismissed for misconduct, was made redundant or left of his own accord.

The Social Security Act 1973 altered the benefits of early leavers considerably with effect from 6 April 1975. Schemes had to provide benefits at or after normal retirement age for scheme members who attained age 26 and who left service having completed five years of scheme membership. The Social Security Act 1985 removed the age 26 qualification. The Social Security Act 1986 reduced the service qualification to two years from 6 April 1988 and provided for 5 per cent revaluation of that part of the early leaver's preserved pension (from a final salary scheme) which related to service after 1 January 1985 in respect of early leavers after 1 January 1986.

The Social Security Act 1990 extended this requirement to revalue preserved pensions in respect of *all* service for leavers after 1 January 1991.

The options normally available to the employee are set out below, although some of the options may not be granted either as a result of the preservation requirements under the Act or because the employer's pension scheme does not provide some of the options.

(1) A deferred pension (sometimes known as preserved, paid up or frozen pensions) may be provided, payable when the member reaches normal retirement age, although early and late retirement options will be permitted.
(2) A deferred annuity may be purchased from an insurance company which issues s 32 annuities, sometimes called 'buy-out plans'.
(3) The assignment of an employee's individual 'earmarked' pension policy to the scheme of a new employer.
(4) A cash transfer of the member's rights under the original scheme to the new employer's pension scheme but not via the member.

(5) A cash transfer of the member's rights under the original scheme to a personal pension scheme.

(6) A refund to the employee of his contributions to the pension scheme.

(7) The assignment by the trustees of the original scheme of an employee's individual pension policy to the employee personally, subject to the provisions of the original scheme. It may be possible for the policy to be written in trust, thereby enabling the proceeds to be paid without attracting a charge to inheritance tax.

(8) Again, in the case of an individual policy scheme, the policy may continue to be held by the trustees and will participate in any future growth. If the original trust deed allows, it may be possible for separate trustees to be appointed to hold the leaver's individual policy.

16.2 DEFERRED PENSIONS

A deferred pension is generally limited to a proportion of the employee's total final remuneration at the date of leaving his employment. For pre-1987 members and 1987–89 members the maximum proportion under Revenue limits is two-thirds of the fraction obtained by taking the number of actual years of service under the number of potential service which the employee could have achieved at normal retirement age.

Example 16.1

An employee aged 45 who is a pre-1987 member leaves the service of a company having completed 20 years' service. His salary on leaving is £22,000. He was a member of a scheme providing a pension of $\frac{1}{60}$ of his final salary for each year of service at age 65. His deferred pension payable from age 65 will be £7,333, ie $\frac{20}{60}$ of £22,000, subject to statutory revaluation which is generally 5 per cent (see below). His maximum deferred pension is:

$$\text{Total remuneration} \times \frac{\text{Actual service to date of leaving}}{\text{Potential service to age 65}} \times \frac{2}{3} = \text{Deferred pension}$$

The deferred pension must be revalued in line with the cost of living between the date of leaving and normal retirement age, subject to a maximum of 5 per cent per annum. Assuming the deferred pension of £7,333 is revalued at 5 per cent per annum it will amount to £19,456 per annum at age 65.

For post-1989 members the maximum proportion is one-thirtieth of total remuneration for each year of service to the date of leaving, subject to an overall limit of two-thirds of salary.

Example 16.2

> An employee aged 45 who is a post-1989 member leaves the service of a company having completed 15 years' service. His salary is £30,000. He was a member of a scheme providing a pension of $\frac{1}{60}$ of his final salary for each year of service at age 65. The deferred pension from age 65 will be £7,500 per annum, ie $\frac{15}{60}$ of £30,000, subject to statutory revaluation. His maximum deferred pension is:
>
> Total remuneration × actual service to date of leaving × $\frac{1}{30}$.
>
> Again, this maximum pension must be increased in line with the cost of living between the date of leaving and normal retirement date.

Defined benefit company pension schemes which are contracted out of the earnings-related part of the state scheme must protect against inflation the guaranteed minimum pension (the proportion of the deferred pension which would have been provided by the state if the employee had not been contracted out) which will have accrued up to 5 April 1997.

Part of the pension may be exchanged for a lump sum on reaching normal retirement date. The maximum lump sum is calculated on the same basis as for early retirement (see Chapter 4).

In the case of a former employee dying before reaching normal retirement age, the scheme may provide benefits for a widow or dependants, in which case maximum benefits are calculated as on death in service.

16.3 PROBLEMS OF THE EARLY LEAVER

16.3.1 Frozen pensions

For a long time anyone who left their job – and their final salary scheme – before reaching pension age lost out on their pension benefits because their pension was frozen at the date of leaving (except to the limited extent of revaluation of the GMP under a contracted-out scheme).

The Social Security Act 1985 provided protection for the early leaver:

(1) The proportion of a deferred pension which relates to pensionable service with the employer from 1 January 1985 must be revalued in line with increases in the Retail Prices Index or 5 per cent per annum if lower. This resulted in little immediate improvement in early leavers' benefits in the short term as no account was taken in respect of service with the employer before January 1985. (With some schemes, particularly large ones where the trustees wish to use up

surpluses, the revaluation was applied in respect of service before January 1985.)

(2) The Social Security Act 1990 has now extended this requirement so that the revaluation must apply to all service for any scheme member leaving the employer's service on or after 1 January 1991.

The following example shows the effect of the Social Security Acts in providing for revaluation at 5 per cent per annum. It assumes that an individual has four jobs, each providing a pension of one-eightieth of final salary for each year of service. Without revaluation the combined total pensions would be £20,080 per annum, approximately less than one-half of the pension which would have been payable had the employee remained in the first job for 40 years, ie $^{40}\!/_{80}$ of £87,548 = £43,774 per annum. With revaluation, the pension is increased by around one-third.

Example 16.3

	Age on leaving	Salary on leaving		Frozen pension entitlement	Pensions revalued at 4% pa
Job 1	35	£10,000	$^{10}\!/_{80}$	= £1,250	£4,054
Job 2	45	£17,081	$^{10}\!/_{80}$	= £2,135	£4,678
Job 3	55	£29,177	$^{10}\!/_{80}$	= £3,647	£5,398
Job 4	65	£49,839	$^{10}\!/_{80}$	= £6,229	£10,944
				£13,261	£25,074

Note It has been assumed that salary increases at 5.5% per annum and that the whole of the deferred pension is revalued at 4% per annum.

16.4 SECTION 32 ANNUITY

Rather than providing deferred benefits under the scheme as above, the trustees may purchase from an insurance company chosen by the member a deferred annuity in the name of an employee. FA 1981, s 32 (now ICTA 1988, s 591(g)) enabled such annuities to be purchased: this may be an attractive option to pension scheme trustees and those leaving or thinking of leaving an employer.

The maximum pension and the maximum tax-free cash lump sum permitted by the Revenue will be endorsed on the policy issued by the insurer. These benefits may be increased between the date on which the transfer is made into the s 32 annuity policy and retirement in line with increases in the retail prices index subject to a maximum of 5 per cent per annum. The projected benefits payable under such a policy should be carefully examined and compared with the alternative deferred pension.

A s 32 policy effected without the consent of the member and following the provision of the required actuarial certification under The Occupational Pension Schemes (Preservation of Benefit) Regulations 1991 has to contain an option allowing the member to surrender or assign the policy in exchange for another s 32 policy, eg of the member's own choice, a personal pension scheme or an occupational pension scheme.

The s 32 annuity itself may include an open-market option and power to surrender the policy and transfer it to a new scheme including a personal pension scheme. The GMP within the s 32 policy may also be transferred to a new scheme.

Benefits (pension *and* tax-free cash lump sum) may be taken from age 50 onwards, but not later than age 75, regardless of whether or not the policyholder has retired or is continuing to work. These benefits may include the GMP element.

On death, before taking benefits, the policy may provide for a lump sum to be paid equal to four times remuneration on leaving the previous scheme, up to the date of death.

16.5 PERSONAL PENSION PLANS

An individual leaving his employer's scheme also has the option of transferring his benefits into a personal pension plan. Although a personal pension plan is generally only available to the self-employed or to those in non-pensionable employment there is an exception: an individual who is in a pension scheme can take out a personal pension plan which is funded by the transfer from another scheme.

This new option may be more flexible than the s 32 annuity described above because the transferred benefits will be subject to the personal pension legislation allowing ongoing contributions to be paid by the member if he has net relevant earnings and also any subsequent transfer payments. If the individual was a member of a contracted-out defined benefit scheme the transfer will include a guaranteed minimum pension (GMP). On transferring into the personal pension there will no longer be any need for the guarantee to continue, but 'protected rights' will have to be provided instead. Protected rights benefits may be paid after the member reaches the age of 60, although the non-protected rights benefits may be paid in stages between the ages of 50 and 75 regardless of whether or not the policyholder has retired or is continuing to work.

On death before taking benefits, one-quarter of the plan's value may be paid as a lump sum with the balance being paid as a widow(er)'s pension. If there is no dependant, the whole amount may be paid as a lump sum.

However, before benefits may be transferred to a personal pension scheme the trustees of the employer's scheme must provide certificates as required in Inland Revenue regulations, as follows:

A controlling director's/high earner's certificate

This certificate is required only in respect of a person who is a controlling director, or was a higher earner (defined as earning £90,600 or more in 1999/2000), at any time during the ten years prior to the date in which the transfer value is applied for. In this instance a certificate cannot be provided, and the transfer to a personal pension may not proceed unless the transfer value is less than the figure produced by the somewhat arbitrary formula set out in reg 6(3) of the Personal Pension Schemes (Transfer Payment) Regulations 1988, as amended.

A cash sum certificate

This certificate applies only in respect of a person who is a controlling director or high earner (as defined above) or who is over age 45 at the date that a right to a transfer value is applied for. This certificate must state the maximum cash lump sum payable under the transferring scheme at normal retirement date based on salary and service at the date of leaving.

The maximum cash sum that may be paid from a personal pension scheme arising from the transfer payment is the lesser of 25 per cent of the accumulated fund (excluding any 'protected rights' if the personal pension plan was effected on or after 27 July 1989) or the certified cash amount increased in line with increases in the Cost of Living Index between the date of transfer and the date benefits are taken under the personal pension scheme.

For persons under age 45 who are not controlling directors or high earners there may be opportunities to transfer into a personal pension scheme in order to increase the amount of cash lump sum at retirement.

16.5.1 Assignment of an individual policy under an executive pension plan

Where benefits are secured by an individual earmarked policy, it is possible for that policy to be transferred, without surrendering it, to a compatible scheme of a new employer. When a policy is assigned in this way, the surrender penalties often associated with the following option may be avoided.

16.5.2 Transfer values

When an employee leaves one employment to take up another employment, his benefits under the original pension scheme may be transferred to the new pension scheme (if it meets standards laid down by the DSS and Inland Revenue) provided the new employer scheme is willing and able to accept a transfer value. Alternatively the trustees may pay the transfer value to an insurance company of the employee's choice to buy a s 32 annuity or to a personal pension scheme as described above, or to a combination of both. However, it is not possible for the transfer value to be paid direct to the individual.

16.5.3 Right to a transfer value

With effect from 6 April 1997, the provisions of the Pensions Act 1995 extend the right to request a transfer value to employees who left an employer's pension scheme before 1 January 1986. Before 6 April 1997, only those employees who left their employer's scheme after 1 January 1986 have a right in law to a transfer value payment, although in fact most schemes will pay a transfer value to an approved scheme.

The Pensions Act also requires final salary schemes to guarantee transfer values for three months, and reduces the period within which the transfer value must be paid by the trustees to six months. Failure to comply with these provisions of the Pensions Act may result in the imposition of monetary penalties on the trustees and/or administrators by the Occupational Pensions Regulatory Authority (OPRA).

16.5.4 Calculation of transfer values

A transfer value is the current cost of providing the benefits to which the employee was entitled under his former scheme and is based on the value of the benefits on the date the transfer value is requested. The transfer value must take into account any increases, statutory or otherwise, that would apply to the benefits if they were to continue to be preserved within the scheme.

In calculating transfer value, trustees must have regard to a Guidance Note published by the Institute of Actuaries (reference GN11) which ensures that members of defined benefit schemes exercising a right to a transfer value can be assured that it reflects the reasonable expectation of benefits otherwise available on withdrawal and ensures that incoming and outgoing transfers are dealt with consistently. The assumptions used in the calculations, however, may be overridden by the transfer regulations which affect controlling directors and high earners, as described above.

Transfer values are a constant source of difficulty as the amount which is transferred from one scheme to another depends on various assumptions, for example:

(1) whether the former scheme provides benefits on a final salary or money purchase basis;

(2) whether the deferred pension otherwise available in the former scheme will be increased between the date of leaving and retirement;

(3) if a transferred payment is regarded by the receiving scheme as purchasing an additional number of years' service (added years), it is usually found that the purchased years will be less than the years of service actually obtained by the employee in the former pension scheme.

The major boost to improved transferability was provided by the liberalising provisions of the Social Security Act 1985.

In some of the large private sector companies, as well as for those in the public sector there is a special basis for calculating higher transfer values between schemes which are members of the 'transfer club'. This ensures that employees moving between member organisations lose less on transferring: in some cases, pensionable service is deemed to continue without a break.

Another factor which may cause a member to delay taking a transfer value is where there is a surplus of scheme assets over liabilities, part of which will be required under the provisions of the Pensions Act 1995 to increase both pensions in payment and future pensions in line with increases in the cost of living, or 5 per cent per annum, if lower. A preserved pension which currently does not increase in payment but which is later improved as a result of the distribution of a surplus will have an increased transfer value. (In practice, however, many defined benefits schemes already provide for increases in payment on part of the pension, and indeed the GMP element already has to increase at 3 per cent per annum.)

16.6 REFUNDS OF MEMBERS' CONTRIBUTIONS

Currently, no refund can normally be made if the employee has completed two years' membership of a pension scheme. 1991 Regulations on preservation removed the option to take a refund of pre-April 1975 contributions as part of short-service benefits. This option had previously been available to early leavers whose pensionable service ended on or after 28 February 1991. Regulations permit trustees to buy out benefits for leavers who have completed between two and five years' membership.

Any refund may include interest on the contributions. If a refund of contributions is made to a former employee (except in the event of his death), the administrator of the scheme has to account to the Revenue for tax at the rate of 20 per cent on the contributions (including any interest) repaid to the member.

16.7 WHICH SCHEMES MAY PERMIT A TRANSFER VALUE?

Table 16.1

Previous scheme		New scheme			
	PPP	Occ	Occ	R Ann	FSAVCs
s 32					
		MP	FS		
Personal Pension Plan (PPP)	✓	✓	✓	✗	✓	✗
Occupational-Money Purchase (Occ Mp)	✓	✓	✓	✗	✗	✓
Occupational-Final Salary (Occ FS)	✓	✓	✓	✗	✗	✓
Retirement Annuity[1] (R Ann)	✓	✓	✓	✓	✗	✗
FSAVCs	✓	✓	✓	✗	✓	✓
Section 32[2]	✓	✓	✓	✗	✗	✓

1 A transfer may only be taken from a retirement annuity by endorsing the policy accordingly.
2 A transfer from a s 32 is only allowed if the previous scheme rules permit. Transfers out of s 32s established before October 1983 are not permitted.

16.8 EFFECTS OF SOCIAL SECURITY ACT 1990

The Social Security Act 1990 made a number of significant changes to occupational pension schemes, including:

(1) Early leavers are entitled to revaluation of all of their deferred pensions, including the portion which accrued before 1 January 1985.
(2) Self-investment by pension schemes is limited to 5 per cent of the scheme assets (see Chapter 9).
(3) A number of measures were introduced to help the individual member: the setting up of a 'Pensions Ombudsman', the development of the role of the Occupational Pensions Advisory Service (OPAS) in providing a conciliation service between scheme members and scheme trustees, and the establishment of a register of occupational and personal pension schemes to provide a tracing service for scheme members.

16.8.1 Deferred pensions

Prior to the Social Security Act 1990, the preserved pension of an early leaver from a defined benefit occupational scheme was subject to limited revaluation: the amount of preserved pension accruing in respect of pensionable service from 1 January 1985 would be subject to increases at the lesser of increase in the Retail Prices Index and 5 per cent per annum. The Social Security Act 1990 extended the compulsory revaluation of the preserved pension in respect of pensionable service accrued up to 31 December 1984 from 1 January 1991.

16.9 GOLDEN HANDSHAKES

Following the issue of a Statement of Practice by the Inland Revenue in October 1991, care must be taken to distinguish between *ex gratia* payments on retirement (or death) and 'golden handshakes' made under s 148 as described below.

If there is an 'arrangement' to make an *ex gratia* payment to a director or employee, and the recipient is not a member of a tax approved scheme of the employer, the payment may receive tax approval from the Revenue and be treated as a relevant benefit. If these conditions are not met, then the payment may be treated as emerging from an unapproved pension scheme.

16.9.1 Application of the 'golden handshake' legislation

Section 148 only applies to payments 'not otherwise chargeable to tax'. Consequently, a payment made under the terms of a contract of service or in respect of services (past, present or future) will be taxable as an emolument under the normal Schedule E rules. It is still, therefore, as important as it was before FA 1981 to ensure that the documentation of the golden handshake is carefully worded so as to avoid reference to past services.

Statutory redundancy payments are taxed under the golden handshake provisions rather than the provisions of Schedule E by ICTA 1988, s 572. The Revenue has also agreed that non-statutory redundancy payments will be taxed in the same way provided there is a 'genuine' redundancy. The Revenue will be satisfied that the redundancy is genuine if:

(1) the payment is only made on account of redundancy as defined in the Employment Protection (Consolidation) Act 1980, s 81;

(2) the employee has been in continuous service for at least two years;

(3) the payments are not made to selected employees only; and

(4) the payments are not excessively large in relation to the employee's earnings and length of service.

On the other hand, certain payments which are not taxable under Schedule E are also exempted from the charge in s 187. The main examples of these payments are:

(1) payments made on the employee's death or on the termination of his employment on account of injury or disability;

(2) considerations for certain restrictive covenants;

(3) payments made under certain approved pension schemes in the United Kingdom and abroad; and

(4) certain payments made by Royal Warrant or Order in Council to members of the forces.

The amount of the redundancy payment which is exempt from taxes in the hands of the employee is £30,000.

16.9.2 Close companies

Two problems arise in connection with golden handshakes made to directors who are shareholders of close companies or to members of their families:

(1) the non-tax deductibility of the payment from the company's point of view; and

(2) the possibility of the payment being treated as a distribution.

Unlike contributions to an exempt approved scheme, golden handshake payments will only be allowed as a deduction for the purposes of Schedule D if it is allowed by the Inspector in accordance with the normal 'wholly and exclusively' rule. It may be that in normal 'arm's length' cases that payment will not be allowed because, for example, the payment is made in conjunction with a cessation of trade or winding-up. In the case of a close company, however, it must be very likely that the payment will be disallowed as being a payment made for the personal benefit of the director or his family.

Potentially more serious, however, is the possibility of the payment being treated as a distribution under ICTA 1988, s 209. It seems that in cases where the distributor holds nearly 100 per cent of the share capital it will very likely be treated as a distribution.

On the other hand there is a good chance of the question of a distribution not being raised if:

(1) the individual has put in genuine service of the quality and length

that would have recommended him for a severance payment were he an arm's length employee;

(2) the shareholding is modest (say around 5 per cent); and

(3) the amount involved is modest (up to £25,000).

Where, as will be common, the case falls between these two extremes, all that can be said is that the payment should not be made while the recipient is still a controlling shareholder and that if de-control is possible, the higher the former shareholding and the more recently de-control took place, the more likely it is that the inspector will treat it as a distribution.

16.9.3 Pensioning 'golden handshakes'

If the employment from which the golden handshake is payable is already pensionable, the payment may not be included in remuneration for the purposes of providing additional retirement benefits through augmentation or voluntary contributions by the employee.

If the employment was not pensionable the individual will be entitled to contribute to a personal pension scheme. However, the golden handshake payment must be excluded from earnings for this purpose. No such restriction applies if the individual has a retirement annuity contract (which must have been in existence on 29 July 1988); in these circumstances the taxable element golden handshake payment may be included in the definition of 'net relevant earnings'.

16.10 'HANCOCKS'

A Hancock annuity is now little more than a way of describing the outright purchase of an immediate or deferred annuity for an employee at the time of or after his retirement, or for the widow(er) or dependant of a deceased employee.

The name is derived from the case of *Hancock v General Reversionary and Investment Co Ltd* (1918) TTC 358 which established that the payment by an employer to purchase an annuity for an employee on his retirement is an allowable expense in the year in which it is paid and is not regarded as additional remuneration to the employee.

The only aspect in which the Hancock precedent may provide a better position than the legislation now provides is that it will not require relief on the payment to be spread forward if it is more than the employer's ordinary annual contribution (see Chapter 6). In such cases, it is understood that the Revenue will direct that the scheme be approved as an exempt approved scheme if it feels that the relief should be spread forward, so the advantage is more apparent than real.

The Hancock procedure is now the only method of providing a pension for an employee or director who has attained age 75. Since the Finance Act 1989 it has not been possible to accumulate funds within an approved pension scheme and provide benefits after age 75, and under personal pension schemes and retirement annuities benefits must be taken by age 75.

17

PENSION LOANS

17.1 INTRODUCTION

Most banks and building societies accept pensions as another means of repaying loan capital. Although the traditional endowment and repayment mortgages are still the most popular, pensions can also be appropriate, especially for people who wish to build up pension benefits at the same time as repaying a mortgage.

The ingredients of a pension loan are as follows:

(1) The individual starts a pension plan which has the following favourable tax advantages:
   (a) income tax is saved on contributions at the highest rate paid on earned income,
   (b) the pension fund accumulates free of UK income and capital gains taxes; however, the fund manager cannot reclaim tax paid on UK and some overseas dividends, and
   (c) at retirement age a substantial part of the benefits may be taken in the form of a tax-free lump sum.
(2) A bank or building society lends money to an individual on a basis similar to an endowment mortgage – interest is paid on the loan throughout the term and the capital is repaid at the end of the term. The lending institution will normally take as security a property owned, or about to be bought, by the individual.
(3) The tax-free lump sum emerging from the pension plan may be used to repay the loan. In this way the borrower has effectively obtained full tax relief on his capital repayments as opposed to the usual method of paying them out of net income.
(4) The balance of the pension plan provides a lifetime income.
(5) The borrower will probably effect a life assurance policy to cover the loan repayment in the event of his death before retirement. In the case of a person who has an existing retirement annuity policy or personal pension scheme the associated life assurance benefit which may be provided is an attractive option because tax relief at the

highest rate on earned income is granted and because the policy can be assigned to the lender.

(6) However, pensions legislation does not permit a pension plan to be used as security for a loan. The policy provisions or pension scheme rules will state that the plan must not be assigned by the member to a lender.

17.2 COMPARING COSTS

Although the contributions for the pension plan may be considerably higher than those for a repayment mortgage or a low-cost endowment assurance, tax relief will narrow the gap between the costs of the different methods. The higher the tax bracket of the borrower, the more cost effective the pension mortgage becomes.

It can be argued by the detractors of pension-related loans that as the cash lump sum under a pension plan is used to pay off the capital at the end of the term, the individual's retirement benefits are being reduced. However, the tax advantages of pension schemes will result in many people enjoying an additional income in retirement, by default. An individual who is currently contributing £100 per month to an endowment insurance policy taken out since March 1984 does not enjoy any tax relief. An equivalent net contribution to a pension plan will result immediately in approximately £130 per month being invested, assuming the individual is a 23 per cent taxpayer. When the benefits of tax-free growth within the pension fund are added, the pension fund at the end of the term would be significantly higher than the endowment fund. The pension fund may be taken partly in the form of a tax-free lump sum, with the balance being used to provide an income.

The only circumstances in which a pension-related mortgage might be said to reduce retirement income would be where an individual arranges a loan on an interest-only basis with the intention of using the cash lump sum from an *existing* pension plan to repay the capital but without making any additional pension provision, for example through additional voluntary contributions. However, in practice most pension-related loans are arranged on the basis that pension contributions will be increased, or started under a new plan.

A pension-related loan alongside a retirement annuity contract or personal pension scheme must result in income in retirement even after the loan is repaid. The reason for this is that it is not possible to fund solely for a cash lump sum.

Under a retirement annuity the amount which may be taken in a form of a cash lump sum is three times the annuity which remains after the cash has been taken, and therefore varies according to retirement age and sex. On retirement at age 65 a male could expect to receive approximately 26 per cent in the form of a cash lump sum, on annuity rates prevailing in August 1999 (for other ages see Chapter 14). This means that if the cash lump sum amounts to £30,000 (sufficient to repay the loan), the total fund would be £115,400.

Under a personal pension scheme one-quarter can be taken in the form of a cash lump sum, regardless of age and sex. This means that if the cash lump sum amounts to £30,000 (ie, is of sufficient size to repay the loan), the total fund would be £120,000 and the cost would be 4 per cent higher than that under a retirement annuity contract. It will be seen, therefore, that an existing retirement annuity, because it is likely to generate more cash lump sum than a personal pension scheme, requires less outlay if the cash lump sum is to be used to repay a loan. In either case, if the cash lump sum is used to repay a loan the bulk of the fund remains to provide an income.

Some personal pension schemes can be particularly useful as they can provide more than one-quarter in the form of a tax-free lump sum: ones taken out before 27 July 1989 and used for contracting out can include in the overall fund of which one-quarter is taken the fund built up by DSS contributions – the 'protected rights fund'.

For example: assume that the protected rights fund amounts to £100,000, and the fund generated by personal contributions amounts to £33,333. One-quarter of the total fund amounts to £33,333. The protected rights fund of £100,000 is not being eroded and the additional contributions generate tax-free cash.

If the cash lump sum of £33,333 were to be used to repay a loan the outlay will be much lower than in the examples in the previous paragraphs because the individual does not have to fund for the pension benefits in addition – they have been financed by contributions paid into the plan by government.

In summary, existing retirement annuity contracts, and personal pension schemes used for contracting-out purposes but to which additional contributions are paid, are likely to be tax-efficient methods of repaying loans at retirement, but certain personal pension schemes taken out before 27 July 1989 are particularly useful.

17.3 INTEREST-ONLY LOANS

Traditionally, loans of all descriptions have been arranged on the basis that there is a fixed term, although there is often provision to extend the term of the loan. From the point of view of tax planning, however, it may be worthwhile to extend the loan indefinitely, especially if the loan is one on which interest payments qualify for tax relief (although the MIRAS system comes to an end in April 2000, so this advantage will be short-lived). Also, having to repay a significant amount of capital at the end of the term may cause cash flow problems for the borrower, even though he might have built up sufficient monies to repay the loan, by means of personal investments including pension funding.

At one time lenders were only prepared to advance monies on an interest only basis to individuals whose pension benefits would emerge from an individual policy such as an executive pension plan: from the point of view of the lender the benefits of an ear-marked policy could be easily identified. However, many lenders are now prepared to arrange interest only loans for individuals whose pension benefits will emerge from group pension schemes (where benefits are not usually ear-marked individually but form part of a common trust fund). The lender will usually require a copy of the benefit statement which is provided for the scheme member by trustees. This statement should confirm that the amount of cash lump sum which is likely to emerge is at least equal to the required loan. The lender may want to see future statements to confirm that the individual is still a member of the pension scheme.

17.4 LOAN PURPOSES

If the loan is for a qualifying purpose, tax relief will be obtained on the interest provided interest is paid. Examples of qualifying loans are as follows:

(1) to purchase a main residence in the United Kingdom (the maximum loan for tax relief purposes is currently £30,000, but reduces to zero in April 2000);
(2) to purchase a share or interest in a partnership;
(3) to contribute capital or loan monies for the use of a partnership;
(4) to purchase shares in a closed company or to make loans to such a company for business purposes;
(5) to purchase plant and machinery for use in a partnership or business.

If the loan is for business purposes, then the interest is deductible from business profits under ICTA 1988, s 74. If, however, the loan is taken for the purpose of a main residence or is taken by an individual for putting into a partnership or close company the interest is offset against personal income and not business profits. To the extent that interest is deductible from business profits, the net relevant earnings on which an individual can contribute to a retirement annuity will be reduced. Personal interest, however, does not reduce net relevant earnings.

17.5 PERSONAL LOANS – DIFFERENCES UNDER EXECUTIVE PENSION PLANS FOR DIRECTORS

The preceding paragraphs related generally to loans which may be obtained by an individual who has effected a retirement annuity policy or personal pension scheme. A director, or executive, however, who is contributing to an approved retirement benefit scheme – an executive pension plan – and who is proposing to use the tax-free cash emerging from his fund to repay loan capital, will have these additional factors to consider.

(1) If the plan is arranged for the purpose of getting a loan, the Companies Act 1985, s 330 may be infringed. This section specifically prohibits companies making or procuring loans to directors. To avoid infringing the Companies Act and to avoid jeopardising approval of the pension plan by the Revenue, the setting up of the plan should not be dependent upon obtaining a loan. The sole purpose of the pension plan should be the provision of 'relevant benefits'.

(2) Any collateral life assurance will have to be effected by an ordinary life assurance policy; the life assurance associated with an executive pension plan will not be satisfactory because it cannot be assigned to a lender and in any case, the destination of the benefits on the death of the member is at the discretion of the trustees.

(3) It is not possible to have a waiver of premium benefit in respect of any contributions paid into an executive pension plan so that in the event of sickness or disability contributions to the plan (in particular those payable personally by the member) are likely to stop or reduce. Consequently the fund at retirement will be lower.

17.6 LIMITATIONS OF PENSION LOANS

The mortgage market generally now provides wider choice in relation to interest rates (eg variable rate, fixed rate, discounts), with 'special offers' encouraging borrowers to change lender. Although this can be attractive from the viewpoint of short-term mortgage payments, the pension plan will still need to be maintained to repay the capital when mortgage payments increase after the initial benefit period.

A change in personal circumstances may result in the need to stop pension contributions (eg redundancy). In this event, the pension plan will not produce the required level of tax-free cash at retirement to pay off the loan. This may mean having to switch to a repayment method for the outstanding loan.

Pension loans linked to executive plans provide tax-free lump sums at retirement based on years of service with the employer and remuneration at retirement. Broken service, restricted service (eg through redundancy) or lower than expected retiring remuneration could result in an insufficient lump sum to pay off the loan.

Critical illness is not permitted under pensions legislation and therefore would have to be provided separately.

Because there is no link between the pension plan and the mortgage, the borrower is responsible for ensuring that the benefits from the pension plan will be sufficient to repay the mortage. The option to repay the mortgage early will be constrained by the pension plan, which usually links early payment of benefits with early retirement.

18

VARIOUS ASPECTS OF EXECUTIVE PENSION PLANS

18.1 INVESTMENT COMPANIES

An investment company is a company the income of which would be treated as investment income for tax purposes if it were the income of an individual. A company which is treated for tax purposes as an investment company cannot set up a pension plan and obtain approval under the Revenue's discretionary power under ICTA 1988, s 591 (see Appendix 4) if the membership includes 20 per cent directors or controlling directors of that employer or directors who while not owning 20 per cent of the shares themselves, or being controlling directors, are members of a family together controlling more than 50 per cent of the shares.

Since controlling directors of investment companies are prohibited from contributing to personal pension schemes (see Chapter 14), this effectively prevents such individuals from making any pension provision except through a scheme approved under ICTA 1988, s 590 (see Appendix 4) which requires the Revenue to approve a scheme if it meets the more stringent conditions of that section. Very few directors would be happy with the benefits which may be provided under that section, and very few life offices are prepared to write s 590 schemes.

The only benefits which can be provided under s 590 are a pension of one-sixtieth of final remuneration for each year of service (part of which may be exchanged for a lump sum which does not exceed three-eighti-eths of final remuneration for each year of service) and a widow's pension which does not exceed two-thirds of a member's pension and is payable only on death in retirement. There is no sliding scale of accelerated accrual, and no death in service benefits are allowed, including a refund of any contributions made by a member. Remuneration which can be pensioned under s 590 is limited, as the Schedule E income which a director can receive from an investment company is usually very low.

There is no Revenue objection to the provision of retirement benefits for employees and non-controlling directors of investment companies.

18.2 SERVICE COMPANIES

Professional firms sometimes establish service companies to provide clerical staff, accommodation and administrative services for the firm, the directors of the company usually being partners in a practice. The question then arises over the possibility of providing the partner who is also a director of the service company with additional pension benefits through an executive pension plan in respect of his Schedule E earnings as a director.

While in principle this is acceptable, the Revenue is not prepared to approve schemes for such directors where the benefits are geared to a level of remuneration exceeding the amount allowed by the local Inspector as a trading expense of the company. The local Inspector will, in turn, generally take the view that the duties which the director performs for the company are minimal and so the remuneration allowable as a trading expense of the company will be correspondingly very small – as his other profit earning activities are in his capacity as partner of a firm. It will be seen that, in most cases, the amount of additional pension which can be provided for a partner/director will be insignificant, although there may of course be exceptions, where the facts of the case warrant them; for example, it may be possible to show as a matter of fact that the main duties of, say, a staff partner related properly to the service company and should be remunerated from the service company.

Once again, there is nothing to prevent service companies from providing pension benefits in the usual way for its employees.

18.3 SPECIAL OCCUPATIONS – RETIREMENT DATES

There are a number of occupations where a reasonable case may be made out for a normal retirement date earlier than the normal range of 60 to 70. Because of the particular characteristics of the occupation, it may be possible for certain jobholders to agree with the Revenue a retirement date in the range 50 to 55, eg airline pilots, advertising executives, money dealers and trawlermen.

However, an earlier normal retirement date is not automatic simply because the individual follows one of these occupations (as is the case with the special occupations for which early retirement dates can be chosen under retirement annuity contracts and personal pension schemes – see Chapter 14) and a case has to be put to the Revenue for each executive pension plan detailing the exact nature of the work.

If the Revenue accepts that a normal retirement date of 50 to 55 is appropriate in a particular case, it will normally insist that benefits have to be taken at normal retirement date and cannot be deferred if the individual works beyond the retirement date, whether in the same or another occupation.

18.4 RETIREMENT DATES BELOW AGE 50

There are also a number of occupations which cannot be continued much beyond the mid-30s and for these the Revenue may agree to much earlier normal retirement dates – even as low as 35. The occupations to which this applies are usually limited to professional sportsmen and women, for example:

> Professional footballers (normal retirement date 35)
> Professional tennis players (normal retirement date 35)
> Professional motor-racing drivers (normal retirement date 40)

If an early retirement date is chosen, severe restrictions will be placed on the benefits, in particular:

(1) the pension is limited to one-sixtieth of final salary for each year of service;
(2) the cash lump sum is limited to three-eightieths of final salary for each year of service;
(3) no early retirement is allowed, except through incapacity;
(4) late retirement is restricted to five years; for example, a footballer still playing in his forties must receive his benefits from the pension plan at age 40;
(5) if the member takes on some other occupation with the same employer, for example a footballer becoming a coach or manager, he must still take his benefits at his normal retirement date.

18.5 INTERNATIONAL ASPECTS OF EXECUTIVE PENSION PLANS

(1) The basic rule is that if an employee is effectively chargeable to UK tax under Schedule E Case I or II, then the employer can provide executive pension plans benefits for him or her.
(2) The benefits of a tax-approved executive pension plan are available to employees who are resident, but not necessarily domiciled, in the United Kingdom, eg the Swiss-domiciled manager of the UK-based agency of a US corporation.

(3) The only exception to the above rule is the provision by a *UK resident employer* of executive pension plan benefits for an employee who is both resident and domiciled outside the United Kingdom, eg the Spanish sales manager of a UK-based company, who is a Spanish national and lives in Spain ordinarily.

18.5.1 Definitions

(1) 'United Kingdom' means England, Scotland, Wales and Northern Ireland – it does not include the Channel Islands, the Isle of Man or the Republic of Ireland.
(2) Domicile refers to the country which is a person's natural home, and for most people would be their country of birth.
(3) Residence for tax purposes is determined by a number of criteria such as the length of time spent in the country during a fiscal year.
(4) Foreign emoluments describes remuneration paid by an employer who is not *resident* in the United Kingdom to an employee who is not domiciled in the United Kingdom. If a UK resident receives foreign emoluments, he will be assessable to tax under Schedule E on their full amount.
(5) An overseas employer is one who is not resident in the United Kingdom for tax purposes and whose trading profits are, if at all, assessable to UK tax only to the extent that they arise from a branch or agency in this country.

18.5.2 Overseas employer with UK-resident employees

The Revenue will tax-approve an executive pension plan established by an overseas employer conditional upon:

(1) the appointment of a UK-resident person as an 'administrator' of the pension plan, who will be responsible for ensuring that Revenue requirements are met. It is usual for the trustee of the executive pension plan to act as the administrator;
(2) an undertaking to exclude from the pension plan UK-domiciled employees who qualify for full income tax relief on account of the length of time spent overseas.

In establishing an executive pension plan, the overseas employer should give critical consideration to whether it is the most suitable vehicle for the particular employee.

(1) For employees who are both UK-resident and UK-domiciled, there is no alternative to a UK tax-approved pension plan.
(2) For employees who are not UK-domiciled, much will depend on

how long they will be resident in the United Kingdom. For highly mobile employees who are unlikely to remain in the United Kingdom sufficiently long to build up a significant benefit, clearly the executive pension plan is not satisfactory as a retirement savings medium.

Other aspects which may affect an overseas employer's consideration of whether to provide retirement benefits through a UK tax-approved pension plan are:

(1) Concern about the obligations, liabilities and expense involved in establishing a UK pension plan, especially where the overseas employer is unfamiliar with UK pensions legislation, and where the business connection is either in its early stages or not intended to be long-term in nature.

(2) The overseas employer may be able to obtain relief in respect of its contributions to the pension plan from its home tax authorities, so that relief will be confined to its UK profits, if any.

(3) The overseas employer may be subject to restrictions which prevent it contracting with a UK insurer or remitting contributions to the United Kingdom. Also the inconvenience of having to comply with accounting requirements under domestic legislation (eg in the United States) covering pensions provisions for employees of overseas subsidiaries may deter overseas employers from establishing UK pension plans.

18.5.3 Offshore plans

Overseas employers with multi-national representation often prefer to adopt a global strategy in relation to retirement provision for overseas employees. They may accordingly establish an offshore plan in a tax-efficient area, such as the Bahamas, or else include their overseas employees in parallel plans to those established for the corporation's home-based employees. The advantages of this strategy are:

(1) Uniform benefits can be provided for all employees regardless of where they are stationed at any time.

(2) The problem of having to comply with local national legislation on retirement provision and social security can be mitigated.

The disadvantages are:

(1) Tax relief may not be available on either the employer's contributions or the fund. Conversely, the employee may be taxed on the employer's contribution paid for his benefits.

(2) Depending on the employee's country of residence at retirement,
    (a) the pension benefit may be subject to double taxation;

(b) the pension may be secured in an unsatisfactory currency;

(c) the emerging benefit may be completely inappropriate. In many countries lump sum benefits on retirement are the norm; elsewhere there are generous state pension benefits giving rise to the problem of over-provision, although the current world-wide tendency is either to reduce these benefits and/or to fund pension liabilities.

18.5.4 Corresponding approval

If it can be shown to the Revenue's satisfaction that a pension plan established offshore for an employee receiving foreign emoluments 'corresponds' to a UK-approved scheme, then tax relief will be permitted both on the employee's contributions and in respect of the employers' contributions to the plan. This means that the benefit structure of the offshore pension plan must be similar to the structure of a pension plan approved under ICTA 1988, s 591. The Revenue is concerned to prevent the encashment of benefits by an employee on leaving service, or in other circumstances before retirement, and may require an undertaking from the plan administrator in that regard.

Employees applying for corresponding approval relief after 23 February 1995 must satisfy additional Revenue requirements in relation to residence of the scheme, etc.

18.5.5 Section 615 plans (known previously as section 218 plans)

A half-way house to a full offshore pension plan, which is operated by some UK-based multi-national corporations for employees who are resident overseas, is a plan established under ICTA 1988, s 615. A s 615 plan enjoys exemption from UK taxation on its investment income and emerging benefits but is otherwise a much less flexible pensions vehicle than a genuine offshore plan established outside the United Kingdom.

18.5.6 Overseas resident employees

With the agreement of the Pension Schemes Office an employee who is resident abroad – perhaps in a succession of different countries and with different employers – may be included as a member of a UK tax-approved scheme for an aggregate period of up to ten years, subject to the following conditions:

(1) written confirmation of a definite expectation that the employee will

eventually either be employed in the United Kingdom by an employer participating in the scheme, or retire in the United Kingdom;

(2) the overseas employer must reimburse the relevant UK employer for the cost of contributions to the scheme;

(3) scheme benefits should be calculated in relation to a level of remuneration appropriate to similar employment in the United Kingdom;

(4) transfers to the UK scheme from overseas arrangements, simultaneously providing benefits in respect of the overseas service, are not permitted.

18.6 PENSIONERS RESIDENT ABROAD

The questions that arise when a pensioner is resident abroad generally relate to the payment of the cash sum and the pension from the UK scheme. As far as the cash payment is concerned, problems will only arise if there are exchange controls in force at the time of retirement (there are none at present) in which case the Bank of England's permission will be needed to effect the transfer abroad. There is no problem about paying pensions abroad but their taxation needs greater consideration. The position is that, as a general rule, all pensions must be paid from the United Kingdom under deduction of Schedule E tax under the PAYE system. There is no general exemption for pensioners resident abroad even where they have worked abroad, but exemption can be granted if the last ten years' service in respect of which the pension is paid was abroad or half the total service and at least ten out of the last twenty years' service was abroad. Alternatively, exemption may be due under a double taxation agreement (DTA) under which the pension is taxed in the country of residence – such DTAs exist with most of the major countries in the West to which pensioners are likely to go, but not the local tax havens – the Channel Islands and the Isle of Man. Where a DTA applies, the Financial Intermediaries and Claims Office is able to authorise gross payments at source.

18.7 OVERSEAS TRANSFERS

It may be possible to transfer benefits from a UK pension arrangement to an overseas arrangement, or vice versa. In general, such transfers can only be made with the prior agreement of the UK Inland Revenue, and considerable information may be needed, depending on the circumstances. There may also be tax implications for the individual, and requirements set by the overseas authorities.

The UK Inland Revenue is particularly concerned to ensure that transfers to and from overseas are made only in circumstances where a person is or has been genuinely resident and working abroad. Agreement to a transfer from overseas is therefore usually only given if the member has been employed in the overseas employment to which the proposed transfer relates for at least two years.

Similarly, a transfer can only be made to an overseas arrangement in the individual's country of residence and confirmation is needed that the person has no intention of returning to the United Kingdom and understands that the transfer is permanent.

Before approving the transfer payment, the PSO requires copies of the receiving scheme's constitutional documentation (the trust deed and rules equivalent) and confirmation of the benefits to be provided by the scheme in respect of the transfer value.

Reciprocal arrangements exist for transfers between the United Kingdom and the Isle of Man, the Channel Islands and the Republic of Ireland, which qualify or set aside some of the requirements for transfers to and from overseas. There are also special arrangements for transfers to the pension scheme for staff of the European Communities.

19

RETIREMENT OPTIONS – INVESTMENT CONSIDERATIONS

It is not the purpose of this chapter to deal with generalised aspects of retirement, but solely with some of the investment considerations which arise when benefits are paid under pension plans.

The options available at retirement have already been discussed in previous chapters – they differ according to whether benefits are paid from an executive pension plan, retirement annuity or personal pension scheme. Investment considerations, however, are similar for both:

- Should the benefits be taken wholly in the form of a pension annuity?
- Or should the maximum tax-free lump sum be taken with a reduced pension annuity?
- What type of annuity should be taken, level, escalating, single life or joint life?

An indication of the different types of annuity purchased by a fund of £100,000 at age 60 is given in Chapter 14 (and is repeated below), as is the effect of using tax-free cash emerging from a pension plan to buy a purchased life annuity which is taxed only on the interest portion.

Another consideration is whether to take advantage of the facility now available under personal pension plans which is to draw an income from the pension fund, deferring the purchase of an annuity until later, age 75 at the latest.

19.1 TYPES OF PENSION AVAILABLE

On taking the benefits from a personal pension scheme or a retirement annuity, the policyholder normally has various options including the facility to take a reduced pension on his own life but which continues in the event of his death to the spouse. For example, £100,000 would purchase the following types of annuity on the open market for a man aged 65. These annuities, based on an investment yield of 5.25 per cent, are not necessarily at the top of the market as annuity rates change frequently.

Table 19.1

Type of annuity	Amount per annum
Single life annuity payable annually in arrears	£9,324
Single life annuity payable monthly in advance	£8,865
Single life annuity payable monthly in advance but for a minimum of five years	£8,720
Single life annuity payable monthly in advance but for a minimum of ten years	£8,328
Single life annuity payable quarterly in advance for a minimum of five years, increasing each year by 3% compound	£6,744
Joint life level annuity, during the lives of the man and his wife, aged 62, payable quarterly in advance	£6,616

19.2 PURCHASED LIFE ANNUITIES

As an example, a fund of £100,000 built up under a personal pension scheme would provide an income payable in monthly instalments in advance throughout the life of a man aged 65, guaranteed for five years, of £8,720 per annum, but subject to tax as earned income at, say, 23 per cent leaving a net income of £6,714 per annum.

Alternatively, the fund could be taken in the form of a tax-free lump sum of £25,000 plus a reduced income of £6,509 (gross), £5,011 (net); the cash of £25,000 could be used to buy a purchased life annuity of £2,223 of which £816 is interest and would be taxable as unearned income. The net income would be £2,035. The combination of the two net annuities amounts to £7,046, an increase of £332 per annum.

A further alternative is sometimes available under personal pension schemes and retirement annuities – the option to take a unit-linked annuity. The planholder may choose a pension which varies with the value of the units, in for example, a managed fund, a property fund, an equity fund, a gilt edged fund, a fixed interest deposit fund, and overseas funds.

The pension is expressed as the value of a fixed number of units determined at the time that benefits start to be drawn and depending upon the planholder's age and upon mortality experience at the time. When each pension payment falls due, the amount of pension is calculated by applying the bid price of the units on the due date to the fixed number of units calculated at the commencement of the pension. The value of the units, and hence the pension, rises to the full extent of the income plus the capital growth of the fund (after charges) in any year so that the pension's growth potential is maximised. The initial pension, however, starts off at a much lower amount than the level pension. If a unit price goes down, so does the pension.

Table 19.2 below shows the history of a unit-linked pension for a man aged 65 secured by a fund of £1,000 commencing on 1 May 1981 and the subsequent payments compared with level and escalating pensions.

Table 19.2

Date	Unit-linked (annuity) (£ pa)		Sterling annuity (£ pa)	
	Pension managed fund	Pension property fund	Level	Escalating at 8½%
1.5.81	61.18	61.18	152.22	89.53
1.5.82	68.36	69.93	152.22	97.14
1.5.83	89.56	73.69	152.22	105.40
1.5.84	104.23	80.92	152.22	114.36
1.5.85	123.37	88.37	152.22	124.08
1.5.86	159.13	93.83	152.22	134.62
1.5.87	188.88	104.43	152.22	146.07
1.5.88	189.29	127.00	152.22	158.48
1.5.89	220.64	156.99	152.22	171.95
1.5.90	228.33	172.08	152.22	186.57
1.5.91	225.46	157.19	152.22	202.43
1.5.92	277.37	152.19	152.22	219.63
1.5.93	321.52	151.62	152.22	238.30
1.5.94	379.13	194.37	152.22	258.56
1.5.95	379.55	209.10	152.22	280.54
1.5.96	446.45	220.71	152.22	304.38
1.5.97	444.93	247.13	152.22	330.25
1.5.98	577.66	287.58	152.22	358.32
1.5.99	630.05	319.44	152.22	388.78

Notes:
1. If the unit price goes down, so will the pension.
2. Pension will be payable for life, quarterly, in advance, guaranteed for at least five years, even if death occurs.

In deciding what type of annuity the planholder should take he will have to consider the following factors:

(1) Is he in poor health, in which case would it be better to opt for a higher level pension rather than a lower escalating or unit-linked

pension? It may be possible to obtain an 'impaired life' annuity from an insurer which specialises in people in poor health

(2) Is there a history of longevity in the family, in which case might he opt for the lower escalating pension?

(3) If he opts for the unit-linked pension and it drops in value, will he have other income to fall back on?

(4) Does his wife have an income in her own right – if not should he perhaps opt for a joint life last survivor pension?

(5) If he opts for a lower escalating or unit linked pension, how long will it take to overtake the level pension in real terms?

(6) It can be seen from the figures in Table 19.1 that the difference in an annuity with a five-year guarantee compared with an annuity with no guarantee is only £145 per annum (cf £8,720 and £8,865). Similarly, the difference in an annuity with a ten-year guarantee is only £537 per annum (cf £8,328 and £8,865). It may be worthwhile taking this reduction in view of the benefit payable should death occur during the guaranteed period.

19.3 PHASED RETIREMENT

Personal pension plans can provide for benefits to be taken in stages, in line with income needs in retirement. Many personal pension plans (and retirement annuities) can be sub-divided into mini-policies or segments, the number of which sometimes depend on the contributions being paid by the planholder.

On 'retirement' the planholder may cash in some of the segments to provide a cash lump sum and an annuity, always maintaining the statutory requirement that only one-quarter of the fund is surrendered and may be taken as a cash lump sum. Further segments can be surrendered subsequently. This facility enables the planholder to avoid taking more of the pension fund as is necessary in relation to his overall financial position at the time. Any remaining segments must be taken by age 75.

Phased retirement is very useful for planholders who are taxpayers and whose personal circumstances do not require them to use the tax-free lump sum for a capital purpose. Instead they may use it to provide income.

The cash lump sums may be used to provide income to top up the annuities taken. For example say the planholder aged 65 paying tax at 40 per cent requires a net income from the personal pension fund of £20,000 per annum. This could be provided by cashing in sufficient segments to provide a tax-free lump sum of £17,400 plus an annuity of around £4,300 per annum gross, £2,600 per annum net after tax at 40 per cent, giving a total net amount of £20,000.

In the second year if the planholder requires a further net income of £20,000 further segments could be encashed to provide a further tax-free lump sum of £14,990 plus an annuity of £4,016 per annum gross, £2,410 per annum net, which with the original annuity of £2,600 gives £20,000.

Deferring the purchase of annuities introduces the risk that the fund will not grow at a sufficient rate to ensure that the total income, both before and after age 75, will exceed that payable if the fund is fully used to buy an annuity at the outset. However, the purchase of annuities each year should be helpful in providing a spread of different annuities bought in different economic conditions. This should be particularly advantageous if annuity rates are low now.

On death before age 75 the fund may be returned to the member's dependant's and if the plan is arranged under a suitable trust the death benefits may be paid free of inheritance tax and these death benefits arise in respect of any segments of the plan which have not been surrendered.

19.4 INCOME WITHDRAWAL OPTION

Personal pension plans now give planholders greater flexibility at retirement. Rather than having to purchase an annuity, the planholder may draw an income from the fund from age 50 onwards, and defer purchasing an annuity up until age 75. The income withdrawn must be within limits set by the Inland Revenue. The pension fund remains invested, benefiting from any future investment growth. These arrangements are sometimes called income drawdown schemes or pension fund withdrawal schemes.

The maximum income that may be withdrawn is 100 per cent of the notional annuity that the planholder could obtain using rates published by the Government Actuary. These rates vary according to the yield on 15-year gilt-edged securities. As economic circumstances change, so too do the notional annuities. However, once income starts to be drawn from the fund the maximum and minimum amounts are fixed, but subject to adjustments every three years. The minimum income which may be withdrawn is 35 per cent of the maximum income. The amounts withdrawn during the year can fluctuate, provided that the total amount withdrawn is between the 35–100 per cent limits.

During the withdrawal period it is not possible to switch pension providers without buying an annuity (unless the plan is a self-invested personal pension (SIPP) which will allow the planholder to choose and switch investment managers and pension providers).

If the planholder dies while withdrawing income from the fund, the remainder of the fund is returned to the deceased's estate, or to the scheme's trustees, minus a tax charge of 35 per cent. Alternatively the dependant may normally continue to draw an income from the fund until such time as the deceased would have reached age 75, or may purchase an annuity.

If the planholder wishes to take a tax-free cash sum Revenue rules require income to be withdrawn from the fund at the same time. Usually the tax-free cash sum is a key requirement and this drives the amount of income which is withdrawn. For example, take a client who has a pension fund valued at £300,000 on retirement which would provide a tax-free cash sum of £75,000 and £225,000 to buy an annuity, or to generate income withdrawals.

The planholder needs a tax-free cash sum now of only £30,000, for example to pay off the remainder of a mortgage or start up a small business. The planholder would like to take only the tax-free cash sum of £30,000 and no income, having sufficient resources elsewhere to satisfy income needs. However, Revenue rules do not permit this, so the minimum income has to be taken from the fund.

The fund which needs to be used is only £120,000 – the minimum needed to give a tax-free lump sum of £30,000. The remainder of £90,000 will fund the income at between £8,370 per annum (the approximate maximum amount) and £2,929 per annum (the minimum amount assuming that the maximum notional annuity is £8,370 per annum for a male aged around 65).

The balance of the total fund of £300,000 (£180,000) can remain invested to provide further tax-free cash and annuity, or income at a later stage. The total fund can be split in this way provided it can be segmented into a number of arrangements or mini-policies: most modern personal pension plans are segmented in this way.

Further contributions may not be paid into the plan when income has been withdrawn unless the plan contains a number of arrangements or mini policies and the contributions are paid into those segments which have not been encashed.

19.4.1 Annuities or income drawdown?

Annuities involve the insurer in an insurance risk: the insurance company will pay an annuity which is guaranteed, for life, regardless of how long the annuitant lives for. If the annuitant dies shortly after buying the annuity, the annuity instalments paid are likely to be less than the purchase price of the annuity. However, some annuitants live for many years and annuities provide a form of insurance against longevity. The insurance company makes a profit from those who die in the early years, but makes losses in respect of those who survive into a very old age.

Many planholders do not like to think of the insurance company keeping the balance of 'their fund' if they die shortly after buying the annuity: they would like to retain the pension fund which they have built up over the years when they were investing contributions. The income withdrawal option is likely to appeal to these people although there are risks.

19.4.2 Risks of income withdrawal

Many people approaching retirement and pensioners are likely to have a cautious attitude to investment. However, the planholder who decides not to buy an annuity is turning down the opportunity to invest in a pooled environment. Instead, the planholder has to bear the investment risk personally. The pension fund has to accumulate at a sufficient rate to ensure that when the annuity is finally purchased the amount of the annuity is at least equal to what it would have been if an annuity had been purchased at the outset. The rate of return on the investment increases with age. The following table indicates the real rate of return needed at various ages and also demonstrates the subsidy inherent in annuities. Note that these figures do not take into account the effects of charges, and the underlying mortality assumes standard insurance industry experience of annuitants.

Table 19.3

Client age	Additional growth required over and above interest rates (%)
50	0.34
55	0.60
60	1.05
65	1.84
66	2.02
67	2.22
68	2.44
69	2.69
70	2.96
71	3.26
72	3.58
73	3.94
74	4.34

In order to obtain real rates of retirement at the above levels, planholders need to hold a proportion of their pension fund in equity-type investments. As age increases this proportion becomes greater, and attitude to risk would have to be speculative to contemplate a real rate of return above 3 per cent. In practice, even a seasoned speculative pensioner would be unlikely to defer purchasing an annuity beyond age 70.

Income withdrawal facilities have increased awareness of the investment options open to people approaching retirement and to pensioners. Because annuity rates are linked to the returns on gilt-edged securities, there may be a case for investing all or part of the investment funds in gilts. However, in practice this is not feasible for individuals because they are unlikely to find an individual gilt which matches their requirements and in any case they will not know in advance when they will want to buy an annuity.

Table 19.4 compares the various options according to annual changes in interest rates and annual growth in the Financial Times All Share Index. The grid shows that at most variables the conventional annuity – shown in black squares – is likely to be the best option except where both annual interest rates and FTSE growth increase.

However, withdrawing income from the fund will be better than a conventional annuity assuming there is FTSE growth combined with low increases in interest rates (and hence annuity rates) or even reductions in FTSE at the same time as more significant increases in interest: the grid indicates this by diamonds.

Withdrawing income from a fund which is invested in gilts will protect the planholder against changes in interest rates. However, this protection is reduced if there is FTSE growth; the grid indicates this by triangles.

The light squares indicate that withdrawing income from the fund while investing in a 'guaranteed fund' would be better than buying a conventional annuity provided that there is high FTSE growth and falling interest rates. The 'guaranteed fund' used in this example would invest in gilts with the dividends being invested in options linked to FTSE. Again this fund would give protection against changes in interest rates but requires high levels of FTSE growth to be effective. Other types of guaranteed funds exist in the marketplace, but in practice provide similar results.

Table 19.5 sets out the common requirements of potential pensioners and the options usually available under personal pensions (although the individual's investment profile will have a significant bearing in the options).

Table 19.4 – Some Investment Options

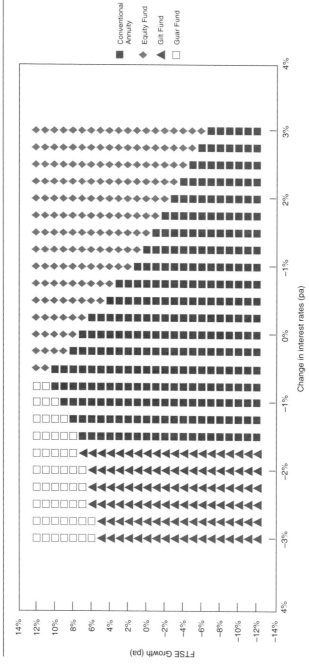

Legend:
- Conventional Annuity
- Equity Fund
- Gilt Fund
- Guar Fund

FTSE Growth (pa)

Change in interest rates (pa)

1. The figures compare an immediate annuity with an annuity purchased after three years under income withdrawal.
2. A dividend yield of 4 per cent per annum is assumed.
3. Interest rates are around 5 per cent at commencement.
4. Figures are based on a man aged 60, taking withdrawals annually in arrears.
5. Figures are based on typical annuity rates as at September 1999.
6. The fund available for investment if a conventional annuity is not purchased will bear an initial charge of 3 per cent and an ongoing charge of 1 per cent per annum.

Table 19.5

Requirements	Options	Favoured Route
1. Maximum cash lump sum plus maximum income	Annuity or income withdrawal	Annuity
2. Maximum cash lump sum plus minimum (or variable) income	Income withdrawal	Income withdrawal
3. Income only	Annuity, phased annuities or phased income withdrawals	Phased annuities

Notes:
(1) The table ignores the effect of death benefits. These could be provided through the remainder of the annuity instalments if a pension is bought on a guaranteed basis, through an annuity continuing to a dependant if a joint life pension is bought, or through the return of the pension fund, minus a 35 per cent tax charge, if the income withdrawal option is used.
(2) Where death benefits are of prime importance, the favoured route would be to defer taking all benefits, so that on death the whole fund would be returned, without a 35 per cent tax charge.
(3) Under requirement 2 above it may be possible to use a combination of unit-linked annuities on a joint life basis in order to minimise the income taken. However, this would not provide the planholder with the ability to vary that income.
(4) Unit-linked annuities and with-profits annuities may provide greater flexibility for those approaching retirement who already have guaranteed income in their portfolios.

19.5 INCREASING CURRENT INCOME

Generally, planholders should not take tax-free lump sums from pension funds unless they are obliged to do so (for example under some occupational pension schemes) or unless there is a definite need for the lump sum.

Withdrawing the lump sum to reinvest it in other investment areas is very unlikely to be financially attractive because the gross investment return within the pension fund will be replaced by a taxed investment return elsewhere. However, where other lump sums are available the following investment areas may be appropriate.

Individuals investing to increase current income will normally be looking at a range of 'money' investments including bank deposits, building societies and fixed interest securities such as gilts. Of these investments,

Table 19.6   Income withdrawal/drawdown comparison between occupational schemes, AVC schemes and personal pension schemes

Occupational schemes	AVC and FSAVC schemes	Personal pension schemes
Available for: • Non-contracted out insured or self-invested money purchase schemes • SSAS which provides only money purchase benefits • EPP • Section 32 contracts	• Group AVC • FSAVC	• any personal pension scheme
Tax-free cash Based on length of service and final remuneration with a maximum of 2.25 times the initial rate of pension before commutation. Where scheme rules directly link amount of pension and tax-free cash, maximum cash is based on amount of income withdrawal *actually drawn*. May therefore be less.	Not normally available except for pre-8 April 1987 arrangements – but see calculation of income withdrawal amount below.	Up to 25% of non-protected rights fund in arrangement may be taken. If benefits are from transfer from occupational scheme, tax-free cash may be restricted to less than 25% of the fund.
Death during income withdrawal period: (a) Lump sums • If five-year guarantee selected at commencement of income withdrawal, balance of instalments payable between	(a) Lump sums • Return of contributions plus interest (or return of fund where secured by unit-linked policy).	(a) Lump sums • Payable subject to 35% tax charge. • Lump sum may be paid as a survivor's

259

Table 19.6 *(cont.)*

Occupational schemes	AVC and FSAVC schemes	Personal pension schemes
date of death and end of guarantee period may be paid based on 100% of GAD annuity at commencement of income withdrawal; *plus* Any difference between 100% of income withdrawal and amount of income withdrawal taken can be paid.		fund* – if a fund is nominated by the member or chosen by the scheme administrator; *or* • If no survivor's fund is nominated by the member or chosen by the scheme administrator, lump sum may be paid under the discretionary powers in the rules. *Survivor's fund needs to be chosen for survivor to have choice of lump sum, income withdrawal or annuity. If no survivor's fund chosen, only a lump sum can be paid.

Example

Five-year guarantee; 100% income withdrawal = £10,000 pa. Member takes £4,000 pa and dies after three years.
Lump sum available on death:
2 × £10,000 = £20,000
3 × £6,000 = £18,000

Total   £38,000

If annuity purchased in guarantee period, any guarantee on annuity is reduced by time elapsed since income withdrawal began.

Table 19.6 *(cont.)*

Occupational schemes	AVC and FSAVC schemes	Personal pension schemes
(b) Survivors' pensions benefits • Any remaining member's fund after provision of lump sum benefits can be used to provide survivors' pensions subject to Revenue limits. • Any surplus dealt with under normal surplus rules for occupational schemes. • Must be aggregated with survivor's own right pension to determine Revenue limits. • Survivor can elect for income withdrawal – annuity must be taken on earlier of survivor attaining 75 and date member would have attained 75.	(b) Survivors' pensions benefits • As for occupational schemes	(b) Survivors' pensions benefits • Only payable if a survivor's fund has been nominated by member or scheme administrator; survivor may then choose: – income withdrawal or – an annuity. • Can take lump sum within two years of member's death if income withdrawal taken. • If survivor under 60, can choose to defer annuity to start at age 60 but cannot then take income withdrawal or lump sum.

Notes:
(1) SSAS = small self-administered scheme; EPP = executive pension plan. Both are used for directors and key executives of companies.
(2) GAD = Government Actuary's Department.

deposit accounts of any kind, whether bank, building society or national savings, are rarely appropriate because the level of income is variable, unpredictable, and the capital base generating the income is fixed. Such investments should be regarded as a store for uninvested cash which may be required at short notice; in other words, as an alternative current account.

Fixed interest securities such as gilts do have a role for investors seeking income because the income flow is predictable and guaranteed. Once again, it might be unwise for an investor to put more than a small percentage of his investment in such an area since guarantees, contrary to popular belief, still represent an investment risk. Investments giving a guaranteed income as such should only be used as a major part of the portfolio if the need for income is very short term.

Individuals seeking a long-term rising income with capital appreciation should consider investing a reasonable portion of their lump sum in asset-backed investments such as unit trusts and insurance bonds, specifically those which invest in companies with good dividend records. Personal equity plans (PEPs) in existence on 5 April 1999 may continue, but further investments into them are not permitted. Any income and capital gains from PEPs will still be tax-free (although the PEP plan manager will only be able to reclaim the tax credit associated with UK dividends until April 2004).

The date 6 April 1999 marked the launch of a new, tax-free savings scheme known as an individual savings account (ISA) which replaced PEPs and tax exempt special savings accounts (TESSAs). Like PEPs, any income or capital growth from ISAs is free of personal taxes and ideally the first tranche of long-term capital should be invested in an ISA up to the current minimum. ISA managers can reclaim the tax credit on UK dividends until April 2004.

In the past, higher rate taxpayers were less interested in receiving investment income and would be more interested in achieving capital growth in order to make use of the CGT exemptions. If a higher rate taxpayer invested in a spread of low yielding unit trusts, there was a reasonable chance that even in the short term one or more of the funds would show a gain, hence giving the investor scope for profit taking within the CGT exemptions. As the top rate of tax on both income and capital is 40 per cent, higher rate taxpayers are unlikely to distort their investment decisions by trying to reduce income and increase their returns through capital growth.

Taking withdrawals from insurance bonds is also a popular way to supplement income in a tax efficient way. Insurance bonds have the further advantage that they have a wider spread of underlying investments than unit trusts, which enable the investor to have some exposure to property or take advantage of the managed fund concept.

To summarise: for individuals who are seeking income, then income producing ISAs, unit trusts and insurance bonds provide a very high quality secure source of income. Income can be received on regular dates throughout the year.

19.6 PRODUCING INCOME IN THE FUTURE

Most planholders who are already taking benefits from pension plans are less likely to require income in the future, but they may wish to provide income for succeeding generations. If this was the case, a broad spread of equities should protect the real value of an investment, while providing a reasonable income, and should form a part of the investment portfolio of any prudent investor.

19.7 GUARANTEED OPTIONS ON RETIREMENT

Scheme members approaching retirement with pension arrangements set up in the 1970s and early 1980s should consider the retirement options available. These arrangements may provide for annuities to be purchased on guaranteed annuity rates set at a time when annuity rates were higher than today. Some arrangements set up in the form of deferred annuities may provide favourable terms for converting part of the annuity into a cash sum. Both of these options may be better than exercising an 'open market option' and transferring the fund to another provider, even one which offers high annuity rates today.

20

PENSIONS – THE FUTURE

20.1 INTRODUCTION

The speed of change which the pensions industry has experienced during the last few years will continue into the future. Most employers and scheme trustees now understand the impact of the Pensions Act 1995 and have gone to great lengths to comply with it. However, these changes are insignificant compared with changes resulting from the stakeholder pensions proposals. These will affect all employees and the self-employed, not just those who are fortunate enough to be members of an employer's scheme. State benefits will change too, affecting the design of employer schemes. Contracting out – a key part of pension scheme design today – will also change.

The Government's proposals are contained in its Green Paper, 'A new Contract for Welfare: Partnership in Pensions'. There have also been six Consultation Briefs from the Government giving further detail on the impact of the pensions changes. Subjects covered in earlier Consultation Briefs are: Minimum Standards (No 1); Employer Access (No 2); Clearing Arrangements (No 3); Regulation Advice & Information (No 4); Governance (No 5); and Tax Regime (No 6). A summary of the Government's proposals is set out below.

20.2 STATE BENEFITS

The basic State pension will continue as now, being the cornerstone of retirement income for all. The Green Paper does not envisage any changes. No means testing will be introduced. The Government will continue to raise the basic State pension annually in line with increases in prices so that, over time, the basic State pension will decline as a proportion of the overall State benefit. There have been calls to increase the basic State pension in line with earnings rather than prices, but this is very unlikely (except possibly, at some stage, in respect of the very elderly, for example those aged 80 and over).

20.2.1 Minimum income guarantee

The Government proposes to target help on the poorest pensioners, providing a minimum income guarantee from April 1999 of £75 per week for a single person and £116.60 per week for a married couple. The minimum income guarantee will be higher for the more elderly.

The Government's aim is to increase the minimum income guarantee each year as resources allow and over the long-term in line with earnings.

20.3 SERPS AND STATE SECOND PENSION

During the first year of stakeholder pensions, SERPS will continue to operate but will be replaced in April 2002 (at the earliest) with the State Second Pension (SSP). At that point, SERPS will be changed to provide better benefits for the lower paid and will be renamed the State Second Pension. The first stage of the SSP will see a doubling of the SERPS accrual for those earning £9,000 a year, greater enhancements for those earning £3,300 to £9,000 per year and more modest enhancements for those earning £9,000 to £18,500 per year. For those earning more than £18,500 a year, SSP will provide the same level of pension as SERPS today.

Carers and the long-term disabled will obtain credits towards the SSP, a significant improvement over SERPS under which no credits are currently available for these people.

Between the start of the SSP in April 2002 and around 2007, SSP will continue to be earnings related but will become a flat-rate benefit for all at that point as if earnings were £9,000 per annum. This two-stage transition will make pension scheme design, and the communication of the inevitable changes, difficult.

20.3.1 Contracting out of SSP

The current basis of contracting out of SERPS will continue up to 2002 and, after that point, contracting out of SSP will be available. As at present, individual members of personal and stakeholder schemes and employers running occupational schemes which are contracted out will have to decide whether the terms for contracting out are attractive enough. It is hoped that the Government may give an indication of the rebates which will be payable into stakeholder pensions towards the end of 1999. As a major plank of the Government's proposals is to encourage more people to contract out of State provision, the levels of rebates will be key to the success of stakeholder pensions.

20.4 INTRODUCTION OF STAKEHOLDER PENSION SCHEMES

Stakeholder pension schemes will operate on a defined contribution basis and will be suitable for contracting out of SSP. Although the target group is primarily those earning between £9,000 and £20,000 per year (who tend not to belong to an occupational pension scheme), stakeholder pensions may also benefit people on high earnings. The aim is to produce more flexible, cost-effective schemes.

20.4.1 Access to employees

Employers which do not provide an occupational pension will have to facilitate access to a stakeholder scheme at the workplace. There will be no exceptions for employer size. An employer with only one employee will still have to provide access, provided that earnings are at least equal to the lower earnings level. The requirement to facilitate access may apply even if the employer operates an occupational scheme or a group personal pension scheme. Many employers offer membership to employees when they have completed an eligibility period and if they fall within certain age limits. Employees who do not satisfy these conditions will be entitled to require the employer to operate a payroll deduction facility under which employees' contributions are deducted from pay and sent to a stakeholder scheme. The employer will have to designate a stakeholder scheme. If an employee would rather the contributions are paid to another scheme, and not one designated by the employer, the employer is not obliged to operate a payroll deduction facility.

The likelihood is that many employers will wish to maintain the often-restricted eligibility conditions which they currently use for their own occupational schemes rather than extending those schemes to make them stakeholder-compatible. They will continue with the current occupational scheme and offer a stakeholder pension scheme for those not eligible to join the occupational scheme.

20.4.2 Minimum standards

Stakeholder pensions will have to comply with minimum standards to include the following:

- A simple charging structure, with a limit on the level of charges, likely to be around 1 per cent per year of the fund.
- Generic advice must be provided within the 1 per cent charge. Fees may be charged for additional advice.

- Allowing members to stop and restart contributions without penalty.
- No additional charges where members wish to transfer out of a stakeholder scheme or to transfer benefits into it from other schemes.
- The provision of regular information for scheme members, at least annually.
- The minimum contribution which schemes would have to accept could be as low as £10.

20.4.3 Contribution levels

Consultation Brief No 6 on stakeholder pensions, published by the Government in September 1999, proposes a single tax regime for all new defined contribution (DC) pensions, including employers' DC schemes, personal pensions and new stakeholder pensions. The contribution limits will be the same for these schemes, namely the age and salary limits as currently applies for personal pensions but with a minimum of £3,600 a year. People with no earned income, for example carers or married women without earnings from employment, may contribute up to £3,600 per year. There will be no limit on the emerging benefits, as with traditional occupational pension schemes. Up to 25 per cent of the fund may be taken as a tax-free lump sum, with the balance being used to provide an annuity (with income withdrawal facilities permitted). Contributions will be paid net of basic rate tax (as applies today for personal pensions for employed people). The system of paying contributions net of basic rate tax will also apply to self-employed people. Higher rate relief will be given by application through the annual tax assessment.

Contributions may be paid for up to five years after earnings have ceased. The upper limit will be based at the highest relief available (by reference to both age and earnings) in either the year of cessation or in the two immediately preceding years. Thereafter, contributions may be paid at up to £3,600 each year. This tax regime will cause significant upheavals in pension scheme design, with scheme trustees and employers attracted by the simplification which should ensue. One of the significant effects will be the ability to pay into a scheme designated as a 'stakeholder' scheme, because, for example, it meets the minimum standards or the maximum charges that can be taken from the fund, as well as a personal pension, at the same time.

20.4.4 Scheme governance

The principal method for governing stakeholder schemes will be based on trust law. Trustees will have to follow statutory requirements and act in the interests of members. They will have to:

- Produce an annual report and accounts
- Appoint professional advisers, including fund managers
- Draw up a statement of investment principles
- Put in place procedures for dealing with internal disputes.

These requirements are very similar for those applying to occupational schemes under the Pensions Act 1995. The Government expects trustees to drive down the costs charged for the running of these schemes by providers. For large occupational-type schemes designated as stakeholder schemes, the use of trust law is unlikely to be burdensome. However, financial services companies may be concerned about acting as providers of stakeholder pension schemes governed by these principles: they may find themselves investing the capital to set up and market stakeholder schemes only to find that after a few years of this operation, the trustees transfer the scheme assets to other schemes, leaving the financial services company with little, or no, profit, and probably a loss from the operation.

Recognising this, the Government has proposed another type of scheme based on a 'secure stakeholder manager' operating on the basis similar to that used by unit trusts where custodian trustees, often banks, protect the interests of individual unitholders. These schemes will look more like individual pension plans or unit trusts, but still subject to the same minimum standards as trust-based schemes.

20.4.5 Scheme information

Occupational, personal and stakeholder pension schemes will be required to provide an annual benefit statement for members, including a forecast of State pension provision. The aim is to provide better, clearer information in order to encourage further provision if necessary. A combined pensions forecast including State and private benefits will clearly be difficult to achieve as many people have accumulated small pension fund pots over a period of time: the protocols for the exchange and passing of information to a 'leading' provider who communicates with the member will require significant systems effort.

Forecasts of DC benefits, including projected values at retirement and the amount of annuity which might emerge, will be based on standard rates of projection.

20.4.6 Regulation

Two regulatory authorities will be involved: the Occupational Pensions Regulatory Authority (OPRA) and the Financial Services Authority

(FSA). OPRA will regulate the conduct of trustees and the access requirements on employers. The FSA will regulate the marketing of stakeholder pension schemes as well as authorising and supervising providers of schemes and fund managers. The FSA will be drawing up 'decision trees' which will simplify the decision-making process for potential scheme members, making it easier for them to join, without having to seek individual financial advice.

20.5 OTHER CHANGES AFFECTING OCCUPATIONAL PENSION SCHEMES

20.5.1 Review of minimum funding requirements

This test of pensions scheme security which applies under salary-related schemes is considered by many to be too inflexible to meet changing market conditions and too complex. The actuarial profession is reviewing the present MFR valuation methods and looking at alternative ways of ensuring security for scheme members.

20.5.2 Member-nominated trustees

The Government currently allows scheme members the right to nominate 'member-nominated trustees' (MNTs), but is considering making the arrangements obligatory on employers who currently have the right to an 'opt-out'. This opt-out facility will be abolished to be replaced with a requirement that all schemes must have a third of trustees as MNTs and for large mature schemes to have a pensioner member on the trustee board.

20.6 OTHER MEASURES

Other measures to strengthen the pensions framework include an extension of protection to pensions of those who are declared bankrupt, an extension of the framework which protects GMPs by preventing increases from being offset against other benefits (known as 'franking') and changes to the reporting requirements to OPRA when employees' contributions are paid late to the schemes. All occupational schemes will be affected in some way by these measures which, generally, have been welcomed by schemes.

20.7 PENSIONS ON DIVORCE

The recently enacted Welfare Reform and Pensions Act (November 1999) allows for pension sharing to be available from December 2000 as well as pension earmarking which is available now. Pension sharing is different from pension earmarking. Under the latter a court order is made against the trustees or managers of a scheme requiring them to pay over the earmarked benefit to the divorced party when the benefit comes into payment. An earmarking order can be made against a member's pension, a lump sum payable on a member's death and a lump sum payable on retirement.

With pension sharing the person who benefits from the order (the 'transferee') obtains an immediate entitlement to pension rights either by means of a cash equivalent of the member's rights which is paid into an approved scheme of the transferee, or by receipt of a pension credit which may be retained by the scheme.

Pension sharing should resolve the main drawbacks of earmarking; the lack of certainty that the ex-spouse will receive the expected amount of benefit (or any benefit at all if the member's benefit on retirement has been earmarked but the member dies before retirement and no benefit therefore accrues to the ex-spouse); and the inability of the earmarking regulations to provide for a clean break of the benefits between the divorcing parties.

20.8 EU TAX HARMONISATION

The EU Commission is studying company taxation in the European Union with a view to addressing tax obstacles to cross-border economic activity in the single market. There are many, including pensions which constitutes a major obstacle as the diversity and complexity of national tax rules currently act as barriers to the free movement of people and the free provision of services. One of the main problems consists of the difficulty in obtaining tax relief (for employer and employee for cross-border contributions to supplementary pension funds). However, it is unlikely that changes will be made through the EU in the near future.

APPENDIX 1
GLOSSARY OF TERMS

This glossary provides an explanation of expressions commonly used by pension scheme practitioners

Accrual rate   The fraction of earnings for each year of service which forms the basis of pension entitlement in a final salary or average salary scheme (for example, 'one-sixtieth' for each year of pensionable service).

Accrued benefits   The benefits in respect of service up to a specific date calculated in relation to current earnings or projected final earnings. Sometimes known as accrued rights.

Actuarial certificate   A certificate given by an actuary, especially a certificate in respect of the solvency test required for contracted-out schemes.

Actuarial valuation   An investigation into whether a pension scheme has sufficient assets to meet its liabilities. The investigation is usually to assess the degree of solvency of the scheme, the funding level and to recommend a contribution rate.

Added years   This is a method of increasing a member's benefits where additional periods of pensionable service are provided, especially when a transfer payment has been made from a previous scheme. Sometimes members have the option of paying additional voluntary contributions in order to purchase added years, for example, an additional three-sixtieths of final remuneration.

Additional component   The state earnings related pension above the *basic component.*

Additional voluntary contributions (AVCs)   Contributions over and above a member's normal contributions (if any), which a member may pay in order to secure additional benefits.

Administrator   The person regarded by the Pension Schemes Office of the Inland Revenue and as being responsible for the management of the pension scheme. Often the trustee or employer or a committee of management.

AEI   Average Earnings Index.

Annuity   A regular guaranteed income, usually payable for life by an insurance company in return for a lump sum investment.

Appropriate Personal Pension A personal pension which is used to contract out of SERPS and which receives only the national insurance rebate, together with basic rate tax relief.

Bridging pension A pension which bridges the gap between early retirement and normal retirement when the state pension becomes payable.

Buy back terms An expression used to describe the payment of a *state scheme premium* to the DSS when a scheme ceases to be contracted out and to reinstate all or part of an individual's SERPS benefits.

Buy out plans The purchase by pension scheme trustees of an insurance policy (a s 32 annuity) in the name of the beneficiary who gives up his entitlement to benefits under the scheme on leaving service.

COMBS The abbreviation for a contracted-out mixed benefit scheme, an occupational pension scheme which has separate defined benefit and money purchase sections and which contracts out on both bases.

COMP The abbreviation for a contracted-out money purchase scheme.

COSRS The abbreviation given to an occupational pension scheme which is contracted out on a salary-related basis.

Continuation option Where a member leaves a pension scheme which also provided life assurance benefits, the insurance company underwriting those benefits will often give him the facility to continue cover under a life assurance policy, without having to provide evidence of health. There is normally a time limit of one month after leaving the scheme for the facility to be taken up.

Contract out Where an occupational pension scheme is used to provide its members with a level of benefits replacing part of the earnings related state scheme benefits that they *would* have enjoyed had they not been members of a contracted-out scheme. Contributions to the state scheme in respect of employees who are contracted out are lower than for employees who are not contracted out.

Contracting-out certificate The certificate issued by the Contributions Agency (an executive office of the Inland Revenue which administers the national insurance contributions system) to a scheme which meets the conditions for contracting out.

Contributions equivalent premium (CEP) A type of state scheme premium which may be paid when a member leaves an occupational pension scheme after a short period of contracted out employment. The state scheme then takes over the obligation to provide the member with his **guaranteed minimum pension**.

Controlled funding A type of funding commonly used in connection with insured final earnings schemes, where the contributions are assessed to the liabilities of the pension scheme as a whole rather than for individual members.

Deductive amount A reduction in pension or pensionable earnings in order to achieve a degree of integration with the state scheme.

Deposit administration   A type of insurance policy where contributions, after expense charges, are accumulated and to which interest and/or bonuses are added. The interest usually reflects prevailing interest rates or building society lending rates.

Director   Special rules apply to persons classed as directors (normally of private limited companies). A 20 per cent director is one who either on his own or with one or more associates beneficially owns or is able to control directly or indirectly or through other companies 20 per cent or more of the ordinary share capital of the company.

Discretionary scheme   A scheme where employees to be included are selected by the employer on a purely discretionary basis. The discretion normally extends to benefits and contributions for each member.

Dynamisation   The index linking of earnings for determining *final remuneration* for the purpose of Revenue limits. The term is sometimes also used to describe escalation or indexation.

Earnings cap   The maximum amount of earnings that may be pensioned, and in respect of which a member may make personal contributions under an occupational scheme, currently £90,600 (1999/2000). Also, the maximum earnings in respect of which contributions may be paid to a personal pension scheme in 1999/2000.

Equivalent pension benefit (EPB)   The benefit which must be provided for an employee who was contracted out of the former graduated pension scheme (sometimes known as the Boyd-Carpenter scheme).

Executive pension plan   A scheme for selected directors or employees.

Exempt approved scheme   An approved scheme established under an irrevocable trust and thus enjoying the tax relief specified in the Finance Acts.

Expression of wish   Where a member makes a nomination indicating his wishes for the destination of death benefits to the trustees of the scheme. They are not bound by the nomination, however.

Final salary scheme   A pension scheme where the benefit is calculated with reference to the member's pensionable earnings at or around retirement or leaving service.

Financial Services Authority (FSA)   The new name for the Securities and Investment Board. The FSA is responsible for the broad framework for investor regulation. It also carries out the work of specific regulatory organisations such as the **Personal Investment Authority (PIA)**.

Fixed revaluation rate   The rate by which a final salary contracted-out scheme may revalue the **guaranteed minimum pension** where a member's contracted out employment ceases.

Free cover   The maximum amount of death benefit which an insurance company covering a group of lives is prepared to underwrite for each individual without requiring evidence of health.

Freestanding AVC   An additional contribution, by a member of an occupational scheme, to another scheme which is completely separate. The total of the individual's contributions to both schemes is limited to 15 per cent of remuneration.

Guaranteed annuity option   Where the proceeds of an insurance policy may be used to buy an annuity at a rate guaranteed in the policy which may also include an open market option.

Guaranteed minimum pension (GMP)   The minimum pension which a contracted-out scheme must provide for pre-6 April 1997 service. The state benefits payable in respect of a contracted out employee are reduced by the amount of guaranteed minimum pension. Future GMPs were abolished from April 1997 and no further GMP entitlement will accrue after that date but existing GMPs will remain within schemes until members reach state pension age.

Hancock annuity   A type of immediate annuity purchased by an employer when an employee retires.

Industry-wide schemes   Multi-member schemes set up by a number of employers operating in a similar industry, eg the printing industry. Members moving between employers within the scheme are deemed to have continuous service.

Integration   Where a pension scheme is designed to take into account part or all of the state scheme benefits.

Joint notice   A document which is completed by an individual and a pension provider and sent to the DSS stating that the personal pension scheme entered into by the individual is to be used for contracting out of SERPS and requesting the DSS to remit the minimum contribution to it.

LAUTRO   The life assurance and unit trust regulatory organisation before it was subsumed into the **Personal Investment Authority**.

Letter of exchange   A letter which constitutes the formal setting up of an individual pension arrangement which comes into effect when the employee acknowledges its receipt in writing.

Limited price indexation (LPI)   The requirement to guarantee pension increases in line with increases in the Retail Prices Index (RPI), subject to a maximum of 5 per cent per annum.

Limited revaluation premium   A type of state scheme premium which may be paid when a member ceases to be in contracted-out employment in return for which any revaluation of **guaranteed minimum pension** above a specified level (currently 5 per cent) is provided by the state scheme.

Lower earnings limit   The minimum amount which must be earned before contributions become payable to the state scheme. Once the limit is exceeded, contributions are payable in respect of earnings both above and below the limit. The level is approximately the same as the basic single person's pension.

Market level indicator   An index giving a weighted comparison of values of fixed interest securities and equities, and used to adjust the amount of state scheme premiums.

Minimum funding requirement (MFR)   A new method which a scheme actuary must use to value the assets and liabilities of a defined benefits occupational scheme.

Money purchase scheme   A scheme where benefits are directly determined by the value of contributions paid in respect of each member as opposed to a scheme which provides benefits related to earnings.

New code   The code of approval of occupational pension schemes which was introduced by FA 1970, Pt II, Ch II.

Normal retirement date   The date at which a member of a pension scheme normally becomes entitled to receive his retirement benefits.

Old code   The code of approval of occupational pension schemes which applied before the passing of FA 1970: approval under the old code ended on 5 April 1980, if it had not already been replaced by new code approval.

Paid up benefit   A preserved benefit secured for an individual member under an assurance policy where premiums have ceased to be paid in respect of that member.

OPRA   The Occupational Pensions Regulatory Authority. Its role is to investigate schemes, to ascertain whether regulatory provisions are being complied with, and to take action to rectify non-compliance.

Pension Schemes Office   The Inland Revenue branch which deals with the approval of pension schemes.

Pensionable earnings   The earnings on which benefits and/or contributions are calculated. Pensionable earnings may differ from actual remuneration in that they may exclude various items such as bonuses, overtime, commission and directors' fees.

Pensioneer trustee   An individual widely involved with pension schemes and accepted by the Revenue as being a trustee of a small self-administered scheme.

Pensioner's rights premium   A type of state scheme premium which may be paid for a member or pensioner over state pension age, when a scheme ceases to be contracted out, in return for which the state scheme will take over the obligation to provide his **guaranteed minimum pension**.

Personal Investment Authority (PIA)   The regulatory organisation formed to replace the separate authorities LAUTRO and FIMBRA but now subsumed into the **Financial Services Authority**.

Pooled Pension Investment (PPI)   A new financial instrument for pension investment primarily intended to help deliver stakeholder pensions.

Practice notes   The vast majority of occupational pension schemes are approved by the Inland Revenue under its discretionary powers currently embodied in Practice Note IR 12 (1997). Further publications describe PSO practice on personal pension schemes, free standing AVC schemes and simplified schemes.

Protected rights   That part of a personal pension scheme or contracted-out money purchase scheme that represents the fund accumulated by contributions paid by the DSS. These rights are separated from any other benefits built up by the member's or the employer's contributions, as restrictions are imposed on the options available in respect of protected rights.

Purchased life annuity   An annuity purchased privately by an individual where instalments of annuity are subject to tax only in part (ICTA 1988, s 656).

Reduction in yield (RIY)   A method used to express the charges and expenses under a personal pension plan. The RIY shows the percentage reduction in annual growth over the term of the plan.

Relevant benefits   Any benefits given in connection with the termination of service except for benefits given only in the event of accident (see ICTA 1988, s 612).

Requisite benefits   The scale of benefits which, prior to November 1986, a pension scheme had to provide as one of the conditions to allow it to contract out.

Reference Scheme Test   The scale of benefits which a salary-related scheme must provide if it is to be used for contracting-out purposes beyond 5 April 1997. The benefits are:

- Benefits under the scheme must be payable at 65, for life.
- Benefits must be not less than one-eightieth of average qualifying earnings in the last three tax years before the end of service, multiplied by years of service.
- Qualifying earnings are to be 90 per cent of the earnings on which National Insurance contributions are paid.
- Pension is not required to exceed 50 per cent of the earnings upon which pension is calculated (which effectively limits the pension to 40 years of service).
- Qualifying earnings are to be 90 per cent of the earnings between the lower and upper earnings limits.
- Spouse's pension: 50 per cent of the member's pension (based on completed service for members who die before age 65).
- All benefits for service after 6 April 1997 must increase by 5 per cent or RPI, if lower.

Retained benefits   Retirement or death benefits in respect of an employee's earlier service with a former employer or an earlier period of self-employment.

Salary sacrifice   An agreement, normally in the form of an exchange of letters between an employer and an employee where the employee gives up part of his salary. The employer is then able to make a corresponding increase in his contribution to the pension scheme.

Section 148 orders   Orders issued each year in accordance with s 148 of the Social Security Administration Act 1992, setting out the rates of increase to be applied in the earnings factors on which the additional component and **guaranteed minimum pension** are based. This revaluation is based on the increase in national average earnings, and was previously known as s 21 orders.

Section 32 policy   An insurance policy which is used to receive a transfer value from an occupational pension scheme. Sometimes called a 'buy out' plan. A section 32A policy is used to secure the protected rights of a member on the winding-up of a COMPS.

Section 226 plan   The old name for a retirement annuity. The current legislative reference is section 620 (of the ICTA 1988).

Self-administered scheme   A scheme (usually small) where the assets are invested by the trustees in a range of media.

Simplified scheme   A money purchase scheme specially designed by the Revenue to speed up the process by which pension schemes are approved. Provided the benefits are exactly as set out in specimen documents produced by the Revenue and membership excludes controlling directors, scheme approval will follow automatically.

SIPP   A self-invested personal pension.

Special contributions   Contributions paid by the employer (or, rarely, by a member) for a limited period or as a single payment to provide augmented benefits for a member or to meet deficiencies in funding levels.

SSAP 24   The abbreviation given to the accounting standard 'Statement of Standard Accountancy Practice'. It refers to the statement which has been issued by the accountancy bodies concerning accounting for pension costs in company accounts: certain items of information must be disclosed about a company's pension arrangements, eg the results of the most recent actuarial valuation and the long-term contribution rate required to meet the cost of pension benefits.

State pension age   The age from which pensions are normally payable by the state scheme, currently 60 for women and 65 for men. By 2020 state pension ages will be equalised at age 65.

Top hat scheme   An alternative term for the executive pension plan.

Transfer payment   A payment made by the trustees of one pension scheme to the trustees of another when a member leaves employment to enable the receiving pension scheme to give additional benefits. Sometimes called a 'cash equivalent'.

Trivial pension   A pension which is so small that it can be exchanged for a cash sum.

Unit-linked pension scheme   Usually an individual arrangement where the amount of retirement benefits is related to the units in an investment fund and the value of the fund varies according to the value of the units.

Upper earnings limit   The amount of earnings (approximately seven times the lower earnings limit) on which contributions are payable to the state scheme.

Vested rights   The benefits under the scheme to which a member is unconditionally entitled if he were to leave service including related benefits for dependants.

Waiting period   Period of service which an employee may have to serve before being entitled to join a pension scheme.

Whistleblower   Under the terms of the Pensions Act 1995 if the scheme actuary or scheme auditor has reasonable cause to believe that any duty relevant to the administration of the scheme is not being complied with and that the failure is likely to be of material significance to OPRA, he must report the matter to OPRA.

Winding-up   The process of terminating an occupational pension scheme and applying the scheme assets to buy annuities for scheme members and their beneficiaries, for example through **section 32 policies**.

APPENDIX 2
EXTRACT FROM INLAND REVENUE PRACTICE NOTES IR 12 (1997, UPDATED AUGUST 1999)

Insured Schemes: Loans to Employers (made on or after 1/12/99)

Background

16.58   Government policy on self-investment (i.e. the investment of pension scheme funds in the employer's business) does not preclude the use of certain pension scheme policies as security for a loan to the employer (or to any *associated employer* whether or not they participate in the scheme) for a genuine business purpose. Only policies (or such part thereof) taken out solely to secure benefits for a *controlling director* are suitable for this purpose and the conditions on which the loan is made must satisfy a number of Inland Revenue requirements.

Purpose of PS 8 certificate

16.59   The PS 8 certificate [reproduced on pp. 288–292] is designed to enable the Pension Schemes Office to dispense with the need to examine documentation relating to the loan and to concentrate on monitoring the circumstances and the use of the loan itself. There is generally no requirement to provide the Pension Schemes Office with any related documentation but the Pension Schemes Office reserves the right to call for documentation in particular cases. If the Pension Schemes Office is satisfied with the circumstances of the loan a simple acknowledgement will be issued within 4 weeks of the receipt of the notification. Otherwise the trustees and the life office will be asked for more information or instructed to obtain immediate repayment of the loan.

Facility not to be abused

16.60   The facility of obtaining loans by using pension scheme policies as security must not be operated in such a way as to call into question the sole purpose requirement of section 590(2)(a). A succession of regular loans to bring the total loan outstanding to the maximum permitted might suggest that the employer is using the facility to only partly fund the scheme while claiming a tax deduction for the total pension contributions . . . If such a succession is not to prejudice the approval of the scheme it should be for a genuine commercial reason and not normally extend beyond 2 years.

Conditions to be Satisfied for a Loan to be Acceptable

Loans must be commercial

16.61   The basic underlying principle is that the loan to the employer (*or associated employer*) should be made on commercial terms. In order to satisfy this basic principle the loan must:

(a) be at a commercial rate of interest (i.e. at least Clearing Bank Base Rate +3% will normally be accepted. See also paragraph 16.62 below)
(b) have a duration commensurate with the purpose of the loan (see paragraphs 16.63 and 16.64 below)
(c) be used for the purpose of the borrowers trading activities (see paragraph 16.65 below)
(d) not be made to companies in financial difficulties (see Update No 43 and paragraph 16.66 below)
(e) be secured against a policy (or part thereof) that is specifically and solely for the provision of benefits for a member who is a *controlling director* of the borrower and who has consented to the policy (or part thereof) being used as security for the loan, and
(f) not exceed 50% of the current value of the policy or policies used to secure the loan (if the lending takes place within 2 years of the establishment of the scheme the amount shall not exceed 25% of the current value of the policy excluding the value of any transfer values received and included therein)

Interest rate less than CBBR+3%

16.62   Where the rate of interest is less than 3% above the current base rate of a particular clearing bank (see paragraph 1(c) of the certificate) written evidence will be required to show that the borrower can obtain a loan on similar terms from an arms-length financial institution.

Duration of loan – maximum

16.63   The maximum duration for such loans is a period expiring 1 year before the *normal retirement date* of the member whose policy (or part thereof) is used as security for the loan.

(a) This is, however, the maximum period for which the loan can be made and will be acceptable only in exceptional circumstances. Normally the duration of such loans would not be expected to be more than 3 to 5 years. For some purposes, e.g. the purchase of stock in trade, a duration of 1 year or less may be more appropriate.
(b) Where the duration of the loan appears to be unusually long in the light of its stated purpose, the Pension Schemes Office may make enquiries and if appropriate insist that the duration of the loan be reduced to a more realistic period.
(c) The duration of the loan will not be permitted to exceed 2 years unless the terms of the loan provide for level capital repayments throughout the loan period with capital repayments being made at least every 6 months.

Amendment to loan agreement

16.64   If the life office and the borrower wish to amend the terms of the loan then fresh documentation and a PS 8 certificate will be required. The Pension Schemes Office may require the loan to be immediately repaid unless the amendment is for acceptable commercial reasons. If the duration of the loan is to be extended, the Pension Schemes Office will normally expect the loan agreement to require regular repayments of capital throughout the duration of the loan as well as interest payments. It is unlikely that the Pension Schemes Office will accept more than two amendments to the terms of the loan.

Restriction on purpose of loan

16.65   The employer (or *associated employer*) may not lend the money on to someone else nor use it for some purely speculative purpose such as the purchase of shares or other investment. It may, however, be acceptable in some circumstances for a holding company to use such monies to make or manage share investments in its 50% trading subsidiaries.

Credit check required

16.66   Before the trustees of the scheme grant security for the loan, a credit check on the borrower must be undertaken and the results disclosed to the Pension Schemes Office when the PS 8 is submitted. There is no requirement for the credit check to take any particular form.

However, the credit check should be undertaken no more than 4 weeks before the loan is made. If the credit check does not provide a rating and a financial strength indicator then it should include at least three or more years of analysed accounts (or from when the company commenced trading), the date of the latest accounts and returns filed, details of any County Court Judgements and mentions in Legal Gazette. Although there is no requirement for the credit check to include any form of rating, the inclusion of such a rating would be preferred and would significantly reduce the probability of the Pension Schemes Office making any further enquiries regarding the loan or requiring the loan to be repaid.

(a) If the Pension Schemes Office do not consider the granting of security to be a judicious act by the trustees the Pension Schemes Office may require the loan to be repaid. Clearly any loan made to an ailing or insolvent company will not be acceptable.

(b) The Pension Schemes Office will take into consideration any other information that the trustees of the scheme wish to attach to the PS 8 in support of their decision to grant security for the loan, e.g. copies of the latest company accounts, cash flow projections etc.

(c) If the trustees wish to have certainty that the Pension Schemes Office is satisfied that a loan was not injudicious then the trustees should ensure that all facts material to the financial health of the borrower are disclosed.

(d) The level of risk considered acceptable will depend on several factors including the financial health of the company, the duration of the loan and whether the terms of the loan provides for ongoing capital repayments throughout the period of the loan.

(e) If there is insufficient information provided by the credit check and the trustees to determine that a loan is judicious then the Pension Schemes Office will require the loan to be repaid unless the trustees can justify the granting of the security.

Injudicious loan can lead to loss of approval

16.67   The PS 8 has been amended to carry a warning that the making of an injudicious loan or the securing of an injudicious loan on scheme policies or failure otherwise to comply with Pension Schemes Office requirements may lead to the loss of approval of the scheme . . .

40% tax charge

16.68   Loss of approval of the scheme will give rise to a tax charge under s591C ICTA 1988 of 40% of the scheme assets . . .

Other significant tax consequences . . . will also apply.

No further loans when arrears exist

16.69   No further loans may be made to an employer (or *associated employer*) secured on scheme policies whilst interest and/or capital is in arrears on an existing loan made to that employer or to an *associated employer* secured on scheme policies. This prohibition extends to loans from any other schemes of the borrower whether or not there are any arrears in respect of loans made by these schemes.

No topping up provisions

16.70   A loan agreement should not include a provision for further topping up. If an additional loan is necessary, it must be the subject of separate documentation and a separate certificate.

Waiving of interest

16.71   In some cases the growth in value of the policy used to secure the loan is linked to the interest paid on the loan. Where there is any link between the loanback and the policy returns the interest payable on the loanback may not be waived nor the rate of interest reduced. It is only permissible to waive the interest or to reduce the rate of interest payable in circumstances where this will not have any effect on the scheme policies or on the growth in value of those policies.

Restrict directors lump sum

16.72   Any reduction of benefits as a result of foreclosure will be first effected against any lump sum retirement benefits payable.
   The restriction on the director's lump sum retirement benefits will be lifted to the extent of the amounts recovered by the scheme trustee(s) under the rights acquired as a result of foreclosure.

Allocation of outstanding interest when paid

16.73   Where interest is not paid by the borrower on the due and payable dates, any payments to life offices intended as repayments of interest or capital will be set off first against current and outstanding interest with any balance then being set off against capital.

PS 8 Certificate

16.74   The certificate PS 8 on which loans to employers (or *associated employers*) are reported must be sent to the Pension Schemes Office within 90 days of the making of the loan) and requires the following information:

(a) The identity of the borrower

(b) The results of the credit check (see paragraph 16.66 above) attached to the PS 8 together with any other information that the trustees may wish the Pension Schemes Office to take into account when considering whether or not the granting of security by the trustee was a judicious act

(c) Certification that the policies used to secure the loan are for *controlling directors* only

(d) Certification of the purpose for which the loan is sought

(e) The duration of the loan

(f) The rate of interest chargeable on the loan and the details of when the interest becomes due and payable.

In addition the PS 8 and certifications should be signed by both the employer (or *associated employer*) and the trustees of the scheme. It is not acceptable for anyone to sign the PS 8 on behalf of the trustees and/or the employer.

If the employer is also the trustee then this may require the employer to sign twice in two separate capacities.

Consequence of Foreclosure

Trustees acquire a right of action

16.75   Where a life office has recourse to security given by the pension scheme trustees, the trustees acquire, under general law, the rights to the original debt. This means that after foreclosure there will be a right of action by the trustees against the employer.

Loan judicious but borrower unable to repay loan

16.76   Where

(a) the granting of security by the scheme trustee(s) was judicious, and

(b) repayment of the original debt has become impossible (e.g. where the employer is in liquidation and the liquidator has indicated that there will be no dividend payable to the scheme), and

(c) the Pension Schemes Office is satisfied that the situation has arisen because of genuine commercial reasons,

the approval of the scheme will not be withdrawn provided that there are no other facts concerning the scheme or its administration that warrant withdrawal of approval.

No charge under s601 ICTA 1988 arises

16.77   Any rights accruing to the scheme as a result of foreclosure in the above circumstances will have no value and can be waived without giving rise to a tax charge under section 601 ICTA 1988 . . . In these circumstances the scheme will not become a self-administered scheme.

Restrict lump sum benefit

16.78   Any reduction of benefits as a result of foreclosure will be first effected against any lump sum retirement benefits payable.

Loan judicious but borrower won't pay rather than can't pay

16.79   Where the granting of security by the trustee(s) was judicious but foreclosure takes place even though the employer is capable of repaying the original debt either at the date of foreclosure or at some future date, e.g. where the employer is continuing to trade or hold assets following foreclosure, the rights acquired by the trustee(s) as a result of foreclosure have value. In this situation the waiving of those rights will be a transfer of value to the employer. This will have tax consequences under section 601 ICTA 1988 and will also be grounds for the withdrawal of the approval of the scheme.

How to avoid loss of approval

16.80   The approval of the scheme will not, however, be withdrawn where the granting of security by the trustees was judicious and, following foreclosure the rights acquired by the trustees have value, provided that the Pension Schemes Office is satisfied that there are no other facts concerning the scheme or its administration that warrant the withdrawal of approval and the trustees have:

(a) immediately enforced their rights against the employer, or
(b) have reached a commercial arrangement whereby the outstanding capital, together with the outstanding interest, will be paid to the scheme trustees within a reasonable period of time.

Continuation of approval will be conditional on the commercial arrangement agreed with the Pension Schemes Office being adhered to.

Scheme may become a SSAS

16.81   Where acceptable arrangements are made the scheme will be holding an asset which is not an insurance policy. Whether or not this is an investment will be a question of fact and the scheme may have become a self-administered scheme as a result. An approved scheme which becomes a small self-administered scheme must comply with the requirements of the 'SSAS Regulations' as subsequently amended as at the time it becomes such a scheme and thereafter . . .

Restriction to benefits and how to avoid it

16.82   The reduction of the *controlling directors* benefits will be lifted to the extent of the amounts recovered by the scheme trustees from the employer under the rights acquired as a result of foreclosure. To avoid a restriction to the lump sum retirement benefits the amounts must be recovered before the lump sum retirement benefits are paid.

Injudicious loan leads to loss of approval

16.83   Where the granting of the security by the trustees was injudicious approval of the scheme will normally be withdrawn. The repayment of the loan and all interest due can usually prevent the loss of approval in these circumstances. Where foreclosure takes place even though the employer is capable of repaying the original debt, a tax charge under section 601 ICTA 1988 will also arise if the acquired rights are waived or not enforced.

How to avoid loss of approval

16.84   Where the granting of security was approved by the Pension Schemes Office then the withdrawal of approval of the scheme on the grounds that the loan was injudicious can only take place if the Pension Schemes Office demonstrates that:

(a) there was information available to the trustees relevant to the financial state of the company at the time the loan was made, which was not disclosed to the Pension Schemes Office with the PS 8 certificate, and which would have affected the decision made by the Pension Schemes Office, or

(b) the information provided to the Pension Schemes Office was incorrect or misleading.

Notifications Required

The PSO must be notified of all loans made

16.85   The Pension Schemes Office must be notified of all such loans within 90 days by means of a completed certificate (PS 8) that the loan and the scheme documentation meet the necessary requirements. The certificate details all the requirements which need to be certified and all the undertakings required. Customers are free to photocopy the certificate for use but must submit them to the Pension Schemes Office on the same coloured paper as the official form as indicated on the . . . specimen [see pp. 288–292]. Customers on our bulk forms users database will be supplied immediately with copies of the new certificate. Any customer who wants to obtain copies of the new certificate should ring the Pension Schemes Office Supplies Line on 0115 974 1670.

Notify PSO of foreclosure

16.86   The lender must notify the Pension Schemes Office whenever foreclosure on a scheme policy takes place within 30 days of the event in question.

Notify PSO if interest is outstanding

16.87   If interest or capital is outstanding 90 days after the due date for payment then the life office should report this to the Pension Schemes Office within a further 30 days.

Notify amendment

16.88   If an existing loan agreement is amended, a new PS 8 certificate should be submitted to the Pension Schemes Office within 90 days of the amendment.

Notify PSO if contributions cease

16.89   If the payment of regular contributions under the scheme for the *controlling director* whose policy (or part thereof) is being used as security for the loan ceases, the Pension Schemes Office must be notified by the life office within 90 days of such cessation. If the life office is aware of the reason for cessation of contributions this information should be included with the notification.

Self-managed Funds

16.90   Where an insured earmarked scheme uses a policy linked to an investment fund (usually held in the name of the insurer) exclusive to that scheme, such investment funds are regarded as self-managed funds and the Pension Schemes Office will, under their discretionary powers (s591(1) ICTA 1988), require as a condition of continued approval that fund to comply with Regulations 4 to 8 of the 'SSAS Regulations' as subsequently amended . . . despite the fact that the scheme is not strictly a small self-administered scheme. Such self-managed funds should therefore be managed in accordance with those Regulations . . . This requirement does not, however, apply to investments made before 31 December 1992.

PS 8 CERTIFICATE

DOCUMENTATION CERTIFICATE: LOAN TO EMPLOYER OR COMPANY ASSOCIATED WITH EMPLOYER

Certificate for the purposes of approval or continued approval under Chapter 1 Part XIV ICTA 1988

This certificate must be sent to the Pension Schemes Office (PSO) within 90 days of making any loan secured on scheme policies to an employer participating in the scheme or to a company associated with such an employer (*see note 1*).

The PSO reserves the right to call for a copy of the loan agreement for any particular loan.

Please remember that the making of an injudicious loan or the securing of an injudicious loan on scheme policies (*see note 2*) or failure otherwise to comply with PSO requirements may lead to the loss of approval of the scheme. This will give rise to a tax charge under S591C ICTA 1988 of 40% of the scheme assets. Other significant tax consequences will also apply as set out in Part 19 of the Practice Notes IR12 (1997).

Please read the notes overleaf before completing this form.

NAME OF PRINCIPAL EMPLOYER ⎯⎯⎯⎯⎯⎯⎯⎯⎯⎯⎯

NAME OF SCHEME ⎯⎯⎯⎯⎯⎯⎯⎯⎯⎯⎯⎯⎯⎯⎯

PSO REF NO SF ⎯⎯⎯⎯⎯ / ⎯⎯⎯⎯⎯⎯

LIFE OFFICE REFERENCE ⎯⎯⎯⎯⎯⎯⎯⎯⎯⎯⎯⎯

I certify

1. that in relation to a loan to the employer or to a company associated with the employer (the borrower) from ⎯⎯⎯⎯⎯⎯ (the lender) on the security of a scheme policy, the borrower, the lender, the trustees of the scheme and the member, being a controlling director of the borrower, whose scheme benefits the policy is intended to secure have entered into a loan agreement satisfying all the following conditions:

a. that the member has agreed to his or her interest in the policy being used as security for the loan;

b. that the policies used to secure the loan are for controlling directors only;

c. that the borrower shall pay interest on the outstanding balance of the loan at a rate of interest which (subject to adjustments not being required more frequently than monthly) shall not at any time be less than either:

   i. 3 per cent greater than the base rate from time to time of a particular named clearing bank, or

   ii. such a lower rate that the borrower can obtain a loan on similar terms from an arms-length financial institution (written evidence of the availability of such a loan must be attached to this certificate);

d. that if the interest is not paid by the borrower on the due and payable dates, any payments made by the borrower to the lender intended as repayments of interest or capital will be allocated by the lender and the borrower first against current interest and outstanding interest, any balance will then be set off against outstanding capital;

e. that there are no outstanding arrears of interest and/or capital on any existing loans secured on scheme policies to this or any associated company;

f. that if any interest is outstanding 90 days after the due date, the PSO will be notified within a further 30 days;

g. that if the terms of the loan are amended, the PSO will be notified within 90 days (*see note 3*);

h. that if the payment of regular contributions for the member ceases, the PSO will be notified within 90 days of such cessation;

i. that the borrower shall repay the loan at or before a specified date no later than twelve months before the normal retirement date specified for the member under the scheme rules;

j. that the outstanding amount of the loan together with any unpaid interest is to be immediately repayable in any of the following circumstances:

    i. if the borrower is in breach of any of the conditions of the loan agreement, or

    ii. if the borrower ceases to carry on business, or

    iii. if the borrower becomes insolvent, within the meaning defined in Regulation 6 of The Retirement Benefit Schemes (Restriction on Discretion to Approve) (Small Self-administered Schemes) Regulations 1991 (SI 1991 No 1614), or

    iv. on the cessation of payment of regular contributions for the member under the scheme (*see note 4*), or

    v. if the borrower applies the loan other than for the stated business purpose of the borrower, or

    vi. if the member dies or retires, or

    vii. if the Inland Revenue gives notice in writing that the loan is not consistent with the approval of the scheme;

k. that the lender shall in the event of default by the borrower notify the PSO within 30 days of having recourse to recovery from the value of the policy; and

2   that the rules of the scheme contain a provision enabling a scheme policy to be applied as security for a loan subject to all the following conditions:

a. that the loan is made to an employer participating in the scheme or to a company associated with such an employer (*see note 1*);

b. that any policy (or part thereof) used as security for a loan must be specifically and solely for the provision of benefits for a member who is a controlling director of the borrower and who has consented to the policy (or part thereof) being charged as security for the loan;

c. that the loan:

    i. is for a fixed term ending not later than 12 months before the Member's Normal Retirement Date,

    ii. is to be applied entirely for the purpose of the borrower's business. In particular it is not to be applied directly or indirectly (other than by increasing the value of the borrower's business) for the benefit of any member or any relative (or the spouse of a relative) of the member or his or her spouse,

iii. is at a commercial rate of interest, and
iv. is evidenced by an agreement in writing which contains all the conditions on which it is made and, in particular, the provisions specified in sub-paragraph d. below,

INFORMATION ABOUT LOANS TO EMPLOYER AND ASSOCIATED COMPANIES

1	Date of loan	
2	Name of borrower and whether employer or associated company (state which (see note 1))	
3	Amount of loan	
4	Amount of loan outstanding	
5	Value of relevant policy at date of loan	
6	Purpose of loan	
7	Repayment date — if more than two years from the date the loan was made, please specify when level capital repayments are due and payable	
8	Rate of interest and when it is due and payable	
9.	Details of member i.e. Name Position in company National Insurance Number Normal Retirement Date	
10	Policy number	

11	Details of all other outstanding loans to employers and 'associated' companies				
	Name of borrower	Employer or associated company (state which)	Date of loan	Amount of loan	Amount of loan outstanding at the date of 1 above

d. the provisions specified in this sub-paragraph are that the loan shall be repaid immediately in any of the following circumstances:
   i.   if the borrower is in breach of the conditions of the agreement, or
   ii.   if the borrower ceases to carry on business, or
   iii. if the borrower becomes insolvent within the meaning defined in Regulation 6 of the Retirement Benefits Schemes (Restriction on Discretion to Approve) (Small Self-administered Schemes) Regulations 1991 (SI 1991 No 1614), or
   iv.   on the cessation of payment of regular contributions for the member under the scheme (*see note 4*), or
   v.   if the borrower applies the loan other than for a business purpose of the borrower, or
   vi.   if the member dies or retires, or
   vii. if the Inland Revenue gives notice in writing that the loan is not consistent with the approval of the scheme;
e. that the total amount of any loans secured on a policy under this provision shall not exceed 50% of the current value of the policy. If the lending takes place within 2 years of the establishment of the scheme the amount shall not exceed 25% of the current value of the policy excluding the value of any transfer values received and included therein,
f. should a loan not be repaid in accordance with these conditions and any amounts outstanding under the loan agreement are recovered from the value of the policy, that any consequent reduction of benefits payable under the scheme will be first effected against any lump sum retirement benefits payable,
g. the trustees of the scheme shall notify the PSO of any loan effected under this provision.

3. that the information set out below in respect of this loan and any other such loans made in the last 5 years is both complete and correct. **A false declaration can lead to the loss of approval of the scheme.**

This certificate must be signed by the employer and (all) the trustee(s) of the scheme. (*See note 5*)

Name	Signature	Date	Capacity (Employer or Trustee)
_____	_____	_____	_____
_____	_____	_____	_____
_____	_____	_____	_____
_____	_____	_____	_____
_____	_____	_____	_____
_____	_____	_____	_____

Notes:

1. For the purpose of this certificate companies are associated if one is controlled by the other or if both are controlled by a third person. Control shall be construed in accordance with section 840 of the Income and Corporation Taxes Act 1988 or, in the case of a close company, with section 416 of that Act.

2. This certificate must be accompanied by a disclosure of the results of a credit check undertaken on the borrower immediately before the trustees agree to permit any policy held by the scheme to be used as security for the loan. The trustees may also attach any other information they consider relevant to their decision that they wish the PSO to take into consideration. If the PSO does not consider the granting of security by the trustees to be a judicious act, the PSO may give notice in writing that the loan is not consistent with the approval of the scheme and require the immediate repayment of the loan.

3. The PSO is unlikely to agree to more than two amendments of a loan agreement, e.g. to extend the period of the loan. The PSO may require the loan to be repaid unless the roll-over is for acceptable commercial reasons.

4. Immediate repayment is not necessary on suspension of regular contributions to meet Inland Revenue funding requirements or otherwise where there is a definite expectation that the contributions will be resumed within 2 years.

5. If the employer is also the trustee of the scheme, please provide a signature in respect of each capacity.

APPENDIX 3
EXTRACT FROM INLAND REVENUE PRACTICE NOTES
(1997, CONTAINING SUBSEQUENT AMENDMENTS INCLUDING SOME DATED 5/99)

PART 20: SMALL SELF-ADMINISTERED SCHEMES

Introduction

20.1   As the term indicates, a small self-administered scheme is a self-administered scheme with a small number of members. The Inland Revenue's discretion to approve a small self-administered scheme is limited by the Retirement Benefits Schemes (Restriction on Discretion to Approve) (Small Self-administered Schemes) Regulations 1991 (SI 1991 No 1614). References in this Part to the 'SSAS Regulations' are to those Regulations and the guidance in this Part should be read in conjunction with those Regulations. The SSAS Regulations define a small self-administered scheme as a self-administered scheme with less than 12 members where at least one of those members is connected with another member, or with a trustee or an employer in relation to the scheme. The Inland Revenue may also require a scheme with 12 or more members to be treated as a small self-administered scheme and to comply with the special requirements set out in this Part. An example would be a scheme established primarily for a few family directors, to whom were added some relatively low-paid employees with entitlement to a very low level of benefits, including as makeweights to bring the total membership to 12 or slightly more. Conversely it will not be necessary to apply 'small scheme' treatment to a scheme with less than 12 members if all the members are at arm's length from one another, from the employer and from the trustees. An approved insured scheme which becomes a small self-administered scheme will lose its approval unless it complies with the requirements of the SSAS Regulations as at the time it becomes such a scheme and thereafter.

20.2   The reasons why the Inland Revenue consider special requirements necessary for the approval of such schemes are:

(a) Under trust law which evolved before the advent of pension schemes, a trust with one or a few beneficiaries is susceptible to being broken regardless of the terms in which the trust is constituted.
(b) The funding of a self-administered scheme for a few members is difficult because the small membership limits the extent to which statistical fluctuations can be smoothed out (eg for mortality).
(c) Small self-administered schemes are usually established to provide benefits for directors. Often the scheme members control the employer company and are also trustees of the scheme. This multiplicity of roles can face a trustee with a conflict of interests leading to actions concerning the scheme being taken for reasons other than the provision of benefits on retirement.

20.3   The special requirements thus fall into three categories viz:

(a) control of the format of the trust,
(b) control of funding, and
(c) control of investments.

The Trust

Pensioneer trustee

20.4   The SSAS Regulations restrict the *Board's* discretion to approve a small self-administered scheme to one whose governing documentation contains provisions requiring one of the trustees to be a 'pensioneer trustee'. A pensioneer trustee is an individual or body recognised by the Inland Revenue as being widely involved with occupational pension schemes and having dealings with the Pension Schemes Office, who has given an undertaking to that Office that he or she will not consent to any termination of a scheme of which he or she is a trustee otherwise than in accordance with the approved terms of the winding-up rule.

20.5   Where a corporate body wishes to be recognised as a pensioneer trustee it is normally essential for the directors, or a majority of them, to be acceptable as such in their own right. The acceptable directors should have the power to direct how the corporate trustee will vote in any proceedings of pension scheme trustees.

20.6   The object of the appointment of a pensioneer trustee is to block any proposal that the trust should be terminated and the funds distributed among the members. It is, however, accepted that trustees have no power to resist such a proposal if all the persons having an interest under the trust are agreed in requiring this action (Saunders v Vautier, 1841). Such a consensus is unlikely in the context of a typical pension scheme where, even if the number of members is small, the existence of further contingent beneficiaries can rarely be excluded.

20.7   The trust provisions of an approved small self-administered scheme must be framed to allow the pensioneer trustee to fulfil his or her function. Thus a provision which allows trustees to act on majority rather than unanimous decisions must be qualified so as not to apply in relation to the termination of the scheme. A scheme subject to Scottish law must expressly require the pensioneer trustee's concurrence in any decision about the scheme's termination.

20.8   A pensioneer trustee should not act as such in any scheme of which he or she is a member. Similarly a corporate trustee should not act in the capacity for a scheme for its own employees. A pensioneer trustee must not be connected with a scheme member, any other trustee of the scheme or any employer in relation to the scheme.

20.9   If a pensioneer trustee ceases to be qualified to act as such or ceases to be a trustee of the scheme, regulation 9 of the SSAS Regulations requires the trustees or the remaining trustee or trustees to:

(a) notify the *Board* in writing within 30 days of such cessation;
(b) within 60 days of the cessation to appoint a successor as a pensioneer trustee; and
(c) within 30 days of the appointment, to notify the *Board* in writing of the name of the successor.

A copy of the document(s) removing and appointing pensioneer trustees should be sent to the Pension Schemes Office.

20.10   The Inland Revenue reserves the right to withdraw pensioneer trustee status should the circumstances warrant it, for example, if the individual or corporate body or any of its directors or staff is found to be involved in or promoting tax avoidance, whether or not the avoidance relates to pension schemes.

Entitlement against the whole trust fund

20.11   It is not permissible for an approved small self-administered scheme to secure a member's benefits against particular trust assets. There is no objection to the calculation of the amount of the member's benefits being notionally linked to the value of particular assets but the trust provisions must ensure that the member's entitlement to benefit is against the funds of the trust as a whole.

Multiple small schemes

20.12   Regulation 3 of the SSAS Regulations prohibits the *Board* from approving a small self-administered scheme in respect of an employer where that employer already has such a scheme approved by the *Board* to which it was or is entitled to pay contributions, and that scheme has not been wound-up. Thus if more than one employee is to be pensioned through this medium they should all be included in one scheme. Where an employee is employed by several companies in a group of associated companies, one centralised small self-administered scheme may be established in which all the relevant companies participate . . . or, alternatively, each employer may set up its own small self-administered scheme to provide benefits for the employee based on his or her salary and service with it alone.

Death benefits

20.13   The scheme rules should provide that lump sum benefits payable on death (including any lump sum payable under a pension guarantee) are, except where paragraph 11.12 [not reproduced] applies, to be distributable at the trustee's/*administrator's* discretion among a wide class of beneficiaries.

Funding

20.14   An approved small self-administered scheme, like any other approved scheme, must comply with the general funding principles set out in paragraph 13.1 [not reproduced]. The more specific requirements of Part 13 are, however, qualified as described in paragraphs 20.15 to 20.24.

Actuarial reports

20.15   An approved small self-administered scheme is required to obtain an actuarial valuation of its assets and liabilities at its inception and thereafter at intervals no greater than 3 years. A copy of each actuarial report must be submitted to the Pension Schemes Office not later than one year from the effective date of the valuation.

Contributions

20.16   No contributions are to be paid to the scheme unless justified by the latest actuarial report. It is not permissible to make contributions when money is available irrespective of the needs of the scheme (it is a popular misconception that a scheme may hold a general reserve equal to one year's *ordinary annual contribution*).

Death benefits

20.17   All death benefits, insofar as they exceed the value of the member's interests in the fund based on his or her accrued pension and other retirement benefits, must be insured.

Purchase of annuities

20.18   To ensure that pensions from small self-administered schemes are pensions for life as required by paragraph 7.31, pensions should normally be secured from the outset by the purchase of an annuity from a life office. The annuity should be non-commutable and non-assignable and in the name of the trustee.

20.19   Annuity rates, however, do fluctuate and when the costs are high the immediate purchase of an annuity may not make economic sense. Rules may, therefore, provide, subject to paragraphs 20.20, 20.21, 20.31, 20.33, 20.36 and 20.42 for the purchase of the annuity to be deferred and the pension to be paid directly from the scheme's resources. Once the pension is in payment, the purchase of annuities may be phased in by the purchase of immediate annuities to provide part of the overall pension. To the extent that pensions are so secured, post-retirement increases in respect of the secured pension must also be immediately secured.

20.20   Deferment of the purchase of annuities may not extend beyond the age of 75. The intention of allowing deferment is to provide the trustees with more flexibility in deciding the most opportune time to purchase the annuity rather than an automatic deferral to age 75. The need to purchase the annuity must, therefore, be kept under continuous review (as a matter of best practice), with trustees taking professional advice on the timing of the purchase. For example, the issue should be considered annually at trustee's meetings and whenever changes occur in interest rates or inflation which have a material impact on the suitability of purchasing an annuity.

20.21   When pensions are paid directly out of scheme resources under paragraph 20.19 above, the scheme actuary must certify the amount of pension payable in accordance with the scheme rules and which can be maintained whilst taking account of:

(a) any contingent widow's, widower's or *dependant's* pension payable; and

(b) the scheme's income and assets, particularly those notionally under-pinning the provision of the member's benefits.

This certificate should compare the pension with an annuity on the same terms that could be secured on the open market at that time with the funds available. Any divergences by more than 10% between the two amounts should be explained by the actuary. The amount of any unse-cured pension in payment must form part of a scheme's triennial actuarial report. Certificates should be provided to the Pension Schemes Office with the next actuarial valuation report, or earlier on request.

Widow's/widower's/dependant's pension

20.22   Subject to paragraph 20.23 the purchase of an annuity to secure a widow's/widower's or *dependant's* pension payable on the member's death either while still in service or after retirement but before the mem-ber attains age 75, may be deferred until the earlier of the attaining by the widow/widower or *dependant* of age 75 or the date on which the deceased member would have attained age 75. As for deferral of mem-bers' pensions, the need to purchase an annuity for a widow/widower or *dependant* should be kept under continuous review. The requirements set out in paragraph 20.21 will apply except that when a widow's/wid-ower's or *dependant's* pension is in payment (a) will not be relevant and the actuarial certificate will take account under (b) only of the scheme's investments and assets underpinning the provision of the widow's/wid-ower's or *dependant's* benefit. The initial certificate should compare the pension with an annuity that could have been purchased at the time of the member's death. Where the member dies in retirement on or after age 75, the widow's/widower's or *dependant's* pension should be secured by the purchase of an annuity not later than the time of the member's death.

Widow's/widower's pension

20.23   A prospective widow's/widower's reversionary pension should be secured by the purchase of a contingent annuity at the same time as the member's own pension is so secured. If, however, the pension is payable to whichever person is the member's spouse when the member dies (ie the entitlement is not limited to the current spouse at the time of retirement), its purchase may be deferred in accordance with paragraph 20.22 above.

Pension increases

20.24   Any cost of living increases granted in respect of a pension already secured in accordance with paragraphs 20.18, 20.19 and 20.23 above should be secured with a life office as soon as they are awarded. Where scheme rules provide for pension increases at a fixed rate of up to 3% per annum compound . . .,the increases should be secured when the basic pension is secured.

Investments

20.25   The Inland Revenue's interest in the investments of a small self-administered scheme flows from the statutory condition of approval that a scheme should be 'bona fide established for the sole purpose of providing *relevant benefits*' (section 590(2)(a)). The concern is that tax exempt investments held for the provision of the scheme benefits should not be of a kind or used in such a way as to produce a non-relevant benefit for the beneficiaries or the employer.

Effect of Regulations

20.26   The SSAS Regulations contain requirements in relation to the power of the trustees of small self-administered schemes to:

(a) borrow money;
(b) hold certain assets as investments;
(c) lend money and purchase shares; and
(d) purchase, sell or lease assets.

The SSAS Regulations restrict the *Board's* discretion to approve such a scheme to one whose governing documentation contains requirements complying with those Regulations in relation to (a) to (d) above. The only exception is where at the date on which the SSAS Regulations were made, the scheme was in existence and either had not been submitted to the *Board* for approval or was before the *Board* awaiting approval. In these circumstances approval will not be precluded by reason of provisions in the scheme's documentation which allow the trustees to retain as an investment of the scheme:

(i)   personal chattels other than choses in action (see paragraph 20.55);
(ii)   residential property other than is described in paragraph 20.52; or
(iii) shares in an unlisted company which carry more than 30% of the voting power in that company or entitle the trustees to more than 30% of any dividends declared by that company (see paragraph 20.57),

provided that such an investment was held by the trustees prior to the date on which the Regulations were made and was acceptable under previous Inland Revenue discretionary practice. Similarly, a provision in the scheme's documentation authorising the trustees to:

(vi) continue to lend money or retain shares in an employer or any *associated employer*, where that money was being lent or the shares were being held prior to the date on which the SSAS Regulations were made and when the money was first lent or the shares were acquired, the scheme had been in existence for 2 years or less and the 25% restriction but not the 50% restriction described in paragraph 20.33 was exceeded; or

(v) sell assets held by them immediately before that date to a member of the scheme or to any person connected with a member of the scheme,

will not prevent approval being given. It should be noted, however, that in relation to (v), the sale must be on an arm's length basis at full market value.

20.27 It is a condition of approval that when actuarial reports are submitted to the Pension Schemes Office (see paragraph 20.15) they must be accompanied by a statement detailing how the funds of the scheme are invested. This enables the Inland Revenue to monitor whether the bona fides of the scheme are being maintained.

20.28 The *Board's* discretion to approve a small self-administered scheme is restricted to one whose governing documentation contains provisions complying with regulation 10 of the SSAS Regulations. That regulation requires the scheme *administrator* to provide to the *Board*, within a period of 90 days after the transaction taking place, information and documents relating to any transaction by the scheme trustees in their capacity as such.

20.29 From 1 January 1996 the requirement to supply information about certain transactions which is contained in regulation 10 of the SSAS Regulations was duplicated in its entirety in regulation 5 of the Information Powers Regulations . . . thus allowing a monetary penalty to be levied under section 98 Taxes Management Act 1970 for failure to comply. The intention is, in due course, to repeal regulation 10 of the SSAS Regulations but this will not affect the ability of the Pension Schemes Office to withdraw approval in appropriate cases under the discretionary powers contained in section 591B.

The types of transaction involved are:

(a) the acquisition or disposal of land including buildings and other structures;

(b) the lending of money to an employer or an *associated employer*;

(c) the acquisition or disposal of shares in an employer or an *associated employer*;

(d) the acquisition or disposal of shares in an unlisted company;

(e) the borrowing of money; and

(f) the purchase, sale or lease from or to an employer; or any *associated employer*, of any asset other than one as described in (a), (c) or (d).

The information and documents required are as may be specified on the relevant form — specimen copies are included in Appendix II.

The relevant forms are:

PS 7012 – for details of the acquisition or disposal of land (including buildings and other structures).

PS 7013 – for the lending of money to an employer or *associated employer*.

PS 7014 – for the acquisition or disposal of shares, in the employer, *associated employer* or unlisted companies.

PS 7015 – for the borrowing of money.

PS 7016 – for the purchase from, or sale or lease to an employer, or any *associated employer*, of any asset other than as described in (a), (c) or (d) above.

All transactions should be notified not later than 90 days after the event.

20.30   Apart from the requirements of regulation 5 of the Information Powers Regulations, when requested, scheme *administrators* should provide full details of any transaction to the Pension Schemes Office. The following paragraphs contain details of the various restrictions which are imposed on scheme trustees by the SSAS Regulations in relation to their powers as described in (a) to (d) of paragraph 20.26 together with some guidance on Inland Revenue views and requirements on particular aspects of investment.

General principle

20.31   The Inland Revenue will not necessarily regard any form of investment as consistent with approval just because it is within the trustees' powers and not prohibited under the terms of the SSAS Regulations. In general the Inland Revenue do not interfere in the way trustees invest trust monies except:

(a) where tax avoidance is suspected; or

(b) where an investment appears to be irreconcilable with the bona fides of the scheme having regard to the sole purpose requirement and the scheme's cash needs for purchasing annuities.

For example, investment in land or buildings may be a good long-term investment when the members are many years from retirement but becomes less appropriate as their retirement approaches and, even if the purchase of a member's, widow's/widower's or *dependant's* annuity is deferred, it is necessary to ensure that the scheme is in a position to buy an annuity between the ages of 70 and 75 without becoming involved in a forced sale of property. This is particularly so if the property purchased is an important part of the employer's own commercial premises and thus potentially difficult to realise.

Loans to members and connected persons

20.32   Regulation 6(1) of the SSAS Regulations prohibits scheme trustees from making loans to a member of the scheme or to any person, apart from an employer or any *associated employer*, who for the purposes of those Regulations is connected with a member of the scheme. Thus if a scheme is to be approved, its trust documents should specifically preclude loans to such individuals or persons. The reasons why this prohibition is considered necessary in small self-administered schemes in particular is because of the possibility (arising from the less than arm's length relationship of all the parties) that such a loan would become, in reality, a charge on the retirement benefit, or that the pension scheme would be used in this sway so as to avoid the tax liability arising on loans direct from a close company to its 'participators'.

Self investment

20.33   Regulation 7 of the SSAS Regulations restricts trustees' investment in loans to and shares in an employer company during the first 2 years from the date the scheme was established, to 25% of the market value of its assets which are derived from contributions made to it by an employer and the members since it was established (but excluding any portion of the funds notionally underpinning retired members', widow's/widower's or *dependant's* benefits in payment where the purchase of annuity has been deferred (prospective widow's/widower's of retired members whose pensions must be secured at the same time as the retired members in accordance with paragraph 20.22 being regarded for this purpose as in receipt of pension)). After the end of the 2 year period the figure increases to 50% of the market value of all the assets of the scheme (but excluding any portion of the funds notionally underpinning retired members', widow's/widower's or *dependant's* benefits in payment where the purchase of an annuity has been deferred (prospective widow's/widower's of retired members whose pensions must be secured at the same time as the retired members in accordance with paragraph 20.22 being regarded for this purpose as in receipt of pension)). Within 5 years of the commencement of pensions to new pensioners, or on attainment by the pensioner of age 70 if earlier, the trustees must ensure an appropriate proportion of any loan to the employer or *associate employer* is repaid. Where the pensioner has already attained age 70 when payment of pension commences, repayment of the loan must take place immediately.

20.34   Where all members of the scheme have retired/died, no new loans or share purchases in the employer or *associated employer* will be permitted following the later of the first payment of the final retiring member's pension and the first payment of the final widow's/widower's or *dependant's* pension (prospective widow's/widower's of retired members whose pensions must be secured at the same time as the retired members' in accordance with paragraph 20.22 being regarded for this purpose as in receipt of pension). Existing loans and shares should be repaid or sold within 5 years of the commencement of such pension payments or on attainment by the pensioner of age 70 if earlier. If the pensioner has already attained age 70 when payment of pension commences, such repayment or sale must take place immediately. Where a scheme holds a policy or policies, including a unit linked policy or policies, as part of its assets, the Pension Schemes Office would regard an acceptable interpretation of the market value of such a policy or policies to be the surrender value (calculated on the same basis as a transfer value). In the context of regulation 7 of the SSAS Regulations investment means both loans to, and the purchase of shares in the employer company and any *associated employer* whether or not they participate in the scheme. The Inland Revenue also apply these limits in relation to loans to, or shares in, other persons connected with a scheme through a member, trustee or an employer. It is not possible to provide a comprehensive definition of a connected party in this context, but broadly it includes:

(a)   an individual who is a business associate of a member of the scheme, or of a trustee or employer in relation to the scheme, or who is a relative of a trustee or employer;
(b)   a partnership where one of the partners is connected as in (a) with a member of the scheme, trustee or employer; and
(c)   a company in which a director or influential shareholder (ie one who controls 20% or more of the voting shares in the company) is connected as in (a).

20.35   An individual is connected with a corporate trustee or employer if he or she is a relative or business associate of any director or influential shareholder (as defined in (c) above) of the trustee or employer company. For practical purposes a 'business associate' means a partner in a partnership, a fellow director of a company, or a fellow influential shareholder in a company. A director of a company is regarded as a business associate of an influential shareholder of the same company and vice versa. Forms PS 7013, PS 7014 and PS 7016 (headings suitably amended where necessary) should be used to provide details of loans to, shares (acquired and disposed of) in, or purchases, sales or leases from or to, connected parties other than an employer or *associated employer*. The required documentation should accompany the completed forms.

20.36   Subject to paragraph 20.33 and Department of Social Security legislation, a scheme may lend funds to an employer or any *associated employer* but if it is to be approved, regulation 6 of the SSAS Regulations requires that such lending may only be made for the purposes of the borrower's business (broadly an activity other than that of making or managing investments, except that a holding company is permitted to make or manage share investments in its 51% trading subsidiaries) and that the loan is:

(a) for a fixed term;
(b) at a commercial rate of interest; and
(c) evidenced by an agreement in writing which contains all the conditions on which it is made and provides for immediate repayment of the loan if the borrower:
   (i)   breaches the conditions of the agreement,
   (ii)   ceases to carry on business
   (iii) becomes insolvent, or

   if repayment is required to enable the trustees to pay benefits which have already become due under the scheme. Where the purchase of an annuity has been deferred (see paragraph 20.19) the funds necessary to purchase the whole annuity must be regarded as required to pay benefits no later than 5 years after the commencement of the pension payments or on attainment by the pensioner of age 70 if earlier. If the pensioner has already attained age 70 when payment of pension commences, the funds necessary to purchase the whole annuity must be regarded as required immediately.

The Inland Revenue will also expect these requirements to be met where a loan is made to connect persons other than an employer or *associated employer* as described in paragraph 20.34.

20.37   Loans should not be of such an amount and frequency as to suggest that the employer is only partly funding the scheme while claiming a tax deduction for the total pension contributions. Regulation 6 of the SSAS Regulations requires that a loan must be for a fixed term. The length of the term is a matter for decision between the parties to the loan agreement but it should be realistic. It is not acceptable for a series of 364 day loans to be made when in reality the intention is that the employer will not repay the loan for, say, 3 years. Nor is it acceptable for the term to be longer than necessary — scheme funds should not lodge unnecessarily with an employer.

20.38   It is an Inland Revenue requirement that a commercial rate of interest (see paragraph 20.36(b)) must be charged and paid. The commerciality of the interest will not be questioned if it is at least 3% above the Clearing Banks' Base Rate and an interest rate on this basis will be acceptable for both secured and unsecured loans. The Pension Schemes Office will be prepared to consider a lower rate of interest only if written evidence is produced demonstrating that the borrower can obtain a loan on similar terms from a bank or other arm's length financial institution at a rate below Clearing Banks' Base Rate +3%.

20.39   Quite apart from the requirements of the SSAS Regulations, the Pension Schemes Office require scheme trustees to act in the best interests of scheme members in their capacity as scheme members and not as employees, shareholders etc. If they fail to do so the Pension Schemes Office are likely to take the view that the scheme is not being properly administered and that exempt approval should be withdrawn . . . Examples of the sort of actions which might result in this course of action being taken are:

(a) loans made solely to keep an ailing business afloat;
(b   loans to employers who are technically insolvent; and
(c) the failure of trustees to take all available legal steps to enforce the repayment of a loan to an employer in the circumstances described in paragraph 20.36(c).

As a rule loans should not be made to an employer or any *associated employer* unless the trustees would be prepared to lend the same amount on the same terms to an unconnected party of comparable standing.

20.40   The SSAS Regulations do not prohibit an outstanding loan from being 'rolled over' into a fresh loan agreement. The Pension Schemes Office will not, however, agree to a loan being 'rolled over' more than twice nor to the 'roll over' of unpaid interest into a new loan. Where a loan is 'rolled over' it must satisfy the conditions described in paragraphs 20.33 to 20.38.

Back to back loans

20.41   Any attempt to circumvent the ban on loans to members and connected persons or the restrictions on loans to employers by entering into arrangements whereby the scheme loans money to an unconnected party on the understanding for instance that a similar loan will be made by that party (or an associate) to the employer or a member, will almost certainly lead to withdrawal of approval from the scheme(s) involved.

Borrowing

20.42   Trustees of schemes sometimes wish to borrow funds to enable them to acquire particular assets. Regulation 4 of the SSAS Regulations restricts trustees' borrowing so that at the time of any borrowing, the aggregate amount borrowed does not exceed the total of:

(a) three times the ordinary annual contribution paid by the employers;

(b) three times the annual amount of the *basic or contractual contributions* paid by the scheme members in the year of assessment ending immediately before the time of borrowing; and

(c) 45% of the market value of the investments held for the purposes of the scheme but excluding from that market value any portion of the funds notionally underpinning benefits in relation to a retired member or to a widow/widower or *dependant* where the pension is in payment (prospective widow's/widower's of retired members whose pensions must be secured at the same time as the retired members in accordance with paragraph 20.23 being regarded for this purpose as in receipt of benefits) but the purchase of annuity has been deferred.

20.43   Any borrowing in existence when a member retires or, when a widow's/widower's or *dependant's* benefits come into payment (prospective widow's/widower's of retired members whose pensions must be secured at the same time as the retired members in accordance with paragraph 20.23 being regarded for this purpose as in receipt of benefits) must be reduced to the levels set out in (c) above within 5 years of those events or on attainment by the pensioner of age 70 if earlier. If the pensioner has already attained age 70 when payment of pension commences, any reductions in borrowing to comply with the level set out in (c) above must take place immediately.

20.44   For the purpose of regulation 4 of the SSAS Regulations, ordinary annual contribution has a different meaning to that contained in the Appendix 1 glossary. For the purpose of regulation 4 it means the smaller of:

(i)   the average annual amount of the contributions paid to the scheme by the employers in the 3 accounting years of the scheme immediately preceding the date of the borrowing, or where at that date the scheme had been established less than 3 years, the total amount of contributions paid to the scheme by the employers up to the end of the last accounting period divided by the number of complete years since the scheme was established (a part year counting as one year where the scheme has been established less than a year), and

(ii) the amount of the annual contribution which, within the period of 3 year immediately preceding the date of the borrowing, an actuary has advised in writing would have to be paid in order to secure the benefits provided under the scheme.

20.45   Monies borrowed by trustees must be used to benefit the scheme. Thus if the borrowed monies are on-lent to the employer (or any *associated employer*) the trustees must receive a higher rate of interest than they have to pay to obtain the finance.

20.46   As an administrative relaxation, the Pension Schemes Office do not require notification of short term borrowing for a period not exceeding 6 months where the aggregate amount borrowed does not exceed the lesser of 10% of the market value of the fund or £50,000 and the borrowing is repaid at or before the due date. If, however, the borrowing or part of it is rolled over into a further term it must be reported.

Purchase of assets from members, connected persons or an employer

20.47   Regulation 8 of the SSAS Regulations prohibits the direct or indirect purchase by scheme trustees of an asset from a member of the scheme or any person, apart from an employer or any *associated employer*, connected with a member of the scheme. For this purpose, the purchase of an asset by the trustees will not be regarded as being an indirect purchase from a member of the scheme or connected person if at the time of purchase 3 or more years have passed since the asset was owned by the member or connected person. Regulation 8 does not preclude the scheme trustees purchasing an asset from an employer or any *associated employer* but it requires that such purchases may only be made:

(a) after the trustees have obtained independent professional advice in writing, and
(b) in accordance with that advice.

20.48   Although the purchase of an asset from an employer or an *associated employer* is permissible, the Pension Schemes Office will need to be satisfied that it is consistent with the scheme's approval. The Pension Schemes Office should, whenever possible, be advised in advance of any such proposed transactions. The Pension Schemes Office will generally need to consult the appropriate Inspector of Taxes to determine whether tax avoidance is involved and whether the acquisition is part and parcel of a 'transaction in securities' to which section 703 might apply. Trustees may wish to satisfy themselves that the vendors have obtained clearance under section 707 (from the Inland Revenue Compliance and Collection Division) before making such an acquisition. If such clearance cannot be given or if tax avoidance is involved, the transaction will not be consistent with the scheme's approval.

Sale of assets to members, connected persons or an employer

20.49   Subject to the exception explained in paragraph 20.26, regulation 8 of the SSAS Regulations prohibits the direct or indirect sale by the trustees of a scheme asset to a member of the scheme or any person, apart from an employer or any *associated employer*, connected with a member of the scheme. For this purpose, the sale of a scheme asset by the trustees will not be regarded as being an indirect sale to a member of the scheme or connected person, if the purchase by the member or connected person took place 3 or more years after the sale by the trustees. Regulation 8 does not preclude the sale by the trustees of a scheme asset to an employer or any *associated employer* but such a sale may only be made subject to the conditions described in (a) and (b) of paragraph 20.47.

Lease of assets to an employer

20.50   Regulation 8 of the SSAS Regulations permits scheme documentation to provide for the lease by the trustees of scheme assets to an employer or any *associated employer* but only where the conditions described in (a) and (b) of paragraph 20.47 are satisfied.

Lease of assets to members or to connected persons

20.51   Regulation 8 of the SSAS Regulations prohibits the trustees from leasing any scheme assets to a member of the scheme or any person, apart from an employer or any *associated employer*, connected with a member of the scheme.

Residential property

20.52   Regulation 5 of the SSAS Regulations prohibits scheme trustees from investing in residential property other than:

(a) residential property which is, or is to be, occupied by an employee who is not connected with his or her employer and who is required as a condition of employment to occupy the property, or

(b) residential property which is, or is to be, occupied by a person, other than a scheme member or a person connected with a scheme member, in connection with that person's occupation of business premises (for example, a shop with an integral flat above) where those business premises are held by the trustees as a scheme asset.

In relation to (a) above, an employee is connected with his or her employer in circumstances where:

(i) the employer is a partnership and he or she is connected with a partner (viz is the partner's spouse, or is a relative, or the spouse of a relative, of the partner or the partner's spouse) in the partnership, or

(ii) the employer is a company and he or she or a person connected with him or her (viz in this context the spouse, or a relative, or the spouse of a relative, of the employee or the employee's spouse) is, or at any time during the preceding 10 years has been a *controlling director* of the company.

20.53   For the purposes of regulation 5 of the SSAS Regulations, the scheme trustees are not regarded as indirectly holding as an investment residential property other than as is described in (a) and (b) above where they hold as an investment units in a unit trust scheme:

(i)   which is an authorised unit trust scheme within the meaning of section 468(6), or
(ii) where all the unit holders would be wholly exempt from capital gains tax or corporation tax (otherwise than by reason of residence) if they disposed of their units.

and the trustees of the unit trust scheme hold such property as an investment subject to the trusts of the scheme.

Holiday property

20.54   Investment by scheme trustees in holiday property is not regarded as being consistent with approval

Pride in possession articles

20.55   Regulation 5 of the SSAS Regulations prohibits scheme trustees from investing in personal chattels other than choses in action (or, in Scotland, movable property other than incorporeal movable property). A 'chose in action' is something which is not corporeal, tangible, movable or visible and of which a person has not the present enjoyment but merely a right to recover it (if withheld) by action. Examples of personal chattels which are prohibited investments include works of art, jewellery, vintage cars, yachts, gold bullion etc. Examples of choses in action which are permitted investments include company shares, copyrights, financial futures etc. If scheme trustees are uncertain as to whether a particular investment would be acceptable, they should consult their professional advisers before making the investment.

Shared Investments

20.56   There is no objection in principle to a scheme joining with other parties to make a single investment (eg in a property) provided that the other parties do not include a member of the scheme or any person, apart from an employer or any *associated employer*, connected with a member of the scheme. The trustees should not, however, allow any restriction of the scheme's freedom to realise its investment how and when it wishes.

Trading

20.57   It is not necessarily inconsistent with approval for the trustees of a scheme to enter into trading activities but, as explained in paragraph 17.11, any profits are outside the protection of section 592(2). There have been, however, instances of scheme trustees either setting up a trading company or acquiring a controlling interest in such a company either directly or indirectly in order to convert non-tax exempt trading profits into tax exempt dividends. This is not consistent with approval and therefore regulation 5 of the SSAS Regulations prohibits scheme trustees from investing in the shares of an unlisted company which:

(a) carry more than 30% of the voting power in the company, or
(b) entitle the shareholder to more than 30% of any dividends declared by the company.

20.58   Where all members of the scheme have retired/died, no new investments in any stock or shares of any unlisted company will be permitted following the later of the first payment of the final retiring member's pension and the first payment of the final widow's/widower's or *dependant's* pension (prospective widow's/widower's of retired members whose pensions must be secured at the same time as the retired members in accordance with paragraph 20.23 being regarded for this purpose as in receipt of pension). Existing stocks/shares should be sold within 5 years of the commencement of such pension payments or on attainment by the pensioner of age 70 if earlier. If the pensioner has already attained age 70 when payment of pension commences, such sale must take place immediately.

20.59   Where the scheme has both non-pensioners and pensioners, any portion of the funds notionally underpinning retired member's, widows', widowers', or *dependants'* benefits in payment where the purchase of annuity has been deferred must be excluded in determining the amount which may be used to buy stock or shares in any unlisted company. Within 5 years of the commencement of pensions to new pensioners or on attainment by the pensioner of age 70 if earlier the trustees must ensure an appropriate proportion of the value of any stock or shares held in any unlisted company is sold. Where the pensioner has already attained age 70 when payment of pension commences, sale of an appropriate proportion of the stock/shares must take place immediately.

Other Requirements

Serious ill-health commutation

20.60   An approved small self-administered scheme may not exercise any provision for full commutation of an employee's pension on grounds of exceptional circumstances of serious ill-health without the specific prior agreement of the Pension Schemes Office.

Employer in liquidation

20.61   Scheme documentation should provide that, if an employer goes into liquidation without a successor, the scheme is to be wound-up or partially wound-up as appropriate. The proceeds are to be used in accordance with the documentation to purchase or transfer the accrued benefits. Any surplus is to be returned to the employer . . .

APPENDIX 4
ICTA 1988, ss 590–612, 618–655
and Schedule 23
(as amended)

(*Note:* Text in square brackets are prospective amendments made by FA 1999, Sch 10. Readers should check whether these provisions are enacted before acting upon them.)

590   Conditions for approval of retirement benefit schemes

(1)   Subject to section 591, the Board shall not approve any retirement benefits scheme for the purposes of this Chapter unless the scheme satisfies all of the conditions set out in subsection (2) below.

(2)   The conditions are—

(a)   that the scheme is bona fide established for the sole purpose [(subject to any enactment or Northern Ireland legislation requiring or allowing provision for the value of any rights to be transferred between schemes or between members of the same scheme)] of providing relevant benefits in respect of service as an employee;

[(aa)   that those benefits do not include any benefits payable to a person other than—
  (i)   the employee or a scheme member's ex-spouse,
  (ii)   a widow, widower, child, or dependant of the employee or of a scheme member's ex-spouse, or
  (iii)   the personal representatives of the employee or of a scheme member's ex-spouse;]

(b)   that the scheme is recognised by the employer and employees to whom it relates, and that every employee who is, or has a right to be, a member of the scheme has been given written particulars of all essential features of the scheme which concern him;

(c)   that there is a person resident in the United Kingdom who will be responsible for the discharge of all duties imposed on the administrator of the scheme under this Chapter;

(d)   that the employer is a contributor to the scheme;

(e)   that the scheme is established in connection with some trade or undertaking carried on in the United Kingdom by a person resident in the United Kingdom;

(f)   that in no circumstances, whether during the subsistence of the scheme or later, can any amount be paid by way of repayment of an employee's contributions under the scheme.

(3)   Subject to subsection (1) above, the Board shall approve a retirement benefit scheme for the purposes of this Chapter if the scheme satisfies all the conditions of this subsection, that is to say—

(a)   that any benefit for an employee is a pension on retirement at a specified age not earlier than 60 and not later than 75, which does not exceed one-sixtieth of the employee's final remuneration for each year of service up to a maximum of 40;

(b)   that any benefit for any widow or widower of an employee is a pension payable on his death after retirement such that the amount payable to the widow or widower by way of pension does not exceed two-thirds of any pension or pensions payable to the employee;

[(ba)   that any benefit for an ex-spouse, or for the widow or widower of an ex-spouse, is a benefit in relation to which the scheme satisfies the conditions set out in subsection (3A) below;

(bb)   that the scheme does not allow any rights debited to a scheme member as a consequence of a pension sharing order or provision to be replaced with any rights which that scheme member would not have been able to acquire (in addition to the debited rights) had the order or provision not been made;

(c)   that no benefits are payable under the scheme other than those mentioned in paragraphs (a), (b) and (ba) above;]

(d)   that no pension is capable in whole or in part of surrender, commutation or assignment, [except—
    (i) for the purpose of giving effect to a pension sharing order or provision, or
    (ii) in so far as the commutation of a benefit for an ex-spouse is allowed by virtue of subsection (3A) below, or
    (iii)] in so far as the scheme allows an employee on retirement to obtain, by commutation of [a pension provided for him], a lump sum or sums not exceeding in all three-eightieths of his final remuneration for each year of service up to a maximum of 40.

[(da)   that, in a case in which—
    (i) a lump sum may be obtained by the commutation of a part of a pension provided for an employee, and
    (ii) the amount of that pension is affected by the making of a pension sharing order or provision,
the lump sum does not exceed the sum produced by multiplying by 2.25 the amount which (after effect has been given to the pension sharing order of provision) is the amount of that pension for the first year in which it is payable;]

(e)   that, in the case of any employee who is a member of the scheme by virtue of two or more relevant associated employments, the amount payable by way of pension in respect of service in any one of them may not, when aggregated with any amount payable by way of pension in respect of service in the other or others, exceed the relevant amount;

(f)   that, in the case of any employee who is a member of the scheme by virtue of two or more relevant associated employments, the amount payable by way of commuted pension in respect of service in any one of them may not, when aggregated with any amount payable by way of commuted pension in respect of service in the other or others, exceed the relevant amount;

(g)   that, in the case of any employee in relation to whom the scheme is connected with another scheme which is (or other schemes each of which is) an approved scheme, the amount payable by way of pension under the scheme may not, when aggregated with any amount payable by way of pension under the other scheme or schemes, exceed the relevant amount;

(h)   that, in the case of any employee in relation to whom the scheme is connected with another scheme which is (or other schemes each of which is) an approved scheme, the amount payable by way of commuted pension may not, when aggregated with any amount payable by way of commuted pension under the other scheme or schemes, exceed the relevant amount.

[(3A)   The conditions mentioned in subsection (3)(ba) above are—

(a)   that any benefit for an ex-spouse takes the form of a pension (with or without an entitlement to commute a part of that pension);

(b)   that any benefit for an ex-spouse is a pension payable only on the attainment by the ex-spouse of a specified age of not less than 60 and not more than 75;

(c)   that any entitlement to commute a part of the pension is exercisable only on its becoming payable;

(d)   that any benefit for the widow or widower of an ex-spouse is confined to a non-commutable pension payable on the death of the ex-spouse at a time when the ex-spouse is already entitled to receive a pension under the scheme;

(e)   that any pension provided for the widow or widower of an ex-spouse is of an amount not exceeding two-thirds of the pension payable to the ex-spouse;

(f)   that, in a case in which a lump sum may be obtained by the commutation of a part of a pension provided for an ex-spouse, the lump sum does not exceed the sum produced by multiplying the amount of the pension for the first year in which it is payable by 2.25.]

(4)   The conditions set out in subsections (2) [to (3A)] above are in this Chapter referred to as 'the prescribed conditions'.

(4A)   In subsection (3)(c) above 'benefits' does not include any benefits for whose payment the scheme makes provision in pursuance of any obligation imposed by legislation relating to social security.

[(4B)   For the purposes of this section, a benefit provided under any scheme is provided for an ex-spouse or the widow or widower of an ex-spouse, and shall be treated as not provided for an employee or the widow or widower of an employee, to the extent (and to the extent only) that—

   (a) it is provided for a person who is, or is the widow or widower of, either—
> (i) an employee who is an ex-spouse; or
> (ii) a scheme member's ex-spouse;
> and

   (b) it is as an ex-spouse, or as the widow or widower of an ex-spouse, that that person is the person for whom the benefit is provided.

(4C) For the purposes of this section a benefit provided for any person under any scheme is provided for that person as an ex-spouse, or as the widow or widower of an ex-spouse, to the extent (and to the extent only) that—

   (a) the benefit is provided in respect of rights of an ex-spouse that are or represent rights conferred on the ex-spouse as a consequence of a pension sharing order or provision; and

   (b) the scheme makes separate provision for the benefit to be treated as provided separately from any benefits which are provided under the scheme for the same person as an employee or as the widow or widower of an employee.

(4D) In this section 'scheme member', in relation to a scheme, means—

   (a) an employee; or

   (b) a person entitled to any relevant benefits under the scheme as a consequence of a pension sharing order or provision.

(4E) The following rules shall apply in calculating for the purposes of subsection (3)(da) or (3A)(f) above the amount of a person's pension for the first year in which it is payable—

   (a) if the pension payable for the year changes, the initial pension payable shall be taken;

   (b) it shall be assumed that that person will survive for the year; and

   (c) the effect of commutation shall be ignored.

(4F) A pension provided for an ex-spouse who is an employee, or for the widow or widower of such an ex-spouse, shall be disregarded in any determination of whether the conditions set out in subsection (3)(e) to (h) above are satisfied or continue to be satisfied in the case of that employee.]

(5), (6) . . .

(7) Subsections (8) to (10) below apply where the Board are considering whether a retirement benefits scheme satisfies or continues to satisfy the prescribed conditions.

(8) For the purpose of determining whether the scheme, so far as it relates to a particular class or description of employees, satisfies or continues to satisfy the prescribed conditions, that scheme shall be considered in conjunction with—

   (a) any other retirement benefits scheme (or schemes) which relates (or relate) or employees of that class or description and which is (or are) approved for the purposes of this Chapter,

   (b) any other retirement benefits scheme (or schemes) which relates (or relate) to employees of that class or description and which is (or are) at the same time before the Board in order for them to decide whether to give approval for the purposes of this Chapter,

(c) any section 608 scheme or schemes relating to employees of that class or description, and

(d) any relevant statutory scheme or schemes relating to employees of that class or description.

(9) If those conditions are satisfied in the case of both or all of those schemes taken together, they shall be taken to be satisfied in the case of the scheme mentioned in subsection (7) above (as well as the other or others).

(10) If those conditions are not satisfied in the case of both or all of those schemes taken together, they shall not be taken to be satisfied in the case of the scheme mentioned in subsection (7) above.

(11) The reference in subsection (8)(c) above to a section 608 scheme is a reference to a fund to which section 608 applies.

590A   Section 590: supplementary provisions

(1) For the purposes of section 590(3)(e) and (f) two or more employments are relevant associated employments if they are employments in the case of which—

(a) there is a period during which the employee has held both or all of them,

(b) the period counts under the scheme in the case of both or all of them as a period in respect of which benefits are payable, and

(c) the period is one during which both or all of the employers in question are associated.

(2) For the purposes of section 590(3)(g) and (h) the scheme is connected with another scheme in relation to an employee if—

(a) there is a period during which he has been the employee of two persons who are associated employers,

(b) the period counts under both schemes as a period in respect of which benefits are payable, and

(c) the period counts under one scheme by virtue of service with one employer and under the other scheme by virtue of service with the other employer.

(3) For the purposes of subsections (1) and (2) above, employers are associated if (directly or indirectly) one is controlled by the other or if both are controlled by a third person.

(4) In subsection (3) above the reference to control, in relation to a body corporate, shall be construed—

(a) where the body corporate is a close company, in accordance with section 416, and

(b) where it is not, in accordance with section 840.

590B   Section 590: further supplementary provisions

(1) For the purposes of section 590(3)(e) the relevant amount, in relation to an employee, shall be found by applying the following formula—

$$\frac{A \times C}{60}$$

(2)   For the purposes of section 590(3)(f) the relevant amount, in relation to an employee, shall be found by applying the following formula—

$$\frac{3 \times A \times C}{80}$$

(3)   For the purposes of section 590(3)(g) the relevant amount, in relation to an employee, shall be found by applying the following formula—

$$\frac{B \times C}{60}$$

(4)   For the purposes of section 590(3)(h) the relevant amount, in relation to an employee, shall be found by applying the following formula—

$$\frac{3 \times B \times C}{80}$$

(5)   For the purposes of this section A is the aggregate number of years service (expressing parts of a year as a fraction), subject to a maximum of 40, which, in the case of the employee, count for the purposes of the scheme at the time the benefits in respect of service in the employment become payable.

(6)   But where the same year (or part of a year) counts for the purposes of the scheme by virtue of more than one of the relevant associated employments it shall be counted only once in calculating the aggregate number of years service for the purposes of subsection (5) above.

(7)   For the purposes of this section B is the aggregate number of years service (expressing parts of a year as a fraction), subject to a maximum of 40, which, in the case of the employee, count for the purposes of any of the following—

    (a)   the scheme, and
    (b)   the other scheme or schemes with which the scheme is connected in relation to him

at the time the benefit become payable.

(8)   But where the same year (or part of a year) counts for the purposes of more than one scheme it shall be counted only once in calculating the aggregate number of years service for the purpose of subsection (7) above.

(9)   For the purposes of this section C is the permitted maximum in relation to the year of assessment in which the benefits in question become payable, that is, the figure found for that year by virtue of subsections (10) and (11) below.

(10)   For the years 1988–89 and 1989–90 the figure is £60,000.

(11)   For any subsequent year of assessment the figure is the figure found for that year, for the purposes of section 590C, by virtue of section 590C(4) to (5A).

590C   Earnings cap

(1)   In arriving at an employee's final remuneration for the purposes of section 590(3)(a) or (d), any excess of what would be his final remuneration (apart from this section) over the permitted maximum for the year of assessment in which his participation in the scheme ceases shall be disregarded.

(2)   In subsection (1) above 'the permitted maximum', in relation to a year of assessment, means the figure found for that year by virtue of subsections (3) and (4) below.

(3)   For the years 1988–89 and 1989–90 the figure is £60,000.

(4)   For any subsequent year of assessment the figure is also *£60,000*, subject to subsection (5) and (5A) below.

(5)   If the retail prices index for the month of September preceding a year of assessment falling within subsection (4) above is higher than it was for the previous September, the figure for that year shall be an amount arrived at by—

    (a)   increasing the figure for the previous year of assessment by the same percentage as the percentage increase in the retail prices index, and

    (b)   if the result is not a multiple of £600, rounding it up to the nearest amount which is such a multiple.

(5A)   If the retail prices index for the month of September preceding a year of assessment falling within subsection (4) above is not higher than it was for the previous September, the figure for that year shall be the same as the figure for the previous year of assessment.

(6)   The Treasury shall in the year of assessment 1989–90, and in each subsequent year of assessment, make an order specifying the figure which is by virtue of this section the figure for the following year of assessment.

591   Discretionary approval

(1)   The Board may, if they think fit having regard to the facts of a particular case, and subject to such conditions, if any, as they think proper to attach to the approval, approve a retirement benefits scheme for the purposes of this Chapter notwithstanding that it does not satisfy one or more of the prescribed conditions; but this subsection has effect subject to subsection (5) below.

(2)   The Board may in particular approve by virtue of this section a scheme—

    (a)   which exceeds the limits is imposed by the prescribed conditions as respects benefits for less than 40 years; or

    (b)   which provides pensions for the widows [and widowers] of employees on death in service, or for the children or dependants of employees; or

    [(ba)   which provides pensions for the widows and widowers of ex-spouses dying before the age at which their pensions become payable and for the children or dependants of ex-spouses; or]

    (c)   which provides on death in service a lump sum of up to four times the employee's final remuneration (exclusive of any refunds of contributions); or

(d) which allows benefits to be payable on retirement within ten years of the specified age, or on earlier incapacity; or

(e) which provides for the return in certain contingencies of employees' contributions; or

(f) which relates to a trade or undertaking carried on only partly in the United Kingdom and by a person not resident in the United Kingdom; or

(g) which provides in certain contingencies for securing relevant benefits falling within subsection (2A) below (but no other benefits) by means of an annuity contract made with an insurance company of the employee's choice; or

(h) to which the employer is not a contributor and which provides benefits additional to those provided by a scheme to which he is a contributor.

(2A) Relevant benefits fall within this subsection if they correspond with benefits that could be provided by an approved scheme, and for this purpose—

(a) a hypothetical scheme (rather than any particular scheme) is to be taken, and

(b) benefits provided by a scheme directly (rather than by means of an annuity contract) are to be taken.

(3) In subsection (2)(g) above 'insurance company' has the meaning given by section 659B.

(4) In applying this section to a scheme which was in existence on 6th April 1980, the Board shall exercise their discretion, in such cases as appear to them to be appropriate, so as to preserve—

(a) benefits earned or rights arising out of service before 6th April 1980; and

(b) any rights to death-in-service benefits conferred by rules of the scheme in force on 26th February 1970.

(5) The Board shall not approve a scheme by virtue of this section if to do so would be inconsistent with regulations made by the Board for the purposes of this section.

(6) Regulations made by the Board for the purposes of this section may restrict the Board's discretion to approve a scheme by reference to the benefits provided by the scheme, the investments held for the purposes of the scheme, the manner in which the scheme is administered or any other circumstances whatever.

591A Effect on approved schemes of regulations under section 591

(1) Subsection (2) below applies where on or after 17 April 1991 regulations are made for the purposes of section 591 ('section 591 regulations') which contain provisions restricting the Board's discretion to approve a retirement benefits scheme by reference to any circumstances other than the benefits provided by the scheme ('relevant provisions').

(2) Any retirement benefits scheme approved by the Board by virtue of section 591 before the day on which the section 591 regulations come into force shall cease to be approved by virtue of that section at the end of the period of

36 months beginning with that day if at the end of that period the scheme—

(a) contains a provision of a prohibited description, or

(b) does not contain a provision of a required description.

unless the description of provision is specified in regulations made by the Board for the purposes of this subsection.

(3)   For the purposes of this section, a provision contained in a scheme shall not be treated as being of a prohibited description by reason only of the fact that it authorises the retention of an investment held immediately before the day on which the section 591 regulations are made.

(4)   In determining for the purposes of this section whether any provision contained in a scheme is of a required description, the fact that it is framed so as not to require the disposal of an investment held immediately before the day on which the section 591 regulations are made shall be disregarded.

(5)   In this section—

(a) references to a provision of a prohibited description are to a provision of a description specified in the relevant provisions of the section 591 regulation as a description of provision which, if contained in a retirement benefits scheme, would prevent the Board from approving the scheme by virtue of section 591;

(b) references to a provision of a required description are to a provision of a description specified in the relevant provisions of the section 591 regulations as a description of provision which must be contained in a retirement benefits scheme before the Board may approve the scheme by virtue of section 591.

591B   Cessation of approval: general provisions

(1)   If in the opinion of the Board the facts concerning any approved scheme or its administration cease to warrant the continuance of their approval of the scheme, they may at any time by notice to the administrator, withdraw their approval on such grounds, and from such date (which shall not be earlier than the date when those facts first ceased to warrant the continuance of their approval or 17th March 1987, whichever is the later), as may be specified in the notice.

(2)   Where an alteration has been made in a retirement benefits scheme, no approval given by the Board as regards the scheme before the alteration shall apply after the date of the alteration unless—

(a) the alteration has been approved by the Board, or

(b) the scheme is of a class specified in regulations made by the Board for the purposes of this paragraph and the alteration is of a description so specified in relation to schemes of that class.

591C   Cessation of approval: tax on certain schemes

(1)   Where an approval of a scheme to which this section applies ceases to have effect, tax shall be charged in accordance with this section.

(2)   The tax shall be charged under Case VI of Schedule D at the rate of 40 per cent on an amount equal to the value of the assets which immediately before the

date of the cessation of the approval of the scheme are held for the purposes of the scheme (taking that value as it stands immediately before that date).

(3)   Subject to section 591D(4), the person liable for the tax shall be the administrator of the scheme.

(4)   This section applies to a retirement benefits scheme in respect of which one or more of the conditions set out below is satisfied.

(5)   The first condition is satisfied in respect of a scheme if, immediately before the date of the cessation of the approval of the scheme, the number of individuals who are members of the scheme is less than twelve.

(6)   The second condition is satisfied in respect of a scheme if at any time within the period of one year ending with the date of the cessation of the approval of the scheme, a person who is or has been a controlling director of a company which has contributed to the scheme is a member of the scheme.

(7)   For the purposes of this section a person is a controlling director of a company if he is a director of it and within section 417(5)(b) in relation to it.

591D   Section 591C: supplementary

(1)   For the purposes of section 591C(2) the value of an asset is, subject to subsection (2) below, its market value, construing "market value" in accordance with section 272 of the 1992 Act.

(2)   Where an asset held for the purposes of a scheme is a right or interest in respect of any money lent (directly or indirectly) to any person mentioned in subsection (3) below, the value of the asset shall be treated as being the amount owing (including any unpaid interest) on the money lent.

(3)   The persons are—

    (a)   any employer who has at any time contributed to the scheme;
    (b)   any company connected with such an employer;
    (c)   any person who has at any time (whether or not before the making of the loan) been a member of the scheme;
    (d)   any person connected, at the time of the making of the loan or subsequently, with a person falling within paragraph (c) above.

(4)   Where the administrator of the scheme is constituted by persons who include a person who is an approved independent trustee in relation to a scheme, that person shall not be liable for tax chargeable by virtue of section 591C.

(5)   A person is an approved independent trustee in relation to a scheme only if he is—

    (a)   approved by the Board to act as a trustee of the scheme; and
    (b)   not connected with—
        (i)   a member of the scheme;
        (ii)   any other trustee of the scheme; or
        (iii) an employer who has contributed to the scheme.

(6)   For the purposes of section 596A(9) income and gains accruing to a scheme shall not be regarded as brought into charge to tax merely because tax is charged in relation to the scheme in accordance with section 591C.

(7)   The reference in section 591C(1) to an approval of a scheme ceasing to have effect is a reference to—

(a)   the scheme ceasing to be an approved scheme by virtue of section 591A(2);

(b)   the approval of the scheme being withdrawn under section 591B(1); or

(c)   the approval of the scheme no longer applying by virtue of section 591B(2);

and any reference in section 591C to the date of the cessation of the approval of the scheme shall be construed accordingly.

(8)   For the purposes of section 591C and this section a person is a member of a scheme at a particular time if at that time a benefit—

(a)   is being provided under the scheme, or

(b)   may be so provided,

in respect of any past or present employment of his.

(9)   Section 839 shall apply for the purposes of this section.

Tax reliefs

592   Exempt approved schemes

(1)   This section has effect as respects—

(a)   any approved scheme which is shown to the satisfaction of the Board to be established under irrevocable trusts; or

(b)   any other approved scheme as respects which the Board, having regard to any special circumstances, direct that this section shall apply;

and any scheme which is for the time being within paragraph (a) or (b) above is in this Chapter referred to as an 'exempt approved scheme'.

(2)   Exemption from income tax shall, on a claim being made in that behalf, be allowed in respect of income derived from investments or deposits if, or to such extent as the Board are satisfied that, it is income from investments or deposits held for the purposes of the scheme.

(3)   Exemption from income tax shall, on a claim being made in that behalf, be allowed in respect of underwriting commissions if, or to such extent as the Board are satisfied that, the underwriting commissions are applied for the purposes of the schemes and would, but for this subsection, be chargeable to tax under Case VI of Schedule D.

(4)   Any sum paid by an employer by way of contribution under the scheme shall, for the purposes of Case I or II of Schedule D and of sections 75 and 76, be allowed to be deducted as an expense, or expense of management, incurred in the chargeable period in which the sum is paid but no other sum shall for those purposes be allowed to be deducted as an expense, or expense of management, in respect of the making, or any provision for the making, of any contributions under the scheme.

(5)   The amount of an employer's contributions which may be deducted under subsection (4) above shall not exceed the amount contributed by him under the scheme in respect of employees in a trade or undertaking in respect of the profits of which the employer is assessable to tax (that is to say, to United Kingdom income tax or corporation tax).

(6)   A sum not paid by way of ordinary annual contribution shall for the purposes of subsection (4) above be treated, as the Board may direct, either as an expense incurred in the chargeable period in which the sum is paid, or as an expense to be spread over such period of years as the Board think proper.

(6A)   Where any sum is paid to the trustees of the scheme in or towards the discharge of any liability of an employer under section 58B of the Social Security Pensions Act 1975 or section 144 of the Pension Schemes Act 1993 (deficiencies in the assets of a scheme) or under Article 68B of the Social Security Pensions (Northern Ireland) Order 1975 or section 140 of the Pension Schemes (Northern Ireland) Act 1993 (which contain corresponding provision for Northern Ireland), the payment of that sum—

> (a)   shall be treated for the purposes of this section as an employer's contribution under the scheme; and
>
> (b)   notwithstanding (where it is the case) that the employer's trade, profession, vocation or business is permanently discontinued before the making of the payment, shall be allowed, in accordance with subsection (4) above, to be deducted as such a contribution to the same extent as it would have been allowed but for the discontinuance and as if it had been made on the last day on which the trade, profession, vocation or business was carried on.

(7)   Any contribution paid under the scheme by an employee shall, in assessing tax under Schedule E, be allowed to be deducted as an expense incurred in the year of assessment in which the contribution is paid.

(8)   Subject to subsection (8A) below, the amount allowed to be deducted by virtue of subsection (7) above in respect of contributions paid by an employee in a year of assessment (whether under a single scheme or under two or more schemes) shall not exceed 15 per cent, or such higher percentage as the Board may in a particular case prescribe, of his remuneration for that year.

(8A)   Where an employee's remuneration for a year of assessment includes remuneration in respect of more than one employment, the amount allowed to be deducted by virtue of subsection (7) above in respect of contributions paid by the employee in that year by virtue of any employment (whether under a single scheme or under two or more schemes) shall not exceed 15 per cent, or such higher percentage as the Board may in a particular case prescribe, of his remuneration for the year in respect of that employment.

(8B)   In arriving at an employee's remuneration for a year of assessment for the purposes of subsection (8) or (8A) above, any excess of what would be his remuneration (apart from this subsection) over the permitted maximum for that year shall be disregarded.

(8C)   In subsection (8B) above 'permitted maximum', in relation to a year of assessment, means the figure found for that year by virtue of subsections (8D) and (8E) below.

(8D)   For the year of assessment 1989–90 the figure is £60,000.

(8E)   For any subsequent year of assessment the figure is the figure found for that year, for the purposes of section 590C, by virtue of section 590C(4) to (5A).

(9)   Relief shall not be given under sections 266 or 273 in respect of any payment in respect of which an allowance can be made under subsection (7) above.

(10)   Subsection (2) of section 468 and subsection (3) of section 469 shall not apply to any authorised unit trust which is also an exempt approved scheme if the employer is not a contributor to the exempt approved scheme and that scheme provides benefits additional to those provided by another exempt approved scheme to which he is a contributor.

(11)   Nothing in this section shall be construed as affording relief in respect of any sums to be brought into account under section 438.

(12)   This section has effect only as respects income arising or contributions paid at a time when the scheme is an exempt approved scheme.

593   Relief by way of deductions from contributions

(1)   Relief under section 592(7) shall be given in accordance with subsections (2) and (3) below in such cases and subject to such conditions as the Board may prescribe by regulations under section 612(3) in respect of schemes—

- (a)   to which employees, but not their employers, are contributors; and
- (b)   which provide benefits additional to benefits provided by schemes to which their employers are contributors.

(2)   An employee who is entitled to relief under section 592(7) in respect of a contribution may deduct from the contribution when he pays it, and may retain, an amount equal to income tax at the basic rate on the contribution.

(3)   The administrator of the scheme—

- (a)   shall accept the amount paid after the deduction in discharge of the employee's liability to the same extent as if the deduction had not been made; and
- (b)   may recover an amount equal to the deduction from the Board.

(4)   Regulations under subsection (3) of section 612 may, without prejudice to the generality of that subsection—

- (a)   provide for the manner in which claims for the recovery of a sum under subsection (3)(b) above may be made;
- (b)   provide for the giving of such information, in such form, as may be prescribed by or under the regulations;
- (c)   provide for the inspection by persons authorised by the Board of books, documents and other records.

594   Exempt statutory schemes

(1)   Any contribution paid by any officer or employee under a relevant statutory scheme established under a public general Act shall, in assessing tax under

Schedule E, be allowed to be deducted as an expense incurred in the year of assessment in which the contribution is paid; and relief shall not be given under sections 266 or 273 in respect of any contribution allowable as a deduction under this section.

(2)   Subject to subsection (3) below, the amount allowed to be deducted by virtue of subsection (1) above in respect of contributions paid by a person in a year of assessment (whether under a single scheme or under two or more schemes) shall not exceed 15 per cent such higher percentage as the Board may in a particular case prescribe, of his remuneration for that year.

(3)   Where a person's remuneration for a year of assessment includes remuneration in respect of more than one office or employment, the amount allowed to be deducted by virtue of subsection (1) above in respect of contributions paid by the person in that year by virtue of any office or employment (whether under a single scheme or under two or more schemes) shall not exceed 15 per cent, or such higher percentage as the Board may in a particular case prescribe, of his remuneration for the year in respect of that office or employment.

(4)   In arriving at a person's remuneration for a year of assessment for the purposes of subsections (2) or (3) above, any excess of what would be his remuneration (apart from this subsection) over the permitted maximum for that year shall be disregarded.

(5)   In subsection (4) above 'permitted maximum', in relation to a year of assessment, means the figure found for that year by virtue of subsections (6) and (7) below.

(6)   For the year 1989–90 the figure is £60,000.

(7)   For any subsequent year of assessment the figure is the figure found for that year, for the purposes of section 590C, by virtue of section 590C(4) to (5A).

Charge to tax in certain cases

595   Charge to tax in respect of certain sums paid by employer etc

(1)   Subject to the provisions of this Chapter, where, pursuant to a retirement benefits scheme, the employer in any year of assessment pays a sum with a view to the provision of any relevant benefits for any employee of that employer, then (whether or not the accrual of the benefits is dependent on any contingency)—

    (a) the sum paid, if not otherwise chargeable to income tax as income of the employee, shall be deemed for all purposes of the Income Tax Acts to be income of that employee for that year of assessment and assessable to tax under Schedule E; and

    (b) where the payment is made under such an insurance or contract as is mentioned in section 266, relief, if not otherwise allowable, shall be given to that employee under that section in respect of the payment to the extent, if any, to which such relief would have been allowable to him if the payment had been made by him and the insurance or contract under which the payment is made had been made with him.

(2), (3) . . .

(4)   Where the employer pays any sum as mentioned in subsection (1) above in relation to more than one employee, the sum so paid shall, for the purposes of that subsection, be apportioned among those employees by reference to the separate sums which would have had to be paid to secure the separate benefits to be provided for them respectively, and the part of the sum apportioned to each of them shall be deemed for that purpose to have been paid separately in relation to that one of them.

(5)   Any reference in this section to the provision for an employee of relevant benefits includes a reference to the provision of benefits payable to that employee's wife [or husband] or widow [or widower or] children, dependants or personal representatives.

596   Exceptions from section 595

(1)   Section 595(1) shall not apply where the retirement benefits scheme in question is—

  (a) an approved scheme, or
  (b) a relevant statutory scheme, or
  (c) a scheme set up by a government outside the United Kingdom for the benefit, or primarily for the benefit of, its employees.

(2)   Section 595(1) shall not apply for any year of assessment—

  (a) where the employee performs the duties of his employment in such circumstances that no tax is chargeable under Case I or II of Schedule E in respect of the emoluments of his employment (or would be so chargeable were there such emoluments), or
  (b) where the emoluments from the employment are foreign emoluments within the meaning of section 192 and the Board are satisfied, on a claim made by the employee, that the retirement benefits scheme in question corresponds to such a scheme as is mentioned in paragraph (a), (b) or (c) of subsection (1) above.

(3)   Where, in respect of the provision for an employee of any relevant benefits—

  (a) a sum has been deemed to be income of his by virtue of subsection (1) of section 595, and
  (b) subsequently, the employee proves to the satisfaction of the Board that—
    (i) no payment in respect of, or in substitution for, the benefits has been made, and
    (ii) some event has occurred by reason of which no such payment will be made

  and makes application for relief under this subsection within six years from the time when that event occurred,

the Board shall give relief in respect of tax on that sum by repayment or otherwise as may be appropriate; and if the employee satisfies the Board as mentioned above in relation to some particular part, but not the whole, of the benefits, the Board may give such relief as may seem to them just and reasonable.

[(4)   Relief shall not be given under subsection (3) above in respect of tax on any sum if—

    (a)   the reason for there having been no payment in respect of, or in substitution for, the benefits, or part of the benefits, in question, or

    (b)   the event by reason of which there will be no such payment,

is a reduction or cancellation, as a consequence of any pension sharing order or provision, or employee's rights in respect of the benefits.]

596A   Charge to tax: benefits under non-approved schemes

(1)   Where in any year of assessment a person receives a benefit provided under a retirement benefits scheme which is not of a description mentioned in section 596(1)(a), (b) or (c), tax shall be charged in accordance with the provisions of this section.

(2)   Where the benefit is received by an individual, he shall be charged to tax under Schedule E for that year.

(3)   Where the benefit is received by a person other than an individual, the administrator of the scheme shall be charged to tax under Case VI of Schedule D for that year.

(4)   Subject to subsection (9) below the amount to be charged to tax is—

    (a)   in the case of a cash benefit, the amount received, and

    (b)   in the case of a non-cash benefit, whichever is the greater of—

        (i)   the amount which would be chargeable to tax under section 19(1) if the benefit were taxable as an emolument of the employment under Case I of Schedule E, or

        (ii)   the cash equivalent of the benefit determined in accordance with section 596B.

(5)   In the case of the charge under Case VI of Schedule D, the rate of tax is 40 per cent or such other rate (whether higher or lower) as may for the time being be specified by the Treasury by order.

(6)   Tax shall not be charged under this section in the case of—

    (a)   any pension or annuity which is chargeable to tax under Schedule E by virtue of section 19(1); or

    (b)   any pension or other benefit chargeable to tax under section 58.

(7)   But where the amount chargeable to tax as mentioned in subsection (6)(a) above is less than the amount which would be chargeable to tax under this section—

    (a)   subsection (6)(a) above shall not apply, and

    (b)   the amount chargeable to tax under this section shall be reduced by the amount chargeable to tax by virtue of section 19(1).

(8)   Subject to subsection (9) below, tax shall not be charged under this section (or section 19(1) or 148) in the case of a lump sum where—

    (a)   the employer has paid any sum or sums with a view to the provision of any relevant benefits under a retirement benefits scheme;

    (b)   an employee has been assessed to tax in respect of the sum or sums by virtue of section 595(1); and

    (c)   the lump sum is provided under the scheme to the employee, [an ex-spouse of the employee,] any person falling within section 595(5) in relation to the employee or any other individual designated by the employee.

(9)   Where any of the income or gains accruing to the scheme under which the lump sum is provided is not brought into charge to tax, tax shall be charged under this section on the amount of the lump sum received less any deduction applicable under subsection (10) or (11) below.

(10)   Subject to subsection (11) below, the deduction applicable is the aggregate of—

    (a)   any sum or sums in respect of which the employee has been assessed as mentioned in subsection (8)(b) above, and

    (b)   any sum or sums paid by the employee,

which in either case were paid by way of contribution to the provision of the lump sum.

(11)   Where—

    (a)   the lump sum is provided under the scheme on the disposal of a part of any asset or the surrender of any part of or share in any rights in any asset, and

    (b)   the employee, any person falling within section 595(5) in relation to the employee or any person connected with the employee has any right to receive or any expectation of receiving a further lump sum (or further lump sums) under the scheme on a further disposal of any part of the asset or a further surrender of any part of or share in any rights in the asset,

the deduction applicable shall be determined in accordance with the formula in subsection (12) below.

(12)   The formula is—

$$D = S \ \times \ \frac{A}{B}$$

(13)   For the purposes of the formula in subsection (12) above—

    D   is the deduction applicable;

    S   is the aggregate amount of any sum or sums of a description mentioned in paragraphs (a) and (b) of subsection (10) above;

    A   is the amount of the lump sum received in relation to which the deduction applicable falls to be determined;

    B   is the market value of the asset in relation to which the disposal or surrender occurred, on the assumption that the valuation is made immediately before the disposal or surrender.

(14)   An individual may not claim that a deduction is applicable in relation to a lump sum more than once.

(15)   For the purposes of subsections (8) and (9) above, it shall be assumed unless the contrary is shown—

    (a) that no sums have been paid, and the employee has not been assessed in respect of any sums paid, with a view to the provision of relevant benefits;

    (b) that the income or gains accruing to a scheme under which the benefit is provided are not brought into charge to tax; and

    (c) that no deduction is applicable under subsection (10) or (11) above.

(16)   Section 839 shall apply for the purposes of subsection (11) above.

(17)   In subsection (13) above 'market value' shall be construed in accordance with section 272 of the 1992 Act.

596B   Section 596A: supplementary provisions

(1)   For the purposes of section 596A the cash equivalent of a benefit in kind is—

    (a) in the case of a benefit other than living accommodation, the amount which would be the cash equivalent of the benefit under Chapter II of Part V if it were chargeable under the appropriate provision of that Chapter (treating any sum made good by the recipient as made good by the employee), and

    (b) in the case of living accommodation, an amount equal to the value of the accommodation to the recipient determined in accordance with the following provisions of this section less so much of any sum made good by him to those at whose cost the accommodation is provided as is properly attributable to the provision of the accommodation.

(2)   Where the cost of providing the accommodation does not exceed £75,000, the value of the accommodation to the recipient in any period is the rent which would have been payable for the period if the premises had been let to him at an annual rent equal to their annual value as ascertained under section 837.

(3)   But for a period in which those at whose cost the accommodation is provided pay rent at an annual rate greater than the annual value as so ascertained, the value of the accommodation to the recipient is an amount equal to the rent payable by them for the period.

(4)   Where the cost of providing the accommodation does exceed £75,000, the value of the accommodation to the recipient shall be taken to be the aggregate of the value of the accommodation to him determined in accordance with subsections (2) and (3) above and the additional value of the accommodation to him determined in accordance with subsections (5) and (6) below.

(5)   The additional value of the accommodation to the recipient in any period is the rent which would have been payable for that period if the premises had been let to him at an annual rent equal to the appropriate percentage of the amount by which the cost of providing the accommodation exceeds £75,000.

(6)   Where throughout the period of six years ending with the date when the recipient first occupied the property any estate or interest in the property was held by a relevant person (whether or not it was the same estate, interest or person

throughout), the additional value shall be calculated as if in subsection (7) below—

    (a)   the amount referred to in paragraph (a) were the market value of that property as at that date, and

    (b)   the amount referred to in paragraph (b) did not include expenditure on improvements made before that date.

(7)   For the purposes of this section, the cost of providing any living accommodation shall be taken to be the aggregate of—

    (a)   the amount of any expenditure incurred in acquiring the estate or interest in the property held by a relevant person, and

    (b)   the amount of any expenditure incurred by a relevant person before the year of assessment in question on improvements to the property.

(8)   The aggregate amount mentioned in subsection (7) above shall be reduced by the amount of any payment made by the recipient to a relevant person, so far as that amount represents a reimbursement of any such expenditure as is mentioned in paragraph (a) or (b) of that subsection or represents consideration for the grant to the recipient of a tenancy of the property.

(9)   For the purposes of this section, any of the following persons is a relevant person—

    (a)   the person providing the accommodation,

    (b)   the employer or former employer; or

    (c)   any person, other than the recipient, who is connected with a person falling within paragraph (a) or (b) above.

(10)   In this section—

    'the appropriate percentage' means the rate applicable for the purposes of section 160 as at the beginning of the year of assessment in question;

    'market value', in relation to any property, means the price which that property might reasonably be expected to fetch on a sale in the open market with vacant possession, no reduction being made, in estimating the market value, on account of any option in respect of the property held by the recipient, or a person connected with him, or by any of the persons mentioned in subsection (9) above;

    'property', in relation to any living accommodation, means the property consisting of that living accommodation;

    'tenancy' includes a sub-tenancy;

and section 839 shall apply for the purposes of this section.

596C   Notional interest treated as paid if amount charged in respect of beneficial loan

(1)   This section applies where a person is chargeable to tax under section 596A in any year of assessment on an amount which consists of or includes an amount representing the cash equivalent of the benefit of a loan determined (by virtue of section 596B(1)(a)) in accordance with Part II of Schedule 7.

(2)   Where this section applies, the person chargeable is treated as having paid interest on the loan of the same amount as the cash equivalent so determined.

(3)   The interest is treated as paid for all the purposes of the Tax Acts (other than those relating to the charge under section 596A) but not so as to make it—

(a)   income of the person making the loan, or

(b)   relevant loan interest to which section 396 applies (mortgage interest payable under deduction of tax).

(4)   The interest is treated as accruing during and paid at the end of the year of assessment or, if different, the period in that year during which the loan is outstanding.

597   Charge to tax: pensions

(1)   Subject to subsection (2) below, all pensions paid under any scheme which is approved or is being considered for approval under this Chapter shall be charged to tax under Schedule E, and section 203 shall apply accordingly.

(2)   As respects any scheme which is approved or is being considered for approval under this Chapter, the Board may direct that, until such date as the Board may specify, pensions under the scheme shall be charged to tax as annual payments under Case III of Schedule D, and tax shall be deductible under sections 348 and 349 accordingly.

(3)   Without prejudice to subsection (1) above, where funds held for the purposes of any scheme which is approved or is being considered for approval under this Chapter are used to acquire an annuity—

(a)   the annuity shall be charged to tax under Schedule E and section 203 shall apply accordingly;

(b)   the annuity shall not be charged to tax under Case III of Schedule D.

598   Charge to tax: repayment of employee's contributions

(1)   Subject to the provisions of this section, tax shall be charged under this section on any repayment to an employee during his lifetime of any contributions (including interest on contributions, if any) if the payment is made under—

(a)   a scheme which is or has at any time been an exempt approved scheme, or

(b)   a relevant statutory scheme established under a public general Act.

(2)   Where any payment is chargeable to tax under this section, the administrator of the scheme shall be charged to income tax under Case VI of Schedule D and, subject to subsection (3) below, the rate of tax shall be 20 per cent.

(3)   The Treasury may by order from time to time increase or decrease the rate of tax under subsection (2) above.

(4)   The tax shall be charged on the amount paid or, if the rules permit the administrator to deduct the tax before payment, on the amount before deduction of tax, and the amount so charged to tax shall not be treated as income for any other purpose of the Tax Acts.

(5)   Subsection (1)(a) above shall not apply in relation to a contribution made after the scheme ceases to be an exempt approved scheme (unless it again becomes an exempt approved scheme).

(6)   This section shall not apply where the employee's employment was carried on outside the United Kingdom.

(7)   In relation to a statutory scheme, 'employee' in this section includes any officer.

599   Charge to tax: commutation of entire pension in special circumstances

(1)   [Subject to subsection (1A) below, where] a scheme to which this section applies contains a rule allowing, in special circumstances, a payment in commutation of an employee's entire pension, and any pension is commuted, whether wholly or not, under the rule, tax shall be charged on the amount by which the sum receivable exceeds—

   (a)   the largest sum which would have been receivable in commutation of any part of the pension if the scheme had secured that the aggregate value of the relevant benefits payable to an employee on or after retirement, excluding any pension which was not commutable, could not exceed three-eightieths of his final remuneration (disregarding any excess of that remuneration over the permitted maximum) for each year of service up to a maximum of 40; or
   (b)   the largest sum which would have been receivable in commutation of any part of the pension under any rule of the scheme authorising the commutation of part (but not the whole) of the pension, or which would have been so receivable but for those special circumstances;

whichever gives the lesser amount chargeable to tax.

[(1A)   Subsection (1) above shall have effect in relation to the commutation of the whole or any part of a pension the amount of which has been affected by the making of any pension sharing order or provision as if paragraph (a) and the words after paragraph (b) were omitted.

(1B)   Where—

   (a)   a scheme to which this section applies contains a rule allowing, in special circumstances, a payment in commutation of the entire pension provided under the scheme for an ex-spouse, and
   (b)   any pension is commuted, whether wholly or not, under the rule,

tax shall be charged on the amount by which the sum receivable exceeds the largest sum which would have been receivable in commutation of any part of the pension under any rule of the scheme authorising the commutation of a part (but not the whole) of the pension.

(1C)   A pension provided for an ex-spouse shall be disregarded when applying subsection (1) above in relation to the commutation of any pension provided for an employee.

(1D)   A pension provided for an employee shall be disregarded when applying subsection (1B) above in relation to the commutation of any pension provided for an ex-spouse.

(1E)   Subsections (4B) and (4C) of section 590 apply for the purposes of subsections (1C) and (1D) above as they apply for the purposes of that section.]

(2)   This section applies to—

    (a)   a scheme which is or has at any time been an approved scheme, or

    (b)   a relevant statutory scheme established under a public general Act.

(3)   Where any amount is chargeable to tax under this section the administrator of the scheme shall be charged to income tax under Case VI of Schedule D on that amount, and section 598(2), (3) and (4) shall apply as they apply to tax chargeable under that section.

(4)   This section shall not apply where the employee's employment was carried on outside the United Kingdom.

(5)   In relation to a statutory scheme, 'employee' in this section includes any officer.

(6)   In applying paragraph (a) or (b) of subsection (1) above[, or in applying subsection (1B) above]—

    (a)   the same considerations shall be taken into account, including the provisions of any other relevant scheme, as would have been taken into account by the Board in applying section 590; and

    (b)   where the scheme has ceased to be an approved scheme, account shall only be taken of the rules in force when the scheme was last an approved scheme.

(7)   Where the pension has been secured by means of an annuity contract with an insurance company and the sum receivable is payable under that contract by the insurance company, the references to the administrator of the scheme in subsection (3) above and in section 598(2) and (4) as applied by that subsection are to be read as references to the insurance company.

(8)   In subsection (7) above 'insurance company' has the meaning given by section 659B.

(9)   In relation to payments made under schemes approved or established before 17th March 1987 to employees who became members before that date, subsection (1)(a) above shall have effect with the omission of the words '(disregarding any excess of that remuneration over the permitted maximum)'.

(10)   In subsection (1)(a) above 'the permitted maximum' means, as regards a charge to tax arising under this section in a particular year of assessment, the figure found for that year by virtue of subsections (11) and (12) below.

(11)   For the years 1988–89 and 1989–90 the figure is £60,000.

(12)   For any subsequent year of assessment the figure is the figure found for that year, for the purposes of section 590C, by virtue of section 590C(4) to (5A).

599A   Charge to tax: payments out of surplus funds

(1)   This subsection applies to any payment which is made to or for the benefit of an employee or to his personal representatives out of funds which are or have been held for the purposes of—

    (a)   a scheme which is or has at any time been an exempt approved scheme, or

(b)   a relevant statutory scheme established under a public general Act,

and which is made in pursuance of duty to return surplus funds.

(2)   On the making of a payment to which subsection (1) above applies, the administrator of the scheme shall be charged to income tax under Case VI of Schedule D at the relevant rate on such amount as, after deduction of tax at that rate, would equal the amount of the payment.

(3)   Subject to subsection (4) below, the relevant rate shall be 35 per cent.

(4)   The Treasury may by order from time to time increase or decrease the relevant rate.

(5)   Where a payment made to or for the benefit of an employee is one to which subsection (1) applies, it shall be treated in computing the total income of the employee for the year in which it is made as income for that year which is—

(a)   received by him after deduction of income tax at the basic rate from a corresponding gross amount, and
(b)   chargeable to income tax under Case VI of Schedule D.

(6)   But, no repayment of income tax shall be made to, the employee.

(7)   . . .

(8)   Subsection (5) above applies whether or not the employee is the recipient of the payment.

(9)   Any payment chargeable to tax under this section shall not be chargeable to tax under section 598, 599 or 600 or under the Regulations mentioned in paragraph 8 of Schedule 3 to the Finance Act 1971.

(10)   In this section—
'employee', in relation to a relevant statutory scheme, includes any officer; references to any payment include reference to any transfer of assets or other transfer of money's worth.

600   Charge to tax: unauthorised payments to or for employees

(1)   This section applies to any payment to or for the benefit of an employee [or an ex-spouse], otherwise than in course of payment of a pension, being a payment made out of funds which are held for the purposes of a scheme which is approved for the purposes of—

(a)   this Chapter;
(b)   Chapter II of Part II of the Finance Act 1970; or
(c)   section 208 or Chapter II of Part IX of the 1970 Act.

(2)   If the payment is not expressly authorised by the rules of the scheme or by virtue of paragraph 33 of Schedule 6 to the Finance Act 1989 the employee [or, as the case may be, the ex-spouse shall] (whether or not he is the recipient of the payment) be chargeable to tax on the amount of the payment under Schedule E for the year of assessment in which the payment is made.

(3)   Any payment chargeable to tax under this section shall not be chargeable to tax under section 598 or 599 or under the Regulations mentioned in paragraph 8 of Schedule 3 to the Finance Act 1971.

(4)   References in this section to any payment include references to any transfer of assets or other transfer of money's worth.

601   Charge to tax: payments to employers

(1)   Subsection (2) below applies where a payment is made to an employer out of funds which are or have been held for the purposes of a scheme which is or has at any time been an exempt approved scheme and whether or not the payment is made in pursuance of Schedule 22.

(2)   An amount equal to 40 per cent of the payment shall be recoverable by the Board from the employer.

(3)   Subsection (2) above does not apply to any payment—

- (a) to the extent that, if this section had not been enacted, the employer would have been exempt, or entitled to claim exemption from income tax or corporation tax in respect of the payment; or
- (b) made before the scheme became an exempt approved scheme; or
- (c) of any prescribed description; or
- (d) made in pursuance of the winding-up of the scheme where the winding-up commenced on or before 18th March 1986; or
- (e) made in pursuance of an application which—
  - (i)   was made to the Board on or before that date and was not withdrawn before the making of the payment, and
  - (ii) sought the Board's assurance that the payment would not lead to a withdrawal of approval under section 19(3) of the Finance Act 1970;

(4)   Subsection (2) above does not apply where the employer is a charity (within the meaning of section 506).

(5)   Where any payment is made or becomes due to an employer out of funds which are or have been held for the purposes of a scheme which is or has at any time been an exempt approved scheme then—

- (a) if the scheme relates to a trade, profession or vocation carried on by the employer, the payment shall be treated for the purposes of the Tax Acts as a receipt of that trade, profession or vocation receivable when the payment falls due or on the last day on which the trade, profession or vocation is carried on by the employer, whichever is the earlier;
- (b) if the scheme does not relate to such a trade, profession or vocation, the employer shall be charged to tax on the amount of the payment under Case VI of Schedule D.

This subsection shall not apply to a payment which fell due before the scheme became an exempt approved scheme or to a payment to which subsection (2) above applies or would apply but for subsection (3)(a) or (4) above.

(6)   In this section—

- (a) references to any payment include references to any transfer of assets or other transfer of money's worth; and
- (b) 'prescribed' means prescribed by regulations made by the Treasury.

602   Regulations relating to surpluses

(1)   In relation to an amount recoverable as mentioned in section 601(2), the Treasury may by regulations make any of the provisions mentioned in subsection (2) below; and for this purpose the amount shall be treated as if it were—

- (a)   an amount of income tax chargeable on the employer under Case VI of Schedule D for the year of assessment in which the payment is made; or
- (b)   where the employer is a company, an amount of corporation tax chargeable on the company for the accounting period in which the payment is made.

(2)   The provisions are—

- (a)   provision requiring the administrator of the scheme or the employer (or both) to furnish to the Board, in respect of the amount recoverable and of the payment concerned, information of a prescribed kind;
- (b)   provision enabling the Board to serve a notice or notices requiring the administrator or employer (or both) to furnish to the Board, in respect of the amount and payment, particulars of a prescribed kind;
- (c)   provision requiring the administrator to deduct out of the payment the amount recoverable and to account to the Board for it;
- (d)   provision as to circumstances in which the employer may be assessed in respect of the amount recoverable;
- (e)   provision that, in a case where the employer has been assessed in respect of an amount recoverable but has not paid it (or part of it) within a prescribed period, the administrator may be assessed and charged (in the employer's name) in respect of the amount (or part unpaid);
- (f)   provision that, in a case where the amount recoverable (or part of it) has been recovered from the administrator by virtue of an assessment in the employer's name, the administrator is entitled to recover from the employer a sum equal to the amount (or part);
- (g)   provision enabling the employer or administrator (as the case may be) to appeal against an assessment made on him in respect of the amount recoverable.
- (h)   provision as to when any sum in respect of the amount recoverable is payable to the Board by the administrator or employer and provision requiring interest to be paid on any sum so payable;
- (j)   provision that an amount paid to the Board by the administrator shall be treated as paid on account of the employer's liability under section 601(2).

(3)   For the purpose of giving effect to any provision mentioned in subsection (2)(c) to (j) above, regulations under this section may include provision applying (with or without modifications) provisions of the enactments relating to income tax and corporation tax.

(4)   Subject to any provision of regulations under this section—

- (a)   a payment to which section 601(2) applies shall not be treated as a profit or gain brought into charge to income tax or corporate tax and shall not be treated as part of the employer's income for any purpose of this Act; and

    (b)   the amount recoverable shall not be subject to any exemption or reduction (by way of relief, set-off or otherwise) or be available for set-off against other tax.

(5)   If the employer is a company and a payment to which section 601(1) and (2) applies is made at a time not otherwise within an accounting period of the company, an accounting period of the company shall for the purpose of subsection (1)(b) above be treated as beginning immediately before the payment is made.

603   Reduction of surpluses

Schedule 22 (which provides for the reduction of certain pension fund surpluses) shall have effect.

Supplementary provisions

604   Application for approval of a scheme

(1)   An application for the approval for the purposes of this Chapter of any retirement benefits scheme shall be made in writing by the appropriate applicant to the Board before the end of the first year of assessment for which approval is required, and shall be accompanied by—

    (a)   two copies of the instrument or other document constituting the scheme; and

    (b)   two copies of the rules of the scheme and, except where the application is being sought on the setting up of the scheme, two copies of the accounts of the scheme for the last year for which such accounts have been made up; and

    (c)   such other information and particulars (including copies of any actuarial report or advice given to the appropriate applicant, administrator or employer in connection with the setting up of the scheme) as the Board may consider relevant.

(1A)   In subsection (1) above 'the appropriate applicant' means—

    (a)   in the case of a trust scheme, the trustee or trustees of the scheme; and

    (b)   in the case of a non-trust scheme, the scheme sponsor or scheme sponsors;

and subsection (9) of section 611AA applies for the purposes of this subsection as it applies for the purposes of that section.

(2)   The form in which an application for approval is to be made, or in which any information is to be given, in pursuance of this section may be prescribed by the Board.

605   Information

(1A)   The Board may by regulations make any of the following provisions—

    (a)   provision requiring prescribed persons to furnish to the Board at prescribed times information relating to any of the matters mentioned in subsection (1B) below;

  (b) provision enabling the Board to serve a notice requiring prescribed
       persons to furnish to the Board, within a prescribed time, particulars
       relating to any of those matters;

  (c) provision enabling the Board to serve a notice requiring prescribed
       persons to produce to the Board, within a prescribed time, documents
       relating to any of those matters;

  (d) provision enabling the Board to serve a notice requiring prescribed
       persons to make available for inspection on behalf of the Board
       books, documents and other records, being books, documents and
       records which relate to any of those matters;

  (e) provision requiring prescribed persons to preserve for a prescribed
       time books, documents and other records, being books, documents
       and records which relate to any of those matters.

(1B)   The matters referred to in subsection (1A) above are—

  (a) a scheme which is or has been an approved scheme;

  (b) a relevant statutory scheme;

  (c) an annuity contract by means of which benefits provided under an
       approved scheme or a relevant statutory scheme have been secured;

  (d) a retirement benefits scheme which is not an approved scheme but in
       relation to which an application for approval for the purposes of this
       Chapter has been made.

(1C)   A person who fails to comply with regulations made under subsection
(1A)(e) above shall be liable to a penalty not exceeding £3,000.

(1D)   Regulations under subsection (1A) above may make different provision
for different descriptions of case.

(1E)   In subsection (1A) above 'prescribed' means prescribed by regulations
made under that subsection.

(2) . . .

(3) It shall be the duty of every employer—

  (a) if there subsists in relation to any of his employees a retirement ben-
       efits scheme to which he contributes and which is neither an approved
       scheme nor a relevant statutory scheme, to deliver particulars of that
       scheme to the Board within three months beginning with the date on
       which the scheme first comes into operation in relation to any of his
       employees, and

  (b) when required to do so by notice given by the Board, to furnish within
       the time limited by the notice such particulars as the Board may
       require with regard to—

     (i) any retirement benefits scheme relating to the employer which
          is neither an approved scheme nor a relevant statutory scheme;
          and

     (ii) the employees of his to whom any such scheme relates.

(4) It shall be the duty of the administrator of a retirement benefits scheme
which is neither an approved scheme nor a relevant statutory scheme, when
required to do so by notice given by the Board, to furnish within the time limited

by the notice such particulars as the Board may require with regard to the scheme.

605A   False statements etc

(1)   A person who fraudulently or negligently makes a false statement or false representation on making an application for the approval for the purposes of this Chapter of—

    (a) a retirement benefits scheme, or

    (b) an alteration in such a scheme,

shall be liable to a penalty not exceeding £3,000.

(2)   In a case where—

    (a) a person fraudulently or negligently makes a false statement or false representation, and

    (b) in consequence that person, or any other person, obtains relief from or repayment of tax under this Chapter.

the person mentioned in paragraph (a) above shall be liable to a penalty not exceeding £3,000.

606   Default of administrator etc

(1)   This section applies in relation to a retirement benefits scheme if at any time—

    (a) there is no administrator of the scheme, or

    (b) the person who is, or all of the persons who are, the administrator of the scheme cannot be traced, or

    (c) the person who is, or all of the persons who are, the administrator of the scheme is or are in default for the purposes of this section.

(2)   If the scheme is a trust scheme, then—

    (a) if subsection (1)(b) or (c) above applies and at the time in question the condition mentioned in subsection (3) below is fulfilled, the trustee or trustees shall at that time be responsible for the discharge of all duties imposed on the administrator under this Chapter (whenever arising) and liable for any tax due from the administrator in the administrator's capacity as such (whenever falling due);

    (b) if subsection (1)(a) above applies, or subsection (1)(b) or (c) above applies and at the time in question the condition mentioned in sub-section (3) below is not fulfilled, the employer shall at that time be so responsible and liable;

and paragraph (b) above shall apply to a person in his capacity as the employer even if he is also the administrator, or a trustee, of the scheme.

(3)   The condition is that there is at least one trustee of the scheme who—

    (a) can be traced,

    (b) is resident in the United Kingdom, and

    (c) is not in default for the purposes of this section.

(4)   If the scheme is a non-trust scheme, then—

    (a) if subsection (1)(b) or (c) above applies and at the time in question the condition mentioned in subsection (5) below is fulfilled, the scheme sponsor or scheme sponsors shall at that time be responsible for the discharge of all duties imposed on the administrator under this Chapter (whenever arising) and liable for any tax due from the administrator in the administrator's capacity as such (whenever falling due);

    (b) if subsection (1)(a) above applies, or subsection (1)(b) or (c) above applies and at the time in question the condition mentioned in subsection (5) below is not fulfilled, the employer shall at that time be so responsible and liable;

and paragraph (b) above shall apply to a person in his capacity as the employer even if he is also the administrator of the scheme, or a scheme sponsor.

(5)   The condition is that there is at least one scheme sponsor who—

    (a) can be traced,

    (b) is resident in the United Kingdom, and

    (c) is not in default for the purposes of this section.

(6)   Where at any time—

    (a) paragraph (b) or (c) of subsection (1) above applies in relation to a scheme, and

    (b) a person is by virtue of this section responsible for the discharge of any duties, or liable for any tax, in relation to the scheme,

then at that time the person or persons mentioned in paragraph (b) or (as the case may be) paragraph (c) of subsection (1) above shall not, by reason only of being the administrator of the scheme, be responsible for the discharge of those duties or liable for that tax.

(7)   Where the scheme is a trust scheme and the employer is not a contributor to the scheme, subsection (2) above shall have effect as if—

    (a) for 'the employer', in the first place where those words occur, there were substituted 'the scheme sponsor or scheme sponsors', and

    (b) for 'the employer', in the second place where those words occur, there were substituted 'scheme sponsor'.

(8)   Where the scheme is a non-trust scheme and the employer is not a contributor to the scheme, subsection (4) above shall have effect as if paragraph (b) and the words after that paragraph were omitted.

(9)   No liability incurred under this Chapter—

    (a) by the administrator of a scheme, or

    (b) by a person by virtue of this section,

shall be affected by the termination of a scheme or by its ceasing to be an approved scheme or to be an exempt approved scheme.

(9A)   Where by virtue of this section any person is the person, or one of the persons, responsible for the discharge of the duties of the administrator of a scheme, any power or duty by virtue of this Part to serve any notice on, or to do any other thing in relation to, the administrator may be exercised or performed, instead, by the service of that notice on that person or, as the case may be, by the doing of that other thing in relation to that person.

(10)   Where by virtue of this section a person becomes responsible for the discharge of any duties, or liable for any tax, the Board shall, as soon as is reasonably practicable, notify him of that fact; but any failure to give such notification shall not affect that person's being responsible or liable by virtue of this section.

(11)   A person is in default for the purposes of this section if—

  (a) he has failed to discharge any duty imposed on him under this Chapter, or
  (b) he has failed to pay any tax due from him by virtue of this Chapter,

and (in either case) the Board consider the failure to be of a serious nature.

(11A)   In determining for the purposes of this section—

  (a) whether all of the persons who are the administrator of a scheme are at any time in default in respect of an amount of tax chargeable by virtue of section 591C, or
  (b) whether a trustee of a scheme is in default in respect of any amount of tax so chargeable,

the persons who at that time are trustees of the scheme or hold appointments in relation to the scheme under section 611AA(4) to (6) shall be deemed not to include any person who by virtue of section 591D(4) is not liable for that tax.

(12)   References in this section to a trust scheme, a non-trust scheme, trustees and scheme sponsors shall be construed in accordance with section 611AA.

(13)   References in this section to the employer include, where the employer is resident outside the United Kingdom, references to any branch or agent of the employer in the United Kingdom, and in this subsection 'branch or agent' has the meaning given by section 118(1) of the Management Act.

(14)   This section does not apply for the purposes of sections 602 and 603 and Schedule 22.

606A   Recourse to scheme members

(1)   This section applies where—

  (a) an approval of a retirements benefits scheme has ceased to have effect;
  (b) a person ('the employer') has become liable by virtue of section 606 to any tax chargeable on the administrator of the scheme under section 591C;
  (c) the employer has failed, either in whole or in part, to pay that tax; and
  (d) a person falling within subsection (2) below ('the relevant member') was a member of the scheme at the time ('the relevant time') immediately before the date of the cessation of its approval.

(2)   A person falls within this subsection in relation to any tax chargeable under section 591C if—

    (a)   at the relevant time or at any time before that time he was a controlling director of the employer; or

    (b)   he is a person by or in respect of whom any contributions were made by reference to which the condition in subsection (6A) of that section has been satisfied for the purpose of the charge to that tax.

(3)   Subject to subsection (4) below, if in a case where this section applies—

    (a)   the employer has ceased to exist, or

    (b)   the Board notify the relevant member that they consider the failure of the employer to pay the unpaid tax to be of a serious nature,

the relevant member shall be treated as included in the persons on whom the unpaid tax was charged and shall be assessable accordingly.

(4)   The amount of tax for which the relevant member shall be taken to be assessable by virtue of this section shall not exceed the amount determined by—

    (a)   taking the amount equal to 40 per cent of his share of the scheme; and

    (b)   subtracting from that amount his share of any tax charged under section 591C that has already been paid otherwise than by another person on whom it is treated as charged in accordance with this section.

(5)   For the purposes of this section the relevant member's share of the scheme is the amount equal to so much of the value of the assets held for the purposes of the scheme at the relevant time (taking the value at that time) as, on a just and reasonable apportionment, would have fallen to be treated as the value at that time of the assets then held for the purposes of the provision under the scheme of benefits to or in respect of the relevant member.

(6)   For the purposes of this section the relevant member's share of an amount of tax already paid is such sum as bears the same proportion to the amount paid as is borne by his share of the scheme to the total value at the relevant time of the assets then held for the purposes of the scheme.

(7)   The reference in subsection (5) above to the provision of benefits to or in respect of the relevant member includes a reference to the provision of a benefit to or in respect of a person connected with the relevant member.

(8)   For the purposes of this section a person is a controlling director of a company if he is a director of the company and is within section 417(5)(b) in relation to the company.

(9)   A notification given to any person for the purposes of subsection (3)(b) above may be included in any assessment on that person of the tax to which he becomes liable by virtue of the notification.

(10)   An assessment to tax made by virtue of this section shall not be out of time if it is made within three years after the date on which the tax which the employer has failed to pay first became due from him.

(11)   Subsections (1) to (3) of section 591D shall apply to the determination of the value at any time of an asset held for the purposes of a scheme as they apply for the purposes of section 591C(2).

(12)   Subsections (7) and (8) of section 591D shall apply for the purposes of this

section as they apply for the purposes of subsection (1) of section 591C and section 591C, respectively.

(13)   Section 839 (connected persons) shall apply for the purposes of this section.

607   Pilots' benefit fund

(1)   The Board may, if they think fit, and subject to such conditions as they think proper to attach to the approval, approve a pilots' benefit fund for the purposes of this Chapter as if it were a retirement benefits scheme and notwithstanding that it does not satisfy one or more of the conditions set out in section 590(2) and (3).

(2)   If a fund is approved by virtue of this section—

    (a)   sections 592, 597 to 600 and 604 to 606 shall have effect in relation to the fund with the modifications specified in subsection (3) below;

    (b)   pensions paid out of the fund and any sums chargeable to tax in connection with the fund under section 600 shall be treated for the purposes of the Income Tax Acts as earned income; and

    (c)   Chapter III of this Part shall have effect as if a member of the fund were the holder of a pensionable office or employment and his earnings as a pilot (estimated in accordance with the provisions of Case II of Schedule D) were remuneration from such an office or employment.

(3)   The modifications referred to in subsection (2)(a) above are as follows—

    (a)   in section 592, for the references in subsection (7) to an employee and Schedule E there shall be substituted respectively references to a member of the fund and Schedule D, and subsections (4) to (6), and in subsection (7) the words from 'incurred' onwards, shall be omitted;

    (b)   in sections 597 to 606 (except sections 601 to 603)—

        (i)   for references to an employee there shall be substituted references to a member or former member of the fund;

        (ii)   in section 599(1)(a) for the reference to a year of service there shall be substituted a reference to a year as a pilot licensed by a pilotage authority or authorised by a competent harbour authority;

        (iii)   section 606(2)(b), (4)(b), (7), (8) and (13) and so much of any other provision as applies to an employer shall be omitted; and

        (iv)   in section 600, for references to Schedule E there shall be substituted references to Case VI of Schedule D.

(4)   In this section 'pilots' benefit fund' means a fund established under section 15(1)(i) of the Pilotage Act 1983 or any scheme supplementing or replacing any such fund.

608   Superannuation funds approved before 6th April 1980

(1)   This section applies to any fund which immediately before 6th April 1980 was an approved superannuation fund for the purposes of section 208 of the 1970 Act if—

    (a)   it has not been approved under this Chapter (or under Chapter II of Part II of the Finance Act 1970); and

(b) no sum has been paid to it by way of contribution since 5th April 1980.

(2)   Subject to subsection (3) below, exemption from income tax shall, on a claim being made in that behalf, be allowed to a fund to which this section applies in respect of—

(a)   income derived from investments or deposits of the fund;
(b)   any underwriting commissions which apart from this subsection would be chargeable to tax under Case VI of Schedule D; and
(c)   any profits or gains which (apart from this subsection) would be chargeable to tax under Case VI or Schedule D by virtue of section 56(1)(a) and (2);

if, or to such extent as the Board are satisfied that, the income, commissions, profits or gains are applied for the purposes of the fund.

(3)   No claim under subsection (2) above shall be allowed unless the Board are satisfied that the terms on which benefits are payable from the fund have not been altered since 5th April 1980.

(4)   An annuity paid out of a fund to which this section applies shall be charged to tax under Schedule E and section 203 shall apply accordingly.

609   Schemes approved before 23rd July 1987

Schedule 23 to this Act, which makes provision with respect to retirement benefit schemes approved before 23rd July 1987, shall have effect.

610   Amendments of schemes

(1)   This section applies to any amendment of a retirement benefits scheme proposed in connection with an application for the Board's approval for the purposes of this Chapter which is needed in order to ensure that approval is so given, or designed to enhance the benefits under the scheme up to the limits suitable in a scheme for which approval is sought.

(2)   A provision, however expressed, designed to preclude any amendment of a scheme which would have prejudiced its approval under section 208 or 222 of the 1970 Act shall not prevent any amendment to which this section applies.

(3)   In the case of a scheme which contains no powers of amendment, the administrator of the scheme may, with the consent of all the members of the scheme, and of the employer (or of each of the employers), make any amendment to which this section applies.

611   Definition of 'retirement benefits scheme'

(1)   In this Chapter 'retirement benefits scheme' means, subject to the provisions of this section, a scheme for the provision of benefits consisting of or including relevant benefits, but does not include any national scheme providing such benefits.

(2)   References in this Chapter to a scheme include references to a deed, agreement, series of agreements, or other arrangements providing for relevant benefits notwithstanding that it relates or they relate only to—

(a) a small number of employees, or to a single employee, or

(b) the payment of a pension starting immediately on the making of the arrangements.

(3)   The Board may, if they think fit, treat a retirement benefits scheme relating to [scheme members] of two or more different classes or descriptions as being for the purposes of this Chapter two or more separate retirement benefits schemes relating respectively to such one or more of those classes or descriptions of those [scheme members] as the Board think fit.

(4)   For the purposes of this section, and of any other provision of this Chapter—

(a) employees may be regarded as belonging to different classes or descriptions if they are employed by different employers; and

(b) a particular class or description of [scheme member] may consist of a single [scheme member], or any number of [scheme members], however small.

(5)   Without prejudice to subsections (3) and (4) above, the Board may continue to treat as two different schemes, for the purposes of this Chapter, any retirement benefits scheme which, in pursuance of paragraph 5 of Schedule 3 to the Finance Act 1971 (schemes in existence before 5th April 1973), they treated, immediately before the coming into force of this Chapter, as two separate schemes for the purposes of Chapter II of Part II of the Finance Act 1970.

[(6)   In this section 'scheme member', in relation to a scheme means—

(a) an employee; or

(b) a person whose rights under the scheme derive from a pension sharing order or provision.]

611AA   Definition of the administrator

(1)   In this Chapter references to the administrator, in relation to a retirement benefits scheme, are to the person who is, or the persons who are, for the time being the administrator of the scheme by virtue of the following provisions of this section.

(2)   Subject to subsection (7) below, where—

(a) the scheme is a trust scheme, and

(b) at any time the trustee, or any of the trustees, is or are resident in the United Kingdom,

the administrator of the scheme at that time shall be the trustee or trustees of the scheme.

(3)   Subject to subsection (7) below, where—

(a) the scheme is a non-trust scheme, and

(b) at any time the scheme sponsor, or any of the scheme sponsors, is or are resident in the United Kingdom.

the administrator of the scheme at that time shall be the scheme sponsor or scheme sponsors.

(4)   At any time when the trustee of a trust scheme is not resident in the United Kingdom or (if there is more than one trustee) none of the trustees is so resident, the trustee or trustees shall ensure that there is a person, or there are persons—

(a)   resident in the United Kingdom, and
(b)   appointed by the trustee or trustees to be responsible for the discharge of all duties relating to the scheme which are imposed on the administrator under this Chapter.

(5)   At any time when the scheme sponsor of a non-trust scheme is not resident in the United Kingdom or (if there is more than one scheme sponsor) none of the scheme sponsors is so resident, the scheme sponsor or scheme sponsors shall ensure that there is a person, or there are persons—

(a)   resident in the United Kingdom, and
(b)   appointed by the scheme sponsor or scheme sponsors to be responsible for the discharge of all duties relating to the scheme which are imposed on the administrator under this Chapter.

(6)   Without prejudice to subsections (4) and (5) above—

(a)   the trustee or trustees of a trust scheme, or
(b)   the scheme sponsor or scheme sponsors of a non-trust scheme,

may at any time appoint a person who is, or persons who are, resident in the United Kingdom to be responsible for the discharge of all duties relating to the scheme which are imposed on the administrator under this Chapter.

(7)   Where at any time there is or are a person or persons—

(a)   for the time being appointed under subsection (4), (5) or (6) above as regards a scheme, and
(b)   resident in the United Kingdom,

the administrator of the scheme at that time shall be that person or those persons (and no other person).

(8)   Any appointment under subsection (4), (5) or (6) above—

(a)   must be in writing, and
(b)   if made after the time when the scheme is established, shall constitute an alteration of the scheme for the purposes of section 591B(2).

(9)   In this section—

(a)   references to a trust scheme are to a retirement benefits scheme established under a trust or trusts;
(b)   references to the trustee or trustees, in relation to a trust scheme and to a particular time, are to the person who is the trustee, or the persons who are the trustees, of the scheme at that time;
(c)   references to a non-trust scheme are to a retirement benefits scheme not established under a trust or trusts, and
(d)   references to the scheme sponsor or scheme sponsors, in relation to a retirement benefits scheme and to a particular time, are references to any person who established the scheme and is in existence at that time or, if more than one, all such persons.

611A   Definition of relevant statutory scheme

(1)   In this Chapter any reference to a relevant statutory scheme is to—

    (a)   a statutory scheme established before 14th March 1989, or

    (b)   a statutory scheme established on or after that date and entered in the register maintained by the Board for the purposes of this section, or

    (c)   a parliamentary pension scheme.

(2)   The Board shall maintain a register for the purposes of this section and shall enter in it the relevant particulars of any statutory scheme established on or after 14th March 1989 which is reported to the Board by the authority responsible for establishing it as a scheme the provisions of which correspond with those of an approved scheme.

(3)   The reference in subsection (2) above to the relevant particulars, in relation to a scheme, is a reference to—

    (a)   the identity of the scheme,

    (b)   the date on which it was established,

    (c)   the authority responsible for establishing it, and

    (d)   the date on which that authority reported the scheme to the Board.

(4)   Where the Board enter the relevant particulars of a scheme in the register maintained by them for the purposes of this section, they shall inform the authority responsible for establishing the scheme of the date of the entry.

(5)   In subsection (1)(c) 'parliamentary pension scheme' means—

    (a)   the Parliamentary pension scheme within the meaning of the Parliamentary and Other Pensions Act 1987;

    (b)   any pension scheme established for members of the Scottish Parliament under section 81(4) of the Scotland Act 1998;

    (c)   any pension scheme established for members of the Welsh Assembly under section 18(2) of the Government of Wales Act 1998;

    (d)   any pension scheme established for members of the Northern Ireland Assembly under section 48(2) of the Northern Ireland Act 1998;

    (e)   the pension scheme established for members of the European Parliament under section 4 of the European Parliament (Pay and Pensions) Act 1979;

    (f)   the pension scheme established under section 3 of the Ministerial Salaries and Members' Pensions Act (Northern Ireland) 1965;

    (g)   the pension scheme established under the Assembly Pensions (Northern Ireland) Order 1976.

612   Other interpretative provisions and regulations for purposes of this Chapter

(1)   In this Chapter, except where the context otherwise requires—

    'approved scheme' means a retirement benefits scheme for the time being approved by the Board for the purposes of this Chapter:

    'director' in relation to a company includes—

    (a)   in the case of a company the affairs of which are managed by a board of directors or similar body, a member of that board or body,

(b) in the case of a company the affairs of which are managed by a single director or similar person, that director or person,

(c) in the case of a company the affairs of which are managed by the members themselves, a member of that company;

and includes a person who is to be or has been a director;

'employee'—`

(a) in relation to a company, includes any officer of the company, any director of the company and any other person taking part in the management of the affairs of the company, and

(b) in relation to an employer, includes a person who is to be or has been an employee;

and 'employer' and other cognate expressions shall be construed accordingly;

'exempt approved scheme' has the meaning given by section 592(1);

'final remuneration' means the average annual remuneration of the last three years' service;

'pension' includes annuity;

'the permitted maximum' has the meaning given by section 590(3);

'relevant benefits' means any pension, lump sum, gratuity or other like benefit given or to be given on retirement or on death[, or by virtue of a pension sharing order or provision], or in anticipation of retirement, or, in connection with past service, after retirement or death, or to be given on or in anticipation of or in connection with any change in the nature of the service of the employee in question, except that it does not include any benefit which is to be afforded solely by reason of the disablement by accident of a person occurring during his service or of his death by accident so occurring and for no other reason;

'remuneration' does not include—

(a) anything in respect of which tax is chargeable under Schedule E and which arises from the acquisition or disposal of shares or an interest in shares or from a right to acquire shares; or

(b) anything in respect of which tax is chargeable by virtue of section 148;

'service' means service as an employee of the employer in question and other expressions, including 'retirement', shall be construed accordingly; and

'statutory scheme' means a retirement benefits scheme established by or under any enactment—

(a) the particulars of which are set out in any enactment, or in any regulations made under any enactment, or

(b) which has been approved as an appropriate scheme by a Minister or government department (including the head of a Northern Ireland department or a Northern Ireland department).

(2) Any reference in this Chapter[, in relation to a scheme,] to the provision of relevant benefits, or of a pension, for employees [or ex-spouses] includes a

reference to the provision of relevant benefits or a pension by means of a contract between the administrator or the employer or the employee [or ex-spouse] and a third person; and any reference to pensions or contributions paid, or payments made, under a scheme includes a reference to pensions or contributions paid, or payments made, under such a contract entered into for the purpose of the scheme.

[(2A)   In subsection (2) above the reference to the employer is a reference to the person who is the employer in relation to the scheme.]

(3)   The Board may make regulations generally for the purpose of carrying the preceding provisions of this Chapter into effect.

Chapter III

Retirement annuities

618   Termination of relief under this Chapter, and transitional provisions

(1)   Nothing in this Chapter shall apply in relation to—

    (a)   a contract made or trust scheme established on or after 1st July 1988; or

    (b)   a person by whom contributions are first paid on or after that date under a trust scheme established before that date.

(2)   Subject to subsection (4) below, the terms of a contract made, or the rules of a trust scheme established, on or after 17th March 1987 and before 1st July 1988 and approved by the Board under section 620 shall have effect (notwithstanding anything in them to the contrary) as if they did not allow the payment to the individual by whom the contract is made, or an individual paying contributions under the scheme, of a lump sum exceeding £150,000 or such other sum as may for the time being be specified in an order under section 635(4).

(3)   Subject to subsection (5) below, the rules of a trust scheme established before 17th March 1987 and approved by the Board under section 620 shall have effect (notwithstanding anything in them to the contrary) as if they did not allow the payment to any person first paying contributions under the scheme on or after 17th March 1987 of a lump sum such as is mentioned in subsection (2) above.

(4)   Subsection (2) above shall not apply—

    (a)   to a contract if, before the end of January 1988, the persons by and to whom premiums are payable under it jointly give notice to the Board that subsection (2) is not to apply; or

    (b)   to a scheme if, before the end of January 1988, the trustees or other persons having the management of the scheme give notice to the Board that subsection (2) is not to apply;

and where notice is given to the Board under this subsection, the contract or scheme shall, with effect from the date with effect from which it was approved, cease to be approved.

(5)   Subsection (3) above shall not apply in the case of any person paying contributions under a scheme if, before the end of January 1988, he and the trustees or other persons having the management of the scheme jointly give notice to the Board that subsection (3) is not to apply; and where notice is given to the Board, the scheme shall cease to be approved in relation to the contributor with effect from the date on which he first paid a contribution under it or (if later) the date with effect from which it was approved.

619   Exemption from tax in respect of qualifying premiums

(1)   Where in any year of assessment an individual is (or would but for an insufficiency of profits or gains be) chargeable to income tax in respect of relevant earnings from any trade, profession, vocation, office or employment carried on or held by him, and pays a qualifying premium then—

   (a)   relief from income tax shall be given under this section in respect of that qualifying premium, but only on a claim made for the purpose, and where relief is to be so given, the amount of that premium shall, subject to the provisions of this section, be deducted from or set off against his relevant earnings for the year of assessment in which the premium is paid; and

   (b)   any annuity payable to the same or another individual shall be treated as earned income of the annuitant to the extent to which it is payable in return for any amount on which relief is so given.

Paragraph (b) above applies only in relation to the annuitant to whom the annuity is made payable by the terms of the annuity contract under which it is paid.

(2)   Subject to the provisions of this section and section 626, the amount which may be deducted or set off in any year of assessment (whether in respect of one or more qualifying premiums, and whether or not including premiums in respect of a contract approved under section 621) shall be more than 17 1/2 per cent of the individual's net relevant earnings for that year.

(3)   Subject to the provisions of this section, the amount which may be deducted or set off in any year of assessment in respect of qualifying premiums paid under a contract approved under section 621 (whether in respect of one or more such premiums) shall not be more than 5 per cent of the individual's net relevant earnings for that year.

(4)   An individual who pays a qualifying premium in a year of assessment (whether or not a year for which he has relevant earnings) may on or before the 31st January next following that year elect that the premium shall be treated as paid—

   (a)   in the last preceding year of assessment; or

   (b)   if he had no net relevant earnings in the year referred to in paragraph (a) above, in the last preceding year of assessment but one;

and where an election is made under this subsection in respect of a premium the other provisions of this chapter shall have effect as if the premium had been paid in the year specified in the election and not in the year in which it was actually paid.

(5)   Where relief under this section for any year of assessment is claimed and allowed (whether or not relief then falls to be given for that year), and afterwards there is made any assessment, alteration of an assessment, or other adjustment of the claimant's liability to tax, there shall be made also such adjustments, if any, as are consequential thereon in the relief allowed or given under this section for that or any subsequent year of assessment.

(6)   Where relief under this section is claimed and allowed for any year of assessment in respect of any payment, relief shall not be given in respect of it under any other provision of the Income Tax Acts for the same or a later year of assessment nor (in the case of a payment under an annuity contract) in respect of any other premium or consideration for an annuity under the same contract; and references in the Income Tax Acts to relief in respect of life assurance premiums shall not be taken to include relief under this section.

(7)   If any person, for the purpose of obtaining for himself or any other person any relief from or repayment of tax under this section, knowingly makes any false statement or false representation, he shall be liable to a penalty not exceeding £3,000.

620   Qualifying premiums

(1)   In this Chapter 'qualifying premium' means, subject to subsection (5) below, a premium or other consideration paid by an individual—

    (a)   under an annuity contract for the time being approved by the Board under this section as having for its main object the provision for the individual of a life annuity in old age, or

    (b)   under a contract for the time being approved under section 621.

(2)   Subject to subsections (3) and (4) below, the Board shall not approve a contract under this section unless it appears to them to satisfy the conditions that it is made by the individual with a person lawfully carrying on in the United Kingdom the business of granting annuities on human life, and that it does not—

    (a)   provide for the payment by that person during the life of the individual of any sum except sums payable by way of annuity to the individual; or

    (b)   provide for the annuity payable to the individual to commence before he attains the age of 60 or after he attains the age of 75; or

    (c)   provide for the payment by that person of any other sums except sums payable by way of annuity to the individual's widow or widower and any sums which, in the event of no annuity becoming payable either to the individual or to a widow or widower, are payable by way of return of premiums, by way of reasonable interest on premiums or by way of bonuses out of profits; or

    (d)   provide for the annuity, if any, payable to a widow or widower of the individual to be of greater annual amount than that paid or payable to the individual; or

    (e)   provide for the payment of any annuity otherwise than for the life of the annuitant;

and that it does include provision securing that no annuity payable under it shall be capable in whole or in part of surrender, commutation or assignment.

(3)   A contract shall not be treated as not satisfying the requirements of sub-section (2) above by reason only that it—

   (a)   gives the individual the right to receive, by way of commutation of part of the annuity payable to him, a lump sum not exceeding three times the annual amount of the remaining part of the annuity, taking, where the annual amount is or may be different in different years, the initial annual amount, and

   (b)   makes any such right depend on the exercise by the individual of an election at or before the time when the annuity first becomes payable to him.

(4)   The Board may, if they think fit, and subject to any conditions they think proper to impose, approve, under this section, a contract otherwise satisfying the preceding conditions, notwithstanding that the contract provides for one or more of the following matters—

   (a)   for the payment after the individual's death of an annuity to a depen-dant not the widow or widower of the individual;

   (b)   for the payment to the individual of an annuity commencing before he attains the age of 60, if the annuity is payable on his becoming inca-pable through infirmity of body or mind of carrying on his own occupation or any occupation of a similar nature for which he is trained or fitted;

   (c)   if the individual's occupation is one in which persons customarily retire before attaining the age of 60, for the annuity to commence before he attains that age;

   (d)   for the annuity payable to any person to continue for a term certain (not exceeding ten years), notwithstanding his death within that term, or for the annuity payable to any person to terminate, or be suspended, on marriage (or remarriage) or in other circumstances.

   (e)   in the case of an annuity which is to continue for a term certain, for the annuity to be assignable by will, and in the event of any person dying entitled to it, for it to be assignable by his personal representatives in the distribution of the estate so as to give effect to a testamentary dis-position, or to the rights of those entitled on intestacy, or to an appropriation of it to a legacy or to a share or interest in the estate.

(5)   Subject to section 621(5), section 619 and subsections (1) to (4) above shall apply in relation to a contribution under a trust scheme approved by the Board as they apply in relation to a premium under an annuity contract so approved, with the modification that, for the condition as to the person with whom the contract is made, there shall be substituted a condition that the scheme—

   (a)   is established under the law of any part of, and administered in, the United Kingdom; and

   (b)   is established for the benefit of individuals engaged in or connected with a particular occupation (or one or other of a group of occupa-tions), and for the purpose of providing retirement annuities for them, with or without subsidiary benefits for their families or dependants; and

(c) is so established under irrevocable trusts by a body of persons com-
prising or representing a substantial proportion of the individuals so
engaged in the United Kingdom, or of those so engaged in England,
Wales, Scotland or Northern Ireland;

and with the necessary adaptations of other references to the contract or the person with whom it is made.

(6) Exemption from income tax shall be allowed in respect of income derived
from investments or deposits of any fund maintained for the purpose maintained
in subsection (5)(b) above under a scheme for the time being approved under that
subsection.

(7) The Board may at any time, by notice given to the persons by and to whom
premiums are payable under any contract for the time being approved under this
section, or to the trustees or other persons having the management of any scheme
so approved, withdraw that approval on such grounds and from such date as may
be specified in the notice.

(8) Nothing in sections 4 and 6 of the Policies of Assurance Act 1867 (obligations of assurance companies in respect of notices of assignment of policies of
life assurance) shall be taken to apply to any contract approved under this section.

(9) For the purposes of any provision applying this subsection 'approved annuities' means—

(a) annuities under contracts approved by the Board under this section,
being annuities payable wholly in return for premiums or other consideration paid by a person who (when the premiums or other
considerations are or is payable) is, or would but for an insufficiency
of profits or gains be, chargeable to tax in respect of relevant earnings
from a trade, profession, vocation, office or employment carried on or
held by him; and

(b) annuities or lump sums under approved personal pension arrangements within the meaning of Chapter IV of this Part.

621 Other approved contracts

(1) The Board may approve under this section—

(a) a contract the main object of which is the provision of an annuity for
the wife or husband of the individual, or for any one or more dependants of the individual,

(b) a contract the sole object of which is the provision of a lump sum on the
death of the individual before he attains the age of 75.

(2) The Board shall not approve the contract unless it appears to them that it is
made by the individual with a person lawfully carrying on in the United Kingdom
the business of granting annuities on human life.

(3) The Board shall not approve a contract under subsection (1)(a) above unless
it appears to them to satisfy all the following conditions, that is to say—

(a) that any annuity payable to the wife or husband or dependant of the
individual commences on the death of the individual;

(b) that any annuity payable to the individual commences at a time after the individual attains the age of 60, and, unless the individual's annuity is one to commence on the death of a person to whom an annuity would be payable under the contract if that person survived the individual, cannot commence after the time when the individual attains the age of 75;

(c) that the contract does not provide for the payment by the person contracting with the individual of any sum, other than any annuity payable to the individual's wife or husband or dependant, or to the individual, except, in the event of no annuity becoming payable under the contract, any sums payable by way of return of premiums, by way of reasonable interest on premiums or by way of bonuses out of profits;

(d) that the contract does not provide for the payment of any annuity otherwise than for the life of the annuitant;

(e) that the contract does include provision securing that no annuity payable under it shall be capable in whole or in part of surrender, commutation or assignment.

(4)   The Board may, if they think fit, and subject to any conditions that they think proper to impose, approve a contract under subsection (1)(a) above notwithstanding that, in one or more respects, they are not satisfied that the contract complies with the provisions of paragraphs (a) to (e) of subsection (3) above.

(5)   The main purpose of a trust scheme, or part of a trust scheme, within section 620(5) may be to provide annuities for the wives, husbands and dependants of the individuals, or lump sums payable on death and in that case—

(a) approval of the trust scheme shall be subject to subsections (1) to (4) above with any necessary modifications, and not subject to section 620(2) to (4);

(b) the provisions of this Chapter shall apply to the scheme or part of the scheme when duly approved as they apply to a contract approved under this section; and

(c) section 620(6) shall apply to any duly approved trust scheme, or part of a trust scheme.

(6)   Except as otherwise provided in this Chapter (and in particular except in section 620), any reference in the Tax Acts to a contract or scheme approved under that section shall include a reference to a contract or scheme approved under this section.

622   Substituted retirement annuity contracts

(1)   The Board may, if they think fit, and subject to any conditions they think proper to impose, approve an annuity contract under section 620 notwithstanding that the contract provides that the individual by whom it is made—

(a) may agree with the person with whom it is made that a sum representing the value of the individual's accrued rights under it should be applied as the premium or other consideration either under another annuity contract made between them and approved by the Board under section 620, or under personal pension arrangements made between them and approved by the Board under Chapter IV of this Part; or

   (b) may require the person with whom it is made to pay such a sum to such other person as the individual may specify, to be applied by that other person as the premium or other consideration either under an annuity contract made between the individual and him and approved by the Board under section 620, or under personal pension arrangements made between the individual and him and approved by the Board under Chapter IV of this Part.

(2) References in subsection (1) above to the individual by whom the contract is made include references to any widow, widower or dependant having accrued rights under the contract.

(3) Where in pursuance of any such provision as is mentioned in subsection (1) above of an annuity contract approved under section 620, or of a corresponding provision of a contract approved under section 621(1)(a), a sum representing the value of accrued rights under one contract ('the original contract') is paid by way of premium or other consideration under another contract ('the substituted contract'), any annuity payable under the substituted contract shall be treated as earned income of the annuitant to the same extent that an annuity payable under the original contract would have been so treated.

623 Relevant earnings

(1) . . .

(2) 'relevant earnings', in relation to any individual means, for the purposes of this Chapter, any income of his chargeable to tax for the year of assessment in question, being either—

   (a) income arising in respect of remuneration from an office or employment held by him other than a pensionable office or employment; or

   (b) income from any property which is attached to or forms part of the emoluments of any such office or employment held by him; or

   (c) income which is chargeable under Schedule D and is immediately derived by him from the carrying on or exercise by him of his trade, profession or vocation either as an individual or, in the case of a partnership, as a partner personally acting therein; or

   (d) income treated as earned income by virtue of section 529;

but does not include any remuneration as director of a company whose income consists wholly or mainly of investment income (that is to say, income which, if the company were an individual, would not be earned income), being a company of which he is a controlling director.

(3) For the purposes of this Chapter, an office or employment is a pensionable office or employment if, and only if, service in it is service to which a sponsored superannuation scheme relates (not being a scheme under which the benefits provided in respect of that service are limited to a lump sum payable on the termination of the service through death or disability before the age of 75 or some lower age); but references to a pensionable office or employment apply whether or not the duties are performed wholly or partly in the United Kingdom or the holder is chargeable to tax in respect of it.

(4) Service in an office or employment shall not for the purposes of subsection

(3) above be treated as service to which a sponsored superannuation scheme relates by reason only of the fact that the holder of the office or employment might (though he does not) participate in the scheme by exercising or refraining from exercising an option open to him by virtue of that service.

(5)   For the purposes of relief under section 619, an individual's relevant earnings are those earnings before giving effect to any capital allowances, other than deductions allowable in computing profits or gains, but after taking into account the amounts on which charges fall to be made under any of the Capital Allowances Acts; and references to income in the following provisions of this section (other than references to total income) shall be construed similarly.

(6)   Subject to the following provisions of this section 'net relevant earnings' means, in relation to an individual, the amount of his relevant earnings for the year of assessment in question, less the amount of any deductions falling to be made from the relevant earnings in computing for the purpose of income tax his total income for that year, being—

- (a)   deductions which but for section 74(m), (p) or (q) could be made in computing his profits or gains; or
- (b)   deductions in respect of relief under Schedule 9 of the Finance Act 1981 (stock relief); or
- (c)   deductions in respect of losses or capital allowances arising from activities profits or gains of which would be included in computing relevant earnings of the individual.

(7)   Where in any year of assessment for which an individual claims and is allowed relief under section 619—

- (a)   there falls to be made in computing the total income of the individual a deduction in respect of any such loss or allowance of the individual as is mentioned in subsection (6)(c) above; and
- (b)   the deduction or part of it falls to be so made from income other than relevant earnings,

the amount of the deduction made from that other income shall be treated as reducing the individual's net relevant earnings for subsequent years of assessment (being deducted as far as may be from those of the immediately following year, whether or not he claims or is entitled to claim relief under this section for that year, and so far as it cannot be so deducted, then from those of the next year, and so on).

(8)   An individual's net relevant earnings for any year of assessment are to be computed without regard to any relief which falls to be given for that year under section 619 to that individual.

(9)   An individual's relevant earnings, in the case of partnership profits, shall be taken to be his share of the partnership income, estimated in accordance with the Income Tax Acts, but the amount to be included in respect of those earnings in arriving at his net relevant earnings shall be his share of that income after making therefrom all such deductions (if any) in respect of payments made by the partnership or of relief given to the partnership under Schedule 9 of the Finance Act 1981 (stock relief) or in respect of capital allowances falling to be made to the partnership as would be made in computing the tax payable in respect of that income.

624 Sponsored superannuation schemes and controlling directors

(1) In section 623 'a sponsored superannuation scheme' means a scheme or arrangement—

    (a) relating to service in particular offices or employments, and

    (b) having for its objects or one of its objects to make provision in respect of persons serving in those offices or employments against future retirement or partial retirement, against future termination of service through death or disability, or against similar matters,

being a scheme or arrangement under which any part of the cost of the provision so made is or has been borne otherwise than by those persons by reason of their service (whether it is the cost or part of the cost of the benefits provided, or of paying premiums or other sums in order to provide those benefits, or of administering or instituting the scheme or arrangement).

(2) For the purposes of subsection (1) above a person shall be treated as bearing by reason of his service the cost of any payment made or agreed to be made in respect of his service, if that payment or the agreement to make it is treated under the Income Tax Acts as increasing his income, or it would be so treated if he were chargeable to tax under Case I of Schedule E in respect of his emoluments from that service.

(3) In section 623 'controlling director' means a director of a company, the directors of which have a controlling interest in the company, who is the beneficial owner of, or able either directly or through the medium of other companies or by any other indirect means to control, more than 5 per cent of the ordinary share capital of the company; and for the purposes of this definition—

    'company' means one within the Companies Act 1985 or the Companies (Northern Ireland) Order 1986; and
    'director' means—

    (a) in relation to a body corporate the affairs of which are managed by a board of directors or similar body, a member of that board or similar body;

    (b) in relation to a body corporate the affairs of which are managed by a single director or similar person, that director or person;

    (c) in relation to a body corporate the affairs of which are managed by the members themselves, a member of the body corporate;

and includes any person who is to be or has been a director.

625 Carry-forward of unused relief under section 619

(1) Where—

    (a) in any year of assessment an individual is (or would but for an insufficiency of profits or gains be) chargeable to income tax in respect of relevant earnings from any trade, profession, vocation, office or employment carried on or held by him, but

    (b) there is unused relief for that year, that is to say, an amount which would have been deducted from or set off against the individual's relevant earnings for that year under subsection (1) of section 619 if—

(i) he had paid a qualifying premium in that year; or

(ii) the qualifying premium or premiums paid by him in that year had been greater;

then, subject to section 655(1)(b), relief may be given under that section, up to the amount of the unused relief, in respect of so much of any qualifying premium or premiums paid by the individual in any of the next six years of assessment as exceeds the maximum applying for that year under subsection (2) of that section.

(2)   Relief by virtue of this section shall be given for an earlier year rather than a later year, the unused relief taken into account in giving relief for any year being deducted from that available for giving relief in subsequent years and unused relief derived from an earlier year being exhausted before unused relief derived from a later year.

(3)   Where a relevant assessment to tax in respect of a year of assessment becomes final and conclusive more than six years after the end of that year and there is an a amount of unused relief for that year which results from the making of the assessment—

(a) that amount shall not be available for giving relief by virtue of this section for any of the six years following that year, but

(b) the individual may, within the period of six months beginning with the date on which the assessment becomes final and conclusive, elect that relief shall be given under section 619, up to that amount, in respect of so much of any qualifying premium or premiums paid by him within that period as exceeds the maximum applying under sub-section (2) of that section for the year of assessment in which they were paid;

and to the extent to which relief in respect of any premium or premiums is given by virtue of this subsection it shall not be given by virtue of subsection (1) above.

(4)   In this section 'a relevant assessment to tax' means an assessment on the individual's relevant earnings or on the profits or gains of a partnership from which the individual derives relevant earnings.

626   Modification of section 619 in relation to persons over 50

In the case of an individual whose age at the beginning of a year of assessment is within a range specified in the first column of the Table set out below, section 619(2) shall have effect for that year with the substitution for the reference to $17\frac{1}{2}$ per cent of a reference to the relevant percentage specified in the second column of the Table.

TABLE

Age range	Percentage
51 to 55	20
56 to 60	$22\frac{1}{2}$
61 or more	$27\frac{1}{2}$

627   Lloyd's underwriters

(1)   Where for any year of assessment an individual—

(a) is chargeable to income tax in respect of relevant earnings derived from Lloyd's underwriting activities; and

(b) there is an amount of unused relief attributable to those earnings,

the individual may, subject to subsection (2) below, elect that there shall be treated as paid in that year any qualifying premium paid by him in the next year of assessment but two.

(2)   An election under this section shall not have effect in relation to so much of any qualifying premium as exceeds the amount of unused relief referred to in subsection (1)(b) above.

(3)   Any election under this section shall be made before the end of the year of assessment in which the premium is paid.

(4)   Where an election is made under this section the provisions of this Chapter, other than section 619(4), shall have effect as if the premium or, as the case may be, the part of the premium in question had been paid in the year specified in the election and not in the year in which it was actually paid.

(5)   In this section—

'unused relief' has the same meanings as in section 625; and

'relevant earnings derived from Lloyd's underwriting activities' means relevant earnings as an underwriting or former underwriting member of Lloyd's or by way of commission calculated by reference to the profits of Lloyd's underwriting business.

628   Partnership retirement annuities

(1)   Where a person ('the former partner') has ceased to be a member of a partnership on retirement, because of age or ill-health or on death and, under—

(a) the partnership agreement; or

(b) an agreement replacing the partnership agreement or supplementing it or supplementing an agreement replacing it; or

(c) an agreement made with an individual who acquires the whole or part of the business carried on by the partnership;

annual payments are made for the benefit of the former partner or a widow, widower or dependant of the former partner and are for the purposes of income tax income of the person for whose benefit they are made, the payment shall be treated as earned income of that person, except to the extent that they exceed the limit specified in subsection (2) below.

(2)   The limit mentioned in subsection (1) above is 50 per cent of the average of the amounts which, in the best three of the relevant years of assessment, were the former partner's shares of the relevant profits or gains; and for this purpose—

(a) the former partner's share in any year of the relevant profits or gains is, subject to subsection (3) below, so much of the relevant profits or gains as fell to be included in a return of his income for that year; and

(b) the relevant profits or gains are the profits or gains of any trade, profession or vocation on which the partnership or any other partnership of which the former partner was a member was assessed to income tax; and

(c) the relevant years of assessment are the last seven years of assessment in which he was required to devote substantially the whole of his time to acting as a partner in the partnership or those partnerships; and

(d) the best three of the relevant years of assessment are those three of them in which the amounts of his shares of the relevant profits were highest;

but where, in any of the relevant years, the circumstances were such that any of the profits or gains of a partnership were not assessable to income tax, paragraphs (a), (b) and (d) above shall apply as they would apply had those profits or gains been so assessable.

(3) If the retail prices index for the month of December in the last of the seven years referred to in paragraph (c) of subsection (2) above is higher than it was for the month of December in any of the other years referred to in that paragraph, the amount which, for that other year, was the former partner's share of the relevant profits or gains shall be treated for the purposes of that subsection as increased by the same percentage as the percentage increase in that index.

(4) If the retail prices index for the month of December preceding a year of assessment after that in which the former partner ceased to be a member of the partnership is higher than it was for the month of December in the year of assessment in which he ceased to be such a member, the amount which under subsection (2) above is the limit for the first-mentioned year of assessment shall be treated as increased by the same percentage as the percentage increase in that index.

(5) Where the former partner ceased to be a member of the partnership before the year 1974–75, subsection (4) above shall have effect as if he had ceased to be a member in that year.

629   Annuity premiums of Ministers and other officers

(1) For the purposes of this Chapter so much of any salary which—

(a) is payable to the holder of a qualifying office who is also a Member of the House of Commons, and

(b) is payable for a period in respect of which the holder is not a participant in relation to that office in arrangements contained in the Parliamentary pension scheme but is a participant in relation to his membership of the House of Commons in any such arrangements, or for any part of such a period.

as is equal to the difference between a Member's pensionable salary and the salary which (in accordance with any such resolution as is mentioned in subsection (3)(a) below) is payable to him as a Member holding that qualifying office shall be treated as remuneration from the office of Member and not from the qualifying office.

(2) In this section—

'Member's pensionable salary' means a Member's ordinary salary under any resolution of the House of Commons which, being framed otherwise than as an expression of opinion, is for the time being in force relating to the remuneration of Members or, if the resolution provides for a Member's ordinary salary thereunder to be treated for pension purposes as being at a higher rate, a national yearly salary at that higher rate;

'qualifying office' means an office mentioned in section 2(2)(b), (c) or (d) of the Parliamentary and other Pensions Act 1987;

'the Parliamentary pension scheme' has the same meaning as in that Act;

and without prejudice to the power conferred by virtue of paragraph 13 of Schedule 1 to that Act, regulations under section 2 of that Act may make provision specifying the circumstances in which a person is to be regarded for the purposes of this section as being or not being a participant in relation to his Membership of the House of Commons, or in relation to any office, in arrangements contained in the Parliamentary pension scheme.

(3) In subsection (2) above 'a Member's ordinary salary', in relation to any resolution of the House of Commons, means—

(a) if the resolution provides for salary to be paid to Members at different rates according to whether or not they are holders of particular offices, or are in receipt of salaries or pensions as the holders or former holders of particular offices, a Member's yearly salary at the higher or highest rate; and

(b) in any other case, a Member's yearly salary at the rate specified in or determined under the resolution.

Chapter IV

Personal pension schemes

Preliminary

630   Interpretation

(1)   In this Chapter—

'approved'—

(a)   in relation to a scheme, means approved by the Board under this Chapter; and

(b)   in relation to arrangements, means made in accordance with a scheme which is for the time being, and was when the arrangements were made, an approved scheme;

but does not refer to cases in which approval has been withdrawn;

'authorised insurance company' has the meaning given by section 659B.

'income withdrawal' means a payment of income, under arrangements made in accordance with a personal pension scheme, otherwise than by way of an annuity;

'member', in relation to a personal pension scheme, means an individual who makes arrangements in accordance with the scheme;

'pension date', in relation to any personal pension arrangements, means the date determined in accordance with the arrangements on which—

(a)   an annuity such as is mentioned in section 634 is first payable, or

(b)   the member elects to defer the purchase of such an annuity and to make income withdrawals in accordance with section 634A;

'personal pension arrangements' means arrangements made by an individual in accordance with a personal pension scheme;

'personal pension scheme' means a scheme whose sole purpose is the provision of annuities, income withdrawals or lump sums under arrangements made by individuals in accordance with the scheme;

'scheme administrator' means the person referred to in section 638(1);

and references to an employee or to an employer include references to the holder of an office or to the person under whom an office is held.

(2)   For the purposes of this Chapter the annual amount of the annuity which would have been purchasable by a person on any date shall be calculated by reference to—

(a)   the value on that date, determined by or on behalf of the scheme administrator, of the fund from which income withdrawals are to be or have been made by him under the arrangements in question, and

(b)   the current published tables of rates of annuities prepared for the purposes of this Chapter by the Government Actuary.

(3)   The reference in subsection 2(*a*) above to the value of the fund from which income withdrawals are to be or have been made under any personal pension arrangements is to the value of the accrued rights to which the person concerned is entitled conferring prospective entitlement to benefits under those arrangements.

Where a lump sum falls to be paid on the date in question, the reference is to the value of the fund after allowing for that payment.

(4)   The Board may make provision by regulations as to the basis on which the tables mentioned in subsection (2)(*b*) above are to be prepared and the manner in which they are to be applied.

631   Approval of schemes

(1)   An application to the Board for their approval of a personal pension scheme shall be in such form, shall contain such information, and shall be accompanied by such documents, in such form, as the Board may prescribe.

(2)   The Board may at their discretion grant or refuse an application for approval of a personal pension scheme, but their discretion shall be subject to the restrictions set out in sections 632 to 638A.

(3)   The Board shall give notice to the applicant of the grant or refusal of an application; and in the case of a refusal the notice shall state the grounds for the refusal.

(4)   If an amendment is made to an approved scheme without being approved by the Board, their approval of the scheme shall cease to have effect.

Restrictions on approval

632   Establishment of schemes

(1)   The Board shall not approve a personal pension scheme established by any person other than—

    (a)   a person who is authorised under Chapter III of Part I of the Financial Services Act 1986 to carry on investment business and who carries on business of a kind mentioned in subsection (2) below;

    (aa) an EC company which—

        (i)   lawfully carries on long term businesses in the United Kingdom, or

        (ii) lawfully provides long term insurance in the United Kingdom;

    (b)   a building society within the meaning of the Building Societies Act 1986;

    (bb) a pension company within the meaning of the Building Societies (Designation of Pension Companies) Order 1987 which is an associate of a building society within the meaning of section 18(17) of the Building Societies Act 1986;

    (c)   an institution authorised under the Banking Act 1987;

    (cc) a body corporate which is a subsidiary or holding company of an institution authorised under the Banking Act 1987, or is a subsidiary of the holding company of such an institution;

    (d)   a recognised bank or licensed institution within the meaning of the Banking Act 1979.

    (e)   an institution which—

        (i)   is a European institution within the meaning of regulation 3(1) of the Banking Coordination (Second Council Directive) Regulations 1992, and

        (ii) in conformity with the conditions and requirements of those Regulations, carries on in the United Kingdom, through a branch established in the United Kingdom for that purpose, or by the provision of services, any activity falling within item 1, 7 or 11 of the list of activities contained in Schedule 1 to those Regulations.

(2)   The kinds of business referred to in subsection (1)(a) above are—

    (a)   issuing insurance policies or annuity contracts;

    (b)   managing unit trust schemes authorised under section 78(1) of the Financial Services Act 1986.

(2ZA)   For the purposes of subsection (1)(aa) above an EC company—

    (a)   lawfully carries on long term business in the United Kingdom if it does so through a branch in respect of which such requirements of Part I of Schedule 2F to the Insurance Companies Act 1982 as are applicable have been complied with;

    (b)   lawfully provides long term insurance in the United Kingdom if such of those requirements as are applicable have been complied with in respect of the insurance.

(2A)   In subsection 1(cc) above 'holding company' and 'subsidiary' are to be construed in accordance with section 736 of the Companies Act 1985 or Article 4 of the Companies (Northern Ireland) Order 1986.

(2B)   For the purposes of this section—

(a) references to an EC company shall be construed in accordance with section 2(6) of the Insurance Companies Act 1982;

(b) references to long term business shall be construed in accordance with section 1(1) of that Act;

(c) references to the provision of long term insurance in the United Kingdom shall be construed in accordance with section 96A(3A) of that Act.

(3)   Subsection (1) above shall not apply in relation to a scheme approved by the Board by virtue of section 620(5) if it was established before 1st July 1988.

(4)   The Treasury may by order amend this section as it has effect for the time being.

633   Scope of benefits

(1)   The Board shall not approve a personal pension scheme which makes provision for any benefit other than—

(a) the payment of an annuity satisfying the conditions in section 634 or income withdrawals with respect to which the conditions in section 634A are satisfied;

(b) the payment to a member of a lump sum satisfying the conditions in section 635;

(c) the payment after the death of a member of an annuity satisfying the conditions in section 636 or income withdrawals with respect to which the conditions in section 636A are satisfied;

(d) the payment on the death of a member of a lump sum satisfying the conditions in section 637 (death benefit);

(e) the payment on or after the death of a member of a lump sum with respect to which the conditions in section 637A (return of contributions) are satisfied.

(2)   Subsection (1) above shall not prevent the approval of a scheme which makes provision for insurance against a risk relating to the non-payment of contributions.

634   Annuity to member

(1)   The annuity must be payable by an authorised insurance company which may be chosen by the member.

(2)   Subject to subsection (3) below, the annuity must not commence before the member attains the age of 50 or after he attains the age of 75.

(3)   The annuity may commence before the member attains the age of 50 if—

(a) it is payable on his becoming incapable through infirmity of body or mind of carrying on his own occupation or any occupation of a similar nature for which he is trained or fitted; or

(b) the Board are satisfied that his occupation is one in which persons customarily retire before that age.

(4) Subject to subsection (5) below, the annuity must be payable to the member for his life.

(5) The annuity may continue for a term certain not exceeding ten years, notwithstanding the member's death within that term; and for this purpose an annuity shall be regarded as payable for a term certain notwithstanding that it may terminate, after the death of the member and before expiry of that term, on the happening of any of the following—

(a) the marriage of the annuitant;
(b) his attaining the age of 18;
(c) the later of his attaining that age and ceasing to be in full-time education.

(6) The annuity must not be capable of assignment or surrender, [except that—

(a) an annuity may be assigned or surrendered for the purpose of giving effect to a pension sharing order or provision; and
(b)] an annuity for a term certain may be assigned by will or by the annuitant's personal representatives in the distribution of his estate so as to give effect to a testamentary disposition, or the rights of those entitled on an intestacy, or to an appropriation of it to a legacy or to a share or interest in the estate.

634A Income withdrawals by member

(1) Where a member elects to defer the purchase of an annuity such as is mentioned in section 634, income withdrawals may be made by him during the period of deferral, subject as follows.

(2) Income withdrawals must not be made before the member attains the age of 50, unless—

(a) they are available on his becoming incapable through infirmity of body or mind of carrying on his own occupation or any occupation of a similar nature for which he is trained or fitted, or
(b) the Board are satisfied that his occupation is one in which persons customarily retire before that age.

(3) Income withdrawals must not be made after the member attains the age of 75.

(4) The aggregate amount of income withdrawals by a member in each successive period of twelve months beginning with his pension date must be not less than 35 per cent or more than 100 per cent of the annual amount of the annuity which would have been purchasable by him on the relevant reference date.

(5) For the purposes of this section the relevant reference date for the first three years is the member's pension date, and for each succeeding period of three years is the first day of that period.

(6) The right to income withdrawals must not be capable of assignment or surrender[, except for the purpose of giving effect to a pension sharing order or provision].

635   Lump sum to member

(1)   The lump sum must be payable only if the member so elects on or before his pension date under the arrangements in question.

(2)   The lump sum must be payable on the date which is his pension date under the arrangements in question.

(3)   The lump sum must not exceed one quarter of the difference between—

    (a)   the total value, at the time when the lump sum is paid, of the benefits provided for by the arrangements in question; and

    (b)   the value, at that time, of such of the member's rights under those arrangements as are protected rights for the purposes of the Pension Schemes Act 1993 or the Pension Schemes (Northern Ireland) Act 1993.

(4) . . .

(5)   The right to payment of the lump sum must not be capable of assignment or surrender[, except for the purpose of giving effect to a pension sharing order or provision].

636   Annuity after death of member

(1)   The annuity must be payable by an authorised insurance company which may be chosen by the member or by the annuitant.

(2)   The annuity must be payable to the surviving spouse of the member, or to a person who was at the member's death a dependant of his.

(3)   The aggregate annual amount (or, if that amount varies, the aggregate of the initial annual amounts) of all annuities to which this section applies and which are payable under the same personal pension arrangements shall not exceed—

    (a)   where before his death the member was in receipt of an annuity under the arrangements, the annual amount (or, if it varied, the highest annual amount) of that annuity; or

    (b)   where paragraph (a) does not apply, the highest annual amount of the annuity that would have been payable under the arrangements to the member (ignoring any entitlement of his to commute part of it for a lump sum) if it had been purchased on the day before his death.

[(3A)   The references in subsection (3) above—

    (a)   to the annual amount or highest annual amount of an annuity of which the member was in receipt before his death, and

    (b)   to the highest annual amount of an annuity that would have been payable if it had been purchased on the day before the member's death,

shall each be construed in a case where payments of that annuity were or would have been affected by the making of any pension sharing order or provision as if the only payments of that annuity to be taken into account were those that have been or would have been so affected.]

(4)   Subject to subsections (5) to (9) below, the annuity must be payable for the life of the annuitant.

(5)   Where the annuity is payable to the surviving spouse of the member and at the time of the member's death the surviving spouse is under the age of 60, the annuity may be deferred to a time not later than—

    (a)   the time when the surviving spouse attains that age; or

    (b)   where the member's annuity is payable to the surviving spouse for a term certain as mentioned in section 634(5) and the surviving spouse attains the age of 60 before the time when the member's annuity terminates, that time.

(6)   The annuity may cease to be payable on the marriage of the annuitant.

(7)   Where the annuity is payable to the surviving spouse of the member, it may cease before the death of the surviving spouse if—

    (a)   the member was survived by one or more dependants under the age of 18 and at the time of the member's death the surviving spouse was under the age of 45; and

    (b)   at some time before the surviving spouse attains that age no such dependant remains under the age of 18.

(8)   Where the annuity is payable to a person who is under the age of 18 when it is first payable, it must cease to be payable either—

    (a)   on his attaining age; or

    (b)   on the later of his attaining that age and ceasing to be in full-time education,

unless he was a dependant of the member otherwise than by reason only that he was under the age of 18.

(9)   The annuity may continue for a term certain not exceeding ten years, notwithstanding the original annuitant's death within that term; and for this purpose an annuity shall be regarded as payable for a term certain notwithstanding that it may terminate, after the death of the original annuitant and before the expiry of that term, on the happening of any of the following—

    (a)   the marriage of the annuitant to whom it is payable;

    (b)   his attaining the age of 18;

    (c)   the later of his attaining that age and ceasing to be in full-time education.

(10)   The annuity must not be capable of assignment or surrender, [except that—

    (a)   an annuity may be assigned or surrendered for the purpose of giving effect to a pension sharing order or provision; and

    (b)]   an annuity for a term certain may be assigned by will or by the annuitant's personal representatives in the distribution of his estate so as to give effect to a testamentary disposition, or to the rights of those entitled on an intestacy, or to an appropriation of it to a legacy or to a share or interest in the estate.

636A   Income withdrawals after death of member

(1)   Where a person entitled to such an annuity as is mentioned in section 636 elects to defer the purchase of the annuity, income withdrawals may be made by him during the period of deferral, subject as follows.

(2)   No such deferral may be made, and accordingly income withdrawals may not be made, if the person concerned elects in accordance with section 636(5)(*a*) to defer the purchase of an annuity.

(3)   Income withdrawals must not be made after the person concerned if he had purchased such an annuity as is mentioned in section 636 would have ceased to be entitled to payments under it.

(4)   Income withdrawals must not in any event be made after the member would have attained the age of 75 or, if earlier, after the person concerned attains the age of 75.

(5)   The aggregate amount of income withdrawals by a person in each successive period of twelve months beginning with the date of the member's death must be not less than 35 per cent or more than 100 per cent of the annual amount of the annuity which would have been purchasable by him on the relevant reference date.

(6)   For the purposes of this section the relevant reference date for the first three years is the date of the member's death, and for each succeeding period of three years is the first day of that period.

(7)   The right to income withdrawals must not be capable of assignment or surrender[, except for the purpose of giving effect to a pension sharing order or provision].

637   Death benefit

The lump sum—

> (a)   must be payable on the death of the member before he attains the age of 75, and
> (b)   must be payable by an authorised insurance company.

637A   Return of contributions on or after death of member

(1)   The lump sum payable under the arrangements in question (or, where two or more lump sums are so payable, those lump sums taken together) must represent no more than the return of contributions together with reasonable interest on contributions or bonuses out of profits, after allowing for—

> (a)   any income withdrawals, and
> (b)   any purchases of annuities such as are mentioned in section 636.

To the extent that contributions are invested in units under a unit trust scheme, the lump sum (or lump sums) may represent the sale or redemption price of the units.

(2)   A lump sum must be payable only if, in the case of the arrangements in question—

> (a)   no such annuity as is mentioned in section 634 has been purchased by the member;
> (b)   no such annuity as is mentioned in section 636 has been purchased in respect of the relevant interest; and
> (c)   no election in accordance with subsection (5)(*a*) of section 636 has been made in respect of the relevant interest.

(3)   Where the member's death occurs after the date which is his pension date in

relation to the arrangements in question, a lump sum must not be payable more than two years after the death unless, in the case of that lump sum, the person entitled to such an annuity as is mentioned in section 636 in respect of the relevant interest—

    (*a*) has elected in accordance with section 636A to defer the purchase of an annuity; and

    (*b*) has died during the period of deferral.

(4)   In this section 'the relevant interest' means the interest, under the arrangements in question, of the person to whom or at whose direction the payment in question is made, except where there are two or more such interests, in which case it means that one of them in respect of which the payment is made.

(5)   Where, under the arrangements in question, there is a succession of interests, any reference in subsection (2) or (3) above to the relevant interest includes a reference to any interest (other than that of the member) in relation to which the relevant interest is a successive interest.

638   Other restrictions on approval

(1)   The Board shall not approve a personal pension scheme unless they are satisfied that there is a person resident in the United Kingdom who will be responsible for the management of the scheme.

(2)   The Board shall not approve a personal pension scheme unless it makes such provision for the making, acceptance and application of transfer payments as satisfies any requirements imposed by or under regulations made by the Board.

(3)   The Board shall not approve a personal pension scheme unless it makes provision, in relation to arrangements made in accordance with the scheme, for ensuring that—

    (a) the aggregate amount of the contributions that may be made in a year of assessment by the member and an employer of his under the arrangements, together with the aggregate amounts of such contributions under other approved personal pension arrangements made by that member, does not exceed the permitted maximum for that year; and

    (b) any excess is repaid to the member to the extent of his contributions and otherwise to his employer.

(4)   In subsection (3) above 'the permitted maximum' for a year of assessment means an amount equal to the aggregate of—

    (a) the relevant percentage of the member's net relevant earnings for the year; and

    (b) so much of any relief given under section 639(1) for that year as is given by virtue of section 642;

and references in subsection (3) to contributions by the member do not include references to contributions treated by virtue of section 649(3) as paid by him.

(5)   In subsection (4) above 'the relevant percentage' means 17.5 per cent or, in a case where section 640(2) applies, the relevant percentage there specified.

(6)   The Board shall not approve a personal pension scheme which permits the acceptance of contributions other than—

(a)   contributions by members;

(b)   contributions by employers of members;

(c)   minimum contributions paid by the Board under section 43 of the Pension Schemes Act 1993 or by the Department of Health and Social Services for Northern Ireland under section 39 of the Pension Schemes (Northern Ireland) Act 1993.

(7)   The Board shall not approve a personal pension scheme which permits the acceptance of minimum contributions paid as mentioned in subsection (6)(c) above in respect of an individual's service as director of a company, if his emoluments as such are within section 644(5).

(7A)   The Board shall not approve a personal pension scheme unless it prohibits, except in such cases as may be prescribed by regulations made by the Board—

(*a*)   the acceptance of further contributions, and

(*b*)   the making of transfer payments,

after the date which is the member's pension date in relation to the arrangements in question.

(8)   A personal pension scheme which permits the acceptance of minimum contributions paid as mentioned in subsection (6)(c) above in respect of an individual's service in an office or employment to which section 645 applies may be approved of by the Board only if—

(a)   the scheme does not permit the acceptance of contributions from the individual or from the person who is his employer in relation to that office or employment; or

(b)   at the time when the minimum contributions are paid the individual is not serving in an office or employment to which section 645 applies.

638A   Power to prescribe restrictions on approval

(1)   The Board—

(a)   may by regulations restrict their discretion to approve a personal pension scheme; and

(b)   shall not approve any such scheme if to do so would be inconsistent with any regulations under this section.

(2)   The restrictions that may be imposed by regulations under this section may be imposed by reference to any one or more of the following, that is to say—

(a)   the benefits for which the scheme provides;

(b)   the investments held for the purposes of the scheme;

(c)   the manner in which the scheme is administered;

(d)   any other circumstances whatever.

(3)   The following provisions of this section apply where—

(a)   any regulations are made under this section imposing a restriction ('the new restriction') on the Board's discretion to approve a personal pension scheme;

(b)   the new restriction did not exist immediately before the making of the regulations; and

(c) that restriction is one imposed by reference to circumstances other than the benefits for which the scheme provides.

(4)   Subject to subsections (5) and (6) below, a personal pension scheme which is an approved scheme immediately before the day on which the regulations imposing the new restriction come into force shall cease to be approved at the end of the period of 36 months beginning with that day if, at the end of that period, the scheme—

(a) contains a provision of a prohibited description, or
(b) does not contain every provision which is a provision of a required description.

(5)   The Board may by regulations provide that subsection (4) above is not to apply in the case of the inclusion of such provisions of a prohibited description, or in the case of the omission of such provisions of a required description, as may be specified in the regulations.

(6)   For the purposes of subsection (4) above—

(a) a provision contained in a scheme shall not be treated as being of a prohibited description to the extent that it authorises the retention of an investment held immediately before the day of the making of the new regulations; and
(b) so much of any provision contained in a scheme as authorises the retention of an investment held immediately before that day shall be disregarded in determining if any provision of the scheme is of a required description.

(7)   In this section—

(a) references to a provision of a prohibited description are references to a provision of a description which, by virtue of the new restriction, is a description of provision which, if contained in a personal pension scheme, would prevent the Board from approving it; and
(b) references to a provision of a required description are references to a provision of a description which, by virtue of the new restriction, is a description of provision which must be contained in a personal pension scheme before the Board may approve it.

Tax reliefs

639   Member's contributions

(1)   A contribution paid by an individual under approved personal pension arrangements made by him shall, subject to the provisions of this Chapter, be deducted from or set off against any relevant earnings of his for the year of assessment in which the payment is made.

Except where subsections (2) to (4) below apply, relief under this subsection in respect of a contribution shall be given only on a claim made for the purpose.

(2)   In such cases and subject to such conditions as the Board may prescribe in regulations, relief under subsection (1) above shall be given in accordance with subsections (3) and (4) below.

(3)   An individual who is entitled to such relief in respect of a contribution may deduct from the contribution when he pays it, and may retain, an amount equal to income tax at the basic rate on the contribution.

(4)   The scheme administrator—

(a)   shall accept the amount paid after the deduction in discharge of the individual's liability to the same extent as if the deduction had not been made; and

(b)   may recover an amount equal to the deduction from the Board.

(5)   Regulations under this section may make provision for carrying subsections (3) and (4) above into effect and, without prejudice to the generality of that, may provide

(a)   for the manner in which claims for the recovery of a sum under subsection (4)(b) may be made;

(b)   for the giving of such information, in such form, as may be prescribed by or under the regulations;

(c)   for the inspection by persons authorised by the Board of books, documents and other records.

(6)   Where relief under this section for any year of assessment is claimed and allowed (whether or not it then falls to be given for that year), and afterwards an assessment, alteration of an assessment, or other adjustment of the claimant's liability to tax is made, there shall also be made such consequential adjustments in the relief allowed or given under this section for that or any subsequent year as are appropriate.

(7)   Where relief under this section is claimed and allowed for any year of assessment in respect of a contribution, relief shall not be given in respect of it under any other provision of the Income Tax Acts for the same or any subsequent year, nor (in the case of a contribution under an annuity contract) in respect of any other premium or consideration for an annuity under the same contract.

(8)   References in the Income Tax Acts to relief in respect of life assurance premiums shall not be taken to include relief under this section.

640   Maximum amount of deductions

(1)   The maximum amount that may be deducted or set off in any year of assessment by virtue of section 639(1) shall be 17.5 per cent of the individual's net relevant earnings for that year.

(2)   In the case of an individual whose age at the beginning of the year of assessment is within a range specified in the first column of the following table, subsection (1) above shall have effect with the substitution for 17.5 per cent of the relevant percentage specified in the second column.

36 to 45	20 per cent
46 to 50	25 per cent
51 to 55	30 per cent
56 to 60	35 per cent
61 or more	40 per cent

(3)   Without prejudice to subsection (1) above, the maximum amount that may be deducted or set off in any year of assessment in respect of contributions paid by an individual to secure benefits satisfying the conditions in section 637 shall be 5 per cent of the individual's net relevant earnings for that year.

(4)   Where personal pension arrangements are made by an employee whose employer makes contributions under the arrangements, the maximum amount that may be deducted or set off in any year of assessment shall be reduced by the amount of the employer's contributions in the year.

(5)   Any minimum contributions treated by virtue of section 649(3) as paid by the individual in respect of whom they are paid shall be disregarded for the purposes of this section.

640A   Earnings cap

(1)   In arriving at an individual's net relevant earnings for a year of assessment for the purposes of section 640 above, any excess of what would be his net relevant earnings for the year (apart from this subsection) over the allowable maximum for the year shall be disregarded.

(2)   In subsection (1) above 'the allowable maximum' means, as regards a particular year of assessment, the figure found for that year by virtue of subsections (3) and (4) below.

(3)   For the year of assessment 1989–90 the figure is £60,000.

(4)   For the year of assessment 1990–91 and any subsequent year of assessment the figure is the figure found for that year, for the purposes of section 590C, by virtue of section 590C(4) to (5A).

641   Carry-back contributions

(1)   An individual who pays a contribution under approved personal pension arrangements in a year of assessment (whether or not a year for which he has relevant earnings) may elect that the contribution, or part of it, shall be treated as paid—

(a)   in the year of assessment preceding that year; or
(b)   if he had no net relevant earnings in that preceding year of assessment, in the year of assessment before that.

(2)   Where for any year of assessment an individual—

(a)   has relevant earnings as an underwriting or former underwriting member of Lloyd's or by way of commission calculated by reference to the profits of Lloyd's underwriting business; and
(b)   there is an amount of unused relief attributable to those earnings,

the individual may elect that there shall be treated as paid in that year so much of any contributions paid by him under approved personal pension arrangements in the next year of assessment but two as does not exceed the amount of the unused relief.

(3)   Subject to section 655(2), references in subsection (2) above to an amount of unused relief attributable to the earnings mentioned in subsection (2)(a) are to an amount which could have been deducted from or set off against those earnings under section 639(1) if—

(a) the individual had paid contributions under approved personal pension arrangements in the year of assessment for which he has the earnings; or

(b) any such contributions paid by him in that year had been greater.

(4) An election under this section must be made on or before the 31st January next following the year of assessment in which the contributions treated as paid in another year are actually paid.

(5) Where an election is made under this section in respect of a contribution or part of a contribution, the other provisions of this Chapter shall have effect as if the contribution or part had been paid in the year specified in the election and not in the year in which it was actually paid.

642 Carry-forward of relief

(1) Where—

(a) for any year of assessment an individual has relevant earnings from any trade, profession, vocation, office or employment carried on or held by him, and

(b) there is an amount of unused relief for that year,

relief may be given under section 639(1), up to the amount of the unused relief, in respect of so much of any contributions paid by him under approved personal pension arrangements in any of the next six years of assessment as exceeds the maximum applying for that year under section 640.

(2) In this section, references to an amount of unused relief for any year are to an amount which could have been deducted from or set off against the individual's relevant earnings for that year under section 639(1) if—

(a) the individual had paid contributions under approved personal pension arrangements in that year; or

(b) any such contributions paid by him in that year had been greater.

(3) Relief by virtue of this section shall be given for an earlier year rather than a later year, the unused relief taken into account in giving relief for any year being deducted from that available for giving relief in subsequent years and unused relief derived from an earlier year being exhausted before unused relief derived from a later year.

(4) Where a relevant assessment to tax in respect of a year of assessment becomes final and conclusive more than six years after the end of that year and there is an amount of unused relief for that year which results from the making of the assessment—

(a) that amount shall not be available for giving relief by virtue of this section for any of the six years following that year; but

(b) the individual may, within the period of six months beginning with the date on which the assessment becomes final and conclusive, elect that relief shall be given under section 639(1), up to that amount, in respect of so much of any contributions paid by him under approved personal pension arrangements within that period as exceeds the maximum applying under section 640 for the year of assessment in which they are paid;

and to the extent to which relief in respect of any contributions is given by virtue of this subsection it shall not be given by virtue of subsection (1) above.

(5)   In this section 'a relevant assessment to tax' means an assessment on the individual's relevant earnings or on the profits or gains of a partnership from which the individual derives relevant earnings.

643   Employer's contributions and personal pension income etc

(1)   Where contributions are paid by an employer under approved personal pension arrangements made by his employee, those contributions shall not be regarded as emoluments of the employment chargeable to tax under Schedule E.

(2)   Income derived by a person from investments or deposits held by him for the purposes of an approved personal pension scheme shall be exempt from income tax.

(3)   An annuity payable under approved personal pension arrangements shall be treated as earned income of the annuitant.

(4)   Subsection (3) above applies only in relation to the annuitant to whom the annuity is made payable by the terms of the arrangements.

(5)   Income withdrawals under approved personal pension arrangements shall be assessable to tax under Schedule E (and section 203 shall apply accordingly) and shall be treated as earned income of the recipient.

644   Meaning of 'relevant earnings'

(1)   In this Chapter, 'relevant earnings', in relation to an individual, means any income of his which is chargeable to tax for the year of assessment in question and is within subsection (2) below.

(2)   Subject to subsections (3) to (6F) below, income is within this subsection if it is—

> (a) emoluments chargeable under Schedule E from an office or employment held by the individual;
> (b) income from any property which is attached to or forms part of the emoluments of an office or employment held by him;
> (c) income which is chargeable under Schedule D and is immediately derived by him from the carrying on or exercise by him of his trade, profession or vocation (either as an individual or as a partner acting personally in a partnership);
> (d) income treated as earned income by virtue of section 529.

(3)   Where section 645 applies to an office or employment held by the individual, neither emoluments from the office or employment nor income from any property which is attached to it or forms part of its emoluments are within subsection (2) above.

(4)   The following are not income within subsection (2) above—

> (a) anything in respect of which tax is chargeable under Schedule E and which arises from the acquisition or disposal of shares or an interest in shares or from a right to acquire shares;
> (b) anything in respect of which tax is chargeable by virtue of section 148.

(5)   Emoluments of an individual as director of a company are not income within subsection (2) above if—

(a)   the income of the company consists wholly or mainly of investment income; and

(b)   the individual, either alone or together with any other persons who are or have been at any time directors of the company, controls the company;

and section 840 shall apply for the purposes of this subsection.

(6)   For the purposes of subsection (5) above—

'director' includes any person occupying the position of director by whatever name called; and

'investment income' means income which, if the company were an individual, would not be earned income.

(6A)   Emoluments of an individual as an employee of a company are not income within subsection (2) above if—

(a)   he is a controlling director of the company at any time in the year of assessment in question or has been a controlling director of the company at any time in the ten years immediately preceding that year of assessment, and

(b)   any of the subsections (6B) to (6E) below applies in his case.

(6B)   This subsection applies in the case of the individual if—

(a)   at any time in the year of assessment in question he is in receipt of benefits under a relevant superannuation scheme, and

(b)   the benefits are payable in respect of past service with the company.

(6C)   This subsection applies in the case of the individual if—

(a)   at any time in the year of assessment in question he is in receipt of benefits under a personal pension scheme,

(b)   the scheme has received a transfer payment relating to him from a relevant superannuation scheme, and

(c)   the transfer payment is in respect of past service with the company.

(6D)   This subsection applies in the case of the individual if—

(a)   at any time in the year of assessment in question he is in receipt of benefits under a relevant superannuation scheme,

(b)   the benefits are payable in respect of past service with another company,

(c)   the emoluments are for a period during which the company mentioned in subsection (6A) above has carried on a trade or business previously carried on by the other company, and

(d)   the other company carried on the trade or business at any time during the period of service in respect of which the benefits are payable.

(6E)   This subsection applies in the case of the individual if—

(a)   at any time in the year of assessment in question he is in receipt of benefits under a personal pension scheme,

(b) the scheme has received a transfer payment relating to him from a relevant superannuation scheme,

(c) the transfer payment is in respect of past service with another company,

(d) the emoluments are for a period during which the company mentioned in subsection (6A) above has carried on a trade or business previously carried on by the other company, and

(e) the other company carried on the trade or business at any time during the period of service in respect of which the transfer payment was made.

[(6EA) Where—

(a) there is a time at which a person would be in receipt of any benefits under a scheme but for any debit to which any of his rights under that scheme became subject by virtue of any pension sharing order or provision, and

(b) the benefits he would be in receipt of are benefits payable in respect of past service with a company,

that person shall be deemed for the purposes of subsections (6A) to (6E) above to be in receipt at that time of benefits under that scheme and the benefits which he is deemed to be in receipt of shall be deemed to be benefits in respect of past service with that company.]

(6F) For the purposes of subsections (6A) to (6EA) above—

(a) a person is a controlling director of a company if he is a director (as defined by section 612(1)), and he is within paragraph (b) of section 471(5), in relation to the company;

(b) 'relevant superannuation scheme' has the same meaning as in section 645(1);

(c) references to benefits payable in respect of past service with a company include references to benefits payable partly in respect of past service with the company [but do not include references to benefits which (within the meaning of section 590) are provided for him as an ex-spouse]; and

(d) references to a transfer payment in respect of past service with a company include references to a transfer payment partly in respect of past service with the company [but do not include references to any transfer payment made for the purpose of giving effect to a pension sharing order or provision].

645 Earnings from pensionable employment

(1) This section applies to an office or employment held by an individual if—

(a) service in it is service to which a relevant superannuation scheme relates; and

(b) the individual is a participant in the scheme; and

(c) subsection (4) below does not apply to his participation in the scheme.

(2) This section applies whether or not the duties of the office or employment are performed wholly or partly in the United Kingdom or the individual is chargeable to tax in respect of it.

(3)   In subsection (1) above 'a relevant superannuation scheme' means a scheme or arrangement—

   (a)   the object or one of the objects of which is the provision, in respect of persons serving in particular offices or employments, of relevant benefits within the meaning of section 612;

   (b)   which is established by a person other than the individual; and

   (c)   which is of a description mentioned in sections 596(1)(a), (b) or (c).

(4)   This subsection applies to an individual's participation in a scheme if the scheme provides no benefits in relation to him other than—

   (a)   an annuity payable to his surviving spouse or a dependant of his;

   (b)   a lump sum payable on his death in service.

(4A)   Where the emoluments from an office or employment held by an individual are foreign emoluments within the meaning of section 192, this section shall have effect with the substitution of the following for paragraph (c) of subsection (3) above—

   '(c)   which corresponds to a scheme of a description mentioned in section 596(1)(a), (b) or (c).'

646   Meaning of 'net relevant earnings'

(1)   Subject to subsections (3) to (7) below and section 646A, in this Chapter 'net relevant earnings', in relation to an individual means the amount of his relevant earnings for the year of assessment in question, less the amount of any deductions within subsection (2) below which fall to be made from the relevant earnings in computing for the purposes of income tax his total income for that year.

(2)   Deductions are within this subsection if they are—

   (a)   deductions which but for section 74(m) (p) or (q) could be made in computing the profits or gains of the individual;

   (b)   deductions made by virtue of section 198, 201 or 332(3);

   (c)   deductions in respect of relief under Schedule 9 to the Finance Act 1981 (stock relief);

   (d)   deductions in respect of losses or capital allowances, being losses or capital allowances arising from activities profits or gains of which would be included in computing relevant earnings of the individual.

(3)   For the purposes of this section, an individual's relevant earnings shall be taken to be those earnings before giving effect to any capital allowances, other than deductions allowable in computing profits or gains, but after taking into account the amounts on which charges fall to be made under the 1990 Act (including enactments which under this Act are to be treated as contained in the 1990 Act); and in subsections (4) and (5) below, references to income (other than references to total income) shall be construed similarly.

(4)   In the case of an individual's partnership profits, the amount to be included in arriving at his net relevant earnings shall be his share of the partnership income (estimated in accordance with the Income Tax Acts) after making from it any such deductions in respect of—

   (a)   payments made by the partnership;

(b) relief given to the partnership under Schedule 9 to the Finance Act 1981; or

(c) capital allowances falling to be made to the partnership,

as would be made in computing the tax payable in respect of that income.

(5)   Where, in a year of assessment for which an amount is deducted or set off under section 639(1) against the net relevant earnings of an individual—

(a) a deduction in respect of such a loss or allowance of the individual as is mentioned in subsection (2)(d) above falls to be made in computing the total income of the individual; and

(b) the deduction or part of it falls to be so made from income other than relevant earnings;

the amount of the deduction made from that other income shall be treated as reducing the individual's net relevant earnings for subsequent years of assessment in accordance with subsection (6) below.

(6)   The deduction shall be made so far as possible from the individual's net relevant earnings for the first of the subsequent years of assessment (whether or not he is entitled to relief under section 639(1) for that year), and than, so far as it cannot be so made, from those of the next year, and so on.

(7)   An individual's net relevant earnings for any year of assessment shall be computed without regard to any deduction or set off under section 639(1) which falls to be made for that year in respect of the individual.

646A   Earnings from association employments

(1)   This section applies where in the year of assessment in question—

(a) an individual holds two or more offices or employments which are associated in that year,

(b) one or more of them is an office or employment to which section 645 applies ('pensionable job'), and

(c) one or more of them is an office or employment to which that section does not apply ('non-pensionable job').

(2)   Where the emoluments for that year from the pensionable job (or jobs) are equal to or exceed the allowable maximum for that year, section 646(1) shall have effect in the case of the individual as if the references to relevant earnings were references to relevant earnings not attributable to the non-pensionable job (or jobs).

(3)   Where the allowable maximum for that year exceeds the emoluments for that year from the pensionable job (or jobs), the individual's net relevant earnings, so far as attributable to the non-pensionable job (or jobs), shall not be greater than the amount of the excess.

(4)   For the purposes of this section two or more offices or employments held by an individual in a year of assessment are associated in that year if the employers in question are associated at any time during it.

(5)   For the purposes of subsection (4) above, employers are associated if (directly or indirectly) one is controlled by the other or if both are controlled by a third person.

(6)   In subsection (5) above the reference to control, in relation to a body corporate, shall be construed—

    (a)   where the body corporate is a close company, in accordance with section 416, and

    (b)   where it is not, in accordance with section 840.

(7)   In this section 'the allowable maximum' has the same meaning as in section 640A(1).

Charge to tax

647   Unauthorised payments

(1)   This section applies to any payment within subsection (2) below which is made—

    (a)   out of funds which are or have been held for the purposes of a personal pension scheme which is or has at any time been approved; and

    (b)   to or for the benefit of an individual who has made personal pension arrangements in accordance with the scheme.

(2)   A payment is within this subsection if—

    (a)   it is not expressly authorised by the rules of the scheme; or

    (b)   it is made at a time when the scheme or the arrangements are not approved and it would not have been expressly authorised by the rules of the scheme or by the arrangements when the scheme, or as the case may be the arrangements, were last so approved.

(3)   The individual referred to in subsection (1)(b) above, whether or not he is the recipient of the payment, shall be chargeable to tax under Schedule E on the amount of the payment for the year of assessment in which the payment is made.

(4)   This section applies to a transfer of assets or other transfer of money's worth as it applies to a payment, and in relation to such a transfer the reference in subsection (3) above to the amount of the payment shall be read as a reference to the value of the transfer.

648   Contributions under unapproved arrangements

Where contributions are paid by an employer under personal pension arrangements made by his employee then, if those arrangements are not approved arrangements and the contributions are not otherwise chargeable to income tax as income of the employee, the contributions shall be regarded for all the purposes of the Income Tax Acts as emoluments of the employment chargeable to tax under Schedule E.

648A   Annuities: charge under Schedule E

(1)   Subject to subsection (2) below, where funds held for the purposes of an approved personal pension scheme are used to acquire an annuity—

    (a)   the annuity shall be charged to tax under Schedule E and section 203 shall apply accordingly;

    (b)   the annuity shall not be charged to tax under Case III of Schedule D.

(2)   As respects any approved personal pension scheme the Board may direct that, until such date as the Board may specify, annuities acquired with funds held for the purposes of the scheme shall be charged to tax as annual payments under Case III of Schedule D, and tax shall be deductible under sections 348 and 349 accordingly.

648B   Return of contributions after pension date

(1)   Tax shall be charged under this section on any payment to a person under approved personal pension arrangements of such a lump sum as is mentioned in section 637A in a case where the member's death occurred after his pension date in relation to the arrangement in question.

(2)   Where a payment is chargeable to tax under this section, the scheme administrator shall be charged to income tax under Case VI of Schedule D and, subject to subsection (3) below, the rate of tax shall be 35 per cent.

(3)   The Treasury may by order from time to time increase or decrease the rate of tax under subsection (2) above.

(4)   The tax shall be charged on the amount paid or, if the rules of the scheme permit the scheme administrator to deduct the tax before payment, on the amount before deduction of tax; and the amount so charged to tax shall not be treated as income for any other purpose of the Tax Acts.

Miscellaneous

649   Minimum contributions under Social Security Act 1986

(1)   Where under section 43 of the Pension Schemes Act 1993 the Secretary of State pays minimum contributions for the purposes of approved personal pension arrangements, the amount of the employee's share of those contributions shall, instead of being the amount provided for in that Part, be the grossed-up equivalent of the amount so provided for.

(2)   For the purposes of this section—

  'the employee's share' of minimum contributions is the amount that would be the minimum contributions if, for the reference in section 45(1) of the Pension Schemes Act 1993 to the appropriate age-related percentage, there were substituted a reference to the percentage mentioned in section 41(1A)(*a*) of that Act;

  'the grossed-up equivalent' of an amount is such sum as, after deduction of income tax at the basic rate in force for the year of assessment for which the contributions are paid, is equal to that amount.

(3)   The employee's share of minimum contributions paid for a year of assessment by the Secretary of State for the purposes of approved personal pension arrangements shall be treated for the purposes of income tax—

  (a)   as the income for that year of the individual in respect of whom it is paid; and
  (b)   as contributions paid in that year by that individual under those arrangements.

(4)   The Board may make regulations—

(a)   providing for the recovery by the Secretary of State from the Board, in such circumstances as may be prescribed by the regulations, of any increase attributable to this section in the sums paid by the Secretary of State out of the National Insurance Fund;

(b)   requiring the Secretary of State to give the Board such information as may be so prescribed about minimum contributions paid by the Secretary of State;

(c)   prescribing circumstances in which this section or any provision of it shall not apply;

(d)   making such provision as appears to the Board to be necessary or expedient for the purposes of supplementing the provisions of this section.

(5)   Any payment received by the Secretary of State by virtue of this section shall be paid into the National Insurance Fund.

(6)   In relation to Northern Ireland, this section shall have effect as if—

(a)   references to the Secretary of State were references to the Department of Health and Social Services for Northern Ireland;

(b)   references to section 43, section 45(1) and section 41(1)(a) of the Pension Schemes Act 1993 were references to sections 39, 41(1) and 37(1)(a) of the Pension Schemes (Northern Ireland) Act 1993 respectively; and

(c)   references to the National Insurance Fund were references to the Northern Ireland National Insurance Fund.

650   Withdrawal of approval

(1)   If in the opinion of the Board the facts concerning an approved personal pension scheme or its administration or arrangements made in accordance with it do not warrant the continuance of their approval of the scheme, they may at any time by notice given to the scheme administrator withdraw their approval of the scheme.

(2)   If in the opinion of the Board the facts concerning any approved personal pension arrangements do not warrant the continuance of their approval in relation to the arrangements, they may at any time by notice given to the individual who made them and to the scheme administrator withdraw their approval in relation to the arrangements.

(3)   Without prejudice to the generality of subsection (2) above, the Board may withdraw their approval in relation to any personal pension arrangements if they are of the opinion that securing the provision of benefits under the arrangements was not the sole purpose of the individual in making them.

(4)   A notice under subsection (1) or (2) above shall state the grounds on which, and the date from which, approval is withdrawn.

(5)   The Board may not withdraw their approval from a date earlier than the date when the facts were first such that they did not warrant the continuance of their approval (so, however, that in a case within subsection (3) above their approval may be withdrawn from the day the arrangements in question were made).

(6)   The power of the Board under this section to withdraw their approval in

relation to any arrangements made under a personal pension scheme shall be exercisable for the purposes of section 650A notwithstanding that the time from which the approval is withdrawn is a time from which, by virtue of section 631(4) or 638A(4), the whole scheme ceases to be an approved scheme.

650A Charge on withdrawal of approval from arrangements

(1)   Where any personal pension arrangements cease to be approved arrangements by virtue of the exercise by the Board of their power under section 650(2), tax shall be charged in accordance with this section.

(2)   The tax shall be charged under Case VI of Schedule D at the rate of 40 per cent on an amount equal to the value (taking that value at the relevant time) of the appropriate part of the assets held at that time for the purposes of the relevant scheme.

(3)   In subsection (2) above—
  'the appropriate part', in relation to the value of any assets, is so much of those assets as is properly attributable, in accordance with the provisions of the scheme and any just and reasonable apportionment, to the arrangements in question; and
  'the relevant time' means the time immediately before the date from which the Board's approval is withdrawn.

(4)   Subject to subsection (5) below, the person liable for the tax charged under this section shall be the scheme administrator for the relevant scheme.

(5)   If, in any case where an amount of tax has been charged under this section and has not been paid—

  (a)   there is at any time no person who, as the scheme administrator for the relevant scheme, may be assessed to that amount of tax, or is liable to pay it,
  (b)   the scheme administrator for that scheme cannot for the time being be traced,
  (c)   there has been such a failure by the scheme administrator for that scheme to meet a liability to pay that amount as the Board consider to be a failure of a serious nature, or
  (d)   it appears to the Board that a liability of the scheme administrator for that scheme to pay that amount of tax is a liability that he will be, or (were there an assessment) would be, unable to meet out of assets held in accordance with the scheme for the purposes of those arrangements,

the Board shall be entitled to assess the unpaid tax on the person who made the arrangements in question as if the tax charged under this section, to the extent that it is unpaid, were assessable under this section on that person, instead of on the scheme administrator.

(6)   An assessment to tax made by virtue of subsection (5)(c) above shall not be out of time if it is made within three years after the date on which the tax which the scheme administrator has failed to pay first became due from him.

(7)   For the purposes of this section the value of an asset is, subject to subsection (8) below, its market value, construing 'market value' in accordance with section 272 of the 1992 Act.

(8)   Where an asset held for the purposes of a scheme is a right or interest in respect of any money lent (directly or indirectly) to any person mentioned in sub-section (9) below, the value of the asset shall be treated as being the amount owing (including any unpaid interest) on the money lent.

(9)   Those persons are—

- (a)   the person who (whether or not before the making of the loan) made the arrangements in relation to which the Board's approval has been withdrawn;
- (b)   any other person who has at any time (whether or not before the making of the loan) made contributions under those arrangements; and
- (c)   any person connected, at the time of the making of the loan or subsequently, with a person falling within paragraph (a) or (b) above.

(10)   In this section 'the relevant scheme', in relation to any personal pension arrangements, means the scheme in accordance with which those arrangements were made.

(11)   Section 839 shall apply for the purposes of this section.

651   Appeals

(1)   Where the Board—

- (a)   refuse an application by notice under section 631; or
- (b)   withdraw an approval by notice under section 650;

the person to whom the notice is given may appeal to the Special Commissioners against the refusal or, as the case may be, the withdrawal.

(2)   An appeal under this section shall be made by notice stating the grounds for the appeal and given to the Board before the end of the period for 30 days beginning with the day on which the notice of refusal or withdrawal was given to the appellant.

(3)   On an appeal under this section against the withdrawal of an approval, the Special Commissioners may, instead of allowing or dismissing the appeal, order that the withdrawal shall have effect from a date other than that determined by the Board.

(4)   The bringing of an appeal under this section shall not affect the validity of the decision appealed against pending the determination of the proceedings.

651A   Information powers

(1)   The Board may by regulations make any of the following provisions—

- (a)   provision requiring prescribed persons to furnish to the Board, at prescribed times, information relating to any of the matters mentioned in subsection (2) below;
- (b)   provision enabling the Board to serve a notice requiring prescribed persons to furnish to the Board, within a prescribed time, particulars relating to any of those matters;
- (c)   provision enabling the Board to serve a notice requiring prescribed persons to produce to the Board, within a prescribed time, documents relating to any of those matters;

(d) provision enabling the Board to serve a notice requiring prescribed persons to make available for inspection on behalf of the Board books, documents and other records, being books, documents and records which relate to any of those matters;

(e) provision requiring prescribed persons to preserve for a prescribed time books, documents and other records, being books, documents and record which relate to any of those matters.

(2) The matters referred to in subsection (a) above are—

(a) any personal pension scheme which is or has been approved; and

(b)) any personal pension arrangements which are or have been approved.

(3) A person who fails to comply with regulations made under subsection (1)(e) above shall be liable to a penalty not exceeding £3,000.

(4) Regulations under this section may make different provision for different descriptions of case.

(5) In this section 'prescribed' means prescribed by regulations made under this section.

652 Information about payments

(1) An inspector may give a notice to a scheme administrator requiring him to provide the inspector with—

(a) such particulars as the notice may require relating to contributions paid under approved personal pension arrangements made in accordance with the scheme;

(b) such particulars as the notice may require relating to payments by way of return of contributions;

(c) copies of such accounts as the notice may require.

(2) A person to whom a notice is given under this section shall comply with the notice within the period of 30 days beginning with the day on which it is given.

653 Information: penalties

A person who knowingly makes a false statement or false representation on making an application under section 631 or for the purpose of obtaining for himself or any other person any relief from or repayment of tax under this Chapter shall be liable to a penalty not exceeding £3,000.

653A Notices to be given to scheme administrator

(1) Where—

(a) the Board, or any officer of the Board, is authorised or required by or in consequence of any provision of this Chapter to give a notice to the person who is the scheme administrator of a personal pension scheme, but

(b) there is for the time being no scheme administrator for that scheme or the person who is the scheme administrator for that scheme cannot be traced,

that power or duty may be exercised or performed by giving that notice, instead, to the person specified in subsection (2) below.

(2)   That person is—

    (a)   the person who established the scheme; or

    (b)   any person by whom that person has been directly or indirectly succeeded in relation to the provision of benefits under the scheme.

(3)   The giving of a notice in accordance with this section shall have the same effect as the giving of that notice to the scheme administrator and, without prejudice to section 650A(5), shall not impose an additional obligation or liability on the person to whom the notice is actually given.

654   Remuneration of Ministers and other officers

(1)   This section applies to any salary—

    (a)   payable to the holder of a qualifying office who is also a Member of the House of Commons; and

    (b)   payable for a period in respect of which the holder is not a participant in relation to that office in arrangements contained in the Parliamentary pension scheme but is a participant in relation to his membership of the House of Commons in any such arrangements, or for any part of such a period.

(2)   So much of any salary to which this section applies as is equal to the difference between a Member's pensionable salary and the salary which (in accordance with any such resolution as is mentioned in subsection (4)(a) below) is payable to him as a Member holding that qualifying office, shall be treated for the purposes of this Chapter as remuneration from the office of Member and not from the qualifying office.

(3)   In this section—

    'Member's pensionable salary' means a Member's ordinary salary under any resolution of the House of Commons which, being framed otherwise than as an expression of opinion, is for the time being in force relating to the remuneration of Members or, if the resolution provides for a Member's ordinary salary thereunder to be treated for pension purposes as being at a higher rate, a notional yearly salary at that higher rate;

    'qualifying office' means an office mentioned in paragraph (b), (c) or (d) of subsection (2) of section 2 of the Parliamentary and other Pensions Act 1987;

    'the Parliamentary pension scheme' has the same meaning as in that Act;

and, without prejudice to the power conferred by virtue of paragraph 13 of Schedule 1 to that Act, regulations under section 2 of that Act may make provision specifying the circumstances in which a person is to be regarded for the purposes of this section as being or not being a participant in relation to his membership of the House of Commons, or in relation to any office, in arrangements contained in the Parliamentary pension scheme.

(4)   In subsection (3) above 'a Member's ordinary salary', in relation to any resolution of the House of Commons, means—

    (a)   if the resolution provides for salary to be paid to Members at different rates according to whether or not they are holders of particular offices or are in receipt of salaries or pensions as the holders or former holders of particular offices, a Member's yearly salary at the higher or highest rate; and

(b) in any other case, a Member's yearly salary at the rate specified in or determined under the resolution.

655 Transitional provisions

(1) Where approved personal pension arrangements are made by an individual who pays qualifying premiums within the meaning of section 620(1)—

(a) the amount that may be deducted or set off by virtue of section 639(1) in any year of assessment shall be reduced by the amount of any qualifying premiums which are paid in the year by the individual and in respect of which relief is given for the year under section 619(1)(a); and

(b) the relief which, by virtue of section 625, may be given under section 619 by reference to the individual's unused relief for any year shall be reduced by the amount of any contributions paid by him in that year under the approved personal pension arrangements.

(2) Where an individual elects under section 641 that a contribution or part of a contribution shall be treated as paid in the year of assessment 1985–86, 1986–87 or 1987–88, the payment shall be treated as the payment of a qualifying premium for the purposes of Chapter III of this Part; and in such a case references in section 641 to an amount of unused relief shall be construed in accordance with section 625.

(3) The references in section 642 to unused relief for any year are, for years of assessment before 1988–89, references to unused relief within the meaning of section 625.

(4) The Board shall not grant any application under section 631 so as to approve a scheme with effect from a date earlier than 1st July 1988.

(5) The Board may by regulations make provision for applications for approval of personal pension schemes to be granted provisionally, notwithstanding that the Board have not satisfied themselves that the schemes comply with the requirements of sections 632 to 638; and such regulations may, in particular, provide—

(a) for the contents and form of certificates or other documents which the Board may require the applicant to give them before they grant an application provisionally;

(b) for the making of such amendments of the rules of the scheme after the provisional grant of an application as are necessary to enable the scheme to comply with the requirements of sections 632 to 638, and for those amendments to have effect as from the date of approval of the scheme;

(c) for the withdrawal of approval of the scheme as from that date if it does not comply with the requirements of sections 632 to 638 and such amendments as are mentioned in paragraph (b) above are not made;

and may make such supplementary provision as appears to the Board to be necessary or expedient.

SCHEDULE 23

OCCUPATIONAL PENSION SCHEMES

SCHEMES APPROVED BEFORE 23RD JULY 1987

Preliminary

1.—(1)   This Schedule shall be deemed to have come into force on 17th March 1987 and, subject to sub-paragraphs (2) and (3) below, applies in relation to any retirement benefits scheme approved by the Board before the passing of the Finance (No 2) Act 1987 (23rd July 1987).

(2)   The Board may by regulations provide that, in circumstances prescribed in the regulations, this Schedule or any provision of it shall not apply or shall apply with such modifications as may be so prescribed.

(2A)   Regulations under sub-paragraph (2) above—

    (a)   may include provision authorising the Board to direct that this Schedule or any provision of it shall not apply in any particular case where in the opinion of the Board the facts are such that its application would not be appropriate;

    (b)   may take effect (and may authorise any direction given under them to take effect) as from 17th March 1987 or any later date;

    (c)   may make such supplementary provision as appears to the Board to be necessary or expedient.

(3)   This Schedule shall not apply to a retirement benefits scheme if, before the end of 1987, the administrator of the scheme gave notice to the Board that it is not to apply.

(4)   Where a notice is given to the Board under sub-paragraph (3) above, the scheme shall, with effect from 17th March 1987 or (if later) the date with effect from which it was approved, cease to be approved.

Accelerated accrual

2.—(1)   This paragraph applies where an employee becomes a member of the scheme on or after 17th March 1987.

(2)   Notwithstanding anything to the contrary in the rules of the scheme, they shall have effect as if they did not allow the provision for the employee of a pension exceeding one-thirtieth of his relevant annual remuneration for each year of service up to a maximum of 20.

3.—(1)   This paragraph applies where an employee becomes a member of the scheme on or after 17th March 1987 and the scheme allows him to commute his pension or part of it for a lump sum or sums.

(2)   If the employee's full pension (that is, the pension before any commutation) is equal to or less than a basic rate commutable pension, the rules of the scheme shall have effect (notwithstanding anything in them to the contrary) as if they did not allow him to obtain by way of commutation a lump sum or sum exceeding in all a basic rate lump sum.

(3)   If the employee's full pension is greater than a basic rate commutable pension but less than a maximum rate commutable pension, the rules of the scheme shall have effect (notwithstanding anything in them to the contrary) as if they did not allow him to obtain by way of commutation a lump sum or sums exceeding in all the aggregate of—

(a)   a basic rate lump sum, and

(b)   an amount equal to the relevant percentage of the difference between a basic rate lump sum and a maximum rate lump sum.

(4)   In this paragraph, as it applies in relation to an employee—

(a)   a 'basic rate commutable pension' means a pension of one-sixtieth of his relevant annual remuneration for each year of service up to a maximum of 40;

(b)   a 'maximum rate commutable pension' means a pension of one-thirtieth of his relevant annual remuneration for each year of service up to a maximum of 20;

(c)   a 'basic rate lump sum' means a lump sum of three-eightieths of his relevant annual remuneration for each year of service up to a maximum of 40;

(d)   a 'maximum rate lump sum' means a lump sum of such amount as may be determined by or under regulations made by the Board for the purposes of this paragraph and paragraph 4 below;

(e)   'the relevant percentage' means the difference between a basic rate commutable pension and the employee's full pension expressed as a percentage of the difference between a basic rate commutable pension and a maximum rate commutable pension.

4.—(1)   This paragraph applies where an employee becomes a member of the scheme on or after 17th March 1987 and the scheme provides a lump sum or sums for him otherwise than by commutation of his pension or part of it.

(2)   If the employee's pension is equal to or less than a basic rate non-commutable pension, the rules of the scheme shall have effect (notwithstanding anything in them to the contrary) as if they did not allow the payment to him, otherwise than by way of commutation, of a lump sum or sums exceeding in all a basic rate lump sum.

(3)   If the employee's pension is greater than a basic rate non-commutable pension but less than a maximum rate non-commutable pension the rules of the scheme shall have effect (notwithstanding anything in them to the contrary) as if they did not allow the payment to him, otherwise than by way of commutation, of a lump sum or sums exceeding in all the aggregate of—

(a)   a basic rate lump sum, and

(b)   an amount equal to the relevant percentage of the difference between a basic rate lump sum and a maximum rate lump sum.

(4)   In this paragraph, as it applies in relation to an employee—

    (a) a 'basic rate non-commutable pension' means a pension of one-eight-ieth of his relevant annual remuneration for each year of service up to a maximum of 40,

    (b) a 'maximum rate non-commutable pension' means a pension of one-fortieth of his relevant annual remuneration for each year of service up to a maximum of 20,

    (c) 'basic rate lump sum' and 'maximum rate lump sum' have the same meanings as in paragraph 3 above, and

    (d) 'the relevant percentage' means the difference between a basic rate non-commutable pension and the employee's actual pension expressed as a percentage of the difference between a basic rate non-commutable pension and a maximum rate non-commutable pension.

Final remuneration

5.—(1)   This paragraph applies where an employee who is a member of the scheme retires on or after 17th March 1987.

(2)   The rules of the scheme shall have effect as if they provided that in determining the employee's relevant annual remuneration for the purpose of calculating benefits, no account should be taken of anything excluded from the definition of 'remuneration' in section 612(1).

(3)   In the case of an employee—

    (a) whose employer is a company and who at any time in the last ten years of his service is a controlling director of the company, or

    (b) whose relevant annual remuneration for the purpose of calculating benefits, so far as the remuneration is ascertained by reference to years beginning on or after 6th April 1987, would (apart from this Schedule) exceed the permitted maximum,

the rules of the scheme shall have effect as if they provided that his relevant annual remuneration must not exceed his highest average annual remuneration for any period of three or more years ending within the period of ten years which ends with the date on which his service ends.

(4)   In the case of an employee within paragraph (b) of subparagraph (3) above who retires before 6th April 1991, the rules of the scheme shall have effect as if they provided that his relevant annual remuneration must not exceed the higher of—

    (a) the average annual remuneration referred to in that subparagraph, and

    (b) his remuneration (within the meaning given by section 612(1) assessable to income tax under Schedule E for the year of assessment 1986–87).

(5)   For the purposes of this paragraph a person is a controlling director of a company if—

    (a) he is a director (as defined in section 612), and

(b) he is within paragraph (b) of section 417(5),

in relation to the company.

Lump sums

6.—(1)   This paragraph applies where an employee becomes a member of the scheme on or after 17th March 1987.

(2)   If the rules of the scheme allow the employee to obtain, (by commutation of his pension or otherwise), a lump sum or sums calculated by reference to his relevant annual remuneration, they shall have effect as if they included a rule that in calculating a lump sum any excess of that remuneration over the permitted maximum should be disregarded.

Additional voluntary contributions

7.—(1)   This paragraph applies where—

(a)   the rules of the scheme make provision for the payment by employees of voluntary contributions, and

(b)   on or after 8th April 1987 an employee enters into arrangements to pay such contributions.

(2)   Notwithstanding anything in the rules of the scheme, they shall have effect as if they did not allow the payment to the employee of a lump sum in commutation of a pension if or to the extent that the pension is secured by the voluntary contributions.

Supplementary

9.   In this Schedule 'relevant annual remuneration' means final remuneration or, if the scheme provides for benefits to be calculated by reference to some other annual remuneration, that other annual remuneration.

INDEX

All references are to paragraph numbers.

Small self-administered scheme—*contd*
    Practice Notes, 4.3
    property, investment in, 9.2.2, 9.2.10, 9.6
    records, 9.4
    self-assessment for tax, 9.3.7
    self-investment—
        generally, 9.1.1
        restrictions on, 9.2
    SFO Memorandum, 9.2
    unlisted company shares, 9.2.4
    works of art etc, investment in, 9.2.7
Solvency, minimum requirements, 2.9
Speedway riders, 14.4
Sportsmen, professional, 18.4
Sportswomen, professional, 18.4
Spouse—
    pension for, 4.14
    self-employed person, of, 4.1
Squash players, 14.4
Stakeholder pension schemes—
    contribution levels, 20.4.3
    development of, 1.3
    employees, access to, 20.4.1
    introduction of, 20.4
    minimum standards, 20.4.2
    regulation, 20.4.6
    scheme governance, 20.4.
    scheme information, 20.4.5
    tax regime for, 14.10
State benefits—
    adequacy of, 11.16
    basic old age pension, 11.1
    earnings-related additional pension, *see*
        SERPS
    future of, 20.2
        minimum income guarantee, 20.2.1
    history of, 2.7, 11.1
    state pension age, 11.1, 16.5
    summary of, 11.14
State earnings-related pension scheme, *see*
    SERPS
State pensionable age, 11.1, 16.5
State Second Pension (SSP), 20.3
    contracting out of, 20.3.1
Surpluses, 3.2.1, 7.7, 14.2.11

Table tennis players, 14.4
Tax—
    approval by Inland Revenue, *see* Inland
        Revenue approval
    inheritance tax, *see* Inheritance tax
    investigation settlements, 14.2.17
    late assessment, 14.2.16
    personal pension scheme, *see* Personal
        pension scheme

Tax—*contd*
    planning, *see* Tax planning
    relief, *see* Tax relief
    retirement annuity, *see* Retirement
        annuity
    unapproved scheme, *see* Unapproved
        scheme
Tax planning—
    executive pension plan, 13.1–13.7, 15.1
    group scheme, 13.7
    loans, 17.1–17.5
    partners, 14.2.8
    personal pension scheme, 15.2
    retirement annuity, 14.4.2, 15.2
Tax relief—
    additional voluntary contributions, 5.15
    carry back provisions, 14.2.14
    carry forward of unused relief, 14.2.14
    deferment of, 5.14
    exempt approved scheme, 5.4
    loan, 17.1–17.5
    personal pension scheme,
        14.2.12–14.2.17
    retirement annuity, 14.2.12, 14.2.13
Teacher's Superannuation Scheme, 4.9
Temporary employees, 4.1
Tennis players, professional, 14.4, 18.4
Term assurance, 7.10, 13.6
Territorial Army members, 14.4
Tiered schemes and matching
    arrangements, 10.10
Top hat scheme, 2.3
Topping up group scheme, *see* Group
    scheme
Transfer of pension rights, 2.8
Transfer values, 3.2.1, 16.5.2–16.5.4, 16.7
Trapeze artists, 14.4
Trawlermen, 18.3
Trivial benefits, 4.16
Trust—
    Board resolution, 3.3.1
    declaration of, 3.3.1, 14.3.4
    discretionary, 14.3.3
    employer, 3.3
    flexible, use of, 14.3.2
    formal deed, 3.3.1
    Inland Revenue approval, 3.3.1, 3.4
    interest in possession, 14.3.3
    setting up, 3.3.1
Trustee, pensioneer, *see* Pensioneer trustee
Trustee in Bankruptcy, powers of, 14.9
Trustees—
    ethical investments, 8.8.2
    holiday property, investment in, 9.2.2
    member-nominated trustees, 2.9